D1737946

This study probes the relationship between two contradictory, or apparently contradictory, pairs of terms: "Depression" and "abundance," and "literature" and "mass culture." It suggests, first, that one can detect in the culture of the American thirties – despite the painful national experience of scarcity and poverty – the now-familiar outlines of an image-mediated, consumer society. It argues, second, that the hierarchical opposition between "high art" and "mass culture" was powerfully contested and challenged in the cultural production of the Depression decade: book clubs, radio, popular exhibitions, and star conductors like Toscanini brought high culture to millions of people; Communist cultural critics agitated (against the usual divide between "high" and "low") for a proletarian and later a more populist notion of art; and writers with "serious" literary interests incorporated the discourse of the media into their writing.

Against this cultural and theoretical background, such writers as Kenneth Fearing and Nathanael West, the central figures in this study, emerge as important and in some sense predictive figures: their poetry and prose illuminate emergent cultural forces that have since become dominant in our postmodern world. The cultural criticism implicit in their work shows interesting connections with the thought of Walter Benjamin and the Frankfurt school, as well as later theorists of postmodern culture. They are concerned, for instance, with the retreat of "real life" into simulacra, the abolition of the auratic power of art, the fragmentation of time and of experience, and – more positively – the critical dimension implicit even in reified dreams and mass-produced objects: the kind of possibility Walter Benjamin expresses in his phrase the "revolutionary energies" of the "outmoded." In a sense, then, Fearing and West can be read as our contemporaries. Despite their sharp and often prescient social critique, Fearing and West were not elitist; writing both in and against the American grain, they recognized both the deceit and the promise of our emergent culture of abundance.

CAMBRIDGE STUDIES IN AMERICAN LITERATURE AND CULTURE

Editor

ERIC SUNDQUIST, *University of California, Los Angeles*

Founding Editor

ALBERT GELPI, *Stanford University*

Advisory Board

NINA BAYM, *University of Illinois, Champaign-Urbana*
SACVAN BERCOVITCH, *Harvard University*
ALBERT GELPI, *Stanford University*
MYRA JEHLEN, *University of Pennsylvania*
CAROLYN PORTER, *University of California, Berkeley*
ROBERT STEPTO, *Yale University*
TONY TANNER, *King's College, Cambridge University*

Continued on pages following the Index

The Great Depression and the Culture of Abundance

The Great Depression and the Culture of Abundance,

Kenneth Fearing, Nathanael West, and Mass Culture in the 1930s

RITA BARNARD
University of Pennsylvania

CAMBRIDGE
UNIVERSITY PRESS

Published by the Press Syndicate of the University of Cambridge
The Pitt Building, Trumpington Street, Cambridge CB2 1RP
40 West 20th Street, New York, NY 10011-4211, USA
10 Stamford Road, Oakleigh, Melbourne 3166, Australia

First published 1995

Frontispiece photo by Dorothea Lange courtesy of the Library of Congress

Library of Congress Cataloging-in-Publication Data
Barnard, Rita.
The Great Depression and the culture of abundance : Kenneth
Fearing, Nathanael West, and mass culture in the 1930s / Rita
Barnard.
p.   cm. – (Cambridge studies in American literature and
culture ; 87)
Includes index.
ISBN 0-521-45034-9
1. American literature – 20th century – History and criticism.
2. Popular literature – United States – History and criticism.
3. Literature and society – United States – History – 20th century.
4. Popular culture – United States – History – 20th century.
5. Fearing, Kenneth, 1902–1961 – Political and social views.
6. West, Nathanael, 1903–1940 – Political and social views.
7. Social problems in literature.   8. Depression in literature.
9. Economics in literature.   I. Title.   II. Series.
PS228.P67B37   1995
810.9'0052 – dc20   94-16668
                                                              CIP

A catalog record for this book is available from the British Library.

ISBN 0-521-45034-9 Hardback

Contents

Acknowledgments

I gratefully acknowledge the support of the Research Foundation of the University of Pennsylvania for two summer research grants, one in 1991 and one in 1994, which enabled me to complete this project. Thanks are also due to my professors at Duke University, where this study had its inception. Frank Lentricchia's confidence in my abilities was an inspiration – as was the example of his lyrical and committed critical writing. Bob Gleckner's scrupulous comments on my work have been a great help to me over the years; if there has been any improvement in my writing since my first essay for him ("marred by breathless, dash-ridden style"), he gets a lot of the credit. James Rolleston, Jan Radway, Tom Ferraro, Susan Willis, Jane Gaines, and Rick Roderick offered words of wisdom and encouragement.

My friends Barbara Ching, Tom Scanlon, Susan Hegeman, Molly Mullin, Sue Poznar, Paul Bauer, and Liz King were a true resource – of good ideas and good cheer. I appreciate, in particular, the help of Bill Maxwell and Andy Lakritz, who offered detailed and shrewd comments on early versions of several chapters. Duncan Fick patiently listened to me as I thought through my initial ideas and helped me with research in the *New Masses*. Jeff Twitchell and Ed Johanningsmeier made helpful suggestions for reading. Gary Weisel brought me yellowed Fearing paperbacks he found at secondhand bookstores and yard sales. Jane Penner bravely traveled to Madison in subzero weather to look through the Fearing manuscripts at the University of Wisconsin for me. Bob Ryley has been more than generous in sharing with me his research on Fearing and in reading Part II of this volume: I owe a huge debt to him. I am grateful, finally, to Cary Nelson, Alan Wald, and Eric Cheyfitz for their interest in my work, and to Eric Sundquist,

Susan Chang, and Mary Racine at Cambridge University Press, without whose support and goodwill this book would not have come into existence.

Dana Phillips put up with me and read this text many more times than any human being should have to. Thanks to him.

I gratefully acknowledge permission to quote the following:

Excerpts from Kenneth Fearing, *Complete Poems,* ed. Robert M. Ryley (Orono, Me.: National Poetry Foundation, 1994).

Excerpts from the uncollected prose of Kenneth Fearing by permission of Russell and Volkening.

Excerpts from Nathanael West, *Miss Lonely Hearts and The Day of the Locust.* Copyright © 1960, 1966, 1968 by Laura Perelman. Reprinted by permission of New Directions Publ. Corp.

Excerpts from Nathanael West, "A Cool Million," in *The Dream Life of Balso Snell / A Cool Million.* Copyright © 1934, renewed © 1961 by Laura Perelman. Reprinted by permission of Farrar, Straus & Giroux, Inc., and Laurence Pollinger Limited.

Excerpts from the unpublished writings of Nathanael West by permission of Harold Ober Associates.

Ezra Pound, "N.Y.," in *Personae.* Copyright © 1926, 1928 by Ezra Pound. Reprinted by permission of New Directions Publ. Corp.

Excerpts from Lionel Abel, *The Intellectual Follies: A Memoir of the Literary Venture in New York and Paris* (New York: W. W. Norton, 1984).

Excerpts from W. H. Auden, *The Dyer's Hand and Other Essays.* Copyright © 1948, 1950, 1952, 1953, 1956, 1957, 1958, 1960, 1962 by W. H. Auden. Reprinted by permission of Random House, Inc.

Muriel Rukeyser, "Movie," in *Collected Poems.* Copyright © Muriel Rukeyser 1978, McGraw-Hill, New York. Reprinted by permission of William L. Rukeyser.

Tillie Olsen, "I Would Like You Women Up North to Know . . ." by permission of Tillie Olsen.

An earlier version of Chapter 7 appeared in *American Literature* 66, no. 2 (June 1994); © Duke University Press.

An earlier version of Chapter 8 appeared in *Novel: A Forum on Fiction* 27, no. 1 (Fall 1993) © Novel Corporation.

PART I

Context

1

Introduction
Literature and Mass Culture in the Thirties

The present study offers a reading of two important writers of the 1930s: Kenneth Fearing and Nathanael West. But a larger project informs my reading, one that I hope will extend our understanding of the lively and still-relevant cultural struggles of the American thirties. This project can be grasped as an attempt to examine the complicated relation between the two contradictory, or apparently contradictory, pairs of terms implicit in my title: "Depression" and "abundance," and "literature" and "mass culture."

The first set of terms captures the historical conundrum that has engaged me: the fact that one can detect in the culture of the thirties the now-familiar outlines of a society of consumption – this despite the painful national experience of scarcity and suffering, and despite the emphasis of a good portion of the decade's literary work on labor and production. My sense of why the thirties are so important for an understanding of our present cultural formation can, at this point, be best expressed imagistically. I am thinking of a 1980 photograph (among the "afterimages" to Susan Buck-Morss's study of Walter Benjamin), which anyone who lived through the Reagan–Bush years can easily visualize: a picture of a bag lady huddled in front of a department store window in which two mannequins in bikinis and sunglasses are displayed. Buck-Morss reads the picture dialectically, as Benjamin would have: it is, she says, the image of a woman consumed by the very society that constructs Woman as the prototypical consumer. The ragged appearance of the bag lady, with all her worldly possessions heaped around her in old shopping bags, expresses a certain demystificatory irony: she is the counterimage of "Mrs. Consumer" returning from a spree at the mall or department store.[1] It has been my experience that a study of consumer culture in the Great Depression, and artists' and critics' responses to consumer culture, constantly brings one up against

3

such juxtapositions – though perhaps not always in such a condensed and oxymoronic fashion. The 1980 photograph of the bag lady clearly has ancestors in those famous and equally ironic images from the Depression such as Dorothea Lange's 1939 photograph of two hoboes walking up a dusty road, next to a billboard that says, "NEXT TIME TRY THE TRAIN," and Margaret Bourke-White's 1937 image of folks in a breadline, patiently waiting beneath a billboard proclaiming "THE WORLD'S HIGHEST STANDARD OF LIVING." With its store of images and texts that uncomfortably juxtapose the fact of scarcity and the promise of abundance (of "prosperity just around the corner"), the cultural history of the Great Depression offers us something of that "political dynamite" that interested Benjamin: it provides clues to the "ur-history" of our present moment and helps us see the contradictions of our own time afresh.[2]

The dichotomy between the second pair of terms, "literature" and "mass culture," is quite old, and nowadays decidedly shaky. It dates back at least as far as Flaubert, as far as the first traces of modernism, when artists started to assume an oppositional stance toward the commercial society and industrial products that surrounded them. In the United States, a related cultural split began to emerge in the late nineteenth and early twentieth centuries with the deliberate attempt of certain elites to stratify expressive forms; it was evident also in "genteel" complaints against popular entertainments in the first decades of the century.[3] The dichotomy between modernism and mass culture was perhaps given its first systematic and historical analysis in 1939, with Clement Greenberg's seminal essay "Avant-Garde and Kitsch." Subsequently, the "Great Divide," as Andreas Huyssen has dubbed this theoretical opposition, shaped the cultural debates of the Cold War, especially the work of the New York intellectuals. In this context of polarized global politics, of us and them, "mass culture" came to be seen as the equivalent not only of poor taste but of totalitarianism, while "art," for some of these critics, came to stand for nothing less than the salvation of the Free World.[4] Since then, however, this strict theoretical dichotomy has been challenged, if not erased, by the emergence of postmodern artistic forms, the single unifying characteristic of which has perhaps been the transgression of the dividing line between "high" and "low." Even more than a matter of new cultural *practices* concerned with "learning from Las Vegas," the postmodern obsolescence of the old "theories of brows" has been a cultural *condition* – a condition determined by the ever-increasing dominance of the commodity, whether as actual sales item or as image, in the era of multinational capitalism.[5] The recognition that "there is now very little cultural production outside the commodity form" forces us to consider very seriously Michael Denning's blunt and polemical announcement of the end of the Great Divide: "The fact is that mass culture has won; there is nothing else."[6]

At this moment of its demise, the constructedness of the theoretical dichotomy between high art and mass culture has become evident (and the rise of Cultural Studies in the 1980s can be seen as both a result and an agent of this paradigm shift). Such texts as Huyssen's *After the Great Divide* and Andrew Ross's *No Respect* suggest that we now have the perspective and capacity to historicize the values, both artistic and political, that have been so powerfully concentrated in this hierarchical opposition.[7] With the postmodern interpenetration of art and mass culture, it has become clear that art can no longer, as Fredric Jameson put it in an important essay of 1979, "serve as a fixed point or eternal standard against which to measure the 'degraded' status of mass culture." We can therefore, Jameson argues, move away from the passionate and highly ideological evaluation that has preoccupied critics for so long and replace this timeless realm of absolute judgments with an approach which demands "that we read high and mass culture as objectively related and dialectically interdependent phenomena, as twin and inseparable forms of the fission of aesthetic production under late capitalism."[8]

Jameson's argument has been massively persuasive; indeed, it is fair to say that (along with Stuart Hall's contemporaneous "Notes on Deconstructing 'The Popular' ") his reformulation of the stakes in the mass culture debate enabled scholars in the eighties to move away from an unproductive and undialectical antagonism: a standoff between optimistic populist theories, celebrating mass culture as a new vernacular, and pessimistic totalitarian theories, denouncing mass culture as manipulation and propaganda.[9] Both Hall and Jameson have insisted on and generated a more nuanced understanding of the contradictory impulses in mass-mediated texts and in the reception of such texts. But it seems to me that even Jameson's value-neutral conception of modernism and mass culture as constitutive and dialectical opposites does not really work all that well for the decade I am interested in. To many intellectuals writing in the thirties, Denning's more radical announcement that "mass culture has won" would already have made perfect sense. From a purely theoretical perspective this suggestion might seem surprising, since in the United States the Great Divide remains (despite its earlier beginnings) largely a product of the cultural criticism of the thirties. The work of Greenberg, Dwight Macdonald, and the Frankfurt exiles in the last years of the decade clearly brought a new level of sophistication and fervor to this increasingly central debate.[10] The very term "mass culture" dates from the thirties (though I doubt we can actually credit Macdonald's claim to have invented the term), emerging out of the decade's earnest discussions of the new electronic media and the rise of "mass societies" in Germany, Italy, and the Soviet Union.[11] But the fact is that the strict opposition between art and mass culture does not apply well to the critical and political writings by Left intellectuals in the earlier years of the Depression, nor does it fit particularly comfortably with the actual literary production of the decade. Indeed, it is arguably the very convergence of "high" and "mass" in the artistic work of the thirties that produced the reactive strictness of the Great Divide in the forties and fifties, and triggered, in particular, a stern disapprobation of "midcult," of "the scandal of the middlebrow" (which such critics as Dwight Macdonald and Robert Warshow came to regard as the baneful legacy of the preceding decade, and especially of the Popular Front).[12]

Setting aside for the moment those much-maligned examples of "midcult" cited by the Cold War critics (such as the all too accessible "masterpiece" *The Grapes of Wrath*), I would like to suggest three areas where the lines between art and mass culture became blurred during the thirties. There is, first, the experiment in proletarian literature, an effort to shape a new radical culture, that would be neither high nor low, and produced neither by a separate class of artists nor from above, by media tycoons. The slogan of the John Reed Clubs, "Art Is a Class Weapon," implied not only a rejection of "Art for Art's Sake." It also promised, as Eric Homberger has argued, to bridge the Great Divide: to heal the separation of art and society that had become so characteristic of nineteenth- and twentieth-century notions of culture.[13] The early cultural work of American Communists, in other words, still shared the dreams and cultural politics of the Soviet avant-garde of the early twenties.

Second, and perhaps most problematically for the theorists of the Great Divide, is the fact that in the thirties high culture itself became a kind of mass culture, a prestige commodity offered for wide-scale consumption. Argue as one might – and the theorists of the Great Divide certainly did[14] – it is hard to justify fully any rigid theoretical separation of high and mass culture when millions listen to radio broadcasts of symphonies sponsored by large corporations, or when millions, even in the smaller cities, visit a Van Gogh exhibition, or when even the strange art of the Surrealists draws massive public interest, to the extent that in 1936 Meret Oppenheim's fur-lined cup and saucer became, perhaps, the most-discussed object in the country.[15] James Agee, for one, was quite aware of this thorny problem:

> People hear Beethoven in concert halls or over a bridge game, or to relax; Cézannes are hung on walls, reproduced, in natural wood frames; van Gogh is the man who cut off his ear and whose yellows

became recently popular in window decoration; . . . Kafka is a fad;
Blake is in the Modern Library; Freud is a Modern Library Giant.[16]

It is simply not possible to dismiss all these instances of popular high art
as inherently middlebrow, as mawkishly sentimental and simplistic.
Such cultural phenomena indicate that the theoretical divide was, from
the thirties on, precisely that: a matter of high theory, not of practice.
Agee's remarks explicitly challenge the possibility, still fervently clung
to by postwar intellectuals, that high art could offer any kind of cultural
salvation. As he rather melodramatically charged, the culture had "distilled of [its] deliverers the most ruinous of . . . poisons." This is not, of
course, to say that Agee did not retain some hope of inventing a new
transforming aesthetic practice of his own: Let Us Now Praise Famous
Men was clearly conceived as an antidote to such ruinous commercial
poisons.[17] But his stern instruction to his readers – "Above all else: in
God's name don't think of it as Art" – articulates the suspicion that all
forms of institutionally recognized "culture" were in danger of being
subsumed by the commodity form and "sold" to a devouring and
treacherous new marketplace that could reside equally comfortably in
the "museum, gallery, or home."[18] It was, in short, possible in the
thirties to foresee the "end of mass culture" in the sense that Denning
intends: that, with increasingly rare exceptions, all artistic practices were
becoming commodified or "mass" in the way they were produced, or
consumed, or marketed, or distributed, or discussed.

Finally, the dichotomy between literature and mass culture is also
negated and undermined by a few writers who incorporated the language of mass culture into the body of their "literary" work. An interest
in this kind of practice was evident in the twenties as well, when certain
American writers came under the influence of Dada and the European
avant-garde. In 1922 Matthew Josephson, for instance, offered his noto-
rious paean to the "Great American Billposter" and to such anonymous
"geniuses" as the one who wrote a line of "pure poetry" – "MEATY
MARROWY OXTAIL JOINTS" – to the glorification of Campbell's
soup.[19] Four years later, Alfred Kreymborg (in one of my favorite
examples) constructed a poem from the latest headlines:

DOUBLE MURDER IN A HARLEM FLAT.
CREW LOST WHEN LINER SINKS AT SEA.
CHINAMAN BOILS RIVAL IN A VAT.
COOLIDGE SURE OF MORE PROSPERITY.
EARTHQUAKE SHAKES THE WHOLE PACIFIC COAST.
MORE FOLK OWN FORD CARS THAN FOLK WHO CAN'T.
KU KLUX WATCH ANOTHER NEGRO ROAST.

THE SHUBERTS ARE REVIVING CHARLEY'S AUNT.
MINE CAVES IN AND MEN ARE BURIED DEEP.
NEVER WAS A YEAR LIKE '26.
VALENTINO DIES AND WOMEN WEEP . . .[20]

This kind of technique became widely familiar to readers of American literature in the thirties through John Dos Passos's *U.S.A.*, with its many collage-like citations of tabloid headlines and news items. Yet Dos Passos's work does not actually offer the best example of the transgressive use of commercial discourses, since he confines his collages to the "Newsreel" sections of *U.S.A.*, neatly separating them from the rest of his novel.

There are other writers, such as Kenneth Fearing and Nathanael West, who took greater risks: writers whose work is radically citational, to the extent that it sometimes seems to foreshadow the work of postmodern artists, writers who understood quite clearly the challenge that the commercialization of culture, high and low, presented to the notion of art as a social panacea. It is in the work of Fearing and West, and the critical implications of their parodic and subversive techniques, that I am primarily interested in this study.

Before I detail its contents, however, I would like to gesture toward another area of the blurring between "high" and "mass culture." I am thinking here of the cultural work produced between 1935 and World War II under the auspices of the Popular Front and inspired, in many ways, by the optimistic and nationalistic climate created by the New Deal. The Communist Party's 1935 shift away from its earlier avant-gardist "proletcult" and "agitprop" cultural agenda and toward a broad antifascist policy involved not only a greater tolerance of a range of progressive political positions, but also a populist embrace of mass-mediated culture (though preferably in its more folksy and rural guise). The Popular Front lies for the most part beyond the scope of the present study. (Fearing and West, though interested in the demotic and local, were never particularly folksy, or affirmative, or nationalistic.) I do feel, however, that it has now become possible to regard the Popular Front without immediately invoking the old categories of inauthenticity, provincialism, or kitsch. Scholars have recognized for some time that the Popular Front's fostering of folk music in the later thirties and early forties remains an important legacy – perhaps the one thing that bridged the gap between the Old Left and the New Left.[21] But there may also be something of substance to discover in the Communists' mass culture criticism from the second part of the decade.

Let me suggest only one brief example. In May 1936 the Party stalwart Isidor Schneider expressed the Communists' new attitude toward mass culture in an article entitled "Mass Writers Wanted." The piece is partly promotional, celebrating what Schneider saw as the growing popularity of radical magazines like *Woman Today, The Sunday Worker,* and *The Fight Against War and Fascism.* But instead of lamenting as usual the decadence of bourgeois "mass" writing, the essay identifies the very idea of what we now call the Great Divide as a product of capitalist culture. Mainstream critics, Schneider argues, present a "monstrous double standard" when they judge the difference between high art and the popular as eternal, since, in fact, this "unwholesome and unnatural division into a good literature segregated from the masses and a popular literature, designedly and professionally bad," is the result of a general schizophrenia in the culture at large. This position strikes me as surprisingly compatible with more recent approaches to mass-mediated culture: the same insight, after all, underpins Jameson's conception of modernism and mass culture as "twin and inseparable forms of the fission of artistic production under late capitalism" or even Adorno's more melancholy observation that mass culture and modernism are "torn halves of an integral freedom to which however they do not add up."[22] Moreover, literary scholars have now come to question, as Schneider does in this piece, the way in which the word "writer" seems almost "automatically [to] exclude from consideration the writers in the mass-circulation media." Essays like this one can, I feel, be reexamined with profit.

The Great Depression and the Culture of Abundance is divided into three parts. Part I contains, along with this introduction, only one chapter: a historical essay in which I attempt to negotiate the contradiction between the terms "Depression" and "abundance." I argue, in essence, that the stock market crash of 1929, which ushered in the Great Depression, also represents a watershed in a general cultural and economic transition to the "culture of abundance," a culture in which the strategic element is no longer production, but consumption. In terms of the history I sketch here, the thirties writers who chose to emphasize the plight of the proletariat and the virtues of simple regional cultures are revealed as engaged in a somewhat residual, even nostalgic, cultural endeavor; I should immediately add that this is not necessarily a criticism: the residual, as Raymond Williams insists, is not to be equated with the archaic, and alternative and oppositional political efforts can often include elements of the nostalgic or romantic.[23] Fearing and West, on the other hand, though no less political, illuminate the emergent cultural forces (the culture of cities, as expressed in the newspaper, radio, cinema, and even TV) – forces that are dominant in the daily life of our postmodern world. This essay provides a broad materialist perspective that will serve as a reminder that mass culture is not simply a superstructural or textual phenomenon, but an integral part of the whole cultural and economic formation in question.

Parts II and III present my readings of Kenneth Fearing and Nathanael West respectively. Each chapter is best understood as a relatively free-standing essay, each taking a new thematic tack on the author's response to mass culture and, more generally, to the culture of abundance. I have not attempted to provide any full or chronological treatment of either author's work, since it is not the author per se who is of interest to me, but rather the cluster of social issues that his work addresses. However, since Fearing is so little known I have decided to open Part II with a polemical introduction that does include biographical information, as well as (more importantly) a discussion of the theoretical and historical aspects of Fearing's literary marginalization, of what I call "the politics of literary failure." This discussion should not be seen as a digression from the main issues at hand, since Fearing's "failure," I argue, is in good measure due to his interest in using the language of mass culture and to his irreverent attitude toward high art: his debunking, "taxi-driver" pose, which I associate with the destruction of what Walter Benjamin has called the aura of the masterpiece. In Chapter 3 I turn more specifically to Fearing's critique of consumer society in the late twenties and early thirties, to his comments on the rise of celebrities, movie theaters, nightlife, and so forth, and consider how his perspective compares with that of other Left writers of the period (notably Muriel Rukeyser and Mike Gold). Chapter 4 traces Fearing's understanding of the psychological effects of mass culture, by which I understand here not only specific forms such as comic strips, radio, tabloids, and popular biographies, but the general organization of experience and leisure. It is in these two essays, which touch on such themes as the fragmentation and rationalization of experience, the loss of historicity, and the rise of a culture of simulacra, that Fearing's relation to certain Frankfurt school positions and to postmodernism is most explicitly explored.

Since Nathanael West has achieved at least minor canonical status, and since we already have the benefit of Jay Martin's enormously helpful biography, I have not opened Part III with a polemical and biographical introduction. Even so, my readings do imply a polemical angle, which I articulate within the chapters. I feel that the revival of critical interest in West in the mid-fifties to mid-seventies depended in good measure on a particular interpretation of his work: one that casts his writing as a battle between art and the cheap clichés and disorder of mass culture, a battle from which art emerges victorious. The value of West's novels, in such readings, transcends and solves the problem of the vacuous and vicious culture represented in them. This kind of interpretation has necessitated the exclusion or slighting of certain interesting aspects of West's work, such as the irredeemably (and deliberately) trashy satire *A Cool Million* and the overtly revolutionary poem "Burn the Cities" – both of which critics have generally preferred to see as aberrations. While it is certainly true that West presents mass culture in negative terms and associates it with fascism and depersonalization, I feel that it is wrong to read his work as representing the formalist victory of "Art." West was too political, too much a man of the thirties, to be satisfied with this kind of mystificatory solution; he was certainly no less scornful of the hallowed category of art than Fearing – or the Berlin Dadaists who influenced both writers.

The section on West, then, opens with an essay on *A Cool Million* in which I examine his critique of the new and self-consciously spectacular culture of abundance. I examine the implicit cultural politics of his highly ironic writing and juxtapose his mode of critique with that of his contemporaries who worked in a more documentary or social realist vein. The two essays that follow are more concerned with West's under-standing of the psychological effects of mass culture. In many ways his critique overlaps with Fearing's: both explore, for example, the fragmentation of experience, the denial of negativity, the ideology of gambling, and, more implicitly, the abolition of auratic "distance" and uniqueness. Chapter 8, focusing mainly on West's Hollywood novel, *The Day of the Locust,* takes off from W. H. Auden's often-reprinted essay, "West's Disease." I suggest that West's conception of wishing (of which mass culture, "the business of dreams," is the institutional guise) is far more unsettling, more postmodern, perhaps, than Auden's reading would have it. Comparing West's presentation of Hollywood with cer-tain aspects of Walter Benjamin's theory of mass culture, I try to empha-size the social and political dimensions of the Westian wish, rather than simply regard it as a "disease." The final chapter is on West's first novel, *Miss Lonelyhearts.* The key issue here is again the fragmentation of experience, which, according to Benjamin's "Storyteller" essay, is dia-lectically intertwined with the emergence of mass culture and the decline of the novel. In the light of this essay, and in the context of new trends in American advertising, I try to tease out what West meant when he thought of writing this novel "in the form of a comic strip."

The similarities between Fearing's and West's preoccupations emerge quite clearly in the course of these discussions, as does the similarity in their parodic techniques, in their fiercely negative, even apocalyptic, sensibilities, and in their attention to the nitty-gritty details of the mass culture of their day. It becomes clear, moreover, that both occupy a transitional position in the history of mass culture criticism: still sharing (in their ironic and subversive incorporation of mass culture materials) the subversive politics of Dada and the historic avant-garde, but also prefiguring in certain ways the mass culture criticism of the Frankfurt school (and of later neo-Marxists), in which such concepts as standardization, reification, and "mass deception" are privileged. It is no wonder, then, that the theoretical work of Walter Benjamin (another apocalyptic sensibility) has seemed so particularly applicable to these writers. Benjamin, too, occupies a transitional position. His work negotiates a space between, on the one hand, his sympathies for the avant-gardist practices of Brecht and the Surrealists, plus his genuine interest in the possibilities of the new media, and, on the other hand, the gloomier, more mandarin cultural politics advocated by his friend Adorno (and justified by the dismal political developments around him). Benjamin's major essays of the thirties provide the theoretical basis and inspiration for much of this book.

Such are the details of the proceedings. From a broader perspective one might say that these essays participate in three projects of current critical interest. First, I would like to think of this study as contributing to the ongoing project of periodizing and defining the postmodern. Second, this study participates in the collective effort to revise and expand the canon of American literature (although the canonization of my unknowns is not exactly the end I have in mind). I wish to help shape a more inclusive – more properly historical – version of American literary history, and hope that the discussion in these pages of Fearing, and of other neglected writers such as Mike Gold, Herman Spector, Nelson Algren, and Muriel Rukeyser, will contribute to this task. Finally, as regards critical methodology, I have been concerned to devise ways of writing literary history and literary interpretation in which the broader cultural history is not simply background, but where history and text are mutually illuminating.

A final word on terminology is needed. It is not without trepidation that one chooses nowadays to use the label "mass culture." Not so long ago, as Michael Denning has observed, the act of choosing one's term – "mass culture" or "popular culture" – meant choosing a side: between structuralism and culturalism (in the United Kingdom) and between populism or liberal pluralism and the Frankfurt school's critical theory (in the United States).[24] I am not sure that things have altogether changed since the critical conjuncture of the late seventies and early eighties that Denning describes here. Andrew Ross, for one, has recently lamented the way in which, through the term "mass culture," the "mandarin Germanic specter of *Kulturpessimismus*" remains to haunt Left cultural criticism.[25] If this shibboleth then renders my work unduly "Frankfurtized" (to use an adjective I once saw in the *Village Voice*), so be it.[26] I am indeed far from convinced that critical theory has lost its usefulness and agree wholeheartedly with Jackson Lears's insistence that "writers as elusive as Adorno cannot merely be used as punching bags for populist self-validation."[27] Nor do I think that the critical potency of the concept of reification or of commodity fetishism has been exhausted. While it is indisputable that consumers and audiences can "make do" with and "make over" the products and texts that are handed to them, it is also true that analyses which emphasize the autonomy of the consumer can easily run the risk of underplaying the power of the producer.[28] Moreover, as Susan Willis has argued, such analyses can all too easily take for granted the fact that people have come not to *make* but to *buy* a living – something that still seemed somehow scandalous to the sociologist Robert Lynd back in 1933.[29] "The critic engrossed in mass culture as a struggle over meanings," Willis warns, "runs the risk of being captured in a system of ricocheting – sometimes revolutionary and sometimes recuperated – meanings," and may not be in the best position to question "the consequences of fetishism on the meanings made."[30] I would put the matter more simply (even perhaps simplistically): the disturbing image of the bag lady in front of the store window raises questions of social power that a celebration of subversive cultural bricolage would seem unable to address.

But I have reasons (beyond the more polemical "choosing of sides") for deciding to use the term "mass culture." In the case of Fearing and West the apocalyptic associations – the sense of *Kulturpessimismus* – it might carry are, in fact, appropriate. They were deeply troubled by the cultural and political situation in which they lived, and we cannot blame them for that. In fact, we must remember that our own ability to think about mass-mediated culture as enabling and open to subversion, rather than merely manipulative and controlling, is also historically determined. We live, as Michael Denning and Paul Buhle have pointed out, in "the age of the cassette": new technologies, as well as the very size and multifariousness of the cultural marketplace, have allowed us to experience mass-mediated culture as a series of "elaborate, interlocking subcultures" rather than a threatening, propagandistic monolithic.[31] For Fearing and West things were different: they were not only consumers, but small-time producers, assembly-line writers, at a time when the culture industry was standardizing its products and consolidating itself as a vast oligopoly (the Hollywood studio system being the most obvious instance). My use of the term "mass culture" should thus be taken as signifying a *distance* (as important as the fascinating *connections*) between us and them, and between then and now.

I have, however, decided to use Warren Susman's phrase "the culture of abundance" in my title, instead of the more negative alternatives, such as "the society of the spectacle." This is, in part, to connect my work to that of Susman and of others in the field of American studies who use the term but, more important, to serve as a reminder, even when things get rather bleak, that this new form of capitalism presented not only dystopian but also distinctly utopian features.

2

Hard Times, Modern Times

Nothing impairs morale like the dissolution of a last pair of shoes. Maybe it starts with a little hole in the sole; and then the slush of pavements oozes in, gumming sox and balling between your toes. . . . You walk and stare in shop windows. A pink and white ham simmers in the Bandbox Lunch. . . . Ye Cozy Radio Shoppe flings harmony for five blocks and a thunderous optimist yammers as from a barrel, bassly: "We are now in the dining room of the Commodore Perry Hotel. Lights! Good food! Music! Youth! Is everybody happy! The orchestra enters into the spirit of the occasion with that tuneful selection: 'Happy Days Are Here Again.' "

Jack Conroy, *The Disinherited*

In Gregory La Cava's 1936 film, *My Man Godfrey*, the "forgotten man," loitering among his fellow trash pickers on the dump, is whisked away to become a butler for a society family; when hardship threatens them too, the butler (who is actually one of the wealthy Parkeses of Boston) saves the day by turning the dump into a nightclub called, *mirabile dictu*, "The Dump." Thus garbage becomes classy decor, and the erstwile trash pickers become costumed waiters – actors of sorts in a profitable theme park based on their former "lifestyle." This entrepreneurial solution to economic hardship would seem to smack of the wishful thinking of the Reagan years, but the film's juxtaposed ingredients of wealth, poverty, and entertaining spectacle are, in fact, observable everywhere in the culture of the Depression decade. There is perhaps a temptation, looking back as we do, to think of what Alfred Kazin has called the "lean and angry Thirties" as the last decade of the real America: a time when politics was politics, and Reds were Reds, when strikes were actually radical, when the faces of sharecroppers bespoke some kind of authenticity; a time before class disappeared, before intellectuals became professors, before culture retreated to the museums, before the shopping malls were built, and before the dump became a nightclub.[1] But it is also possible to argue, as Jean Baudrillard does in *The Mirror of Production,* that the stock market crash of 1929 marked the birth of our present social formation, of a culture that theorists have characterized by various and much-disputed terms like the "society of the spectacle," the "culture of abundance," "postindustrial" or "postmodern" society, and "late capitalism." "The feudal system died," or so Baudrillard announces,

> because it could not find the path to rational productivity. The bourgeoisie knew how to make the people work, but it also narrowly escaped destruction in 1929 because it did not know how to make them consume. It was content, until then, to socialize people by force and exploit them through labor. But the crisis in 1929 marked the point of asphyxiation: the problem was no longer one of production but one of circulation. Consumption became the strategic element; the people were henceforth mobilized as consumers; their "needs" became as essential as their labor power. By this operation, the system assured its economic survival at a fantastically expanded level. . . . By allowing for the possibility of expanding and consuming, by organizing social distribution (social security, allotments, salaries that are no longer defined as the strict economic reproduction of labor power), by launching advertising, human relations, etc., the system created the illusion of symbolic participation. . . . [T]his entire symbolic simulation is uncovered as leading to superprofits and super-power.[2]

Despite his marked and perhaps even paralyzing negativity (which I shall address specifically later on), Baudrillard is not alone in identifying 1929, or, more broadly, the interwar years, as a watershed in the history of capitalism. His thumbnail sketch of the origins of late capitalism concurs, in its broad outline, with the more detailed investigations of the historian Warren Susman, who has argued that the thirties marked the climactic phase of the fundamental conflict of twentieth-century America: the transformation from a "Puritan-republican, producer-capitalist culture" to a "culture of abundance" – terms that have achieved wide currency in American studies.[3] Richard Wightman Fox, likewise, has noted that it was in the twenties and thirties that the characteristic institutions and habits of consumer culture – the motion picture, the radio, the automobile, the weekly photo-newsmagazine, installment buying, the five-day work week, suburban living, and (I would add) the self-service supermarket – assumed the central position they still occupy in American life.[4] And while Fox cautiously defines this period as marking the consolidation, not the birth, of modern American consumer society, it is hard not to feel that something quite new is brought about by the simultaneous arrival of so many constitutive elements of the "commodity spectacle." I am thinking, for example, of the advent of the first sound picture, the first national broadcasting networks, the first radios with standardized AC plugs, the first Fords and bed linens ever to be offered in a range of colors, the first telephone service between London, New York, and San Francisco, the first cheaply manufactured Bakelite plastics, and the first huge newsmaking celebrity, Charles Lindbergh – all coming on the scene in that remarkable year of 1927.[5] Such developments strongly suggest that the interwar years were the formative period, the "ur-history," of our consumer society and that this era might very well hold (as the historian Lizabeth Cohen has also argued) "the key to understanding the larger significance of mass consumption in this century."[6]

PERIODIZATION AND OTHER PROBLEMS

Nevertheless, the magisterial abstraction of the Baudrillard passage is unlikely to find favor with all readers; and I would like to start my own reading of the culture of the thirties by discussing three caveats that we must keep in mind as we consider this periodization. To some degree I will be playing the devil's advocate here, since later on in this chapter I will offer further data to support the idea that consumption does in fact become the "strategic element" for the capitalist system around 1929. But it seems to me important to indicate first some of the complications and problems one encounters in writing about consumerism and mass culture in the period.

One might certainly object, first of all, that such a schematic presentation of historical change as Baudrillard's is inevitably simplistic and too neatly theoretical. Major social transformations are never experienced – even during a time of crisis – as the kind of clean break suggested by a word like "henceforth." There is certainly a danger inherent in all attempts to pinpoint a historical watershed (including my own fascination with 1927) of masking the necessary continuities of everyday life, as well as the realities of struggle and resistance. In actual fact, the mobilization of workers as consumers did not happen by the sudden fiat of Capital. Since such a process involves a radical transformation of the daily habits, the ethical convictions, and even the psychological makeup of millions of people, it could and did take place only as a very gradual cultural transformation, starting perhaps in the last two decades of the preceding century and still not complete. After all, people still work, still do not devote all of their leisure to commodified pursuits, and, even in such pursuits, find ways to resist and subvert what Baudrillard so portentously terms "the code."[7] We should not forget, moreover, that many people, even in the United States, are still confronted in their daily lives by more direct forms of oppression than the "repressive desublimation" of hegemonic consumption.

As regards the specific history of the thirties, this caveat against a too neatly schematic periodization is raised, for instance, in the work of the historian Lawrence Levine. Levine has argued that there are important continuities between the "folk" and "mass culture" of the Depression decade – indeed, that commercial mass culture functioned as the "folk-lore of industrial society" and as such provided a sense of community to Americans and helped them "cope" with the hardships of the time.[8] More persuasive (to me at least) is the rather more commonsensical caution that ideological changes often, perhaps always, occur more gradually than material ones. We should therefore not assume too readily that the economic crisis that ushered in the Great Depression entailed a similar collapse of the nation's favorite mythologies.[9] Busi-nessmen in the thirties in fact proved rather reluctant to effect the "mobilization" of mass consumers and to let go of their old, and by now self-defeating, methods of enforcing or cajoling the worker to produce.

Accelerated assembly lines, reduced salaries and layoffs, the clubs of company goons, and the tear gas of Pinkertons were much in evidence throughout the decade. So was the old parable that had served competi-tive capitalism so well: the rags-to-riches story, which held out the promise of success in exchange for hard work. Though patently irratio-nal at a time when unemployment was rife and new businesses were likely to fail, the myth died hard. In 1936, for example, the *Saturday Evening Post* carried an article entitled "Horatio Alger at the Bridge," which argued quite vociferously that the old-style success story was still an accurate index of possibilities and grumbled at the New Deal child labor laws that prevented one from starting one's career at the optimal age of thirteen.[10] The death of John D. Rockefeller, as Levine has argued, brought further evidence that the ideology of production-oriented capitalism had by no means breathed its last. The national press used the occasion to revive dozens of Rockefeller's aphorisms – the same saws that Nathanael West had so bitterly laughed out of court in *A Cool Million*: "Work! Persevere! Be Honest! Save!" "Live Within Your Means." "You won't have a happy life if you don't work."[11] Today it is relatively easy for a historian (the late Charles Eckert, for instance, in his delightful essay on the cultural significance of Shirley Temple) to dis-miss such absurdities as merely an expedient recourse to "the deities who dwelled at the deepest recesses of the capitalist ethos," and even to describe this ideological effort in a mock-heroic vein: "Initiative, Work, and Thrift," Eckert remarks, were duly "summoned forth, blinking at the light."[12] But we should remember that for many of the men and women who lived through the Depression, these values still meant a great deal. In the years preceding the New Deal the countless descriptions of the emotional suffering of the jobless, the personal feelings of shame and inadequacy, and especially phenomena such as "Depression impotence" suggest the extent to which people had internalized the moral strictures of a puritan-capitalist ethos. In short, though consumption may indeed, as Baudrillard argues, have emerged by the thirties as the "strategic element" for the economy, many individuals still based their sense of self on a work ethic – and many still do.

A second objection to the Baudrillard passage is that his dystopian view of consumer culture as a superpotent system of symbolic manipulation is too one-sided and conspiratorial. This view has been challenged on two (not always separate) fronts: on the one hand, there is a new vein of research in American cultural history that has attempted the difficult task of determining the actual experience of mass audiences and consumers; on the other, there is the emerging field of Cultural Studies, with its turn to the more flexible Gramscian conception of hegemony as a terrain of contestation – as a struggle over meanings, rather than a superpotent "code."[13] Baudrillard's gloomy totalization is, of course, no private nightmare: his negativity partakes of a long tradition of Left criticism of mass society. The theorists of the Frankfurt school, for example, discerned in the standardization of consumer culture something akin to fascism and barbarism; and the Situationists of the sixties perceived in the "commodity-spectacle" a ubiquitous threat – a veritable "Godzilla of alienation," as Greil Marcus once put it.[14] Even Fearing and West, the writers who are the focus of this study, often tended to see mass-produced commodities as exhibits in a kind of cultural horror show, and mass culture as the end of "bona-fide life."[15] But despite this tradition (which I, as a born pessimist, find dangerously seductive), it is important to consider Warren Susman's warning that it may be a serious methodological error not to make an attempt to understand the "culture of abundance" on its own terms, which were in fact utopian.[16] Even if consumption functions as a form of social control, it remains one that offers substantial consolations. As one feminist critic has phrased it, "The pleasure of eating an ice cream cone may be minor compared to the pleasure of meaningful autonomous work, but the former is easily available and the latter is not."[17] We should at the very least, she suggests, regard consumer society not as a universal rip-off in which the masses are mindless dupes, but as a bribe – a transaction that offers concrete benefits, including, for most Americans, a degree of comfort unparalleled in history.

A similar argument obviously applies to mass-mediated culture. As Fredric Jameson, Stuart Hall, and many others writing in their wake have argued, it is inconceivable that a culture of pure manipulation could take hold of an audience's hearts and minds: "The works of mass culture," notes Jameson, "cannot be ideological without at one and the same time being implicitly or explicitly Utopian as well: they cannot manipulate unless they offer some genuine shred of content as a fantasy bribe to the public about to be so manipulated."[18] Other theorists of popular culture would, of course, emphasize the element of resistance and subversion even more strongly: Michel de Certeau, for example, would insist that the consumer can control the use of the spaces, objects, and texts of consumer culture through all manner of subversions and irreverent bricolage. The public, in this view, is not merely paid hush money; it cunningly resists the terms that are offered; it "poaches" or steals from the powers that be.[19]

When we apply this caveat – against the supercilious dismissal of the consuming masses as passive dupes – to the history of the thirties, several received ideas are shown to be in need of reevaluation. It becomes clear, for instance, that we cannot simply denounce as a sellout the efforts of labor leaders to win a larger slice of the capitalist pie for workers. While the Keynesian position of Sidney Hillman (of the Amalgamated Clothing Workers' Union) may finally have served the interests of American business, his argument that "unless a great majority of people have the money to buy, nothing significant can be accomplished in the way of recovery" was perhaps the only line that had any chance of being persuasive under the circumstances.[20] We should bear in mind that, by the end of the twenties, the rationalization of the factory through "scientific management" had given owners almost total control of the work process, so that the radical aim of transforming the workplace had already been rendered extremely difficult.[21] Contrary to radical expectations, the possibility of effecting such a transformation was jeopardized rather than furthered by the economic crisis: militant workers were placed in a vulnerable position by the legions of job-hungry Americans outside the factory gates.[22] The fact that labor managed to wrest even short-term victories from management should then be seen as a substantial achievement under the circumstances; and a Left history that presents the thirties only in terms of manipulation and loss is disrespectful of those very people it would presumably hope to empower.

Moreover, cultural historians have recently begun to complicate the idea that socialism faltered in the United States on " 'roast beef and apple pie,' or, by the interwar era, automobiles and refrigerators."[23] The research of Lizabeth Cohen on the actual practices and consciousness of mass consumers in the thirties suggests that we need to think a little more dialectically about what happens when workers enter the mass market as consumers. Her evidence clearly suggests that the standard-ized marketing of goods (through national chain stores and supermar-kets), as well as mass-mediated culture (through commercial broadcast networks and studio-owned movie theaters), made enormous advances during the Depression: in this limited sense, it did "win over" the working class. But it also appears that this increased exposure to mass culture did not necessarily destroy a working-class consciousness. Rather, Cohen suggests, the common experience of such forms created a new, shared culture that transcended old ethnic divisions and ultimately contributed to the forging of the first permanent industrial unions. Cohen's work, like that of Lawrence Levine on the audiences of popular culture, intends, in other words, to remind us that consumers retain a certain degree of autonomy – something that the more schematic ac-counts of the rise of consumerism tend to leave out of the picture.[24]

Another objection to Baudrillard's outline can be stated more briefly. It seems counterintuitive, if not a little perverse, to pick 1929 – the year that ushered in the Great Depression – as the birthdate of consumer society. "Abundance" and "hegemonic consumption" are not the terms that come to mind when one thinks of those famous photographs of breadlines, apple vendors, and impoverished sharecroppers, or when one reads some of the letters that ordinary Americans sent to the Roose-velts during the decade: letters like the one from a woman who begs the First Lady for discarded clothing, "any thing from an old bunch of stockings to an old Sport Suit or an old afternoon dress," or the one from a father who feels guilty because he cannot give his children "the little things in life such as a cone of cream or a 1 *cts* piece of candy or a soft drink once a week."[25] The list of such examples of Depression scarcity, from the devastating to the undignified, could be extended almost indefinitely: they are part of our popular iconography of the period.

I must confess, however, that it is precisely the paradoxical implica-tions of Baudrillard's dating which interest me and which suggest that, despite the objections I have discussed, his outline may be quite accurate. (Besides, it seems to me that paradox always offers, in its defamiliarizing tensions, the heuristic possibilities of a critical rupture.) For the thirties were, if anything, a decade of bizarre contradictions and jarring juxtapo-sitions. These were certainly "hard times," as Studs Terkel's collection of oral accounts of the period reminds us, but as other histories suggest, the years of the Great Depression were also self-consciously "modern times" and modernity (as the visions of "Tomorrow" promoted in the decade's great fairs suggest) was generally understood as having to do with the comfort, mobility, and pleasure promised by "the dime-store dream parade" of commodities.[26]

This view is satirized with precision (and a touch of melodrama) in Kenneth Burke's poem "For a Modernist Sermon" (1938):

You'll have an eight-cylinder car in heaven –
Air-conditioning –
Indirect lighting –
A tile bathroom and a white porcelain kitchen.

.   .   .   .

Despite the phenomenal growth of population,
there'll be no traffic problem,
if you would drive out
to the Garden of Eden
for a week-end.

O the celestial sundaes –
all the flavors made with the purest chemicals.

.   .   .   .

In heaven,
when you want something,
you just fill out an order
and your want is met like magic
from the Power-plants

.   .   .   .

And Blast-Furnaces
of hell.[27]

The best illustration of this kind of contradiction, however, is Charlie Chaplin's 1935 film, *Modern Times* (a text that the title of this chapter must inevitably bring to mind). Though clearly intended to strip the phrase "modern times" of its associations with technological boosterism, the film perfectly encapsulates the period's curious doubleness. *Modern Times*'s tale of hunger, poverty, and drudgery, of the inhumanity of the factory where the worker is dwarfed (or even swallowed) by the gigantic wheels, gears, and belts of incomprehensible machinery, undermines the official optimism of the Alger success story: that old parable explicitly evoked in the opening titles calling the film a "story of industry, of individual enterprise, of humanity crusading in the pursuit of happiness." Despite its presentation of contemporary social ills, however, the film's utopian moments are finally extremely "modern" in their endorsement of consumerism. While the film criticizes the mindless drill to which the worker is subjected in the factory, it in effect celebrates the institution that trains the worker as a consumer – the department store. Some of the happiest scenes in the film are set after hours in a land of wishes, where the delights of the deli counter are free, where the tramp sleeps on the finest bed linen, and where the tattered gamine can don a fur and (for a frame or two) be transformed into a glamour girl. And while the only home that the tramp and his gamine manage to put together is a ramshackle shed, their dream (which Chaplin subjects to only the gentlest of parody) is to own the suburban home we see in a fantasy sequence: the living room crammed with furniture, the bright curtains, the frilly apron, the well-appointed kitchen, the orange tree near the window. It is the most mundane of paradises.[28]

The experience of scarcity during the Depression, as Chaplin's film suggests so vividly, did not immunize Americans against dreams of abundance or modest luxuries. The same era that, even in our distant memory, remains haunted by the specter of a nation "ill-housed, ill-clad, ill-nourished" (as Roosevelt described it in his second inaugural address) brought new meaning to such words as "streamlined," "glamorous," and "sophisticated" and produced that self-congratulatory phrase "the American way of life."[29] The decade produced innumerable contrasts of this sort: while many were deprived of their living by the Dust Bowl, Rudy Vallee crooned, "Life is just a bowl of cherries"; while thousands lined their worn-out shoes with cardboard, Fred Astaire danced elegantly in his patent leathers; and while the 1937 recession cost thousands of factory workers in basic industries their jobs, the factories of the Sieberling-Latex company ran day and night to fulfill a massive demand for a range of products whose use-value certainly seems negligible: statuettes of Dopey and the other Disney dwarfs.[30] Indeed, even the father's letter to Roosevelt mentioned earlier encapsulates an odd cultural contradiction: its poignant lament rests on the assumption that kids are entitled to the consumerist pleasures of the "little things in life." It is this kind of suffering, more than anything else, that seems to me to characterize the thirties. After all, *not having* was nothing new, as the reminiscences of African-Americans from the decade amply attest.[31] But the father's sense that he should be able to offer ice-cream cones and soft drinks may well hint at a historic transition.

A "DEMOCRACY OF GOODS"

Depression statistics, surprisingly, suggest that a number of factors (lower food prices, installment buying, and the availability of cheap plastics) helped keep alive the boom years' trend toward a "higher standard of living." Expenditures on such things as automobiles and personal appearance even showed a marked increase.[32] More and more new commercial products – from electrical gadgets to trailers to bermuda shorts to cocktail bars to small cameras – came on the market, causing the sociologist Robert Lynd to describe the nation in 1935 as "a culture hypnotized by the gorged stream of new things to buy."[33]

Lynd's remark is, of course, hardly devoid of hyperbole: the continued sluggishness of the economy well into the next decade indicates that the transition to a "culture of abundance" remained in the thirties a matter more of commercial ideology than of actual practice. But the ideological dimension of this culture, the discourses and economic structures put into place by the producers of culture and of goods, remains extremely important (even if we grant the relative autonomy of consumers to contest these structures).[34] It seems to me that if we regard the Baudrillard passage not as a *cultural* history so much as an *ideological* history – an account of the producers' shifting perceptions of cost and social control – it often seems uncannily accurate. In the twenties and thirties a variety of professional ideologues – public relations officers, businessmen, advertising people, and "home economists" – expressed themselves in terms very similar to Baudrillard's. In 1927 Bernard Baruch used the very same metaphor of *asphyxiation* to express the anxieties of his class: "We have learned how to create wealth," he announced. "But we have not learned to keep that wealth from choking us and bringing on widespread poverty to the producers in the midst of their abundance."[35] And by 1929, if not earlier, one finds the historic solution to Baruch's problem formulated quite explicitly: it is what Mrs. Christine Frederick describes (in *Selling Mrs. Consumer*) as the "new doctrine" of "consumptionism." This doctrine, she claims, "is admitted today to be the greatest idea that America has to give the world; the idea that workmen and the masses be looked upon not simply as workers or producers, but as *consumers*. Pay them more, sell them more, prosper more is the equation."[36]

This element of deliberate marketing "propaganda" was even more evident after the stock market crash. While the optimism of the "equation" from *Selling Mrs. Consumer* was not so easy to muster during the Depression, the belief in the panacea of "consumptionism" did not fade from sight. In the early thirties the nation's advertising firms obliquely acknowledged an asphyxiating squeeze on the system. They blamed the Depression on a "buyers' strike" – a notion illustrated in the pages of their trade magazines by a dramatic photograph of a clenched fist tightly clasping a few bills with the caption "America Has Closed Its Fist."[37] The phrase "buyers' strike" reveals more than a blind callousness to the sufferings of the masses. One senses behind it a kind of righteous indignation, suggesting that, somehow, consumption had already come to be seen as one of the duties of the working people and that their failure to buy thus constituted a new species of oppositional truculence. The odd phrase and its accompanying iconography thus suggest a crucial insight: in a depressed market with unemployment figures over 10 million, the tight fist of the consumer "refusing" to buy may present a greater threat to the system than the clenched fist of the militant striker refusing to work. What we see in the last years of the Hoover administration, with this perception of a new kind of danger, is a power elite awakening to new strategies of control. A "buyers' strike," quite evidently, is to be overcome not by calling in the National Guard, but by handing out fatter paychecks and creating needs and desires.

While Roosevelt himself was at best a reluctant Keynesian, and on occasion presented the tribulations of the Depression as a deserved punishment for the excesses of the twenties, his administration was certainly cognizant of the need for a strategic shift. A series of federally sponsored budget studies from the mid-thirties (the Bureau of Labor Statistics's investigation, *Family Expenditures in Selected Cities 1935–1936*, the Civil Works Administration's *National Survey of Potential Product Capacity*, and the Works Progress Administration's 1935 inquiry to determine an adequate income for workers) provide some idea of the federal government's attitude toward consumption.[38] The WPA study, for example, suggested that even a barely livable "emergency budget" should set aside a certain amount of money for items like "tobacco, 'treats' of various kinds, games, athletic equipment, and a variety of other leisuretime accessories, serving no particular purpose but contributing something to life's more frivolous moments."[39] Both the "emergency budget" and the slightly more ample "maintenance budget" specifically allotted funds to enable each family member to attend the movies: once a month on the former, and once a week on the latter. The most interesting aspect of these budget studies is, perhaps, the difficulty the authors seem to have had in distinguishing between needs and luxuries. Is a rug, for example, necessary for physical comfort, or is it an extra, an "amenity of living"? And are the movies an indulgence or a necessary escape for those confronted with the stress of hard times and the quickened pace of contemporary life? It is tempting to see such questions as evidence of the disappearance of use-value in a culture increasingly dominated by exchange value – by Guy Debord's "commodity-spectacle" or by Baudrillard's "code." Indeed, for Baudrillard the process culminates in the "uncontrollable play of floating capital," the autonomy of exchange and finance capital, which accompanies the abolition of the gold standard, an event that Roosevelt announced in 1933.[40] But the more cautious claim is perhaps more accurate. These federal budget studies reflect a significant change in official (top-down) attitudes toward consumption, the very change that the Baudrillard passage would lead us to expect: it would appear that, by the mid-thirties, the notion of an "adequate" income for the worker had moved beyond the mere reproduction and maintenance of labor power, toward a wage scale that would ensure a level of purchasing power "adequate" to the needs of the *nation's* economic metabolism.[41]

It is significant that these federal studies are devoid of any old-fashioned moralizing on the triviality and sinfulness of pleasurable expenditures by the working class. However, the thirties also marked the emergence of a voluminous body of critical commentary from the Left and Left-center expressing what Daniel Horowitz has termed a "modern moralism" – a pessimistic and frequently nostalgic analysis of mass society, with its loss of authenticity and meaningful work.[42] It can be argued that the work of best-selling authors such as Robert Lynd, Alfred Bingham, and Stuart Chase contributed significantly to a perception that consumption was the key characteristic of "the American way of life." Richard Wightman Fox has even suggested that Lynd's work, for all its oppositional and demystifying intent, may ultimately have served the ideological function of fostering the very trends it was decrying.[43] It is not easy to know exactly what factual value to put on the more radical conclusions of these "modern moralists" (Fox explicitly reminds us that Lynd's work was generously leavened with opinion). But that does not mean that Lynd's jeremiads are not deeply interesting as a subjective record of a disturbing cultural change and as an important contribution to a decade's discourse about mass culture.

There is, for instance, an intriguing diagnostic moment in Lynd's 1933 essay, commissioned by President Hoover's Committee for Research on Social Trends (an essay he decided to call "The People as Consumers" rather than to give it his editors' preferred title, "Recent Trends in Consumption"). He here expresses something of the shocking novelty of the idea that people had come, with the expansion of the mass market, not to *make* but to *buy* a living.[44] Though recognizing the survival of a "lingering Puritan tradition of abstinence," of the doctrine of "rigorous saving," and of a "deep rooted philosophy of hardship," Lynd reports the advent of a "new gospel which encourages liberal spending to make the wheels of industry turn as *a duty of the citizen*" (my emphasis). He also describes the economic situation using a metaphor similar to that of asphyxiation: the act of buying has become the "neck of the bottle through which the varied output of America's industrial machinery must somehow flow." Like Baruch and Baudrillard, in other words, Lynd identifies the strategic problem not as one of the *production of commodities* (since "the manufacturer and business man" were already being "pushed from behind by the momentum of modern technology and merchandising"), but one of *circulation* – or, even more basically, a problem concerning the *production of needs*. This process signified, he sensed, not merely a qualitative change in the economy, but a momentous psychological adaptation, involving nothing less than a fundamental challenge to the old view of classical economics and philosophy that people were "rational, soberly constant being[s]." Lynd seemed to fear, in these early years of the Depression when the nature of consumer society was only barely becoming evident, something remarkably like the postmodern "death of the subject." The new species, the "people as consumers," appeared to him as encodable "bundles of impulses and habits shaped in response to an unsynchronized environment" – manipulable, passive, and conformist.[45]

This prognosis is not unlike the apocalyptic cultural pessimism of Baudrillard or the Frankfurt school. We may discover here an early counterpart to Max Horkheimer's prediction that the advance of corporate industrialism and consumerism (no less than fascism) required that "the objects of organization [be] disorganized as subjects."[46] Indeed, at the end of *Middletown in Transition*, Lynd sounds the gloomy warning (particularly resonant in 1935, the year marking the first Fascist military adventures) that, with the mobilization of the people as consumers, "the way may be paved for an acceptance of a type of control that will manhandle life deliberately and coercively at certain points to the end of rescuing a semblance of control over [the] all-important economic institutions."[47] The personality of Lynd's irrational consumer differs little from the "authoritarian personality" that Adorno and his colleagues were later to investigate. Moreover, like the Frankfurt school theorists, Lynd and other American observers of the period identified the mass media as the chief agents of this "disorganization" of the subject. Lynd had already argued in *Middletown* (1929) that it was impossible to overestimate "the rôle of motion pictures, advertising, and other forms of publicity in this rise in subjective standards" of what was needed for a decent living.[48] A decade later, when the Lynds revisited Muncie, this tendency seemed to them even more pervasive: American business, they felt, tempted people in "every waking minute with adroitly phrased invitations to apply the solvent remedy of more and newer possessions and socially distinguished goods and comforts to all the ills that flesh is heir to – to loneliness, insecurity, deferred hope, and frustration."[49]

The content of Hollywood films of the thirties does indeed offer some evidence that the transformation of the worker into a consumer was progressing apace. We should, of course, approach this kind of evidence cautiously: analyses of mass-mediated texts do not tell us much about the way audiences actually responded to them and can overemphasize the "propagandistic" and ideological dimensions of the text. But, even so, there is reason to give some credence to the content of the media, and especially of the movies, as a rough index of social trends. Commercial culture is, after all, under a compulsion to be liked; and even if we assume that some went to the movies to scoff, some to sleep, some to kiss, and some to win the Fiesta ware, the attendance figure of 80 million per week by 1940 is rather staggering.[50] And so, arguably, were the absurdities moviegoers witnessed. Frederick Allen, a writer for *Harper's* during the thirties, observed that Depression America, as portrayed in popular magazine fiction, advertisements, and movies, was a country where everybody was rich or about to become rich, where the ownership of a swimming pool or the employment of a butler (complete with English accent) not only failed to raise embarrassing questions, but seemed accepted as "the normal lot of mankind." The "inveterate movie-goer," Allen remarked,

> was unlikely to be surprised to find a couple of stenographers pictured as occupying an apartment with the newest built-in kitchen equipment and a living-room 35 feet long and 20 feet wide; or to hear Bette Davis, in "Dark Victory," expressing satisfaction that she had given up the life in which she "had had everything" for a life in which she "had nothing" – "nothing," in this case, being a remodeled Vermont farm-house which (according to the careful computations of E. B. White in *Harper's Magazine*) must have cost at least $11,000 or $12,000 a year to live in.[51]

This amusing passage rather overstates the exclusiveness of Hollywood's fascination with the rich and glamorous: Allen's comments ignore, for instance, the darker messages of films such as *I Am a Fugitive from a Chain Gang,* or the affectionate romanticizing of the humble auto parks and Greyhound buses in *It Happened One Night,* or even the complex "psychic compromise or horse-trading" between subversive wishes and moralistic containment that seem to be acted out in the gangster movies of the time.[52] But even a film like *Modern Times,* which does present the audience with a sympathetic figure of the factory hand, could hardly have allayed Lynd's fears about the ubiquitous appeal of consumerism. The film's critique of the sweatshop, as I suggested earlier, is balanced by the appeal of the department store and the suburban home; and it invites the audience to identify not only with the worker as worker, but also with the tramp's dreams of security, with the gamine's transformation into a show biz star, and most of all with Chaplin himself, the fabulously wealthy celebrity, who of course only plays at being a factory hand.[53]

Hollywood's celebration of consumption, moreover, was not confined to luxurious mise-en-scènes and visual representations of consumer goods and fashions. The plots of many films of the decade can certainly be read as symbolic narratives advocating the key values of the "culture of abundance": enjoyment of the present moment, self-fulfillment, consumption, and leisure. George Cukor's 1936 film, *Holiday,* for example, offers something of a parable on the struggle between the ethos of production and the ethos of consumption, with the latter winning out in the end. The hero, a charming and energetic naïf (played by Cary Grant), is destined by the demands of the romantic plot to marry one of the two beautiful daughters of a millionaire, a stern self-made man in the classic bourgeois mold. The hero first gets engaged to the elder sister, who endorses her father's rigid values and who cannot accept the young man's vague desire for an extended holiday, or an early retirement, during which he might "find himself" and discover what life has to offer outside the daily drudgery of work. Fortunately, it is revealed that this sister loves the young man only for what he might eventually become in her father's world of business, and the engagement is broken off. The hero thus becomes available to the other sister, played by Katharine Hepburn, who can accept him for the zany fun-loving soul he is. The ideological burden of the film is identical to that of several self-help books of the mid-thirties (such as *Life Begins at Forty, The Importance of Living,* and *Orchids on Your Budget*): all of them best-sellers which argued that work is no longer the only sphere for self-making, and thrift and discipline no longer the only keys to success.[54] The utopian aspects of this message are undeniable; but it is nevertheless remarkable how this idea became current at the very moment when, as Baudrillard put it, the problem the system faced was no longer one of production, but one of circulation – of consumption.

There is further evidence for this cultural shift in Leo Lowenthal's influential 1944 study of the biographical articles in *Collier's* and the *Saturday Evening Post.*[55] Lowenthal and his collaborators found that while the magazine biographies in the first quarter of the twentieth century commonly selected as their subjects "heroes of production" (industrialists, inventors, "serious" artists, or politicians), the biographies appearing by the end of the Great Depression almost exclusively featured "idols of consumption" (actresses, models, sportsmen, or radio announcers): people involved in the sphere of leisure. His data suggests that the celebrities who held the public's fascination at the end of the thirties were pretty much the direct antithesis of the "worker" (an image I shall discuss more fully anon) and that the contested ideological terrain was no longer related to the control of production, but to the control of consumption. This elimination of work (on the level of ideology, that is) is not easily construed as liberating or empowering; on the contrary, it reflects a narrowing of the possibilities of individual achievement in an increasingly monopolized and mechanized economic system. It is no accident, surely, that the turning point (the rise of the idols of consumption) seems to have coincided roughly with the economic crisis of 1929. With their emphasis on hard work and persistence, the older biographies share the ideological project of Horatio Alger's fictive parables: they celebrate the rewards that inevitably await the eager, disciplined worker. The "idols of production" are presented as a call to action, as exemplars of a success that the individual reader with sufficient vigor and determination might conceivably imitate. The "idols of consumption," on the other hand, offer no such object lessons. In the later biographies, success is presented not as a reward for hard work, but as accidental and irrational, a matter of a "lucky break": "being discovered" or "being in the right place at the right time." Success thus assumes the aspect of a game of chance – a cruel game, as Lowenthal points out, which "open[s] the doors to success for a handful, while all the others who were not present when it happened are failures."[56]

The later biographies, in other words, would seem to place the audience in a position of awed or, at best, expectant passivity: they inspire no action, but seem to demand from the ordinary reader the same attitude they bring to "the priceless pictures in our galleries or the fabulous palaces of the rich."[57] The success of the idols of consumption, like the magazine in which we read about it, becomes something to look at: goods for consumption. No wonder then, Lowenthal points out, that the language of these biographies, with its reliance on superlatives, on fancy words with mythological or legendary associations, and on a contrived person-to-person intimacy with the reader, resembles nothing so much as the language of advertising.

Writers such as Susman and, before him, David Riesman have developed the insight implicit in Lowenthal's research that society's conception of the ideal psychological type has shifted from the moral inner-directed "character" to the likable, externally defined "personality."[58] But Lowenthal's essay seems to me even more significant for the shift it traces in the ideology of democracy: a shift that forces us to consider some of the most negative implications suggested in the passage from *The Mirror of Production* already cited. While the earlier success stories assume a *democracy of equal opportunity,* in which the most vigorous and more meritorious workers may excel, the later biographies seem to put forward an entirely spectacular version of democracy, or, to use Baudrillard's phrase, a *"symbolic simulation of participation."* The biographers of the "idols of consumption" seem to take for granted that few of us will ever have the "lucky break"; they nevertheless are at pains to assure us that we are all equal – if not identical – *as consumers.* As Lowenthal points out, the reader is constantly reminded that (like the actor Chris Martin and Adolph Hitler) he might prefer not to smoke or that (like Greer Garson and Mahatma Ghandi) she might have a taste for potatoes or goat's milk.[59] With this propagation of a pseudoequality and a pseudo-*Gemeinschaft,* the later biographies share the same ideological project as those memorable advertisements from the period, which assured men that they could at least buy the same tires as the ones on the glittering limousine, and promised women that they could own the same vacuum cleaner as Mrs. Vanderbilt or use the same soap as Joan Crawford. These texts all preach a now-familiar line, what Roland Marchand has neatly termed "the parable of the democracy of goods": assuring people that they can partake of the *signs* of power, while they remain as powerless as ever to influence matters of production and political policy.[60]

THE LITERARY LEFT AND THE CULTURE OF ABUNDANCE

The question of how the literary Left conceived of its cultural strategy vis-à-vis this emerging "democracy of champagne" (as Muriel Rukeyser ironically called it) is one that I shall frequently return to in this study. But I would like to sketch here a very general and preliminary sense of the Communists' shifting attitudes. We might note, first of all, that the thematic content of the art and writing encouraged by the "proletarian" cultural movement, as well as that produced under the auspices of the New Deal, often emphasized work and production. Proletarian fiction depicted factory workers, bad bosses, and strikes, whereas WPA murals later in the decade tended to represent images of satisfying (often agricultural) labor. There may be a contradiction implicit even in this fact: one could argue that, despite these artists' and writers' left-wing sympathies, such projects shared something of the productionist orientation of the decade's conservative magazines, Republican politicians, and elderly millionaires.[61] This problem was evident to contemporary observers. Floyd Dell once observed that the effusive rhetoric of the literary "proletarians" could nicely serve the interests of the industrialist: Mike Gold, he joked, "has come back from the stoke-hole talking about how beautiful Strength and Steam and Steel and Noise and Dirt are. If so, I say, why abolish capitalism?"[62] In a certain sense, this common ground between the Left and the values of industrial capitalism is only to be expected. Marxism is itself a product of the nineteenth century; it partakes of the older capitalist culture's belief in the central importance of labor, and all too often displays its stoical and puritanical face. Thus, for many Marxists, even in the twentieth century, material possessions have seemed to represent not greater freedom and pleasure but further bondage to the capitalist system; even higher wages, in this view, would only reveal to workers "that the weight and strength of the golden chain is such that its tension can be slackened a little."[63] The American Communists of the late twenties and early thirties, forgetting perhaps that Marxism also offers a powerful critique of scarcity, thus often defined themselves against the hedonistic impulses of the new "culture of abundance."

Such considerations might illuminate the otherwise perplexing antimodernism of the *New Masses,* which after all was aggressively "modern" in its visual style, with its bold designs reminiscent of Bauhaus, Berlin Dada, or the *Neue Sachlicheit.* The journal's antimodernist stance expressed a determination to resist the "decadent" frivolities and luxuries of consumer culture and its emphasis on leisure: a culture for which the artistic bohemians of the twenties (for all their opposition to the cruder materialism of the "booboisie") formed a vanguard. As Malcolm Cowley pointed out in *Exile's Return,* the defiant mores of the "lost generation" were quite comfortably, and even profitably, accommodated by business:

> *Self-expression* and *paganism* encouraged demand for all sorts of products – modern furniture, beach pajamas, cosmetics, colored bathrooms with toilet paper to match. *Living for the moment* meant buying an automobile, radio, or house, using it now and paying for it tomorrow. *Female equality* was capable of doubling the consumption of products – cigarettes, for example – that had formerly been used by men alone. Even *changing place* would help to stimulate business in the country from which the artist was being expatriated. The exiles of art were also trade missionaries: involuntarily they increased the foreign demand for fountain pens, silk stockings, grapefruit and portable typewriters.[64]

While we now tend to see modernism as an oppositional force, as the last stand of the alienated artist confronting the inimical world of commerce, the literary proletarians of the thirties could, for reasons Cowley suggests, associate modernism with the consumerist values of a group of "lounge lizards and jazz hounds and sex degenerates" (a group that in many cases included the new Communist converts' earlier selves).[65]

It is not surprising, then, that several of the Left's prized texts in the proletarian mode demonstrate a traditionalism which goes beyond their artistically conservative sociorealist style. Marcus Klein has noted, for example, that in *Call Home the Heart* and *To Make My Bread,* Fielding Burke's and Grace Lumpkin's novels on the Gastonia strike, the narrative places the dangerous lures of the town – especially the installment plan – in an even worse light than it does the mill management.[66] From Burke and Lumpkin to James Agee, the decade's many evocations of impoverished agrarian or traditional working-class communities could be seen as constituting what Raymond Williams has termed a *residual* cultural force. This insight is implicit, I think, in William Empson's description of proletarian literature as a kind of "Covert Pastoral."[67] Like the more traditional pastoral, these texts represent ways of life and values that were shaped in an earlier historical period but are still active in the cultural process and antagonistic to capitalism, especially in its emergent guise of abundant consumption.[68]

Williams's terms – "dominant," "residual," and "emergent" – suggest something of the complexity of the social forces involved at any moment in any cultural formation and, I think, open up interesting interpretative possibilities. The idea that a residual cultural element might be present in "proletarianism" enables us, for example, to discover more than a garden-variety sexism in the obnoxious machismo of the *New Masses* (which, as Dell once complained, always depicted women with square breasts), in particular that of Mike Gold (who made a point of scoffing at pansies, wearing sombreros, and spitting on the floor).[69] The virile posture expresses, at least in some measure, an oppositional response to the new promises of abundance and leisure. At a time when all kinds of newly invented home accessories and time-saving devices combined to make life more comfortable and aesthetic, but also more "weightless" and unreal, this he-man bravado expresses a certain nostalgia for an age when things were plain and useful – and men, of course, were men, regardless of what car they drove.[70]

In saying this I do not mean to throw all feminist criticisms overboard – rather the contrary. As Williams has noted, residual cultural projects reveal the characteristics of the dominant and, perhaps especially, the emergent culture. Thus the nostalgic agrarianism of the Fugitives, for example, reveals the urban, centralizing, rationalizing tendencies of consumer culture, while the "virility" of the Left's resistance reminds us that the full force of advertising's efforts to produce consumer desire was directed at women. Not only did the advertisers conceive of their target as *Mrs.* Consumer, but they also attributed to the mass public in general those qualities traditionally attributed to women: emotionality, instability, irrationality.[71] In this context, the literary proletarians' annoying celebration of hard-boiled male vigor seems of a piece with their positive contribution: an attempt to elevate the worker as subject of art and history, and to represent the workplace, at a time when (at least in the images and texts of advertising) productive labor was increasingly effaced by the celebration of commodities. The candid advice that Helen Woodward, a leading copywriter in the twenties, offered her colleagues underscores this point:

> If you are advertising any product, never see the factory in which it is made. Don't know too much about it. Don't watch the people at work. Just know all you can about the finished article and the man who is going to buy it, and the conditions of selling in the business. Because, you see, when you know the truth about anything, the real, inner truth – it is very hard to write the surface fluff which sells it.[72]

Next to this comment it seems all the more laudable that many writers on the left at least made a visit "to the stoke-hole" and factory and made an effort to tell this truth. In short, one cannot finally assess the importance and implications of the experiment in proletarian literature without also taking into consideration the work of their cultural adversaries.

The relationship between the advertising industry and the Left, however, was not always so clearly antithetical. The image of working-class virility and vitality, for instance, proved not to be the exclusive property of the Communists. While the *New Masses* was conjuring up images of heroic workers tearing down the bulwarks of bourgeois society, the advertising trade journals were conjuring up "heroic images of ad men in dungarees, with sweat on their brows." Copywriters prided themselves on their new hard-sell approach to the task of saving American business; and the distinctive look of thirties advertising – black-and-white photographs with loud, tabloid-style lettering – deliberately signaled a break from the elegant, flowing, richly colored designs of the twenties. The trend on Madison Avenue in the early thirties was, as a 1933 contributor to *Advertising and Selling* put it, toward "Advertising in Overalls."[73] The socialist realism of the proletarians and the Popular Front and the "Capitalist Realism" of advertising, it would seem, had more in common than either party would have liked to admit.[74] In 1933, only a year or so after a delegation of writers went to Kentucky to demonstrate solidarity with the Harlan County miners in their strike, the advertising firm B.B.D.O. bragged, in a promotional presentation, about its close contact with the working stiffs: the agency proudly told the story of a copywriter who "covered up his typewriter, went to Pennsylvania, got into miner's clothes," and went underground with the men – all in order to write copy for Exide batteries in the miners' very own language.[75] The efforts of literary leftists (James Rorty, the former copywriter, is a good example) who crossed the country in search of the "voice of the people" were paralleled by the efforts of those copywriters who (so they claimed) "got up at six in the morning and donned uniforms to work with a biscuit company salesman." Both sides tried (with various degrees of posturing and hype) to forge a connection with the masses they hoped to convert.[76] Moreover, the Communist writers and the admen also shared certain stylistic aims: both strove for mass comprehensibility, both aspired to a kind of reportorial realism, and both claimed that artistic beauty was an effete indulgence of the decadent twenties. The trend toward "advertising in overalls," in other words, suggests that a kind of discursive tug-of-war over an appealing image was being waged (not necessarily consciously or by design) between the dominant and the would-be alternative culture.

This conception squares quite well with the Gramscian notion of hegemony – or at least with Kenneth Burke's notion that political contestation, in the form of a constant "stealing back and forth of symbols," was always taking place between Left and Right.[77] It would seem that even Mike Gold's idea of the manly proletarian "joker in overalls" could be appropriated by the white-collar "captains of consciousness."[78] But more important than the appropriation of any single symbol was the fact that consumer society had, arguably, stolen away the most potent appeal of Marxism – the promise of an end to material scarcity. Lincoln Steffens had warned in 1929 that "big business in America is producing what the Socialists held up as their goal: food, shelter and clothing for all"; and even though during the Depression big business did not in fact deliver the goods, it managed to keep up the impression that it could and would do so some day.[79] By 1935 it seemed to Kenneth Burke that the purveyors of "Capitalist Realism" were calling the shots in the struggle for hearts and minds, and that the symbol of the worker had lost its appeal. In his speech to the American Writers' Congress, Burke declared:

> "Adult education" in capitalist America to-day is centered in the efforts of our economic mercenaries (our advertising men and sales organizations) to create a maximum desire for commodities consumed under expensive conditions – and Hollywood appeals to the worker mainly by picturing the qualities of life in which this commercially stimulated desire is gratified. The question arises: Is the symbol of the worker accurately attuned to us, as so conditioned by the reactionary forces in control of our main educational channels?[80]

This reading of the contemporary situation certainly accords with Baudrillard's position, which I discussed earlier: it seemed to Burke that a social and ethical transformation of the worker was proceeding apace and that those who would turn the worker into a revolutionary would have to change strategies pretty quickly to reverse the trend. His suggestion was that the Left "propagandist" adopt the rallying symbol of the "people," an idea that troubled some at the Writers' Congress because of its associations with fascism, but which for Burke had a more specifically American ring than "the worker." The term may also have been chosen as an attempt to "steal back" the symbol of "the people" from those other propagandists who, as the title of Lynd's 1933 paper suggests, were engaged in defining "the people" as "consumers."

With the Communists' shift to the antifascist Popular Front shortly after the Writers' Congress, one might say that Burke's disputed suggestion was, unofficially, adopted as part of a larger strategy: the Popular Front would try, as Warren Susman puts it, to capture the idea of "Americanism" (a whole set of treasured symbols) as a "device for turning Americans into conscious socialists."[81] But the word "Americanism," like "the people," also had certain associations – associations that were to change not just the strategic appeal but the politics of the Left. (Words, after all, are not merely tools to be used clinically; they shape the user in return.) With its apparently mild slogan, "Communism is twentieth-century Americanism," the Popular Front was also struggling to reclaim something of the idea of material comfort and modernity that had been so successfully deployed by the culture industry. The word "Americanism," as used in the twenties, not only carried populist and nationalist connotations, but also referred specifically to American technology and mass production.[82] It is this kind of "Americanism" that a 1938 advertisement for the *New Masses,* for instance, seems to endorse: " 'If you like America . . . if you like its Rocky Mountains, its Storm King highway, its low-priced automobiles, the hot and cold running water in your well-tiled bathroom' *i.e.,* if you enjoyed the pleasures of middle-class life in America, you had better join with the Marxists to struggle for them."[83] This bit of Communist copywriting reminds one of Burke's "For a Modernist Sermon," except that everything that gave the poem its bite, especially the notion of "heaven" and "hell," of a cruelly stratified class society, is missing.

The effects of this kind of symbolic reappropriation and the remaking of the Communists' image as "just folks" have been much contested. It is hard not to feel a certain diminishment of political and intellectual vigor when we contrast Mike Gold's heroic image of the man in overalls, "fit to stand up to skyscrapers," with the image of the Young Communist Leaguer as descibed in a university group's literature:

> Some people have the idea that the YCLer is politically minded, that nothing outside of politics means anything. Gosh no. They have a few simple problems. There is the problem of getting good men on the baseball team this spring, of opposition from ping-pong teams, of dating girls etc. We go to shows, parties, dances and all that. In short, the YCL and its members are no different from other people except that we believe in dialectical materialism as a solution to all problems.[84]

In Susman's view this "effort to partake of Americanism led to a gross comedy in which ideas – to say nothing of ideology – took a back seat."[85] The result is, he argues, that the Popular Front's reclamation of nationalistic symbols for the Communist movement, in the end, did little to advance our thinking about what our YCLer would call "dialectical materialism" but that it did bring new meaning and shape to the notion of "Americanism" – one that eventually found an outlet in Hollywood: in Frank Capra, John Ford, and others.[86] The historical irony (which the New York intellectuals never failed to point out in the decades that followed) is, then, that the cultural work of the Communist Party in the thirties, especially of the Popular Front, may in the end have fostered the advance of commercial culture in the United States.[87] While a political agenda without a cultural and symbolic dimension is certainly unimaginable, one does feel that something is lost when *symbolic* participation in the "democracy of goods" becomes the predominant preoccupation of a movement that originally presented itself as an alternative and oppositional cultural force.

It was not until the fifties that a full-blown "democracy of goods" emerged. The celebratory rhetoric of the Nixon–Khrushchev "Kitchen Debate" of 1959, in which Nixon evoked the strength of the American system by referring to the 56 million cars, 50 million TVs, and 143 million radios owned by 44 million U.S. families, would not have worked in the "lean and angry" thirties; but it was, I think, imaginable – to judge, for instance, from the massive hype about the World of Tomorrow at the New York World's Fair of 1939. It is likely, as Jackson Lears and Richard Fox have surmised, that by the forties most Americans probably did call consumer goods to mind when they heard the phrase "freedom of choice."[88] If so, the significance of the ideological and material changes I have attempted to trace in this chapter for our understanding of the emergence of consumer society can hardly be underestimated. The shape of society after the war indicates the extent to which the work of the ideologues of the thirties bore fruit: the consumer boom of the postwar years was fostered by the deferred dreams of consumerist pleasure and luxury that were kept alive during the Depression.[89]

In the chapters that follow, I will consider the work of Kenneth Fearing and Nathanael West in relation to the ideological and material history of the thirties (the "ideological" and "material," of course, become increasingly conflated during the period). The relation of this history to aesthetic expression is not, as I see it, that of a *background* for a central object of attention. I would prefer to see this relationship in the way Walter Benjamin did, as one of mutual decoding or mutual demystification.[90] The turbulent and conflicted history of the thirties keeps one from reading Fearing and West simply as cultural treasures – valuable in themselves, praiseworthy (as some critics have held) for transmuting the ephemera of mass culture into Art.[91] My interest in the culture and politics in which these writers were immersed, and which both criticized and reflected, permits a reading of their work that is not merely concerned with the question of their aesthetic value. Conversely, Fearing and West force us to read the history of the thirties in a new way. They offer what Susan Buck-Morss has called a "critical iconography for deciphering [the] material history" of their time, enabling us to recognize in the culture of the thirties certain images (like that of the nightclub on the dump) that still retain critical potency in relation to the present.[92] Such images of decay and redemption, of cultural poverty and utopian desire (West's "dream dump" of civilization in the studio backlot, Fearing's billboard that says "Mama I Love Crispy Wafers So," over which someone has scrawled the words "Jesus Saves") seem to me curiously familiar; they seem more a part of the world we live in today than the heroic images of proletarian literature, or even the Popular Front's America (an America that I think we can now experience only as camp). Fearing and West, in showing the contradictions of their time, enable us to read the history of the thirties as both "hard times" and "modern times," and as our own prehistory.

PART II

Kenneth Fearing

3

The Politics of Literary Failure
Fearing, Mass Culture, and the Canon

News, common sense, good literature – these are whatever the voices of communication unanimously, and often, say they are.

Kenneth Fearing, "Reading, Writing, and the Rackets"

What evaluation finds is precisely this value: what can be written (rewritten) today.

Roland Barthes, *S/Z*

Kenneth Fearing's name and work have largely fallen into oblivion, but in the thirties he was regarded as a leading light among the writers on the left and was praised as the rebel poet who most accurately recorded the social circumstances and political atmosphere of that turbulent decade.[1] The latter commendation would probably have pleased Fearing: though his poetry shares, to some degree, the experimental impulse we associate with literary modernism, he never claimed (as did some of the paradigmatic high modernists) a nonreferential autonomy for his writing. He valued, above all, those "very few modern writers who ha[ve] detected the existence of a world outside [themselves], and forsaking the great esthetic cliché, the exploitation of life for the sake of art, have written about it."[2] Perhaps because of this consciously held principle – of relevance and a connection between art and life – Fearing's poetry offers a particularly vivid document of the Great Depression. His Whitmanesque enumerations often have the effect of a newsreel shown at double speed: rapid-fire montages juxtapose shots of the statesman at the microphone, of the aviator stepping from his monoplane, of scabs arriving in guarded trucks, of vag tanks and limousines, of breadlines and blackjacks. The ominous rumblings on the international arena likewise echo through his poems, haunted as they are with memories and rumors of war: conspiracies in the "sewers of Berlin," Communist prisoners behind the bars of Moabit, cheering crowds, mobilized fleets, and gleaming bayonets. His poem "The Program," published in 1938, is even darkly prophetic of the decade's end.[3]

> ACT ONE, Madrid-Barcelona, Time, the present,
>   ACT TWO, Paris in springtime, during the siege,
>   ACT THREE, London, Bank Holiday, after an air raid,
>   ACT FOUR, a short time later in the U.S.A.
>
> . . . .
>
> (Scenes by Neville Chamberlain
>   costumes, courtesy of Daladier
>   Spanish Embargo by the U.S. Congress
>   Music and lighting by Pius XI)
>
> SMOKE EL DEMOCRACIES
>
> . . . .
>
>   (DR, 32)

The historical interest of his poetry, however, extends far beyond such direct references to the political events and figures of the decade. If, as Warren Susman has argued, an effective cultural history must deal with those cultural forms most characteristic of their times, Fearing's work, deeply absorbed as it was in the popular discourses of the moment, offers a particularly rich interpretation of the thirties.[4] He firmly believed that poetry "should be based on the materials being written about," that one should not only write *about* the news, or the newspaper, but experiment with writing *like* a newspaper – or a movie, or a comic strip, or a radio show, as the case may be.[5] Susman's provocative remark that Mickey Mouse might be as important for an understanding of the thirties as Franklin Roosevelt is one that Fearing would surely have savored.[6] His writing is equally attuned, as the lines from "Program" suggest, to a speech by Chamberlain and a cigar ad; and he would even suggest a sinister connection between the two – or between Roosevelt and a movie hero.

In the three chapters that follow I hope, therefore, to contribute to our cultural history of the thirties by reading Fearing's poetry and essays somewhat as Walter Benjamin reads Baudelaire: as a rich source of clues to and interpretations of the forms and structures of experience of his time, and to the material conditions that shape them. In the present chapter, however, I intend to suggest that a study of Fearing's work can also contribute to the more specific project of the American literary historian. This contribution can be assessed, I think, only if we explicitly address the issue of literary value, which, despite the currency of historicist and broadly cultural approaches to literature, sooner or later seems to confront a study of a noncanonical figure. It seems to me important, in the case of Fearing, that we raise the naive question "But is it any good?" precisely because the character and reception of his work present us with a particularly sharp and useful sense of the political contingency of our notions of literary worth.

REMEMBERING FEARING

Before we investigate this vexed question of canon making and value more fully, it seems appropriate to provide a brief biographical sketch – especially since an outline of Fearing's life indicates some of the reasons he has seemed to me such a key figure for a discussion of the relation between literature and mass-mediated culture in the thirties.

Kenneth Fearing was born in 1902 and raised in Oak Park, Illinois, the same comfortable Chicago suburb where Ernest Hemingway grew up.[7] In fact, the two attended the same high school, and Fearing recalled Hemingway's return appearance at the school as a war hero, when he showed off his old army pants riddled with bullets and read some of his early stories. After a brief stint at the University of Illinois, Fearing transferred to the University of Wisconsin, where he majored in English. There he encountered the work of Eliot, Cummings, and Stevens, but was influenced more by E. A. Robinson's early poems and preferred the worldly satire of the *Smart Set* to the highbrow verse of the *Dial*. As editor of the *Wisconsin Literary Magazine,* Fearing ran into some trouble with the university authorities over his irreverent treatment of poetic pieties: his editorials vigorously attacked signs of "literary sogginess" and "ready-to-wear emotions, social commodities."[8] It seems that even as an undergraduate he had homed in on some of his enduring targets. Some of his early poems, like "Moral (Op. 1)" (CP, 11), already have a certain sardonic bite; and others forecast his abiding interest in probing our notions of the literary: "Poem?" he asks in "Blair and Blair's Friends" (CP, 8), "You call that a poem – that little line / Etched between his eyes and down his cheeks?"

Yet it was only after Fearing became a "Greenwich villager" that he began to write the unconventional, hard-boiled satirical verse that was to become his trademark. His move to New York in 1924 was one of the determining events of his life and work. His new life in the city fostered in the young poet three great admirations: H. L. Mencken, Dashiell Hammett, and the Communist Party. New York figures prominently in his poems and novels, occasionally as the modern metropolis of the heroic (and then brand-new) skyscrapers, but more often as the seedy geography of the gangster movie, with its speakeasies, el trains, rotted wharves, and "fly-specked" stores. One can glean from the memoirs of his contemporaries, in which Fearing tends to feature only as an elusive figure, that the "Village Bobbie Burns" (as he was dubbed in the late twenties) used to hang out around Eleventh Street or at the gin mills on Fourteenth, a cigarette always dangling from his lips.[9] He was also known as "the leader of the taxi-driver school of verse." He wrote and thought, as Kenneth Rexroth once explained, "like a taxi driver reading a billboard while fighting traffic" – a description which suggests that he was seen as something of a specialist in those discontinuous, demotic experiences that Walter Benjamin described as "urban shock." Fearing never actually drove a cab. On the contrary, he was determined to live by his writing alone, which often meant supporting himself by writing for the mass media: detective stories for "the Street & Smith boys" at one cent a word on acceptance and "True Confessions" for the sex pulps at half that rate. These involvements suggest that Rexroth was probably correct in observing that "no one else so completely immersed himself in the lingo of mass culture."[10]

Digressing for a moment from the strictly biographical, I would like to note that it is precisely this immersion in the popular that enabled his distinctive contribution to the literature of the thirties – a poetic strategy most eloquently characterized by Kenneth Burke in a 1938 review:

> Confronted by all the alloys, substitutes, and canned goods that are offered us by the priesthood of business, the catch phrases of salesman-ship and commercialized solace, Fearing has put the utilitarian slogans to a use beyond utility, as he rhythmically sorrows, with their help, assigning them to an interpretative function in his poems that they lack in their "state of nature."[11]

One might say that Fearing deploys, thirty years before the Situationist International advocated the practice, a kind of literary "détournement": an ironic plagiarism that causes the "spectacle" to speak against itself and forces a consumer society's received ideas of happiness (what Fearing might call the "perfect denouement[s]" [CP 115]) to reveal their own mechanical triteness.[12]

While this ironic protest remains constant, it is possible to distinguish three ways in which Fearing's familiarity with the procedures and prod-ucts of the culture industry inform his work. First, his poems often cite slogans or tabloid headlines outright, creating the jarring effects of a Dadaist collage. "The Program" is a case in point:

EAT ZEPHYR CHOCOLATES
(do not run for the exits in case of fire
the Rome-Berlin Theater has no exits)
SUZANNE BRASSIERES FOR PERFECT FORM (DR, 32)

Second, Fearing frequently incorporates the celebratory language of advertising more indirectly, by way of an insistent ironic hyperbole. We see this technique, for instance, in "Dear Beatrice Fairfax: *Is it true that Father Coughlin and Miss Aimee Semple McPherson and Mr. H. L. Mencken and Peter Pan?*" – his poem addressed to the well-known sob columnist of the day:

> Foolproof baby with that memorized smile,
> Burglarproof baby, fireproof baby with that rehearsed appeal,
> Reconditioned, standardized, synchronized, amplified, best-by-test
> baby with those push-the-button tears. (CP, 100)

Third, and most rarely, his "collisions" with the industry also provided a direct source of material. "Yes, the Agency Can Handle That," for instance, is based on Fearing's experience at a story conference, where, with the help of a few media executives, he learned how to write a "heartbreak series exactly the same as the cycle that preceded it" (NS, xxiii). The poem describes the technique – a process of rigorous subtraction, a weeding out of every possible sales deterrent (along with "every last shred of plausibility") from a "true-to-life" saga:

> You recommend that the motive, in Chapter 8, should be changed
> from ambition to a desire, on the heroine's part, for doing good;
> yes, that can be done.
> Installment 9 could be more optimistic, as you point out, and it will
> not be hard to add a heartbreak to the class reunion in Chapter 10.
> Script 11 may have, as you say, too much political intrigue of the
> sordid type; perhaps a diamond-in-the-rough approach would take
> care of this. And 12 has a reference to war that, as you suggest, had
> better be removed; yes. (CP, 183)

I shall have much more to say about the poetry in the pages that follow. Suffice it to note for the moment that while such writing elicited (from William Rose Benét) the usual rearguard response ("But is it poetry?") Fearing's reputation – especially around 1935, the high point of leftist solidarity – was quite substantial and extended well beyond the offices of the *New Masses*.[13] It was high enough to persuade the University of Wisconsin to send him, out of the blue, his B.A. degree – in grateful acknowledgment of the "enhanced prestige" that his "public recognition" and "considerable notice by the literary establishment" had brought the university. It also earned him two Guggenheim Awards, one in 1936 and one in 1939, on the strength of *Poems* (1935) and *Dead Reckoning* (1938) respectively.[14]

Since much of Fearing's work was done on a free-lance basis and pseudonymously, it is rather difficult to patch together an exact sense of his career, connections, and professional activities. We know that he was associated with Eliot Cohen's *Menorah Journal,* but could criticize the sentimentality of hackneyed "ghetto novels"; that he published poetry in the *New Masses,* and even once sold tickets for the *New Masses* ball, but felt free to complain about the revolutionary bathos of Mike Gold's writing; that he was friendly with Horace Gregory, but felt that Gregory's poetry lingered a trifle too fondly over the "corpse" of the capitalist system; that he was signed up, along with James T. Farrell, to be the film critic for the early *Partisan Review,* but ended up sending most of his lively reviews to the *New Masses;* that in 1936 and 1937 he spent some time in Europe; that he was twice married, but that both marriages eventually dissolved.[15]

Some fictional material helps to fill in a few of the blanks: in Albert Halper's *Union Square,* the character Jason Wheeler, the "ex-poet and ex-communist," who writes trashy sex stories for a living, is based on Kenneth Fearing. Certain details of the portrait are quite accurate: like his fictive counterpart, Fearing wore horn-rimmed glasses, won a literary prize at "a large Mid-Western university," and was once acclaimed as one of the most promising young poets of the Left. Wheeler's drunken babbling at one point in the novel ("blow, bugles, blow . . . and answer, hotdogs, answer . . .") is clearly a parodic imitation of Fearing's early poem "Ballad of the Salvation Army" (CP, 30), which uses the "Blow, bugles, blow" line as a refrain. Fearing's fascination with the language of mass culture is also shared by his fictional double, whose conversation in the first part of Halper's novel is based largely on a Chrysler advertisement (a phrase from which in fact appears in Fearing's poetry): "But just because I'm not famous myself is no reason why I shouldn't drive a famous car. I *do.* I drive a Chrysler – with that patented Floating Power everybody is talking about." If Halper's portrait is as accurate in its overall sense of Fearing's personality as in these details, he was a person whose wit, offbeat eloquence, and intellectual acuity combined dangerously with passionate self-hatred, cynical despair – and a drinking problem.[16]

The evidence suggests, however, that by 1933 (the year Halper's novel came out) Fearing was not, like Jason Wheeler, an "ex-poet," or quite an "ex-communist." In 1935 the reviewers of *Poems* almost unanimously referred to Fearing as a Communist poet. Horace Gregory wrote, for instance, that Fearing had always been "revolutionary in his intentions" and that "the Communist Party and the activity surrounding it, ha[d] always been the source of his material." Even as late as 1939, one still finds a critic referring to Fearing as a "Party poet."[17] It is true that some of Fearing's family members and friends have represented him as completely "apolitical" and "innocent of any political bias," and have insisted that he cared only for art, and only used the Communist Party to get published.[18] But these assertions fly in the face of the work he produced – or, at the very least, rely on a far too narrow definition of the political. Fearing did, on occasion, declare that his political convictions were a mystery to him and that he never joined the Communist Party, because "for one thing, the meetings were too boring"; yet he was clearly a man of the Left, voting for La Follette in 1924 and William Z. Foster in 1932.[19] Kenneth Rexroth recalls that in the opinion of the Communist Party Fearing was always independent and suspect. While the remark may be colored by retrospect (it was not always easy to identify a unified party position), it is likely that Fearing's loose association with the *Partisan Review* group presented a problem to the more orthodox Left in the latter part of the decade, and that his pessimistic tone may have come to seem out of kilter with the relatively upbeat approach of the Popular Front.[20] Even so, the Communist literati certainly published and respected him; and unlike many far more ardent Communists, he never recanted or backtracked during the McCarthy era. He was, like Walt Whitman (whom he cited as a literary ancestor) and Carl Sandburg (to whom he is sometimes compared), radically democratic in temperament: a despiser of bureaucracies, "stuffed shirts," and snobbish lovers of "Beauty." Rexroth (himself no stranger to the seamier sides of society) believes that "no other American poet of his time so closely identified himself with the working class, with the *lumpen* proletariat, with the impoverished stratum of the underworld, with hustlers, grifters, 'nifties, yeggs, and thirsties.' "[21]

Whether this identification would at any stage have moved Fearing to call himself a "proletarian poet" or a "poet for workers" is debatable.[22] It would again be helpful to know how faithfully the "Fearing" character in *Union Square* represents the actual man. In the novel, Jason Wheeler is shown to have nothing but scorn for the affected "Leftism" of the early thirties. He berates a gathering of earnest and admiring "literary workers" for writing poetry that "st[i]nk[s] to high heaven" and for being a bunch of Village bohemians with nothing to offer the Revolution. Earlier in the novel he launches into a harangue against the Communist Party's Soviet orientation:

> Do you really think . . . that a movement appealing to the American masses can be successful as long as the agitators of the movement are not Americanized themselves and have not de-Russianized the propaganda they're trying to hammer into the heads of American labor?[23]

Whether Fearing would have made such a speech remains a matter of speculation. But to judge from his poetic attempts to "create a technique indigenous to the whole country's outlook," it would seem that he may very well have concurred with Wheeler's position on the matter of the Left's Russophilia. After all, the imagery and language of Fearing's poetry derive from local billboards and tabloids, and firmly avoid the red dawns and sturdy peasant girls that inspired other leftist poets (such as H. H. Lewis, Sol Funaroff, and Maxwell Bodenheim).[24] Even that European-sounding designation "worker" is rare in his writing, as Kenneth Burke (who also stressed the importance of developing specifically American "revolutionary symbolism") might have noted with some satisfaction.[25]

On the question of proletarian culture and even the political influence of the avant-garde, Fearing certainly showed some of Wheeler's skepticism. Though he was associated in the mid-thirties with the *Dynamo* poets (a group that acknowledged the influence of Eisenstein and attempted to translate the "miniature dialectic" of his filmic techniques into poetry), Fearing at times questioned the avant-gardist belief that "revolution and modernist technique and good plays are, by some curious magic, a Holy Trinity of which the members are One and the Same." Good artists (and even good Marxists), he argued in a review of Mike Gold's *Hoboken Blues,* do not necessarily make good revolutionaries; on the contrary, sentimental, dishonest "tripe" (such as, in his opinion, *Uncle Tom's Cabin*) might actually be ideal from the point of view of winning new converts.[26] This position clearly differs from the belief of other Communist literati (such as Malcolm Cowley, Michael Gold, Joseph Freeman, and even the young Philip Rahv) that Marxist political zeal represents a definite boon to the work of the committed artist.[27] Fearing also apparently had few illusions that the audience for his poetry extended far beyond the usual readership of liberal middle-class people.[28]

In other respects, however, he seems to have been in general sympathy with at least some of the aims of the experiment in proletarian literature, and certainly with the leftward tendency of literature during the thirties. He believed, for instance, that poetry should ideally reveal its meaning at the ordinary pace of reading – a view that would seem to correlate with the party's demand for clear and accessible literature.[29] And while (in his discussion of the New Playwrights' work) he might use words like "sentimentality" and "dishonesty" in describing agitprop art, he seems quite willing to consider the idea that plays of novels might serve as vehicles for revolutionary propaganda, without disparaging the aim. In 1939 we find him, in response to a *Partisan Review* questionnaire, giving a cautiously positive account of the decade's literary achievements:

> At the risk of being banal, I will have to say that American literature
> since 1930 has been marked as a whole by an increased economic

awareness, which has expressed itself, politically, in a heightened partisanship for one or another organization, vogue, or tradition favoring the cause of the economically exploited and insecure. I believe that although a good deal of such writing staggered and all but fell beneath the burden of its message, this by-now familiar battle was a necessary and healthy one, with results that are satisfying at the present date.[30]

But this was early in 1939. The political earthquake of the Hitler–Stalin pact, and the outbreak of World War II, was soon to change, almost beyond recognition, the cultural terrain he surveyed. In fact, Fearing himself was quick to record some of these changes: writing for *Poetry* magazine in 1940, he predicted (correctly, if one considers the emergence of the Cold War and the "military–industrial complex") a state of permanent warfare, a consequent need for ideological smoke screens (what we might now call "spin control"), and a resulting narrowing of artistic possibilities for "creative as opposed to commercial or state literature." The situation, he surmised, would affect the individual writer profoundly. It would, for instance, become more difficult "for the unknown writer to win a hearing and a following" (again a shrewd guess, if one considers the consolidation of a restrictive academic canon after World War II). It would also diminish, and had perhaps already diminished, the writer's sense of what writing could achieve in the world. Noting that no literary crusader had ever radically changed the "stream of history," Fearing announced bluntly that individual writers might as well forget about themselves as molders of public opinion: it would be enough, he wrote, "if the writer refuses to lend himself to the more prodigious lies that mushroom in times like these." The continuity of the cultural work accomplished by American writers in the thirties, he felt, was being threatened from within and without.[31]

One might think that the project of naysaying in the face of official lies would suit Fearing's artistic temperament quite well, but in fact the context he sketched out in the 1940 essay did not prove to be one in which he could operate very happily. The continuity of his own work, one might say, was disturbed – a fact signaled by his increased attention to fiction and steadily diminishing interest in poetry. By 1953 Nelson Algren wrote to Maxwell Geismar that "Fearing, the truest poet, for my money, of the decade, was repeating himself" and, like several other promising writers of the thirties, was hacking: "When the thirties were done," Algren lamented, "they were done."[32] In Fearing's case there is much to support such a view: many of his later poems read like melancholy reworkings of older themes, and his novels, all published after his heyday in the thirties, would do little to persuade a new reader that he was an important talent, as he was once thought to be. Even in an obituary homage, an anonymous writer for *Mainstream* (the descendant of the *New Masses*) described his novels as potboilers and asserted that he had never managed, after the Depression decade, to "transcend his high-water mark."[33]

Fearing continued, as before, to work in and around the culture industry. By the end of the thirties he found, for a while, a position in Henry Luce's media empire and later wrote book reviews for the *New York Times* and *Newsweek*.[34] These experiences are recorded in his 1946 thriller, *The Big Clock*. Ironically, this novel, which presents the vast media corporations with a curious combination of humor and paranoia, became his one best-seller and was made into a successful Hollywood film, starring Ray Milland and Maureen O'Sullivan. But as far as poetry was concerned, he felt that he had written himself out. Though he did produce a series of new poems for the 1956 collection of his *New and Selected Poems*, his editor at Indiana University Press recalls that he agreed to write them only reluctantly. For some time before his death (of lung cancer) in 1961, Fearing seems to have suffered from severe depressions. His medical records reveal that he had been an alcoholic for many years – drinking one to two pints of whiskey per day plus "an undetermined amount of beer."[35]

Though the last years of his life clearly tell a story of decline and defeat, Fearing did not totally disappear from critical view. His "hacking," moreover, should not necessarily be seen as a renunciation of his earlier acerbic satire. For all their faults, Fearing's novels all have something of a "film noir" quality – a pervasive and even perverse suspicion of a conspiratorial "society necrobiotic with the rackets" (NS, xx). As Charles Humboldt observes (in one of a very small number of good articles on Fearing), the thriller, like science fiction, functioned as a refuge for forbidden thoughts in a conservative age and as the progressive writer's one corridor open to a mass audience.[36] In the sixties, when U.S. politics again took a leftward turn, which produced a mild revival of interest in the thirties, Fearing was reread as a precursor to Pop Art; and the Beats recognized in his long-breathed lines a kindred spirit.[37] His poems were included in some of the radical anthologies of the day, such as Walter Lowenfels's collection of protest poetry, *The Writing on the Wall,* and George Quasha and Jerome Rothenberg's *America: A Prophecy.* He is one of the many heroes of Kenneth Rexroth's anticanonical (and underrated) history, *American Poetry in the Twentieth Century.* Sy Kahn, at one point, planned to write a book on Fearing; and M. L. Rosenthal, Allan Guttman, and Daniel Aaron kept at least some memory of his work alive.[38]

Though no new literary history has devoted much attention to Fear-

ing, the recent debates on the politics of canon formation have articulated a new theoretical stance that helps to make sense of his contribution. Such new books as Cary Nelson's *Repression and Recovery* and
Alan Wald's *The Revolutionary Imagination* mention Fearing's work with
respect. Most recently, Walter Kalaidjian has traced what he calls a
"transpersonal" poetics linking the avant-gardist projects of the twenties
and thirties with those of the postmodern eighties, and has argued that
Fearing could be seen as a hidden ancestor to the contemporary Language poets.[39] Even the trendy *Village Voice Literary Supplement* carried
an article on Fearing under the heading of "Save These Books," and
expressed the hope that a publisher would again make Fearing's work
available. It argued that Fearing's work – "edgy, syncopated, alive to
the pathos of inarticulateness, the sound of American speech, and the
media static that keeps us from knowing what we think or feel – has
lost neither its jagged music nor its emotional whallop."[40] Moreover,
The Big Clock (though admittedly stripped of its paranoid vision of a
world shaped and controlled by media empires) was remade into yet
another Hollywood film: the 1987 Kevin Costner vehicle, *No Way Out*.
The novel is also back in print.

Perhaps the oddest sign that Fearing's ghost was stirring, even in the
Reagan–Bush years, is the poem that in 1983 found its way onto the
pages of *boundary 2:* "letter to kenneth / epistle to pop," by Fearing's
only son Bruce. Amid confessions of his own poetic failure and revelations of a painful life as a drifter and religious fanatic, "Bruce Goose"
invokes memories of an old poem from the twenties and an almost
forgotten poet:

> or that night back on bleeker street up on the top floor
>
> when i must have asked you what you "were" besides my dad
>
> & you said you were a poet
>
> & when i asked next what was poetry you got out that
>
> book & read me the one with lines like
>
> "rat-a-tat-tat stammered the gat of louis the rat while blam blam blam
>   went the officers of the law"
>
> & i thought it was great & sounded just like You
>
> only somewhat More So.[41]

These lines offer, I think, a fittingly ambiguous homage to the elusive
poet, who somehow "sounded just like" the impersonal hard-boiled
slang of the comic-strip detective story.

AMERICAN LITERATURE AND THE "AMERICAN INVESTIGATION"

With the revival of critical interest in the politics of canon formation, the naive question I set out with ("But is he any good?") has been shown to beg all manner of other questions: What does "good" mean? "Good" for whom? What is literature (let alone "good" literature)? And so forth. It is therefore insufficiently probing simply to invert the notions of literary success and failure in the disarming way that Bruce Fearing does in his "epistle to pop":

> . . . i don't Mind the fact that
>
> i'm a total failure, a real Flop, speaks quite well of me
>
> since, to give just 1 "reason" Failure or Success should
>
> be a matter of Complete Indifference to any real poet, yes
>
> we're pushing out the line of what a poet *is*
>
> and i believe, in fact, we've pushed it right around the bend.[42]

There is something deeply romantic in this kind of celebration of the man whom M. L. Rosenthal has called "America's one adult poet-in-a-garret."[43] Yet the strategy of calling Fearing a failure, rather than putting forward an argument for his literary excellence, is in many ways compelling. For Fearing often seems (as I shall argue more fully in the next section) resolutely un-literary. He is, one might say, irredeemably "minor."

And that may perhaps be the very reason we should bother to read his work. The category of "minor" literature, as Cary Nelson has argued, is challenging and destabilizing: as long as notions of greatness remain inherent in our definition of literature, the notion of something "minor" yet "literary" is likely to constitute an epistemological disruption.[44] It is no wonder, then, that many critics working on noncanonical figures have felt compelled to argue that the writer in question is, after all, assimilable to certain modified conceptions of literary worth – and as such is also a candidate for the admiration and attention of experts. But whether conservative or revisionist, the familiar conception of literary history as a struggle for admission to the canon distorts the fact that often this *kind* of success was not of great importance to the writer concerned, and that he or she might have had a different cultural project in mind.[45]

Rather than demonstrate Fearing's virtues, I would therefore prefer to consider him in relation to what we might call "the politics of literary failure" – the underside of the systematic project that Barbara Herrnstein Smith has termed "the economics of literary value."[46] It would be all too easy to find personal reasons for Fearing's failure in terms of his alcoholism, a slender talent, and so forth; but it seems to me that one should take seriously Cary Nelson's advice to literary historians in this regard:

> We need to stop thinking of artistic failure as a statement only about individual tragedy or the weakness and limitations of individual character and begin to see it as culturally driven, as a complex reflection of social and historical contradictions, as the result of the risks of decisions made in a network of determinations.[47]

What makes Fearing particularly interesting as a case study of this sort is the fact that he himself was perfectly clear-sighted about the social determinations that made for his own marginalization, and for the elimination of the cultural space in which his work would have made sense. Very early in his career Fearing observed that "grotesque as it possibly seems to think of the arts as competitive, it is nevertheless true, and fairly obvious, that works of art tend to destroy or invalidate each other."[48] This point is starkly underscored if we consider Robert Penn Warren's retrospective assessment of the poetry of the thirties in a 1939 essay for the *Kenyon Review*.[49] Warren's opening gambit is to insist (in an ideologically charged tautology) that a poem be valued as "nothing more than a poem." This move essentially dismisses the referential dimension of a poem (a dimension Warren regards as particularly "importunate and immediate" in the case of contemporary poetry) as something that can only distract the reader from a contemplative immersion in the poem's verbal design and formal textures. To us these remarks sound like just another familiar assertion of the superseded doctrines of the New Criticism. But in 1939, this radical formalism – this move to suppress a poem's relevance to "the present world, in which the reader holds numerous and valuable vested interests" – had a strong polemical charge. The challenge is strikingly evident if we recall Fearing's conception of literary value: his laconic insistence, for instance, that a poet must "detect[] the existence of a world outside himself" and write about it. By Warren's standards, declared so bluntly at the end of a decade of politically engaged writing, the work of Fearing, and many of his fellows, becomes "little more than a kind of journalism"; and his experimental investigations of popular discourses becomes not only insignificant, but grounds for disqualification from the very designation of "poetry."

While the criticism of the past two decades or so has successfully challenged this formalist sealing off of the reader's "vested interests" from the experience of poetry, the New Critics' retrospective evaluation of American poetry of the preceding decade still has its effects: among them the cultural invisibility of figures like Fearing. Of these effects, Fearing was all too aware. His essay "Reading, Writing, and the Rackets," which appeared as the introduction to the 1956 edition of his *New and Selected Poems,* offers an idiosyncratic but shrewd account of the process of literary canon making, and its inglorious underside of failure. The piece must have struck Samuel Yellin, his editor at Indiana University Press, as an odd performance. Instead of offering the usual retrospective apologia for his poetic work, it starts off as an invective against the activities of the House Un-American Activities Committee, or as Fearing calls it "the American Investigation." But it soon becomes clear that Fearing views the operations of Senator McCarthy and his "Americaneers" (NS, xxiii) as inseparable from the rise of the mass media, and the mass media, in turn, as inseparable from literature.

For one thing, he notes, those public disavowals of earlier Communist associations (the favorite form of the Investigation's widely televised performances) have a literary prototype in a lowly genre of popular fiction: the true confession story. The formula for confessions new and old is abiding, as Fearing (who himself worked in this genre) explains. The story always starts with phase one, "The Temptation":

> ("Little did I dream when the suavely handsome stranger first visited our simple home, and his glib talk about the glittering life of the underworld set my pulses racing, that soon this would lead . . .")
> ("Little did I dream when my new-found friend, all too aware of my innocence, set my youthful idealism on fire with his roseate picture of a better life for the underprivileged, that this soon would lead . . .")
> (NS, xii)

From there, it moves inexorably to phase two, "The Fall," phase three, "The Sad Awakening," and finally phase four, "The Regeneration" (for the new variety of confession adheres faithfully to the famed editorial dictum defining the genre: "The heroine may fall, but she must *fall upward*" [NS, xii]). At this moment of moral restoration, the text is all too familiar:

> Come what might, and at whatever cost, I resolved to break with my infamous past and henceforth lead a better life . . . to atone for my past misdeeds I would begin by making a clean breast of everything, I would tell all, including the names. . . . (NS, xiii)

The theoretical implications of the essay go far beyond this kind of bitter but fairly local satire. Fearing's term, the "Investigation," should be understood as symbolically inclusive of more than these televised "True Confessions" before the House committee. It refers to nothing less than a new kind of society, a "giant syndrome" affecting the entire political and cultural terrain: a system of surveillance and espionage, adjustment and proscription – a national panopticon, in short, manned by the "tribunals of the Investigation, whose legions keep sleepless watch upon [us] all" (NS, xii). The "Investigation" is comparable to Guy Debord's "Spectacle," which includes far more than the communications media, but also signifies the total usurpation of the space of representation by the commodity form. Both terms point to an institutionalization and materialization of ideology: the transformation of culture into a kind of permanent advertisement, into the "laudatory monologue" of the political system.[50] Like Debord's Spectacle, the Investigation operates on the apparently benign, but in fact totalitarian decree that "that which appears is good, and that which is good appears."[51] Fearing vividly describes the effects of this paradoxical kind of censorship:

> The eye can scarcely penetrate beyond the blinding haloes revealed on the electronic screen; the ear catches nothing beneath the repetitions that flow from the loudspeaker; the mind discovers no fresh information between the lines of standard bulletins – all of these in resolute agreement that the circuits of communication defend their freedom and independence of expression. (NS, x)

The Investigation, in short, directs the peculiarly devious mode of social control at work in an apparently free and open society. Thence Fearing's dark suspicions that "the richest prize of the Investigation" may be "its absolute power to prevent investigation" and that the Cold War's "prolonged public drama of Good versus Evil" may be nothing but a kind of decoy: "a glittering, noisy substitute for the total darkness, total silence, total secrecy desired" (NS, x).

If all this talk about McCarthy, ideology, and television seems, at first blush, to be unconnected to such literary matters as canon making, there may be something amiss with our notions of the canon. The repressions and exclusions and silences of the canon correspond, after all, to the repressions and exclusions and silences of the culture at large. Therefore, as Fearing's essay implies, the political purges of Senator McCarthy serve as a metaphor for the dystopian aspects of tradition or canon making. Moreover, it is impossible not only to separate literature from politics, but also, as Fearing was so well aware, to isolate high culture and literature from "what is happening now in the matrix of all communications" (NS, xv). This point, implicit in Fearing's poetic style with its deliberate inclusion of mass discourses, is restated at various moments in "Reading, Writing, and the Rackets." Fearing argues, for instance, that books – those "archaic medi[a]" – have themselves become a kind of mass culture. Theoretically, he admits, a solitary individual could still write a book, but if one considers not only the writing of a book, but the entire mode of literary production – publication, distribution, advertisement, and reviewing – the imaginative writer's claim to independent artisanal craftsmanship becomes rather dubious (NS, ix). High art, furthermore, is no different from any other cultural practice in its historical contingency, no less inviolate from political determinations than TV. Indeed, what happens on TV may determine what is permissible and possible in the literary sphere. As Fearing explains:

> News, common sense, good literature – these are whatever the voices of communication unanimously, and often, say they are. Conversely, distortion, false reasoning, base and degenerate writing, these, too, are whatever the concerted organs of communication repeatedly denounce as such. Still more conveniently, those topics and views not mentioned in the forums of communication, at all, do not exist; certainly, if some unpleasant subject does win a momentary, unauthorized interest, under the magic eraser of silence it soon dies. (NS, xv)

The passage seems strikingly contemporary in its concern to denaturalize the self-evident obviousness of such ideological categories as "common sense" and "literature." But it implies another key point, namely that, whether in the sphere of politics or literature, the production of a hegemonic discourse (or, to use Fearing's less jargony language, of "approved rhetoric") involves two processes: that of forgetting and that of whitewashing whatever we remember.[52] Earlier in the essay Fearing describes the first process as "erasing memories" (or, even more simply, eliminating the person with something to remember) and the second as "arranging far better horizons for all of us" (NS, ix). The one task, of course, serves as a tidy alibi for the other; indeed, Fearing suggests, it is somewhat like the high-toned cause of Prohibition, which in fact permitted the Protection rackets to proliferate underground (NS, xx). Cast in this kind of gangster-movie metaphor, the whole business perhaps sounds too sinister to be credible. But the identical point has recently been made in more "reasonable" academic tones with regard to the operations of literary historians and canon makers: "Custodians," Cary Nelson notes, "concern themselves not only with conserving the past but also with selectively disposing of much of it, though the two impulses become deceptively conflated in the imagination of academic disciplines – so that a self-congratulatory process of conservation remains primarily in view."[53]

This insight, I believe, is the source of Fearing's long-standing suspicion of any form of literary celebrity. A few of his essays from the late twenties already suggest that, in his view, official acclaim meant either a containment of any truly challenging and disruptive writing or, otherwise, a validation of what is already politically safe. He saw the award of two Pulitzer Prizes to Edwin Arlington Robinson (whom he read with great admiration in his years at Wisconsin) as a kind of "fumigation"; but he regarded Amy Lowell (whom he disparagingly referred to as a "teacup revolutionist") as a perfect Pulitzer recipient, since she seemed to amalgamate revolutionary "modernity" with the cozy culture of the New England antique shop: "How dear she was," Fearing remarks, "to the heart of anyone, any magazine editor or critic, wishing and wishing that he, too, might be known as modern and daring, and yet, after all, safe!"[54]

Even more irksome to the young Fearing was the invention of the Book-of-the-Month Club, the Literary Guild, and so forth. He admitted that the book clubs, with the help of their editorial boards of "guaranteed Grade A" critics, were unlikely ever to select a thoroughly bad and uninteresting book. Yet he felt equally certain that this attempt to certify the excellence of a selection of books, destined (or so the Literary Guild claims) to become "a permanent part of your life . . . a classic of the future," would lead not only to great profits for the guaranteed Grade A authors and critics, but to a pernicious standardization by a kind of culture police. Fearing's ironic solution to the question of how one decides which is the best of the book-of-the-month clubs makes his point perfectly clear:

> Let us ask Mr. Van Doren to be Editor-in-Chief of an International Culture Guild. His associates will be Mr. Hugh Walpole, the greatest living English lecturer, and the ghost of Matthew Arnold. It will be the task of these three not only to select the book of the month but the best Book-of-the-Month Club; and to select The-Play-of-the-Week, the Thought-for-the-Day.[55]

The implication of the final item is, of course, that the Culture Guild's selection will help eliminate all other less excellent thoughts.

For Fearing, then, at the beginning and at the end of his career, the preservation and certification of the officially excellent seemed necessarily to involve a degree of censorship, or (to use the language of his 1956 essay) the judicious application of "the magic eraser of silence." His work implies further that whatever can be officially celebrated must itself be celebratory and safe, stripped of any element of surprise and any discordant thought: a "loss-proof package" and (in the years of the Cold War) "risk-proofed against steadily multiplying taboos" (NS, xix, xxii).

"Reading, Writing, and the Rackets" occasionally indicates the character of "approved rhetoric" in the fifties: as regards political discourse it seems to Fearing to allow only "an innocent recital of endless prosperity, occasionally interspersed with grim but imperative demonstrations against super-demons that endanger this idyl" (NS, xix); as regards mass culture, it includes only "sponsored salesmanship," filled with "the easier types of true thoughts, but wholly pruned of thoughts everybody knows are false" (NS, xx); and, as for literature, it permits only "marginal topics" – "bold tales of explorations and adventure, heroic stories about the Civil War, amusing anecdotes about ones' intrepid (elder) relatives" (NS, xv). But the total exclusion of the negative in these neat "loss-proof" ideological packages is itself the product of exclusion: of a prolonged process of "hammering and grinding," a process that may, he sinisterly suggests, involve the removal of "a few human heads" (NS, xix). Along with these heads, of course, go the works and the memories of the erased and, cumulatively, the whole history of "the terrible drama of the past decade, in which a long phase of our society died" (NS, xv).

From our perspective, at a distance of almost forty years, Fearing's assessment might very well seem overly pessimistic, and his metaphors (of a "total eclipse," of a "magic eraser of silence," of a society "necrobiotic with the rackets") unduly apocalyptic; after all, one might feel compelled to point out, there have certainly been books on subjects other than harmless adventures and intrepid relatives. The rhetorical mode of Fearing's essay is obviously hyperbolic and relies on a gloomy polemical insistence (which also, incidentally, marks the dystopian propositions of contemporary theorists such as Debord and Baudrillard). But before we discount Fearing's position as a matter of style or personal paranoia, we should note that he is recording as a lived experience the elimination of certain possiblities, which for most of us has always been a fait accompli. It is for us an imaginative effort to retrieve a sense of the variety of literary, cultural, and political projects that seemed open to writers before the stark dichotomies drawn by the Cold War and the retreat of intellectual life into the separate tribal homeland of academia. We do not notice, like Fearing (or like Nelson Algren, who lamented Fearing's demise), the gaps left by those who disappeared like so many shadows into "the limbo of the proscribed" or the erased (NS, x). Even now if one reads their names – Sol Funaroff, Herman Spector, John Wheelright, Genevieve Taggard, Anna Louise Strong, Abraham Lincoln Gillespie, Joseph Kalar, Edwin Rolfe, Isidor Schneider, H. H. Lewis – there is perhaps still a residual sense that these forgotten people were probably inherently forgettable: "no good."

Where contemporary critics have engaged in the work of retrieval of which I spoke, they have recounted (though in less anguished and bitter terms) the same story of narrowed possibilities that I haved traced in Fearing's essay. Let us consider only one example: Jane Tompkins's polemical conclusion to *Sensational Designs*. This essay – entitled "But Is

It Any Good?" – examines the varying contents of anthologies of American literature and indicates rather convincingly the emergence of a more restrictive definition of "literature" in the fifties and early sixties (coinciding, significantly, with the McCarthy era, the Cold War, and the heyday of New Criticism). She finds that in the thirties anthologies were generously inclusive: cowboy songs, Negro spirituals, songs and prayers of Native Americans, letters, travel literature, philosophical essays, and political speeches were for the first time incorporated into such collections. Moreover, the editors argued for such texts on the basis of "ethical as well as aesthetic ideals," on their value as documents of the political and social history of the age, and as demonstrations of the connection between American literature and American life and thought. These texts, one might say, attempted to represent "the voice of the people." Twenty years later, around the time Fearing was writing the strange introduction to his *Selected Poems,* the key anthologies confined themselves to a dozen or so "great" authors. Gone was any populist ideal or any sense that the nature of literariness might be open to debate; one editor (in a tautology reminiscent of the Warren essay) vindicated "the study of literature primarily because the matter is *literature.*" The editors, moreover, no longer saw themselves as concerned with the social relevance of literature, but with a dualistically conceived task of evaluation: of identifying the "few peaks" of the literary landscape as opposed to "the many low-lying hills."[56]

"Reading, Writing, and the Rackets," rant that it may be, enables us to see this high-minded project from the perspective of the "low-lying hills," the mere "background" to the looming Alps of individual fame. Moreover, Fearing's perception of the homologies between the political proscriptions of the House Un-American Activities Committee, the peculiar mode of censorship deployed by the mass media, and the processes of silence and celebration by which literary fame and failure are decreed emphasizes the fact that the fate of literature is inseparable from the fate of the culture at large. Fearing's quirky retrospective of his own career, in other words, demands that we see both his relegation to insignificance and his potential significance as politically driven.

THE TAXI-DRIVER POET AND THE LOST HALO

The second reason a study of Fearing's poetry is of interest and significance to the literary historian follows from the first: if literary failure is not only personal, but dependent on an ideologically contingent definition of literariness, then the "failed" poets may preserve for us an alternative and subversive sense of what literature may be and what cultural work it might do. Fearing admittedly had a somewhat less defined sense of his own project than other "interesting failures" such as

Mike Gold (who fervently believed in the value of literature as a cultural tool in the class struggle) and Vachel Lindsay (who saw his poems as prophetic blueprints for a truly participatory culture and a material world redeemed by beauty).[57] But even if it is hard to come up with an equivalent thumbnail sketch of Fearing's aims, the profound bitterness of "Reading, Writing, and the Rackets" suggests that he had a clear enough sense of his intentions to know that the business of "literature" turned out to be inimical to the hope and expectation he cherished when he decided to become a writer: the possibility of finding "some fascinating way to be of public service, particularly one that avoided too much humdrum routine in an office cluttered with, well, books" (NS, xxii).

To best define the nature of Fearing's subversions a brief recapitulation is in order. I have already implied that with the waning of the radical culture of the thirties, the range of possible projects for literature was substantially narrowed. Above all, as Cary Nelson argues so forcefully in *Repression and Recovery*, the exclusion of any overtly political aim became not merely incidental but constitutive of the dominant notion of literariness. This notion was one that, in effect, managed to rearticulate modernism (or at least certain aspects of that vast spectrum of often adversarial and disruptive literary practices) with an academic version of the same old genteel tradition it originally seemed to challenge. As read and taught by the New Critics, modernism was transformed into a latter-day version of affirmative culture, recontained in what Peter Bürger has termed the "institution of art."[58] While it is indisputable that in the postwar period the academic canon bestowed a certain kind of cultural power on a few writers, the nature of that power was also quite carefully circumscribed (though the cultural hegemony of literature spills over into other forms of power in myriad unstated ways). Officially, at least, the institution of literature presented itself, by the mid-fifties, as the special domain of the great individual talent and of universal cultural value: a territory bought at the cost of political efficacy and even of Fearing's modest "public service."

This much has already been implicit in the preceding discussion. But the notion of literariness by which Fearing's work has been practically erased has also relied on another of modernism's constitutive exclusions: that of mass culture. In some ways this opposition was even more profoundly "naturalized" than the opposition between universal poetic value and political "propaganda"; and literary intellectuals have, until quite recently, been far more reluctant to dislodge and challenge it. It provided, after all, a high moral ground, an unalienated space, not only for the New Critics but also for anti-Stalinist New York intellectuals, for Marxist theorists like Adorno and (at times) Marcuse – and indeed for artists themselves. But whatever its exact political value, it is clear that this hierarchical opposition has been just as carefully "produced" – especially since the late thirties. In the fifties the Modern Language Association even established a new section for the study of "Literature and General Culture," with the expressed aim of "learn[ing] what clearly separates the best-seller from the work of distinction, and . . . offer[ing] our students the necessary exercises in discrimination."[59] I was myself required, years ago, in an old-fashioned Leavisite English department, to instill in students the connoisseurship required in this kind of distinction. The idea was never put in quite this fashion, nor did I see my work in this light at the time; but what else is finally achieved by those classic exercises in "practical criticism," requesting the student to "analyze and compare," say, an advertisement and a poem, or a character description from a popular romance and one from Jane Austen? My inexperienced readers quickly learned that the passage they might instinctively prefer because it was "clear" was the one of which they were supposed to disapprove. The result is that "Literature" comes to seem a special kind of language with a special "structure of feeling": ironic, serious, complex, cagily indirect, and, for many students, often confoundingly opaque.[60]

Now it would be difficult, if not impossible, to use a Fearing poem as the touchstone of value in the kind of exercise I have described. Consider, for instance, the following samples of his verse:

> Then Louis sagged and fell and ran.
> With seven bullets through his caved-in skull and those feeble brains spilling out like soup,
> He crawled behind a water hydrant and stood them off for another half minute.
> "I'm not shot," he yelled, "I'm not shot." (CP, 32)
>
> And Zorrocco, not knowing Mabel loves Jim, has returned to use her for his criminal scenes; but in a motor crash he is killed, Mabel winning at last to happiness in Jim's arms,
> Directed by Frederick Hammersmith and produced by National.
> (CP, 103)
>
> Glamorous, gripping, moving, try it, send for a 5 cent, 10 cent sample.
> (CP, 113)

My selective citation obviously exaggerates the point; but even so, it seems undeniable that Fearing's imitation and incorporation of media clichés create a challenge to the notion of literariness that the "analyze and compare" exercise strives to promote. Fearing's work instigates a negotiation across the Great Divide – the conceptual gulf between literature and mass culture.[61] These lines are singularly lacking in those linguistic intensities that literary folks are trained to value: that distance and difference from everyday expression which brings to the text, however indirect and evasive it may be, the stamp of a singular personality – of "style." Fearing's writing, in contrast, depends on the discourse of displaced citation, the style he seems to describe (in the poem "Twentieth-Century Blues") by way of punctuation marks: the unoriginality of the "quote, unquote," the eternal sameness of the "ditto, ditto, ditto," and the empty superlatives of "that . . . million-volt exclamation mark" (CP, 125). Such writing finds its ideal muse in the media sob columnist, whom Fearing apostrophizes in the poem "Dear Beatrice Fairfax" in the language of product guarantees: "standardized, synchronized, amplified, best-by-test" (CP, 100). She is, as Edward Dahlberg suggested, an impersonal mass-marketed Beatrice for the audience of a Paramount movie version of *Vita Nuova,* likely to inspire only cliché, only the pseudopersonal lyricism of the advertising slogan.[62]

But before I even try to specify the meaning of these ironic strategies, we should first consider the skeptic's question: is the incorporation of language and imagery from the mass media into the fabric of the poem necessarily destabilizing? After all, even *The Waste Land,* that most canonical of all modernist texts, includes fragments of popular songs in its poetic midden of Western ruin. Indeed, as Fredric Jameson has noted, high modernism has frequently managed to define its own difference and shape its idiosyncratic styles precisely by a homeopathic incorporation of its opposite: elements of a "scandalous and intolerable external irritant," as Jameson puts it, can be "drawn into the aesthetic process itself and thereby systematically worked over, 'acted out,' and symbolically neutralized." One might think, he suggests, of the work of writers like Stein and Robbe-Grillet who deploy the relentless repetition of machinery as an artistic strategy.[63]

A similar argument can easily be put forward with regard to the "irritant" of mass culture. Thomas Strychacz, for instance, has recently argued that modernist writers like Henry James, Theodore Dreiser, John Dos Passos, and also Nathanael West (though West presents, as Strychacz admits, a more complicated, perhaps undecidable case) have "writ[ten] in mass culture in an effort to write it off." The character of these authors' work, indeed, its very "literariness," is radically shaped by their various and shifting responses to mass culture – whether "assimilation" (as in the case of Faulkner's rather seamless use of cinematic techniques) or "accommodation" (as in the case of John Dos Passos, who incorporates elements from mass-mediated culture – such as popular songs and newspaper headlines – into his text in a more obvious, rough-edged fashion). But even in the case of such ostensibly heteroglossic "accommodations," Strychacz argues, the incorporated fragments are subjected to a process of modification and subversion, so that the authors ultimately succeed in reinstating the cultural authority of their literary work and in marking its difference from its mass cultural "other."[64]

Such arguments are by no means negligible, and I shall address them again in the chapters on West. Suffice it to say for the moment that a critic's conclusions in this regard are hardly independent from his or her strategies of interpretation and that these have often involved a kind of redemptive reading in which critical and disruptive moments are assimilated and subsumed under the "success" of the work of art.[65] Such interpretations are based on a limited notion of possible authorial intentions and on the assumption that academic validation or canonicity is the ne plus ultra of literary power. But the fact that we are institutionalized as literary critics does not entitle us to ignore the possibility that an author may have had antiliterary impulses and might have seen this putative triumph of "art" not as a victory but as a loss.

All the evidence suggests that Fearing (and West too, in my view) intended the exact opposite of reinstating the cultural authority of the literary work. Fearing's discursive bridging of the Great Divide between literature and mass culture was conceived not as culturally redemptive, but as a task of destruction and negation whose (often deeply hidden) positive implications were inseparable from hopes of radical political change. It is no accident that Fearing cites the German Dadaist Georg Grosz as an influence on his poetry. His work should be seen as participating in the project of the historic avant-garde.[66] This is a project that the New Masses (at a time when Fearing was a regular contributor) described as the destruction of "the superstition of the sanctity of art" – an attack on all those false idealizations that conspire to make an intolerable life tolerable, especially on what Fearing calls "that mystical and mysterious faith in the myth of art and culture as a consummate panacea."[67] Admittedly, the fact that he still produced poems implies that Fearing never took the avant-gardist attack on art as far as the outrageous exhibitors at the Café Voltaire, or their more political counterparts in Berlin. But, then, it is hard to imagine anyone getting away with such "bohemian" displays in the serious and politically committed literary climate of the American thirties. And when Fearing, in the poem "$2.50," announces that glamour, faith, the beauty of literature, the clever best-seller all "Reek of something blown away from the muzzle of a twenty-inch gun," it seems to me that we can still hear – undiluted – the acidic accents of the more political forms of Dada: "a voice of teeth ground down to points . . . a near-absolute loathing of one's time and place, the note held until disgust turns into glee."[68]

Fearing's connection with Dada emerges even more clearly if we extend our understanding of the historic avant-garde to include Walter Benjamin's seminal interpretation of its significance. Benjamin perceived the performances, collages, and word-salads of the Dadaists as homologous to other forms of contemporary experience: the "urban shock" of the man in the street in big-city traffic and the sensory discontinuities of new forms of mass-reproducible art, especially film. These forms of experience – fragmentary, irreverent, democratic – appeared to him similarly destructive of "aura," of contemplative immersion, depth, and distance.[69] In the light of these insights, Fearing's reputation as "the leader of the taxi-driver school of verse" becomes particularly suggestive. For the poet who writes like "a taxi driver reading a billboard while fighting traffic" any protective separation between art and the bustle of everyday life has disappeared. The nickname suggests that Fearing might be the ideal candidate for the role of the Baudelairean poet who lost his halo amid the moving chaos of city traffic, the poet whose role would become (as Baudelaire foresaw) "the creation of a cliché." The distracted taxi-driver poet, bombarded by urban stimuli, showed little sympathy with the autonomous work of art or the dignity of those elevated poetic souls who fail to confront their changed status in a metropolitan culture, who (as Baudelaire puts it) seem to think that they "drink beef tea made of ambrosia" and "eat cutlets from Paros."[70] In the poem that probably earned him both the title of "Village Bobbie Burns" and of "taxi-driver poet," Fearing mocks the melancholy posturing of the Genius:

> Hey? What saith the noble poet now,
>   Drawing his hand across his brow?
>   Claude, is the divine afflatus upon you?
>   Hey? Hey Claude?
> Here are a million taxi drivers, social prophets,
>   The costume for an attitude
>
>   . . . .
>
> Here is a statue of Burns.
>   There is the modern moon.
>   That song is the latest dance.
> Hey? Of what doth the noble poet brood
>   In a tragic mood? (CP, 58)

While he did not include this poem in his *Collected Poems,* Fearing seems to have adopted it as something of a theme song – no doubt because of its irreverent mood, its "costume for an attitude."[71]

This iconoclastic "taxi-driver" stance is evident in a group of self-consciously hard-boiled urban poems ("St. Agnes' Eve," "Ballad of the Salvation Army," "Death and Transfiguration of Fourteenth Street," and the "Aphrodite Metropolis" series) that mount guerrilla attacks against the aura of artistic classics and traditional poetry through debunking allusions. The best example is perhaps "St. Agnes' Eve" (which Bruce Fearing recalls in his "epistle to pop"). This poem is not the tender maiden's dream that the Keatsian title might lead us to expect, but a gangster story, a genre then still quintessentially modern: urban, tough-minded, and worldly-wise, flaunting the unabashed violence of "brains spilling out like soup." Moreover, it assumes the form of a film script, which allows Fearing to expose the deliberate construction of the poem's devices – a method resembling Brecht's alienation effects in its overt "display of technology," its deliberate inclusion of the artistic apparatus in the poem itself.[72] For instance, Fearing explicitly announces the dramatis personae ("The characters: six policemen and Louie Glatz") and the locations ("The settings include a fly-specked Monday evening, / A cigar store with stagnant windows, / Two crooked streets"); he gives instructions for camera angles and montage ("Close-up of Dolan's widow. Of Louie's mother. / Picture of the fly-specked Monday evening, and fade out slow"); he provides comic-strip sound effects ("Rat-a-tat-tat!" and "Blam! Blam! Blam!"); and he stages a climax in the form of a bizarre moment of pseudometaphysical animation:

> Louie's soul arose through his mouth in the form of a derby hat that danced with cigarette butts and burned matches and specks of dust where Louie sprawled. (CP, 33)

These effects, which one critic has described as "Pop Art" qualities, undercut the atmospheric and associative effect of the melancholy descriptions of the urban scene (the "vacant galleries of night," the "vibrant throats of steamships," and bricks that "bulge and sag") – phrases that might otherwise remind us of the emotive objective correlatives of Eliot's "Preludes."[73] Fearing's alienation devices seem to strip such phrases of their artsy aura, so that we cannot take them too seriously: the line "Soft music, as the wind moans at curtained windows," for example, seems like yet another sound effect.

My contrast of Fearing's technique with T. S. Eliot's famous objective correlatives is not simply thrown in for the delightful incongruity of juxtaposing so unlikely a pair. It seems to me that another way of illustrating Fearing's subversive and antiliterary intentions would in fact be to compare his work with Eliot's. After all, Eliot was the archantagonist of many American leftist writers in the thirties, and Fearing appears quite often to have worked in conscious opposition to this major poet of the day. In the poem "American Rhapsody (1)" he hails the literary superstar with mocking fanfare (and offers a retort to Eliot's infamous comment on the undesirability of "free-thinking Jews"):

That genius, that littérateur, Theodore True,
St. Louis boy who made good as an Englishman in theory, a deacon in
    vaudeville, a cipher in politics,
Undesirable, in large numbers, to any community. (CP, 88)

The two poets, moreover, share certain overlapping concerns that provide specific grounds for comparison: Eliot was also interested in devising an impersonal poetic discourse, open to cited fragments from a
variety of contexts, including, occasionally, that of mass culture; and
both poets were concerned with the possibilities of poetry in and of the
modern city.[74]

On the question of impersonality, the positions are readily contrasted.
The more recent biographical work on Eliot has emphasized what one
could sense in his work all along: that for Eliot poetic impersonality was
really a matter of obliquely asserting that personality from which he
claimed to flee but which he never denied or doubted. We need only
recall here the ponderous snobbery of his remark that "only those who
have personality and emotions know what it means to want to escape
from these things."[75] For Fearing, on the other hand, personality itself
was in danger of becoming a fiction or, more exactly, a commodity.
The poem "Portrait (2)" vividly illustrates the point:

The clear brown eyes, kindly and alert, with 12–20 vision, give confi-
    dent regard to the passing world through R. K. Lampert & Com-
    pany lenses framed in gold;
His soul, however, is all his own;
Arndt Brothers necktie and hat (with feather) supply a touch of youth.

.   .   .   .

But Mercury shoes, with special arch supports, take much of the wear
    and tear;
On the course, a custombuilt driver corrects a tendency to slice;
Love's ravages have been repaired (it was a textbook case) by Drs.
    Schultz, Lightner, Mannheim, and Goode,
While all of it is enclosed in excellent tweed, with Mr. Baumer's
    personal attention to the shoulders and the waist;

All of it now roving, chatting amiably through space in a Plymouth 6,
With his soul (his own) at peace, soothed by Walter Lippman, and
    sustained by Haig & Haig. (CP, 140–41)

For him, therefore, poetic impersonality, allusiveness, and citation are,
simultaneously, an unavoidable imposition of the economic system and
a protest against it.[76] I am tempted to say that the Chrysler advertisement, with its humble and (in Jason Wheeler's reading) ironic deference
to the commodity, appears a particularly apt slogan for a fictional and
real Fearing: "I'm not famous, but my car is. . . ." The basis of his

artistic (and political) strategy is a conscious decision not to be "famous," not to claim for himself the laurels of the great poet, or for his poetry the halo of great art.

The point is evident from his prosy, ironic, and irreverent style generally; but the early poem "Aphrodite Metropolis (III)" provides a neat contrast with Eliot in this respect. The poem describes two working-class lovers, Myrtle and Harry, on their Sunday picnic. In the park, the couple read – and then sit on – a newspaper whose headlines are incorporated into the poem: "GIRL SLAYS BANKER-BETRAYER"; "BATH-TUB STIRS JERSEY ROW" (CP, 26). Wondering what Harry, confronted with such samples of contemporary language, might actually say to Myrtle, Fearing offers a contrasting set of interspersed citations: one, a paraphrased cavalier love lyric ("What will your chastity amount to when your flesh withers in a little while?") and the other, a sampling of advertising copy (" 'Ziggin's Ointment for withered flesh / Cures thousands of men and women of moles, warts, red veins, flabby throat, scalp and hair diseases, / Not expensive, and fully guaranteed' "). Harry wisely avoids the decision with a kiss; and Fearing seems satisfied to juxtapose these snippets of discourse without privileging one over the other. In *The Waste Land,* on the other hand, the allusions to Marvell's "To His Coy Mistress," however comically distorted, have a resonance of power, a trace of something lost to a contemporary world filled with the likes of Sweeney, Albert, Lil, the typist, and her spotty young man. I am not suggesting that Fearing's citations from mass culture are reproduced uncritically: in this case the ridiculousness of Ziggin's therapeutic promises are quite evident. Yet the purpose of the sample of contemporary language is not to shame us back into the ivory tower of high culture.

In Eliot's case, the opposite is true: his poetic project can be understood precisely as regaining a "halo" for art and culture – and laurels for himself. *The Waste Land,* as I have already mentioned, includes some exhibits of what is clearly figured as the debased culture of the contemporary world. But the placement of these fragments is telling: the typist's gramophone record fades into Shakespeare's magical music from *The Tempest;* the raucous ballad of Mrs. Porter and her daughter is silenced by the holy sounds of the "*voix d'enfants, chantant dans la coupole*" – and of course the cultural prestige of Verlaine and Wagner to whom the line alludes. Eliot, in other words, is ever mindful of supporting his individual talent with the authoritative bulwark of tradition. In spite of his impersonal allusive discourse, he remains quintessentially "famous" – and it is this ambition that Fearing homes in on when he ironically acclaims Eliot as "genius" and "littérateur."

Moreover, despite the fragmentary multiplicity of its textures, Eliot's poetry constantly reaffirms a belief in the redemptive value of a monadic and mythically conceived culture. One could argue that the possibility of redemption is only tenuously sketched out in *The Waste Land,* with the final admonitions to give, sympathize, and control. But it seems to me that this argument would ignore the way in which the allusive and associative method privileges the importance of memory: memory, that most auratic of capacities, which, in Eliot's poetic practice, reaches across the distance of time to unify and resacralize the ruin of the present – at least in the minds of the poet and the equally erudite reader. At the core of Eliot's allusive and associative descriptions of the modern city lies an aesthetic and a politics of nostalgia. His cities constitute a kind of formal, even mythic, palimpsest. Consider, for example, the opening scene of "The Fire Sermon," where the departed nymphs and their faithless lovers have left behind their cardboard boxes, sandwich papers, empty bottles, and cigarette ends, the "testimony of summer nights." Beyond the dismal present prospect of debased love, the poet still discovers the redemptive traces of Spenser's joyous *Prothalamion;* and beyond the neurotic modern woman at her boudoir table, strewn with cosmetics, sits Pope's gorgeous Belinda and Cleopatra in her regal barge. This is a poetry not of absence, but of the deferred and therefore only more auratic presence of the culture of the past. Eliot's textual layers create a sense of historical depth and plenitude. The geography of his contemporary London is constantly superimposed on that of Baudelaire's Paris, Dante's Inferno, and so forth. Even in one of his early poems, "The *Boston Evening Transcript,*" Eliot could imagine that "the street were time" and that, while other lesser beings might read their banal newspaper, he could exchange a superior nod with the stern seventeenth-century moralist La Rochefoucauld at the far corner.

Fearing's city, on the contrary, is the space of forgetfulness. Poems such as "Memo" lament the inability of the urban geography of coffee-pots, haberdashers, pinball arcades, heel-pocked pavements, and hurrying feet to retain even the shadow of personal memory – let alone the rich store of mythic associations that enable Eliot to endow the city or its crowds with auratic and symbolic resonances. "Yesterday," as the poem "Nocturne" puts it, "has shrunk to a newsbulletin." Fearing's urban palimpsest is not the high modernist one of Eliot's "unreal city," but the literal one described in the poem "Aphrodite Metropolis (II)": a billboard, where several "perplexed citizen[s]" have left their graffiti, along with the "popcorn wrappers and crushed cigars" (CP, 25). Over the image of a blonde lady, someone has drawn a moustache; and over the slogan "Mama I Love Crispy Wafers So," someone has written "Myrtle loves Harry," and "Jesus Saves. Jesus Saves." The poem presents, I am tempted to say, the depthless cultural palimpsest of postmodernism. It offers only a flat surface inscribed with multiple texts, but invites no redemptive recourse to the mythic resonance of submerged inscriptions. If anything, the citizens' rather banal messages of love and salvation are mocked and trivialized by the prior banality of the consumer's love of Crispy Wafers, just as the moustache mocks the image of the sexy blonde.

A similar point is expressed by the idea of Fearing as the taxi-driver poet who writes poetry that mimics the experience of reading a billboard while fighting traffic. It is poetry that refuses us the possibility of contemplative immersion, and refuses the dream of the Baudelairean flaneur: to endow the city and its crowds with "soul."[77] This high-minded project had already, by the mid-twenties, become something of a set convention in urban poetry. A 1926 anthology (which Fearing seems to have read) was even entitled *The Soul of the City*.[78] This volume consisted largely of indifferent poems deploying the dated dichotomies of the pastoral tradition and, in many cases, the rather hackneyed topos of beautiful music revitalizing a dreary city. Oddly enough, both Pound and Eliot, despite their erudite irony, could be said to participate in this same project and to use the identical conventions. Pound's "N.Y." is a case in point:

> My City, my beloved, my white! Ah, slender,
> Listen! Listen to me, and I will breath into thee a soul.
> Delicately upon the reed, attend to me!
>
> *Now do I know that I am mad,*
> *For here are a million people surly with traffic;*
> *This is no maid.*
> *Neither could I play upon any reed if I had one.*
>
> My city, my beloved,
> Thou art a maid with no breasts,
> Thou art slender as a silver reed.
> Listen to me, attend me!
> And I will breathe into thee a soul,
> And thou shalt live for ever.[79]

Fearing's poem "Death and Transfiguration of Fourteenth Street" seems to be a response to these conventional tropes. Here the hallowed music of late romanticism – first announced by the allusion to Richard Strauss in the title – fails to transform the sordid sounds of the street: the "sleet, sleet, sleet / Of noise it had somehow sired by hoofs and gears / Drumming the xylophones of its deep stones." Union Square remains a "corpse," and Fourteenth Street merely chokes a bit on the "opera-tainted air" exuding from Murray's radio shop. The fact that this music is mechanically reproduced and transmitted further attenuates its connection with a contemporary scene it can only berate and bewail:

> The angels weep while Murray, in the mist,
> Paddles the pants of Fourteenth Street with Liszt. (CP, 34)

The poem seems to be mocking the attempts of a poet like Eliot, who essentially "paddles the pants" of the squalid contemporary city with Wagner and fragments of Elizabethan lyrics in the hope of effecting a cultural transformation. Fearing's poem, on the contrary, does not presuppose the superiority of the past to the present. The malingering Fourteenth Street produces noises of surprising vitality, while the strains of classical music are figured as unappealing and phony relics from Greek mythology: "stuffed" versions of Laocoön's choking serpents – "too glistening, and sweet."[80] The failure of Murray's civilizing efforts can thus be met with an attitude of amused indifference.

Though this awkward and totally forgotten little poem does not spell the matter out, it seems to me what is finally being questioned is the locus of salvation, of "transfiguration." Fearing implies in this, and in his other early poems, that the contemporary American city is no longer the space of high culture, and is unlikely to be transformed, even imaginatively, by any appeal to tradition and art. My sense is that he understood this as the first and necessary assumption to make if poetry was to have any social relevance.

There is a certain ironic logic (perhaps not entirely foreseen by the poet himself) in the fact that Fearing, who rejected the auratic poetics of nostalgia and memory, and who maintained a subversive attitude toward the hallowed artistic tradition, should be consigned to extracanonical oblivion. How do we then remember the poet who would not be "famous"? The best answer may be: as a kind of agent provocateur. The demystifying irreverence of his poetic provocations is, as I have suggested, especially challenging in juxtaposition to what we might call (in Guy Debord's phrase) Eliot's "imperialist" cultural politics – his efforts at reconsecrating everyday life under the auspices of the poetic tradition.[81]

The questions that Fearing provokes could be framed as follows. Is there value in poetry that engages in the possibly self-negating task of questioning its own value; in poetry, not of affirmation, but of negation and critique; and in poetry that will constantly have to be remade – like the protest placards or manifestos it sometimes imitates?

No more breadlines. No more blackjacks. No more Roosevelts. No
    more Hearsts.
No more vag tanks, Winchells, True Stories, deputy sheriffs, no more
    scabs.
No more trueblue, patriotic doublecross leagues. No more Ku Klux
    Klan. No more heart-to-heart shakedowns. No more D.A.R.
    . . . .
no more 14, 16, 18 inch shells. (P, 45–46)

I would not pretend that these questions of value have no final or fixed
answer. But perhaps we may invoke, in conclusion, Roland Barthes's
nonessentializing definition of literary value that I cited as one of the
epigraphs to this chapter: "What evaluation finds is precisely this value:
what can be written (rewritten) today."[82] If, as many have argued, it is
impossible to reinvent the project of the historical avant-garde in the
utterly commodified space of postmodernity, it is surely even more
impossible to reinvent and to rewrite the ambitious dreams of the imperial culture of high modernism. Fearing's ephemeral city of graffiti and
slogans and billboards is still rewritten, for instance, in the citational,
"transpersonal" writings of the Language poet Bob Perelman or in the
negations of an artist like Barbara Kruger, with her ironic use of commercial posters.[83] It seems, therefore, that our understanding of American cultural history should expand to include Fearing's provocations and
his hope for a writer's life that was not only a matter of books – even if
it has seemed for so long that this hope had failed.

4

The Undercover Agent and the Culture of the Spectacle

> In societies where modern conditions of production prevail, all of life presents itself as an immense accumulation of *spectacles*. Everything that was directly lived has moved away into a representation.
>
> Guy Debord, *Society of the Spectacle*

> Would you like to tune in upon your very own life, gone somewhere far away?
>
> Kenneth Fearing, "Radio Blues"

The cover of Guy Debord's *Society of the Spectacle* reproduces a famous photograph from *Life* magazine: that of a movie audience staring at the screen through identical pairs of white-framed 3-D spectacles. The photograph vividly illustrates Debord's critique of a culture of images and simulations, a world in which our perceptions and experiences are thoroughly mediated by commodities. It also tells us something about the stance that often characterizes the more negative theories of mass culture: the critic, adopting a camera angle like that of this photograph, tends to assume a position facing the crowd and to cast what is essentially a satirical glance at the silly-looking people absorbed in the spectacle on screen.

With this image in mind, it is both amusing and intriguing to learn that Kenneth Fearing was once a member of just such a bespectacled audience. Back in 1936, he put on a pair of special goggles – the left lens dark green, the right dark red – in order to view a 3-D film entitled *Audioscopiks*. The experience evoked in him ominous imaginings of a future where people who never left "the dim and hushed cathedrals of the cinema" would be forced to develop strange new protective characteristics in order to cope with this new environment.[1] His dark fantasy, however, did not prevent Fearing from relishing the novelty of a new technique that allowed "something [to] come out of the screen

72

and smack the spectator square in the eye" or from fantasizing about the "enormous possibilities" of being able to see Mae West in three dimensions.

This coincidental connection between Debord and Fearing strikes me as suggestive in two ways. It underlines the curiously proleptic character of Fearing's work and its similarities with Debord's dystopian reading of late capitalist culture (a reading that relies on such critical notions as reification, standardization, and ideological control). But it also reminds us of a difference, namely Fearing's habitual sense of himself as a fan – as a fascinated member of the mass audience.

I suggested in the preceding chapter that, by the mid-fifties, Fearing's conception of mass culture (and the society of which he saw mass culture as the "nerve center") had come to seem very similar to what we tend to think of as the postmodern "society of the spectacle." For example, in "Reading, Writing, and the Rackets" Fearing comments on the fact that all radio and television messages, since they "permit no rejoinder," are perforce received passively; that participation and control by individuals are eliminated by the cost and centralization of the technology; that the communications enterprise is entirely commodified ("All time and all space in every medium is merchandise"); and that mass culture operates as a tautological exercise of self-justification: as the "self-declared corroboration and celebration of itself," as not only the "latest," but also the "first word, and the only word" (NS, xix, xvii).

This negative view of mass culture as an all-pervasive grid of alienation, manipulation, and censorship would seem to contradict our preceding discussion of Fearing's connections with the Dadaists, for whom the incorporation of mass-produced language and images into the work of art appeared to hold liberatory possibilities. How exactly do we connect the pessimistic writer of "Reading, Writing, and the Rackets" with the "taxi-driver" poet who would as happily read a billboard as a poem by Marlowe? In order to do so at all, we must consider Fearing's career in relation to the complicated fate of the historic avant-garde of the twenties and thirties. The dream of a transformed and *lived* culture (which underlies the period's various experimental negotiations with the commercialized technologies of mass production and reproduction) was, in turn, inextricably and fatally linked to the fate of the period's radical political movements. In Europe, these movements met their nemesis in 1933, with the rise of Hitler, and in the United States after World War II, with the apparent "consensus" of an affluent society. Given this historical context, the avant-garde's irreverent courting of the commercial, the technical, and the mass-produced presented something of a risk; for as the erstwhile Dadaist Matthew Josephson put it, "there were as yet no helpful social arrangements" by which the artist who tried to bring technology into the fabric of art might "escape the peril of being caught and mangled by the assembly lines."[2] The question, simply put, is this: can the artist who hopes for a transformed social order still court mass culture when it appears that people's lives are being transformed daily, not by avant-gardist provocations, but by vast historical forces – and, notably, by the technologies of mass production and reproduction?

I am suggesting, in short, that certain historical developments help us account for the contradictions discernible in Fearing's attitude toward mass culture. During the years spanned by his career, the nature and social meaning of mass-mediated culture did in fact change. It became more administered, more bureaucratized. In the twenties the idea of "mass culture" would perhaps have brought to mind the hard-boiled modernity of the Black Mask detective stories, the linguistic and pictorial inventiveness of Krazy Kat, the distinctively personal comedy of Chaplin, and the raucous shorthand of tabloid headlines. But by the forties, the term would have signified vast new institutions: mass culture had come to mean NBC, CBS, Time, the Hollywood studio system, and the nationally syndicated soaps, with their corporate sponsors. The shift from entrepreneurial to corporate control of commercial entertainment brought about important changes in the very character and form of mass-mediated culture (evident in the styles and plots of films, comic strips, and advertisements alike): changes that Jackson Lears has characterized as a shift "from a carnivalesque exploration of performative language and playful imagery to a literalist, didactic narrative realism."[3] Mass entertainment, furthermore, became not just an urban, but a national, phenomenon; and with larger markets, the tendency to standardize, to keep profits predictable, was inevitably increased. Perhaps most important, the political developments of the thirties exacerbated the fears that were always attached to the term "mass": by the end of the decade people would probably have seen newsreels of Hitler addressing torchlight rallies; they would have listened to the broadcast speeches of demagogues like Huey Long and Father Coughlin; they might even have been frightened by Orson Welles's radio drama, The War of the Worlds, or given some thought to the much discussed (and misinterpreted) hysteria it triggered.[4] Moreover, along with the more empirical changes I have cited, we must recall that the thirties also marked the consolidation of a certain theoretical discourse (especially with the rise to prominence of the anti-Stalinist New York intellectuals), which cast mass culture in an extremely negative light: as a threat to individualism and authentic artistic production.

All of these developments inevitably affected Fearing's work. Whereas at first mass culture, with its democratic irreverence, seemed capable of knocking off the mystificatory and auratic halo of the work of art, it eventually came to assume a mystificatory and auratic aspect itself – with the result that (as Fearing puts it in "Reading, Writing, and the Rackets") "the eye can scarcely penetrate beyond the blinding haloes revealed on the electronic screen" (NS, x). Mass culture, the remark suggests, had taken over the affirmative ideological function of high culture: the suspect task of "restor[ing] faith in the flophouse, work-house, warehouse, whorehouse, bughouse life of man" (CP, 113).

This said, I would be reluctant to identify a specific moment at which Fearing's attitude toward mass culture changed. Despite his generally deepening pessimism, the critic and the aficionado are never easily sepa-rated in his writing. Even in the late twenties, at the same time that he was using snippets from the media in his guerrilla attacks on the hal-lowed and the highbrow, Fearing wrote poems that present the opera-tions of the media very pessimistically. The 1929 poem "JACK KNUCKLES FALTERS (*But Reads Own Statement at His Execution While Wardens Watch*)" (CP, 22–23) is a good example. Here Fearing intersperses the tabloid headlines with the words of Knuckles's testi-mony, a technique reminiscent of John Dos Passos's collages in the Newsreel sections of *U.S.A.* But whereas Dos Passos frequently seems to use his headlines only as indices of a particular historical moment, Fearing deploys the device to disclose something about the political role of the news media. The poem exposes the manner in which the newspa-pers suppress, rather than express, the final words of the condemned man. Not only do the inserted headlines, in loud boldface, interrupt the hapless Knuckles's statement, but they shift to sensationalism ("STAG-GERS WHEN HE SEES ELECTRIC CHAIR" and "BODY PLUNGES AS CURRENT KILLS") or misrepresentation ("POSI-TIVE IDENTIFICATION CLINCHED KNUCKLES VERDICT") whenever he asserts the injustice of his conviction. At the end of the poem, the tabloids seem simply to lose interest in this minor drama: the last headlines veer off distractedly to a "FISHERY DISPUTE" and an "EARTHQUAKE REPORTED IN PERU." Thus the tabloids of the twenties, no less than the electronic media of the fifties, are presented as engaged in a peculiar kind of censorship: they serve as what Fearing calls (in his 1956 essay) "a noisy substitute" for the "total darkness, total silence" that the system really desires (NS, x).

The fact is, I think, that throughout his career Fearing's attitude toward mass culture was marked by a certain ambivalence – his stance was always dialectical, if you will. All of his humorous film reviews for the *New Masses* show evidence of real interest and enjoyment, and he addresses his imagined audience of "genuine, dyed-in-the-wool movie hopheads" as one of them.[5] Yet even as he includes himself with the other "unfortunate sub-humans (moving blindly in our shadowy half-world)," he retains a deep suspicion of some ominous ideological cover-up.[6] His list of specifications for acceptable movies (which I glean here from a couple of reviews) is only ironically tolerant: the "celluloid opera" should "give[] the eyes and ears a gentle two-hour massage," should "not gag us," should "leave[] no hang-over," should "contain no Shirley Temple and no social implications (Will Hayes variety)," and should "never under any circumstances, makes us think – think, that is, about the screwballs who glue these things together and their frequently sinister purposes."[7] Fearing is, in short, best understood as a kind of double agent. On the one hand, he casts himself as a mole from the Communists' Movie Department, an "underpaid, undercover agent" who concerns himself with Hollywood only under "long-standing orders from Moscow"; on the other hand, he admits to being a "genuine addict," one who regards Hollywood "dream powder" as "the lowest form of opiate on earth," but who still "can't get enough of it."[8] Even at the end of his career, when Fearing condemns the culture industry in the most paranoid terms and finds it impossible to define literary value except by firm exclusion of commercial products, we still find him looking back with a certain nostalgia to a time when the border between "inventive writing" and mass culture did not appear to be so absolute: before it became the Great Divide or, to use Fearing's much angrier language, "a desolate no man's land patrolled by reformed spies, saboteurs, traitors, monitored by converted Russian Intelligence officers and cultured plantation owners" (NS, xxii). The metaphor suggests to me that Fearing retained the desire to infiltrate, to operate somewhere in the no-man's-land between the anti-Stalinist Left and the New Critics, in the domain of what had become the scandalously middlebrow.[9]

"BIG GOLD DOME": COMMERCIALIZED LEISURE

The ironic and ambivalent vantage point of the double agent may, in fact, be the ideal one from which to view the culture of the thirties. As I suggested in Chapter 2, the decade marks a transitional moment in U.S. history. It was a moment when the impact of a new culture of consumption and leisure – inextricably connected to the new communications media – was increasingly evident, but was still hard to define or assess. Did the flood of brand-new consumer products and entertainments bespeak utopian promises of greater leisure and freedom, of a more varied, colorful, and exciting life? Or did they (as Robert Lynd and other sociologists of the time feared) spell the end of authentic culture, creativity, and even the rational individual, and thus pose the threat of insidious new forms of social control?[10] And by which moral standards could one judge? By the values of the new culture of abundance: self-fulfillment, entertainment, the appeal of "personality" – values that were daily fostered by advertising, self-help manuals, and the movies? Or by the spartan, "virile" standards of the culture of production: self-discipline, hard work, thrift, and integrity of character – values that regained credibility after the economic collapse, a catastrophe earned (or so many thought) by a decade of debauch?

As a "proletarian" poet, and as a writer for the culture industry, Kenneth Fearing straddled the perspectives of the cultures of production and consumption: a position that enabled his illuminating diagnoses of the contemporary scene. His experience in the culture industry, combined with the radical's disgust with the chaos of contemporary capitalism, rendered him an acute critic not only of mass culture per se, but of the new conditions of production and consumption of which the mass media were the most obvious manifestation.

This is not to say, of course, that Fearing's vantage point as a cultural critic did not also have its historical limitations. For instance, he found it difficult to imagine, in the turmoil of the Great Depression, that capital could ever be sufficiently benevolent – even if only to save itself – to pay workers wages high enough for them to become mass consumers. In 1936 he derided H. G. Wells for holding what now seems to be a perfectly reasonable Keynesian view. Wells had argued in a review of Fritz Lang's *Metropolis* that it was unlikely that modern workers would actually become subject to the grim enslavement portrayed in the film. Fearing (while confessing his own love for sinister science fiction movies, fantastic machinery, and laboratory thunderbolts) completely disagreed. He mockingly summarized Wells's cheerfully pragmatic criticism of Lang's dystopia as follows:

> How was it possible, [Wells] asked, to find purchasers for the goods made by workers, if this great majority of the population were to be removed from the purchasing class? No, no, a thousand times no, the whole trend of industry was the other way, the huge working class, according to Wells, must and therefore would receive ever-increasing wages – the development of the proletariat as a healthy, prosperous body of consumers was necessary to capital, and therefore inevitable.[11]

In Fearing's view this optimism had been shown up as "thoroughly empty" by the "sad, subsequent events" of the economic crisis. And yet, in the long run, Wells had it right, and labor leaders in the late thirties used precisely these arguments to win concessions from big business.

But even if his explicit economic prognostications were not unerring, Fearing's writing demonstrates a keen awareness of the advent and character of the new consumer culture. This derives, in part, from his fascination with the city, which, in the twenties and thirties, was broadly perceived as a center for pleasure and play, nightclubs and entertainment – the paradigmatic space of the lifestyle of the new abundance.[12] The poem "Saturday Night," first published in 1928, explores and criticizes this new phenomenon of nightlife (new, that is, for the middle class):

> That is not blood on the shiny street
> Where heroes and heroine appear, in taxis bound for bright cabarets.
> That is not blood along the pavement, though it could be;
> It is dirty water,
> Not the blood you think might be there after crowds have scraped and cursed and hammered upon it all day.
>
> 9:29 Saturday night;
> Elite Max;
> Charlotte, the beautiful magazine girl;
> They only want to hear music;
> They only want to hear some music play.
>
> A packed house in Madison Square Garden finds delirium in a prize fight,
> And elsewhere, others are entertained by Senator Horgan's speech.
> But suave Max and lovely Charlotte seek their pleasure at the *Blue Swan*.
>
> 10:38 P.M.;
> Battling Bolinska sleeps on the canvas mat;
> Senator Horgan is a true statesman of the old school;
> Shall we go to the *Parakeet* instead of this place?
> It is kind of dull here.
> Yes. Give the waiter ten dollars.
>
> That sum represents one day's mental travail on the part of nonchalant Max,
> Elite haberdasher whose cut-priced hosiery shines in a modest window.
> But there is no blood on the street,
> Though crowds have struggled and lied and hurried upon it all day long;
> There is no blood along the pavement from Max, Charlotte, or anyone,
> To pay for the hosiery, the *Blue Swan,* and the fatigue.
>
> 11:45 Saturday night,
> On penny arcade and gin palace and senator alike.
> 11:45, the great leveller.
>
> That is rain-water on the shiny street,
> Not eyes, not blood, not fingers, nerves, rags, glass, bones,

> Where now in a taxi suave Max and exquisite Charlotte roll onward in
>   each other's arms,
> Roll on into the big silhouette of gaiety,
> Roll on through Saturday night. (CP, 66–67)

The structure of the poem is perhaps influenced by Eliot's "Rhapsody
on a Windy Night," where the sinister gas lamp calibrates each half
hour; but Fearing's city of spectacular abundance is not congenial to the
earlier poem's modulations between the present and memory. With the
commodification of leisure, time, it seems, has come to be measured
with an absurd meticulousness ("9:29," "10:38"). Experience and consciousness are confined to the banalities of the present moment, which
unifies all the fun seekers – so that "11:45" becomes "the great leveller"
of all consumers.

Under the illusory "silhouette of gaiety," consumption and leisure
define the social identity of the "heroes and heroine"; even a "modest
haberdasher," no longer confined by the "mental travail" of work hours,
may purchase such flattering epithets as "lovely," "elite," "suave," and
"exquisite." Since in the world of "Saturday Night" work is rendered
invisible, and the "fatigue" thus inexplicable, the hosiery, restaurant,
and cabaret appear as an opaque miracle to be enjoyed (rather like those
mysteriously delivered goods in the Melanesian cargo myth, which, as
Baudrillard has suggested, captures the fetishistic character of consumer
society).[13] Or to put it in the poem's grimmer terms: nobody's "blood"
pays for these commodities. "Saturday Night," in other words, both
imitates and criticizes the tendency of consumer culture to veil the
sphere of production. On the level of assertion, the poem insistently
denies the contrast between the glistening new world of abundant consumption and the harsh grind of work; but on the level of image and
mood, it clearly implies that the "shiny street" of the entertainment
seekers does in fact take its glitter from the "blood . . . fingers, nerves,
glass and bone" of the "crowds" that "have scraped and cursed and
hammered upon it all day." This dual gesture of "Saturday Night" is
characteristic of Fearing's poetic strategy. He re-creates the optimistic
ideological surfaces of consumer culture and simultaneously undermines
them, not by constructing an alternative ideal, but by revealing what is
ignored in the official accounts of the world.

In his other "nightlife" pieces from the late twenties, Fearing's criticism of commercial entertainment is somewhat more tolerant, or at least
more humorous. In "It Was All a Mistake," an article for the *New
Masses,* he addresses a subject that social historians such as Lewis Erensberger and Lary May have begun to explore: namely how the film
industry helped to propagate the habits and values of consumption – not
only through the glamorous lives represented in the movies, but also

(in the late twenties) through the physical environment of lavish new theaters.[14] The designers of these movie palaces (and the word is precisely to the point) set themselves the explicit aim of providing the audience with a concrete experience of luxury, so that ordinary folks, who could never hope to own such riches in real life, could escape from their daily drudgery in the exotic ambience of the Egyptian, Chinese, Baroque, or Moorish decor. Fearing's essay describes a visit to one of the first of these "monument[s] to the moving picture industry" – the Paramount Theater in New York – and his description leaves no doubt as to the enticingly utopian dimensions of both the film and the theater:

> Inside, we have all the exquisite appointments of all the homes not owned, but often dreamed of, by the thousand clerks, shop-girls, taxi-drivers, college professors, pimps and poets who have been waiting for admission. It is our home. My footman bows and indicates the stairs to the main-floor balcony. You look at the hundreds of pictures framed in heavy gold that make your chateau complete. We walk on our heavy carpets and are blinded by the brilliance of our own mammoth cut-glass chandelier.[15]

As the piece continues, the description of the audience's possessive bedazzlement is interwoven with an outline of the movie's plot, blocked out in capitals, and framed, so as to replicate the intertitles of a silent movie. I reproduce a sampling:

> HAROLD STUYVESANT, JR., SCION OF AN ARISTO-CRATIC FAMILY. HE LOVES THE CIRCUS GIRL, WHOSE PARENTAGE IS A MYSTERY.

> . . . SON YOU MUST GIVE UP THIS VULGAR CREATURE. I HAVE AMBITIOUS PLANS FOR YOUR FUTURE. FA-THER, I WILL NOT GIVE UP THE GIRL I LOVE EVEN THOUGH SHE BE A GIRL OF THE COMMON PEOPLE JUST LIKE YOU BIMBOES OUT THERE IN THE AUDIENCE

> . . . HOW WAS HE TO UNDERSTAND IT WAS ALL A MIS-TAKE AND SHE WAS REALLY SO LOYAL AND TRUE AND LOVING TO HAROLD ONLY?

> LOOK AT ME. I – I AM YOUR MOTHER!

This device exposes the silliness of the film's formulaic plot ("Oi, hev I seen it dis pitcher somevere before?" an audience member appropriately asks at the end of the piece). But, more important, the alternation of the descriptive passages and the title cards allows Fearing to suggest how the experience of vicariously "owning" the luxurious palace reinforces the audience's identification with the lives of the wealthy displayed on the screen. For instance, after the title card introducing the hero, Fearing imagines that the audience, thrilling at the sounds of the world's greatest cinema organ in its very own chateau, readily responds: "We are now Harold Stuyvesant Jr., scion of an aristocratic family. Look at our wonderful home on the screen. That's our home. But we give it up for the girl we love. Gladly!" This magnanimity is of course entirely empty, because vicarious; and as Fearing suggests, the audience members' source of concern and satisfaction in the contrived denouement (the circus girl turns out to be Mrs. Stuyvesant's own daughter) lies in their short-lived sense of relief that they (or rather Harold) won't have to lose their luxurious home. Fearing's final assessment of this manipulation of people's desires is sharply critical. But while he finally denounces the movie palace as a "monument" to "the rotten cheapness in our souls," he does not pretend that the promises and solace it offers are unappealing. After all, even professors and poets are not immune to these charms: they are part of the record-breaking crowd that nightly flocks to the Paramount.

The utopian promise of spectacular consumption is also the theme of "Ballad of the Salvation Army" (the poem to which Albert Halper alludes in *Union Square*). Fearing evokes the blare of a Salvation Army band to announce the raucous arrival of a new secular redemption – the utopian dreams of spectacular consumption:

> Heaven is a free amusement park,
>   Big gold dome, big gold dome.
> Movies at night: "The Life she Led."
> Everyone sleeps in one big bed.
> The stars go around inside your head.
>   Home, sweet home.
>
> On Fourteenth street the bugles blow,
>   Bugles blow, bugles blow,
> The torpid stones and pavements wake,
> A million men and street-cars quake
> In time with angel breasts that shake,
>   Blow, bugles, blow! (CP, 30)

The ballad is clearly not meant to be taken too seriously. It casts a parodic glance at two earlier poems: Tennyson's melodic and sentimental song from *The Princess* (from which Fearing steals the refrain "Blow, bugles, blow") and Vachel Lindsay's poem "General William Booth Enters into Heaven" (which, also to the tune of a Salvation Army band, announces the spiritual salvation and transformation of the masses). Fearing's parody substitutes the mass entertainment of the "big gold dome" for Lindsay's populist pieties, his "golden air" and "transcendent dyes"; and he offers the rather banal classless heaven of the movie house and the "one big bed" in lieu of Tennyson's (equally banal) fairyland of aristocratic romance:

> The splendour falls on castle wall
> And snowy summits old in story:
>   The long light shakes across the lakes,
>   And the wild cataract leaps in glory.
> Blow, bugle, blow, set the wild echoes flying,
> Blow, bugle; answer, echoes, dying, dying, dying.
>
>   O hark, O hear! how thin and clear,
>   And thinner, clearer, farther going!
>   O sweet and far from cliff and scar
>   The horns of Elfland faintly blowing!
> Blow, let us hear the purple glens replying:
> Blow, bugle; answer, echoes, dying, dying, dying.[16]

Like "It Was All a Mistake," "Ballad of the Salvation Army" hints at Fearing's ironically ambivalent perspective on the emergent culture of abundance. While the poem makes fun of the tawdriness of the demotic buglers in their "burlap petticoats" and their promises of cheap thrills, this "dime-store dream parade" clearly issues in a salvation and renascence of sorts, while the late Victorian echoes of a separate cultural Elfland are certainly in comparison "dying."[17]

MASS CULTURE AND THE NEW MASSES

Fearing's conception of the emergence of consumer culture as something quite new, his willingness to consider (however ironically) that the American moving picture industry may not be dead, but may yet be "putting forth its finest flower," is surprisingly rare among the leftist writers of the late twenties and early thirties.[18] Communist intellectuals were very much aware of the political importance of mass culture. Yet it is fair to say that (before the adoption of a broadly based antifascist Popular Front generated a more tolerant attitude toward popular forms) they often regarded mass culture from the position of a nineteenth-century production ethic. This meant that the writers for the New Masses and the Daily Worker tended to disparage consumer culture from the moral heights of revolutionary austerity. As I suggested earlier, Raymond Williams's distinction between residual and emergent cultural processes is helpful in characterizing this tendency.[19] Inspired by the historical precedent of the Soviet Union and the scientific certainties of teleological Marxism, many American Communists identified proletarian culture as the heroically emergent force. The confident, even arrogant, tone of the *New Masses* (Richard Pells has singled out Mike Gold and the journal's film critic, Robert Forsythe, as key culprits) makes perfect sense in this light: it derives from an epochal and theoretical version of history, rather than from any analysis of actual American circumstances.[20] According to this Marxist historical blueprint, the capitalist era is to be succeeded, inevitably, by a communist mode of production. Mass culture, therefore, is merely the decadent phase of the dominant bourgeois culture. For this reason, Forsythe can even on occasion adopt an attitude of mock pity, noting that there are "so many indications of the breakdown of capitalist civilization that we are inclined to become tender and sympathetic in the midst of the debacle, much in the manner of 'don't cheer boys; the poor devils are dying.' " This terminal cultural disease is epitomized for him by that "First Artist" of the rotting republic: Fearing's beloved Mae West, whose campy impersonation of the Statue of Liberty Forsythe regarded as a veritable "treatise on decay."[21]

Mike Gold's cultural criticism offers many instances of this leftist version of "negative classicism" – the pervasive tendency to theorize mass culture as a form of social decadence and decline.[22] We could take as an example the 1926 story entitled "Faster, America, Faster! A Movie in Ten Reels," a piece that invites comparison with Fearing's "It Was All a Mistake."[23] Gold uses the same formal devices that we saw in the Fearing piece: an ironic narrative interrupted by boldface representations of silent movie title cards, bearing, in this case, such familiar and melodramatic legends as

I LOVE YOU! MAY I MISS SMITH? I KNOW I'M JUST A POOR COWBOY, BUT –

AND TWO SHOTS RANG OUT!

MEANWHILE A LONE RIDER –

But whereas Fearing uses the interaction of his description and the narrative intertitles to give some account of the appeal of the movies and their vicarious offers of luxury, Gold's narrative proceeds without any response to, or comment on, these fragments from the movies.

This is hardly surprising, since the piece is essentially a parable on the apocalyptic text that Gold parenthetically inserts at the beginning and reiterates at the end of the story: "America is a private train crashing over the slippery rails of History." With the outcome mapped out with such inevitability, there is clearly no need to waste any analytical effort on these samples of cultural dry rot. Gold can safely use his allusions to mass culture as ready-made metaphors of the triviality of his set of wastrels and pleasure makers, bound for Hollywood on a private train: the fatal pace of their journey is like that of a silly Keystone comedy, and the little flapper's face is "beautiful as a flat magazine cover done by a Hearst artist." Their triviality is, for Gold, a sign and omen of their imminent demise. With a melancholy irony worthy of Spengler or Pound, he can announce that the radio, with its transmission of a "ya-hooing" jazz band playing "Yes Sir, She's My Baby," "brought the history of science to a grand climax." Finally, when at the end of the story, the train – predictably – crashes, Gold stages over the wreckage what now reads as an exaggerated bit of heroic allegory:

> A pale farmer came running from the dark. He had a sickle in his hand. A pale worker in overalls came up, with a hammer. They soberly began the rescue work. Dawn grew. The red morning star appeared.

The producers, the story announces, will come to bury the consumers, and an austere new culture will replace the debased indulgence of the travelers to Hollywood.

The undeniable touch of bathos in Gold's stylized social realism should not obscure the historical and cultural interest of the piece, which illustrates perfectly the way in which mass culture theory was affected by an orthodox Marxist teleology. The same position, moreover, informs some rather fine political writing. Muriel Rukeyser's interesting poem "Movie," originally published in the New Masses in 1934, expresses essentially the same attitude toward mass culture, and the same revolutionary certainties:

> Spotlight her face   her face has no light in it
> touch the cheek with light   inform the eyes
> press meanings on those lips.
>   See cities from the air,
> fix a cloud in the sky, one bird in the bright air,
> one perfect mechanical flower in her hair.
>
> Make your young men ride over the mesquite plains   ;
> produce our country on film : here are the flaming shrubs,
> the Negroes put up their hands in Hallelujahs,
> the young men balance at the penthouse door.
> We goggle at the screen : look   they tell us
> you are a nation of similar whores   remember   the Maine
> remember you have a democracy of champagne –

And slowly the female face kisses the young man,
over his face the twelve-foot female head
the yard-long mouth enlarges and yawns
                                        The End

Here is a city   here the village grows
here are the rich men standing rows on rows,
but the crowd seeps behind the cowboy the lover the king,
past the constructed sets America rises
the bevelled classic doorways   the alleys of trees are witness
America rises in a wave a mass
pushing away the rot.
                        The Director cries Cut!
hoarsely CUT   and the people send pistons of force
crashing against the CUT! CUT! of the straw men.

Light is superfluous upon these eyes,
across our minds push new portents of strength
destroying the sets, the flat faces, the mock skies.[24]

Rukeyser conceives of the movie (synecdochically indicative of mass culture in general) as a form of false consciousness, fabricated by a "Director" with a capital "D": the representative of the ruling class. Its "produced" version of America is depicted as unreal and deceitful: a world of "constructed sets" peopled by the romantic rich and the happy Negro singing "Hallelujah" and sustained by a self-congratulatory jingoism (concisely evoked by the old slogan "remember the Maine").[25] The poem rejects the false promises of this American "democracy of champagne" as decadent "rot," denounces the goggling audience as "whores," and responds with a somewhat puritanical revulsion to the voyeuristic indulgence of the gigantic kiss. The movie, in short, is the product of the "straw men" of a decaying dominant culture; and the emergent force, though referred to as "the people," is clearly made up of workers, associated with the "pistons of force" of heroic industry and heralding "new portents of strength." These are representations of an ostensibly "real" America that will demolish all false representation: the "unproduced" producers, who need no spotlight on their eyes, need no meanings pressed on their lips.

The poem achieves a satisfying formal closure with the final three lines, which negate the poem's opening descriptions of the vacant but ideologically "made-up" movie star. Yet it is also contradictory, in ways that are perhaps symptomatic of the larger cultural project in which it participates. The poem posits mass culture as its inauthentic Other; yet it figures the emergent oppositional culture as something rather like a movie. It begs the question as to exactly who these agents of change, vaguely apostrophized as "America ris[ing]," might be: not "you" or "they," it would seem, since those pronouns are associated with the suspect producers of the movie, but apparently also not "we," the gogglers, whose experience of the destruction of the "sets, the flat faces, the mock skies," and "the eyes moving across our minds" seems little different from the earlier experience of watching the romantic finale with the lovers' kiss. The Director's cry of "CUT! CUT!" not only indicates his impotent misapprehension, but also, unintentionally, draws our attention to the uncertain status of the uprising that the poem attempts to represent as untainted by representation. The key conceptual problem is that the people are at one moment imagined as entirely passive, subject to the fantasy on screen, and at another moment as the agents of change – without much sense of how these contradictory notions might be bridged.

The Rukeyser poem indicates a problem that besets the Left's essentially avant-gardist project of imagining a new proletarian culture *for* the people. In opposing the *representations* of abundant consumption with *representations* of the heroism of production, it comes to share something of the dominant culture's spectacular and nonparticipatory character. Both Gold and Rukeyser conceptualize the American "people" as, in some sense, "natural" and the working class as authentic: as antithetical to mass culture, which is associated with everything that is artificial and superficial. In both cases, the "flat" face of the Hollywood starlet is a sign of her unreality, her status as a mere simulacrum. Yet Gold's "pale farmer" and "pale worker" are, arguably, equally one-dimensional; the adjective renders them quite ghostly, and their arrival is certainly no less contrived than that of the "lone rider," whose triviality we are expected to take as prima facie evidence of social decay. In the end, therefore, it becomes hard to say whether the political idealization of Gold's or Rukeyser's conclusion is any less contrived than the romantic idealization of the movie finale; or whether, in its technique, especially in relation to its audience, the utopian narrative of socialist realism is all that different from that of "Capitalist Realism."[26]

The Communist writers of the early thirties were quite conscious of the fact that their work, with its populist and propagandist impulse, shared the field of operations and, to some degree, the methods of the culture industry. An advertisement for the *New Masses* provides some comical evidence of this awareness. Reappropriating the format of the new confessional advertisements, the journal recommends itself to a bourgeois airhead as a cure to "mental halitosis":

HER BEST FRIEND WOULDN'T TELL HER . . .

For years she had been reading all the news unfit to print, the Saturday Evening Pest and Sloppy Stories. All her reading matter, her ideas, her thoughts, had been concocted in a capitalist sewer, strained through a bourgeois filter, and then half-baked in a progressive oven . . .

THEN A REAL FRIEND

told her the truth and backed it up with a copy of the

NEW MASSES

and a lively breeze of fresh air swept through her brain and freshened up her whole mental apparatus.

She is getting better. She is sitting up and taking notice. Specialists tell her that with care and a monthly dose of NEW MASSES she will someday be able to think for herself. And the entire treatment, for a whole year, cost her only $2.00.[27]

The blend of Marxist invective and advertising jargon makes this a fascinating period piece, and it recalls the idea of "stealing back and forth" of images and forms discussed in Chapter 2.

A more serious and influential exposition of this same cultural contestation, however, is outlined in Gold's "Towards an American Revolutionary Culture" of 1931. This essay alerts *New Masses* readers to the ubiquitous "capitalist propaganda" presented in "every short story, every piece of newpaper reporting, every advertisement, child's primer, popular jazz song" propagating a particular set of attitudes toward all aspects of life.[28] It describes leftist writers as engaged in an ideological struggle with the culture industry: a struggle to release the working class of its addiction to the "daily dope" provided by the Hearst and Scripps "coke-peddlers" and to reappropriate the techniques and imagery of the mass media for revolutionary ends. This position is echoed by other writers, who felt, as Gold did, that "you cannot build Communism with masses whose emotions are still of the capitalist world."[29] The drama critic Robert Gessner, for example, argued in 1934 that "all revolutionary artists aiming to undermine the ideological structure of the middle class and consolidate the working class must, in order to be at this time effectively heard, consider seriously the question of working through Hollywood."[30] Even Kenneth Burke's address to the American Writers' Congress of 1935, "Revolutionary Symbolism in America," advocates what we might see as a discursive version of such a struggle, in suggesting that the Left needs to wrest certain linguistic tools – symbols and words with which Americans can readily identify – from the forces of capitalism and consumerism. Such appeals for progressive writers to deploy the techniques of popular culture were only to increase after the official Communist Party policy, initiated at this Writers' Congress, shifted further away from the original strategy of developing a "proletarian" counterhegemony.[31]

With their emphasis on the cultural and subjective dimensions of political activism, the literary intellectuals associated with the Communist Party were at odds with, and perhaps ahead of, the party at large, which slighted the importance of culture in favor of practical tasks such as union organizing.[32] But while we cannot dismiss the importance of these writers' efforts at devising a kind of cultural expression that was "neither high nor low," the notion of cultural revolution held by Gold and his comrades can be criticized in at least two respects.[33] There is, first, the general notion of the mass audience as addicts who cannot keep themselves from gobbling up the harmful dope offered to them by the exploitative culture industry (an attitude that is evident even in such *New Masses* titles as "Sex, An Opium of the People" and "Dope – For the Workers"). This position has troubled historians who insist that audiences can take from popular forms what they need, and can even exert an influence on the content of mass cultural products.[34] Indeed, one might quite reasonably ask why workers should be regarded as dupes if they prefer a romantic kiss to the grim task of clearing up the train wreck of history? Second, there is the problem that, despite the common rhetorical move of attaching class labels to forms of expression (this is "design for a parasite class," that is "poetry for workers," and so forth), the prescriptive and proleptic character of the experiment in proletarian culture in fact assumes a fairly substantial separation of cultural forms from material conditions. To say that culture can be used as a weapon implies that its forms and institutions are more or less neutral – an assumption that becomes increasingly problematic as culture itself becomes integrated into the economic sphere. Critics like Gold, Gessner, Isidor Schneider, and even, to a degree, Kenneth Burke conceived of the media, and perhaps culture itself, in a fairly instrumental manner. Gold, for instance, often seemed to oppose technical experimentation in literature (though it must be said that his positions were not as rigid as has often been claimed) and argued that a literature for the proletariat should be as accessible and emotionally straightforward as mass culture. This position fails to consider whether the forms of didactic literature might not foster authoritarian rather than critical habits of mind, and perhaps exaggerates the degree to which even a deliberately oppositional culture is able to separate itself from the determinations of the dominant culture.[35] To what extent, one may ask, can countercultural products free themselves from the reifying tendencies of the culture at large?

REIFICATION AND RIGOR MORTIS

While Fearing's work bears certain connections to the critical positions discussed in the preceding section (he also playfully applies, for instance, the addict metaphor to himself and to his audience), he does not seem to have shared the certainties of an orthodox Marxist teleology. His work confronts, moreover, the possibility of a more radical determination of literary and cultural forms by the dominant culture and probes rather more darkly the potential subjective and experiential implications of the media. While nobody in the United States could fail to see the connection between mass culture and big business, Fearing traced pervasive signs of reification and commodification in language, in high culture, and in the very core of people's emotional lives. This pessimistic analysis often resembles the work of the Marxist theorists of the Frankfurt school (and subsequent theorists who similarly privilege the concept of reificiation); and it presents a complex set of problems for political activists who regard culture simply as a weapon in the class struggle.

Several of Fearing's poems and essays suggest not only that capitalist culture affects the emotions in order to foster consumerism (as Gold and Burke had asserted), but that the emotions, and culture itself, have become commodities – indeed, the privileged commodities of American society. This "second industrial revolution," fueled by the production and sale of images, implies that the base-superstructure model, still discernible in the instrumental approach to culture, no longer applies. Society could no longer be conceptualized as divided between the solidity of the economic realm and the ephemeralities of culture; it had already, Fearing seems to suggest, assumed the structure of a "continuous superimposition of geological layers of commodities" – the structure Guy Debord was much later to describe in *Society of the Spectacle*.[36]

In "Have You a Fairy in Your Home?" – a humorous piece published in the *New Masses* in 1927 – Fearing hints at this radical incorporation of culture into the economic system. Prompted by Charles Lindbergh's appointment as a "good-will ambassador of the United States" to South America, the essay probes the process by which a person, an event, an emotion, a debate, or a platitude can be transformed into a salable item. The fanciful title (taken from a contemporary slogan) suggests the pervasive mystification that accompanies the marketing of commodities.[37] The essay wittily links such "illogic" with the vaunted no-nonsense values, the brisk, "modern" practicality of U.S. production:

> It is our national characteristic, the speed, efficiency, and illogic with which we turn our spontaneous emotions into patented sentimentalities. Doubtless there are other people who do the same thing; but none of them convert their emotions into institutions as relentlessly as we do, nor do they, the instant *rigor mortis* has occurred, market the cold body in such subtle and profitable ways.[38]

The piece argues, in other words, for a connection between the mode of economic production and the mass consumption of spectacles – of which Lindbergh became a prime example.

Like many later social critics (Adorno, Lowenthal, Boorstin, Debord, and others), Fearing identifies the figure of the celebrity as a particularly alarming and characteristic product of an oversymbolic society: the image of a human being as a "pseudo-event," a perfect example of how what "was directly lived has moved away into a representation."[39] Charles Lindbergh, the essay argues, had become a kind of monument to what were once the living emotions of living human beings. The feelings that the young aviator evoked in people (the desire for romance or simple admiration for an act of daring) are not allowed to "slip away and die a natural death," but become packaged in the image of Lucky Lindy – frozen, one might say, in a kind of simulacral limbo. Thus, while the transatlantic flight was nothing more than a brilliant stunt, the aviator came to represent a "convenient substitute for personal romance" and, indeed, for personal life. As Fearing suggests in his poem "American Rhapsody (4)," the star stands in for a displaced experience, for that "bona-fide life [which] will arrive at last," stepping, like Lindbergh, "from a non-stop monoplane with chromium doors and a silver wing and straight white staring lights" (CP, 146).

This transformation of a person into a celebrity, the representation of once-real human lives and needs, parallels the mystification of labor, needs, and value in the exchangeable commodity. And a commodity is precisely what Lindbergh had become. Neither the idol's refusal of many offers of lucrative product endorsements, nor his (much-publicized) distaste for publicity could bring this process of commodification to a halt. Indeed, by making himself scarce, Lindbergh simply added to his own value as a rare product; he simple moved himself into a higher level of commodification. The aviator's refusal to turn himself into an "institution," as Fearing puts it, was the "hottest institution that had ever happened." This immediate assimilation of opposition seems strikingly contemporary, prefiguring the capacity of a postmodern culture (as many critics have described it) to simply recontain any cultural rebellion on a higher "geological layer" of spectacularization. The fact that the rude, reluctant star – Sinead O'Connor is perhaps the latest example – has become such a familiar feature in contemporary culture is perhaps an index of how accurately Fearing identified an emergent phenomenon.

For all of its topicality and humor, "Have You a Fairy in Your Home?" seems to suggest the beginnings of a theory of ideology, involving two levels or varieties of what Fearing calls "institutions." There are the "little institutions," which can be sold directly "in tins and capsules"; and then there are the "major institutions," which involve larger political issues and appear to be as "universal and indefinable as air." Fearing's "little institutions" include "prosperity speeches," "the latest ax-murder," pseudo-controversial debates ("*Is the Younger Generation Really Immoral?*"), or easy, stock abstractions such as "innocence" (sold in all kinds of moral posturing or earnest debate) or "horror" (sold in the tabloids). These can all be measured and defined, he argues, by the amount of money they cause to change hands. Fearing notes, for example, that the sensational murder case involving Ruth Snyder (then condemned and facing execution) had received so much publicity that it had become a small commercial and ideological institution, keeping a set of knee-jerk responses alive and profitable.[40]

The "major institutions," on the other hand, are the broader political ideologies, like "Bolshevism vs. Democracy" or "Uncle Sam the Santa Claus." Unlike the ephemeral small institutions, which "like thieves at a fair . . . operate busily for a time, then vanish when the star performers move on," the major institutions are durable and so valuable that they are not directly bartered: to measure their power in "dollars and cents," Fearing argues, is "to underestimate them grossly." They are, in other words, truly spectacular; they are (to use a phrase from Debord) "the money which one *only looks at,* because in the spectacle the totality of use is already exchanged for the totality of representation."[41] For a while, the essay notes, it seemed as though Lindbergh might attain this status: on his South American mission, he almost became (rather like Kennedy's Peace Corps) the "portable . . . expression of America's good-will to all, a living proof of her essential virtue and unselfishness." But in the end, the disinterested aviator who could not be bought proved too "inexpensive" to make the major leagues. He was finally, Fearing argues, only a replaceable synecdoche for that vast institution of American goodness and innocence summed up in a phrase like "Uncle Sam the Santa Claus" – the justificatory ideology so essential (as Ariel Dorfman has much more recently suggested) to U.S. imperialism.[42]

I have focused on this article in so much detail because the issues it raises resonate not only throughout Fearing's poetry, but throughout much subsequent mass culture criticism. Many of these themes are echoed and amplified, for instance, in the poem "American Rhapsody (1)," the first version of which was published in 1930. The poem presents a scathing diagnosis of the nation's ills in the form of an ironic gala event, an "evening of illusion," starring the privileged cultural commodities of the day. These institutions include, as we might expect, several celebrities: the "talking-picture queen," the "senator at the microphone," the "spinster sybils in the rotogravure," and even our old friend, "Theodore True," the "genius" and "littérateur" from St. Louis.

One particular media hero draws together the points made in the *New Masses* essay about the social function of the celebrity: "That popular ghost, Franklin Devoe, serial hero of the current magazines, / the exact, composite dream of those who read . . . " (P, 25–26). A reference, no doubt, to the jovial Franklin Roosevelt, this magazine hero is an "artist in innocence" and functions as the symbolic representative of the desires of others. His "profitable smile" (which we may relate to the "deathray smile of president or priest" in the poem "Sunday to Sunday" [CP, 104]) invisibly surveys the contemporary landscape of skyscrapers, tenements, and breadlines; it is like an "ectoplasm" that "hovers inescapably everywhere about us." The commodified personality is once again associated with a kind of limbo: not so much the rigor mortis of the monument as that undefinable, ubiquitous substance of the living dead.

"American Rhapsody" announces, furthermore, the closing prices on a stock exchange, dealing in precisely the kind of phony debates and ideological institutions discussed in "Have You a Fairy in Your Home?":

> Closing Prices: Is this Really a Commercial Age? – 100. That Anguished Soul of Marcel Proust – 150. Liberty or Dangerous Freedom, Which? – 210. That Unknown, Patriotic, Law-abiding Corpse – 305.

This cutting little summary of the day's cultural trading implies that even the most meticulous high modernist art, on the one hand, and the tritest nationalistic pieties, on the other, are at the close of day valued only insofar as they display and protect the commercial interests invested in them. Next, a series of lesser commodities, scraps of clichéd language from the movies, profitable lies, hackneyed justifications, make their appearance: "I killed her because she had an evil eye." "We are not thinking now of our own profits, of course." "Nothing can take back from us this night." "Let me alone you God damn rat." Although these fragmentary, depersonalized utterances are presented without exposition or comment, their implications are not hard to guess. They represent what Robert Warshow was later to describe (in his essay on the legacy of the thirties) as "conventionalized 'responses' " – verbal and emotional institutions that threaten to take the place of personal feelings and a more direct experience of life.[43] Like all the other exhibits in the "evening of illusion," these fragments of speech are defined, in the metaphor suggested in the final stanza, as "merely close-ups": spectacular stand-ins for real people, real communication, keeping the attention away from the historical background of "the expiation of living," of "that breadline," and of the mission offering "salvation before coffee and rolls."

One final celebrity close-up deserves some comment, albeit speculative. Along with the spinster sybils and the senator, the poem introduces a mysterious character: "that proprietor of the revolution, Oracle Steve." While "American Rhapsody" gives little indication as to "Steve's" identity, the name is consistently associated in Fearing's work with sinister, cold-blooded organization men.[44] In the poem "No Credit," "Steve" is described in a way that could well apply to this "proprietor" of revolutionary hope:

> Only Steve, the side-show robot, knows content; only Steve, the mechanical man in love with a photo-electric beam, remains aloof; only Steve, who sits and smokes and stands in salute, is secure;
> Steve, whose shoebutton eyes are blind to terror, whose painted ears are deaf to appeal, whose welded breast will never be slashed by bullets, whose armature soul can hold no fear. (P, 42)

The mechanized man, who no longer feels any emotion, save his love of the "photo-electric beam" of the new media, can hardly be turned into a revolutionary; thus, in the phrase from "No Credit," the "shadow, of even a Communist, is gone from the wall" (P, 41–42). This image of the sideshow robot with his button eyes is the specter that finally haunts all of Fearing's poems (and even his novel *The Big Clock*). He is the man we are all in danger of becoming and the greatest obstacle to any critical class consciousness: the man who feels no pain, representing, on the one hand, the passive consumer of high-tech images and, on the other, the metallized body of the fascist and futurist aestheticization of war.

Both "Have You a Fairy in Your Home?" and "American Rhapsody (1)," then, not only present a satirical look at the operations of the culture industry, but raise important questions about the chances for success of the kind of cultural revolution envisaged by Gold and his comrades. First, if the very mode of experience and feeling becomes infected by a vast process of reification – a rigor mortis – the task of winning over the emotions of the masses, as Gold hoped to do, becomes infinitely complicated. And second, if the process of representation, of symbol making, is dogged so closely by an all-encompassing process of commodification, the oppositional potential of culture is drawn into question.

Since I first raised these problems in connection with Muriel Rukeyser's "Movie," with its affirmation of a new revolutionary American culture, it seems appropriate to compare this poem with one of Fearing's: the first part of "Denouement" (or "Denoument," as the title is misspelled in the 1935 version from which I cite).

> Sky, be blue, and more than blue; wind, be flesh and blood; flesh and blood, be deathless;
> walls, streets, be home;

> desire of millions, become more real than warmth and breath and
>   strength and bread;
> clock, point to the decisive hour and, hour without name when
>   stacked and waiting murder fades, dissolves, stay forever as the
>   world grows new;
>
> Truth, be known, be kept forever, let the letters, letters, souvenirs,
>   documents, snapshots, bills be found at last, be torn away from a
>   world of lies, be kept as final evidence, transformed forever into
>   more than truth;
> change, change, rows and rows and rows of figures, spindles, fur-
>   rows, desks, change into paid-up rent and let the paid-up rent
>   become South Sea music;
> magic film, unwind, unroll, unfold in silver on that million mile
>   screen, take us all, bear us again to the perfect denou[e]ment,
>
> Where everything lost, needed, each forgotten thing, all that never
>   happens,
>   gathers at last into a dynamite triumph, a rainbow peace, a thunder-
>   bolt kiss
>   for you, the invincible, and I grown older, and he, the shipping
>   clerk, and she, an underweight blonde journeying home in the last
>   express. (P, 57)

In "Movie," as we have seen, the silver screen finale gives way to the
ostensible "truth" of revolutionary history, with the people sweeping
away the facade culture of the movie sets. In Fearing's poem, however,
the opposite possibility is indicated: the apocalyptically real revolutionary moment (when the "clock . . . point[s] to the decisive hour," "murder fades," and "the world grows new") is metaphorically transformed
into a movie finale. The legitimate and potentially revolutionary hopes
mentioned at the beginning of the poem – that the "desire of millions"
become real, that the rent be paid, and that the forgotten and lost be
given a place – seem by the end of this opening movement to have
receded into an ironic distance, with exotic dreams of "South Sea music"
or hyperbolically happy endings: "a dynamite triumph, a rainbow peace,
a thunderbolt kiss." Fearing confronts us, in short, with the potential
merger of the utopian dreams of revolution and social transformation
with the corny "perfect denouement[s]" of a "million mile" silver
screen. Unlike Rukeyser, he seems concerned with the possibility that
the revolution itself may be "televised" (if I may anachronistically apply
the phrase from the sixties). In a world of spectacles, the representations
of revolution, too, can readily be turned into an institution: an experience provided *for* the passengers of the last express but not effected *by*
them. Fearing suggests, in other words, that in a context where com-

mercial mass culture has become such a powerful force, it may no longer
be possible to avail ourselves of notions like "the people" or any such
holdout of cultural authenticity.

THE DECLINE OF HISTORICITY

Compared with that of his contemporaries, Fearing's cultural
politics, then, appears strikingly postmodern. His acute interest in the
technologies of communication (3-D movies, radios, recording devices,
information systems, even jukeboxes) underscores this connection with
things to come. In 1938, for instance, Fearing already refers to television, and its endless store of images, to epitomize the culture of the
twentieth century:

> Electric razors;
> I am the law, said Mayor Hague;
> The lynching was televised, we saw the whole thing from beginning
>   to end, we heard the screams and the crackle of flames in a sound-
>   proof room,
> THE TWENTIETH CENTURY COMES BUT ONCE. (CP, 144) [45]

Though lynchings have since been replaced by other violent spectacles,
this fragmentary sequence of advertised commodities, politicans-turned-
media-figures, and sensational crimes are not that different from the
images that flash across today's news broadcasts. In fact, one can discover in "C Stands for Civilization" (the poem from which these lines
are taken) several of the key themes that have surfaced in the contemporary debates around the definition of postmodern culture.

The poem is concerned, first of all, with the prepackaging of experience in a world increasingly dominated by images and representations.
The last line of the citation raises a now-familiar (if not compulsory)
question about the nature of representation, by leaving it open to doubt
whether the lynching has an actual referent or whether it originates, as a
ghoulish simulacrum, in the soundproof rooms of the broadcasting
studio. Furthermore, the poem records the culture's obsession with the
up-to-the-second freshness of those "accurate pictures of the latest disaster exactly on time." It may also hint, through the lack of connection
between its sinister snippets, at a social incapacity to assimilate this new
flood of information into any kind of coherent experience or narrative.
Even the poem's refrain, "THE TWENTIETH CENTURY COMES
BUT ONCE," printed in capital letters like a tabloid headline, suggests
a kind of fragmentation: a transformation of a whole period of human
history into a media event that we might forget to attend. In short, "C
Stands for Civilization" is one among many of Fearing's poems which

suggest that the cultural landscape he surveyed in the thirties demonstrated certain emergent characteristics of a cultural formation that has now become dominant.

It seems appropriate, therefore, that an examination of Fearing's response to mass culture should not only place him in relation to his contemporaries, but also suggest the ways in which his work may be "telescoped" through the present (as Walter Benjamin might express it).[46] His work, it seems to me, diagnoses two tendencies that Fredric Jameson has defined as characteristic of the "cultural logic" of postmodernism: first, a decay of the culture's sense of historicity through the fragmentation of time into a series of perpetual presents; and, second, the transformation of reality into images, or, as Jameson puts it in a later essay, the rise of "a whole new culture of the image or the simulacrum."[47] These two phenomena (which have already been identified in this discussion of Fearing and mass culture) are interconnected in a circular and contradictory economy: one could, simply, say that images make us forget, but since we have become so forgetful, we need more and more images – souvenirs that crystallize the past into frozen moments, removed from the flux of continuous life, and the possibility of historical agency.

I turn now to a more systematic exploration of these two phenomena in Fearing's work, but with the following preliminary caution. When I say that he seems concerned with the fragmentation of time and the decay of the culture's sense of history, I am not suggesting that his writing itself bears any close resemblance to Jameson's contemporary examples of this tendency: the disconcerting loss of time in the strange vastness of the schizophrenic's "hysterical sublime," or the unbearably fragmented, unconnectable sounds of John Cage's compositions, or the curiously ahistorical "pastness" of such indefinably citational and nostalgic texts as, say, Lawrence Kasdan's film *Body Heat*.[48] Fearing's work is diagnostic and critical rather than symptomatic; he records rather than exemplifies this emerging condition.

Even so, there are certainly moments in his poetry when Fearing evokes a flatly *present* world that seems quite remote from what Jameson has described as "the great high-modernist thematics of time and temporality, the elegiac mysteries of *durée* and of memory."[49] I have already noted, in the analysis of "Aphrodite Metropolis (II)," that Fearing's urban "palimpsest," as opposed to that of Eliot, is constituted by flat textual surfaces, devoid of any of those elegiac traces of cultural memory and tradition. Fearing's poem, one might say, reproduces the billboard with layers of graffiti (like the legend "Myrtle loves Harry") scribbled on it by people who, as the poem suggests, find it hard "to *remember* a thing like that" (CP, 25, my emphasis). Fearing's poetic treatment of time, though never exactly hallucinatory or schizoid, always seems to suggest the fragmentation of personal experience. And without some sense of continuity, development, or tradition, time does become an elusive, meaningless category: it takes the shape, perhaps, of the meticulously measured packages of consumable time one sees in the poem "Saturday Evening" or of the numbed fixation in the present ("Breakfast in the morning; office and theater and sleep; no memory") one sees in the poem "Now" (CP, 65). Walter Benjamin has described the matter with precision: "The man who loses his capacity for experiencing feels as though he has dropped from the calendar."[50]

This very condition, a kind of contextless bottoming out of temporality, is evoked in an unusually lyrical fashion (for Fearing) in the early poem "Nocturne":

> The floor of the blue night,
> Steeped in ether,
> Is fixed beneath the muffled floor of time.
>
> In the blue, ether night,
> Buildings rise in marble streams that do not end.
> Night does not end.
> Motionless vapor on the vacant streets thins the barren cries that strike
>   through distance,
> And drains the heatless lamps that stretch away forever in a scene that
>   does not change.
> Night does not change,
> Yesterday has shrunk to a news bulletin
> Read under a grey light in an all-night restaurant on the floor of the
>   blue night that will not end because there is no end to the cold night
>   that seeps through marble walls.
>
> . . . .
>
> On the floor of night there is no time.
> Men cough and walk away. (CP, 70)

The massive architecture of the city, with its vast, nearly hallucinatory spatial extension, seems to abolish all temporal consciousness. In the meaningless present of a night that does not end or change, memory dissolves; what was once directly lived (to use Debord's phrase again) has moved into a representation or, as Fearing would have it, "has shrunk to a news bulletin."

This last image strikes me as particularly resonant in the connection it implicitly draws between the mass media and the decay of a sense of history. It captures, in metaphorical terms, a central idea suggested by Jameson in his essay "Postmodernism and Consumer Society":

> Our entire contemporary social system has little by little begun to lose
> its capacity to retain its own past, has begun to live in a perpetual

present and in a perpetual change that obliterates traditions of the kind which all earlier social formations have had in some way or another to preserve. Think of the media exhaustion of news: of how Nixon and, even more so, Kennedy are figures from a now distant past. One is tempted to say that the very function of the news media is to relegate such recent historical experiences as rapidly as possible into the past. The informational function of the media would thus be to help us forget, to serve as the very agents and mechanisms for our historical amnesia.[51]

One readily recognizes in Jameson's remarks the influence of Benjamin's comments on the function of newspapers in his essays of the 1930s.[52] But these insights are also prefigured in "Reading, Writing, and the Rackets" (1956), where Fearing comments on the intangibility and inaccessibility of the "electronic past" and describes a phenomenological experience very much akin to the "perpetual present" in which the postmodern world, according to Jameson, appears locked. "In these media," Fearing declares, "today's message is always authentic; it is permanently the latest word, of course, but it is more. Because it can never be confronted with a previous message that might contain material to contradict it, it is also the first word, and the only word." Indeed, to judge by the media, Fearing jokes, it would seem that "only singing commercials," the "authentic classics of our age," merit repetition: the rest is lost in the current of information (NS, xvii). The idea that the media induce a pervasive cultural amnesia is also a key motif in the 1938 poem "Manhattan," where the city is characterized by a forgetfulness that is only exacerbated by the very wealth of sensational happenings:

> Do you remember the missing judge, the bigshot spender and the hundred dollar bills (did he do three years?)
> The ballgame of ballgames (the fourth in the series, or was that the sixth?),
> The reform party and the gambling clean-up (a ten-day laugh), the returning champion (what about it?), the abortion (so what?), the rape (who cares?). (CP, 165)

The daily pulse of information and sensational news effects an erasure of narrative and historical continuity.[53] Thus the city's consciousness, as the last lines of the poem finally reveal, includes "only the day," only the present moment, that is itself wrapped in the "ghost horizons" woven by the switchboards and cables of its information network (CP, 166, 164).

There are further examples of the ephemerality and fragmentation of urban experience in Fearing's poetry – for instance in "Memo," which laments the inability of the urban landscape to retain even a "shadow" of reminiscence: the "mark of a certain toe" on a "heelpocked pavement" or "the butt of a particular dropped cigarette" (CP, 153). There are also other examples in the poetry of how the media erase expression – as in "JACK KNUCKLES FALTERS," which (as we have seen) demonstrates how the sensational headlines distort and eventually discard the true story of an executed man. But the (officially) more ephemeral text of Fearing's movie reviews, seems to me to reveal his interest in the question of mass culture and historical memory even more explicitly; they also indicate his sense, however jokingly expressed, that the loss of memory is a serious obstacle to political consciousness. In an article on the 1936 film *Fury*, for instance, Fearing imagines the truly serious movie addict as the man "who can come out of his coma in front of the theater" and completely forget "how he got there, let alone recall the title and plot of the film that has been enthralling him for the last 60 minutes."[54] Not only do such moviegoers forget the brutalities of actual events, such as the lynching that provides the film in question's subject matter; they can hardly remember as far back as the previous movie of any substance (in Fearing's judgment, the 1933 film *I Am a Fugitive from a Chain Gang*). This lack of memory, the review suggests, effectively eliminates the "hophead" from participation in "the revolutionary dance."

Further, in a 1936 review for the *Partisan Review,* Fearing notes how efficiently – and paradoxically – history is eliminated in Hollywood's historical films:

> History as presented by Hollywood . . . is an album of very pictur-esque Christmas cards, book-marks and tin-types thumbed over very, very rapidly. . . . The surface detail is always reasonably accurate, and the success of these pictures is measured by the determination with which their producers have stuck to the surface, refusing to attempt any explanation at all for any social phenomena whatsoever. The trick is to concentrate on the lovers' close-up and to let the multitude in the background go its own – purely spectacular – way.[55]

What seems particularly contemporary about Fearing's grumblings is his recognition that none of these films makes any attempt to copy "real" history: they are remakes, if not repeats, of earlier movies. *Captain Blood,* he notes, "already seemed perfect in 1926," and *A Tale of Two Cities,* except for a new guillotine, is "exactly like every picture of the French Revolution that you ever saw." Moreover, the pastness is spurious, ahistorical, a matter of styling and stars, of whizzing through a pack of celebrity postcards. Fearing ironically offers the plot outline for his own superfilm, a jumbled pastiche that satirically exaggerates Hollywood's Christmas-card or tintype version of history:

> George Washington has just signed a pardon for John Brown, because
> Sylvia Sydney asks him to, and General Sheridan's justly famous ride
> brings it to the foot of the gallows in the nick of time . . . the picture
> proceeds at top speed to a terrific conclusion that shows a group of
> Bolsheviks mourning at the bier of Nicholas II.[56]

The silly scenario suggests a serious point. History, in the world of the
spectacle, seems to have lost all narrative continuity, to have shattered
into disconnected bits of information and myth: the past becomes a
souvenir collection, a series of incongruous images.

This idea is emblematically presented in the poem "Museum," in
which the contemporary world is shrunken, or more exactly "crèchi-
fied" (to steal a coinage from Umberto Eco), as a reduced simulacrum
of itself. In Fearing's museum, time is spatialized and objectified in a
series of entertaining exhibits, fixed in displays for "the Second Age of
Innocence, the Era of Torrents, the Third Age of Fire," and so forth
(CP, 246). "Museum" brings even to the frozen contemporary scene –
("See the telephone? And the ashtray and the desk pad, to the very
life. . .") – a touch of that ahistorical nostalgia Jameson associates with
postmodernism, where history has become precisely a *museum* of anti-
quated styles. Not only, then, does Fearing see experience in general as
slipping away into representations; but the past, in particular, becomes
unreal, a matter of display.

THE CULTURE OF SIMULACRA

With this idea of history as a souvenir or exhibit, we have
already moved toward the second postmodern tendency mentioned earlier: the rise of a culture of images and simulacra. This theme has,
inevitably, been present in this discussion of Fearing's cultural criticism
from the start: from the image of the poet in 3-D specs. It is fair to say
that Fearing's acute awareness of the emergence of what Vachel Lindsay
called a "hieroglyphic society" provides the dominant theme of his
entire poetic career.[57]

The 1929 volume *Angel Arms* already suggests that Fearing saw American culture as one where people are increasingly socialized as passive
consumers of images, as masses who are "aroused to stare," who "have
no voices" but do have "mouths and eyes": crowds that can see and
desire, but are losing the ability to express themselves (CP, 64). In the
allegorical poem "The Cabinet of Simplicity," Fearing hails the very
process of turning reality into images as a "new magic" – the invention
of one "Dr. Barky," who has patented a box in which the universe has
been projected and life reduced to its simplest terms. At times Dr.
Barky's cabinet, alluding as it does to the film *The Cabinet of Dr.*

Caligari, seems to refer specifically to cinema, which by the late twenties had established itself as a major cultural force (indeed, as one of the ten biggest industries in the United States):

> Upside down in a darkened room
> Among an excitable audience, credulous and naive,
> The creaking of the cabinet's hinges could be mistaken
>
> . . . .
>
> For discords struck from violent streets,
> For the giant harmonies of death itself. (CP, 79)

More broadly speaking, however, Fearing's "cabinet of simplicity" functions – again rather like Debord's omnipresent spectacle – as ideology made visible and audible. It is "no dream"; in fact, as these lines suggest, it manages to seem more immediate than the unpleasant realities of social discord and death of which we may "mistakenly" be reminded. On the other hand, this projected "fixed" world itself represents a kind of death. Its "mechanical heart," as Fearing remarks (in lines reminiscent of Yeats), "draws into itself / The veins and arteries of chaos" (CP, 81). But this particular kind of "life-in-death" represents anything but a Yeatsian unity of being: it spells the end of genuine, unmediated experience. The poem thus ends with a telling revision of Whitman's line from "So Long!" – "Camerado, this is no book, / Who touches this, touches a man":

> Comrade, this is no poem,
>   Who touches this
>   Touches Dr. Barky's patented magic cabinet of certified, strictly
>   guaranteed simplicity and truth. (CP, 81)

Even a poet, so the parodic lines suggest, can no longer offer any guarantee of authentic personality or authentic personal voice. While Whitman asserts the identity between the self and the expression, Fearing's poem seems to suggest a peculiar anxiety both about the self and about poetry in the world of mass-mediated culture.

It is an anxiety that persists throughout his career. In the thirties Fearing's poetry became even more obsessed with the loss of authenticity – and so, arguably, did the culture at large. We may bear in mind here Miles Orvell's argument, in *The Real Thing,* that the vast proliferation of mass-produced and -reproduced goods in the twentieth century generated an expressive culture based essentially on the desire to find or re-create some residue of authenticity.[58] Such an impulse was certainly part and parcel of the documentary art of the Depression decade (Agee and Walker Evans are Orvell's most striking exemplars), when an interest in the "real America" inspired so many intellectuals to undertake ethnographic explorations to southern sharecroppers, to Okie farm workers, and to Kentucky miners. Fearing and also Nathanael West, who may at first glance seem atypical and anomalous among the writers of the period, should in fact be seen as working within the same paradigm – but as presenting the other side of the coin. Their writing emphasizes an emergent culture of simulacra (the "unconscious" or ground, one might say, of such texts as *Let Us Now Praise Famous Men*): a culture that would gradually, as it became dominant, render the very notion of the "real thing" problematic.

In contrast, then, to the documentarists' rather Wordsworthian project of finding a residual authenticity in rural America, Fearing's (also somewhat documentary) explorations into the mass-mediated culture of cities, led to destabilizing, and rather anti-Romantic, observations. His poems frequently expose the catch-22 of the impulse to seek guarantees for the reality of feelings in the images of the culture industry – the very agents, in his analysis, of alienation and emotional rigor mortis.[59] In the poem "Lunch with the Sole Survivor," for example, the speaker tries to find an exact simile for an emotion or state of mind:

> Feeling as it does to drive a car that rides and rides like a long, low, dark, silent streak of radio waves;
> Just the way the hero feels in a smash-hit show;
> Exactly like the giant in a Times Square sign making love across the sky to a lady made of light; (CP, 131)

Such commercial images, depthless signs like that amorous giant of Times Square, offer a kind of parody, not only of the essentially Romantic impulses of the period, but also of the poetics of the objective correlative. The high modernists' symbolic dramatization of inner feelings is hollowed out in the attempts of Fearing's speaker to match a particular feeling with some or another mass-produced signifier of a prefabricated emotional intensity. These attempts resemble nothing so much as the effort of a consumer to color-coordinate an ensemble or find a commodity to "match her mood."[60] Unlike, say, Eliot or Stevens, Fearing is interested not in creating symbols to express private emotions, but in probing the cultural and political meaning of an increasing reliance on symbolic mediation: a tendency to displace experience into spectacular substitutes.

Reading his poems of the thirties, one therefore has to bear in mind the surprisingly overt marketing of emotions as therapeutic commodities in the advertisements and radio broadcasts of the period. Hollywood, for example, quite explicitly presented its narratives as substitutes

for life – as in the wonderfully excessive advertisement cited by the
Lynds in *Middletown:*

> "Go to a motion picture. . . . and let yourself go" . . . "Before you
> know it you are *living* the story – laughing, loving, hating, struggling,
> winning! All the adventure, all the romance, all the excitements you
> lack in your daily life are in – Pictures. They take you completely out
> of yourself and into a wonderful new world. . . . Out of the cage of
> everyday existence! If only for an afternoon or an evening – escape!"[61]

Next to this kind of copywriting, Fearing's satirical hyperbole seems
much less distorted than one might think at first glance. His bitter irony
over the possibility of finding "a greater, deeper, more perfect love, by
courtesy of Camels, over NBC" (CP, 105) becomes much more pointed
when one discovers that there was in fact a radio program entitled
"Your Lover" (which featured, against the background of muted organ
music, an intimate, sweet-talking male voice). Love did, it appears, have
its corporate sponsor.[62]

   The effects of this intrusion of the new, pseudopersonal voice of radio
into the private space of the living room, and into the even more
intimate realms of desire and self-expression, are explored more fully in
"Radio Blues." The poem takes the form of a series of unanswered
questions addressed to another of Fearing's "perplexed citizens" (CP,
25): a person desperately turning the radio dial in the hope of finding
(amid the random snatches of sound, the offers of cocoa samples and
commercially sponsored classics, the imitation disasters and imitation
friends) yet another match for a particular feeling. The poem's insistent
repetitions underscore the absurdity of this obsession with tuning in to
the exact megahertz of affect:

> 20, 25;
> Is that what you want, static and a speech and the fragment of a waltz,
>   is that just right?
>
> . . . .
>
> 30, 35, 35 to 40 and 40 to 50;
> Free samples of cocoa, and the Better Beer Trio, and hurricane effects
>   for a shipwreck at sea,
> But is that just right to match the feeling that you have?
>
> . . . .
>
> 1000, 2000, 3000, 4000;
> Is that just right to match the feeling that you want?
> 5000, 6000;
> Is that just right?
> 7000, 8000;

Is that what you want to match that feeling that you have?
9000, 10,000;
Would you like to tune in upon your very own life, gone somewhere
  far away? (CP, 150–51)

"Radio Blues" resembles "Lunch with the Sole Survivor" in its insistence that the representation of each feeling must be "exactly like" or
"just right." However, its insistent repetitions also seem intended to
destabilize the whole idea of representation or emotional expression by
causing us to doubt whether in fact there is any original, authentic
feeling to be reproduced or matched: what exactly is "that feeling" after
being subjected to this nearly hysterical scrutiny? It is appropriate, then,
that the question which concludes the poem suggests that personal
experience has already slipped into the intangible realm of the radio
broadcasts: "Would you like to tune in upon your very own life, gone
somewhere far away?" The abstract and minute calibrations of the dial –
in terms of which "just the ghost of an inch . . . divides Japan and
Peru" – have come to replace and, in effect, abolish the lived space of
world geography.[63] As the new communications media make the world
smaller, "the feeling that you have" is no longer rooted in a unified
personal experience, but is instead disseminated across the commercialized spectrum of the airwaves.
    The 1943 poem "Museum," which I have already briefly discussed,
takes these ideas perhaps even a step further. Once again Fearing presents the "real" world as having been displaced, or rather replaced: this
time by a kind of waxwork simulacrum, its size shrunk to a scale of one
to a thousand. The insistent questions of "Radio Blues" give way to the
blandishments of a proud tour guide:

And now you see the artificial sun come up, everywhere suffusing a
  marvelously painted sky;
It is dawn, revealing leagues of earth, and a taxidermist's frozen version
  of the actual life –

There is the Executive in his office; he is serious, but pleasant; a man
  of great importance in and to his day.
(See the telephone? and the ashtray and the desk pad, to the very life);
Here is the smiling Junior Clerk; the Typist;
And that one is the Salesman, laughing as he seems about to light a
  fresh cigar –

HABITAT: N. AMERICA, it says,
.   .   .   .

(The scene is indescribably real, and this is a gay, casual little tableau).
                                                          (CP, 245–46)

The poem's relevance to the emergence of a culture of simulacra, of the society of the spectacle, requires no gloss. With the inane gaiety of these pocket-sized bureaucrats in their cute little offices and the bland contentment of the lilliputian secretary eternally painting her nails, any trace of negativity and of "bona-fide life" seems to have been finally erased; the poem presents a perfect image of Herbert Marcuse's one-dimensional society – if we understand that one dimension as a facade. There is no life, only a designated "habitat"; and no one is any longer him- or herself, only an exhibit or a sample of a particular social type. I am tempted to say that Fearing's tour guide in this poem finally conducts us out of the turbulent anxieties and hopes of the "angry decade," into the realm of the postmodern.

PARODY AND PASTICHE

But there are, of course, important differences as well. This much is clear when we consider, for instance, Fredric Jameson's distinction between "parody" (a satirical and normative practice of textual mimicry) and "pastiche" (a disconcertingly neutral form of citationality in which any sense of satire or "healthy linguistic normality" has been "amputated").[64] While Jameson, arguably, overstates the extent to which the satirical – indeed, the political – has disappeared from contemporary expressive forms, there still is much value in his emphasis on mood and tone (or even something like Raymond Williams's "structure of feeling") for any periodizing project.[65] Fearing's citations from mass culture are seldom, if ever, neutral. In the poem "Sunday to Sunday," for instance, the lives of the characters (such as Mabel, the cook) dissolve rather ludicrously into a movie scenario:

> And Zorocco, not knowing Mabel loves Jim, has returned to use her
>   for his criminal schemes; but in a motor crash he is killed, Mabel
>   winning at last to happiness in Jim's arms,
> Directed by Frederick Hammersmith and produced by National.
>   (CP, 103)

But Fearing's invocation of the human suffering of this time provides a perspective from which these representations can be decried as ideological fabrications, or even forms of censorship. The "perfect denouement" of Mabel's Hollywood romance is followed by the bitter repetitions of the following lines:

> As hundreds, thousands, millions, search the want ads, search the
>   factories, search the subways, search the streets, search to sleep in
>   missions, jungles, depots, parks, sleep to wake again to gutters,
>   scrapheaps, breadlines, jails.

> Unknown to the beautiful, beautiful, beautiful Mabel; unknown to the
> deathray smile of politician and priest; unknown to Zorocco, Jim, or
> the unknown soldier; unknown to WGN and the bronze, bronze
> bells of Sunday noon. (CP, 103–4)

This juxtaposition identifies the language of the love story (the "beautiful, beautiful, beautiful Mabel," and so forth) as cited and "abnormal";
it underlines, as it were, the quotation marks around the happy finale.

In other poems Fearing could lash out in sarcastic indignation at the
"face of the fool, radiant on newspaper and screen," question the value
of escapist finales ("True Confession lover, when her eyelids flutter shut
at last, what have you really, really won?"), or mock the empty hyperbole of the "million-volt exclamation mark" (CP, 92; P, 53–54). Even a
poem like "Museum," which *describes* an affectless, one-dimensional
world, does not exactly *replicate* this emotional flatness. The satiric
impulse is still palpable, for example, in the implicit scorn for those
banal simulated objects, the ashtray and the desk pad, replicated (ironically) "to the very life." It is a perspective no longer evident in, say,
Warhol's mesmerized fascination with the Campbell's soup can. Indeed,
though some of Fearing's poems have on occasion been likened to Pop
Art, nothing could be more antithetical to his cultural politics than
Warhol's program, as defined in a 1963 interview:

> Everybody looks alike and acts alike, and we're getting more and more
>   that way.
> I think everybody should be a machine.
> I think everybody should like everybody.
> *Is that what Pop Art is about?*
> Yes. It's liking things.[66]

Fearing, in contrast, seemed to fear nothing more than the signs of
vacuous happiness he detected in the culture of his day, which seemed
to spell for him that alienation from the critical moment of alienation
itself. His poems again and again explore and expose such a doubly
alienated consciousness. In "American Rhapsody (4)," for example,
Fearing envisions a world in which all negativity has been erased, or at
least kept from view:

> Tomorrow, yes, tomorrow,
> There will suddenly be new success, like Easter clothes, and a strange
>   and different fate,
> And bona-fide life will arrive at last, stepping from a non-stop mono-
>   plane with chromium doors and a silver wing and straight white
>   staring lights.
>   .   .   .   .   .   .

> Rockets, rockets, Roman candles, flares, will burst in every corner of
>   the night . . .
>
> Tomorrow, yes, tomorrow, surely we begin at last to live,
> With lots and lots of laughter,
> Solid silver laughter,
> Laughter, with a few simple instructions, and a bona-fide guarantee.
> (CP, 146)

These lines describe something very like the consciousness of Debord's
"prisoners of a flattened universe," bemused by the "the shimmering
diversions of the spectacle" and without access to authentic experience.[67]
The imagined speakers of the poem (as I suggested earlier) conceive of
"bona-fide life" as the image of Lindbergh stepping from his monoplane
and of "bona-fide" response as a prefabricated commodity with a product guarantee. But even so, the predominant mood, somehow, remains
that of a nearly hysterical anger and loss. The celebratory fireworks are
there "to veil with snakes of silvery fire the nothingness that waits
and waits":

> There will be a bright, shimmering, silver veil stretched everywhere,
>   tight, to hide the deep, black, empty, terrible bottom of the world
>   where people fall who are alone, or dead,
>
> Sick or alone,
> Alone or poor,
> Weak, or mad, or doomed, or alone. (CP, 146)

There is, in other words, a distance between the consciousness the poem
describes and the ironic, even bitter, consciousness that controls it.
Though it imitates a kind of vacuous euphoria, the "Rhapsody" also
reveals through the language of negation – through those small, painful
adjectives that lay bare the abyss of alienation – the void hidden by the
triumphant glitter of the firework show.

   In a later poem, "Mrs. Fanchier at the Movies," Fearing presents the
case of another "prisoner of the spectacle," whose fate (though less
painful than that of the erased legions of the lonely, the "sick," "weak,"
"mad," and "doomed" of "American Rhapsody") is somehow even
more pathetic. Onomastically designated the uncritical consumer of
media images, Mrs. Fanchier is grateful for the automatic sympathy
extended to her by the "electrical voices" of her ersatz companions, and
regrets only that she cannot "Add somehow to the final outburst of
triumphant music" of the happy finales. She remains nevertheless
numbly aware that her "friends" may have cheated her of her ability to
speak and retains a vague memory of authenticity: "But wondering,

too, what it really was I at one time felt so deeply for, / The actual voice, or this muted thunder? These giant shadows, or the naked face?" (CP, 272). These lines represent, I think, a dialectical moment in Fearing's work. At the point when capitulation to the one-sided "communication" of the spectacle seems complete, the poem articulates those buried positives on which Fearing's singularly negative body of work rests: the "actual voice" and the "naked face" – personal speech and direct encounter. The poem reveals, albeit negatively, the sense of linguistic normality that is missing, or so Jameson feels, in pastiche.

With "Mrs. Fanchier at the Movies" our discussion of Fearing's mass culture criticism, as well as his relation to the society of the spectacle, ends where it began: in the movie theater. Himself also a "fan," Fearing could recognize contemporary forms of mass culture not merely as debased "rot," but as an agent of a new culture of abundant commodities, and not merely as a propaganda "weapon" to be wielded at will, but as a material institution, inextricably intertwined with the interests of capitalism and nationalism. His writing, moreover, raises political problems of particular urgency in our postmodern society, where obituaries for the avant-garde and for revolutionary politics confront us daily, and seem to confirm the assimilative power of the spectacle. Unlike other writers of the thirties, Fearing did not dream away the obstacles that stood in the way of the transformation and empowerment of the masses. And while we cannot properly call his work postmodern (if we understand postmodernism as the "cultural logic of late capitalism," and not merely a collection of styles and themes), his work suggests that certain "late capitalist" tendencies were already discernible in the thirties, though they might not yet have formed what Jameson would call the dominant "force field." Writing at this time of transition, however, Fearing was able to note these emergent social trends with a particular acuity. For all these reasons, he reads as a forgotten ancestor, or even as our contemporary.

5

"Zowie Did He Live and Zowie Did He Die"

Mass Culture and the Fragmentation of Experience

Yesterday a mere stenographer, tomorrow a world figure, like Gloria
Swanson or Valentino, no less. Don't it thrill you, my little Cinderella?
                            Mike Gold, "Faster, America, Faster!"

Shall we move to the Ritz if rails go up, or live in potter's field if the
market goes down?
                            Kenneth Fearing, "Hold the Wire"

One who has renounced using his life can no longer admit his death.
. . . This social absence of death is identical to the social absence of life.
                            Guy Debord, *Society of the Spectacle*

In his 1939 essay on Baudelaire's Paris, Walter Benjamin explores the
very same tendencies we have discovered in Fearing's work: the fragmentation of time and the proliferation of mechanically reproduced,
repeatable images. For Benjamin these phenomena were associated with
the gradual decay of what he termed *Erfahrung* (that is, experience in the
sense of a continuous development of personal memory and skill) and
its replacement with atomistic *Erlebnissen* (that is, experiences in the
sense of momentary sensations).[1] These key terms in Benjamin's materialist theory of experience have great explanatory force with regard to
Fearing's poems and essays of the thirties. And their applicability is not
all that surprising. The Baudelaire essay, in accordance with Benjamin's
characteristic effort to reappropriate history for the present, is marked as
much by the concerns of his own day as by those of nineteenth-century
Paris. The essay comments on a topic that also interested American
observers of the period: the fact that funfairs, with their Dodgem cars
and joyrides, flourish in times of unemployment, such as the Great
Depression. The sociologist Maurice Davie, for instance, noted with
some irony that such amusements hardly represented an escape from the
"artificial" and "mercenary" life of the city, and marveled at the fact that

109

in troubled times people actually "pay to get artificial bumps."[2] Benjamin takes this idea a step further, suggesting that these entertainments proliferate when the capitalist system is in trouble because they keep even workers who have lost their jobs in step with the tempo of machines. Even at leisure, he argues, workers are subject to a taste of that *drill* which in the factory makes up the "entire menu": a kind of training distinct from *practice,* since it is sealed off from any development of skill and experience (*Erfahrung*). The image of the amusement park in Fearing's poetry ("Stranger at Coney Island"), as well as the more frequently recurring images of billboards, traffic, and movies, would then, in Benjamin's view, represent an array of sensory exercise machines that serve only to develop "the art of being off center."[3]

As cultural history this analysis can perhaps be faulted for considering cultural forms from the point of view of the political homeostasis of the system, and not from that of actual consumers (who may have had more complicated and more resistant ways of regarding their leisure). It hinges on one of the key positions of the Frankfurt school's critical theory, namely that in late capitalism the sphere of consumption replicates the experiential structures of the sphere of production. But Benjamin's concrete example, the image of those colliding Dodgem cars, expresses this conception in a very vivid and metaphorically suggestive way – and in a way that suggests parallels with several of Fearing's poems and with other texts from the period.

The experiential connection between the amusement park and the assembly line is given a concise and emblematic expression in Fearing's satirical fantasy, "Travelogue in a Shooting-Gallery." The poem describes a "jungle," the conventional image of all that is natural and untamed, which is now made to fit nicely into the spatial and temporal order of the modern city:

> There is a jungle . . .
> Open to the public during business hours,
> A jungle not very far from an Automat, between a hat store there, and
>   a radio shop. (CP, 224)

This "civilized jungle" resembles something between a factory and a funfair: in its regulated environment, nature comes to have a mechanical seriality and regularity. Lions stalk their prey on treadmills, and the "tom-toms" of "savages" are conveniently equipped with silencers. Even the weather is made predictably comfortable, and the flight of birds rationalized:

> Under the hot, blazing, cloudless, tropical neon skies that the management always arranges there,

Rows and rows of marching ducks, dozens and dozens and dozens of
ducks, move steadily along on smoothly-oiled ballbearing feet
(CP, 224)

This standardization is imposed not only on nature, but on people. What
the amusement-park "jungle" produces are docile human beings: here
psychoanalysts attend to the hunters, once "leanfaced" with "windswept
eyes," but are now content just to watch the animals (" 'There . . .
there . . . / There they come, and there they go' "). Here "smoking is
permitted"; and weighing machines, at a penny at a time, will "read
your soul" and "tell you all" – all, no doubt, about a life that has become
completely homogenized and managed.

FRAGMENTED LIVES AND SUCCESS STORIES
  In the work of the Frankfurt school, capitalist society functions
rather like this shooting gallery. Max Horkheimer once described its
mechanized logic as follows:

> Doing and getting have become identical in this society, the mecha-
> nisms which govern man in his leisure time are absolutely the same
> [as] those which govern him when he works. . . . the key for the
> understanding of the behaviour patterns in the sphere of consumption
> is the situation of the man in industry, his schedule in the factory, the
> organization of office and working place. Consumption tends to vanish
> today, or should I say, eating, drinking, looking, loving, sleeping
> become "consumption," for consumption already means that a man
> has become a machine outside as well as inside the workshop?[4]

This is exactly the same kind of life that Fearing was later to describe as
controlled by the "Big Clock," a central machine "more powerful than
the calendar, and to which one automatically adjusts [one's] entire life,"
a vast "hook-up," compared to which "the man with the adding machines was still counting on his fingers."[5] Fearing's work of the thirties
already foresees, even as it records the insecurities of the Great Depression, the threat of this kind of experiential adjustment. I would like, in
this chapter, to examine this theme in Fearing's poetry and in other texts
from the Depression, to suggest the ways in which this general reification of experience is associated in these texts with mass-mediated culture, and, finally, to discover, in Fearing's 1935 poem "Denouement," a
moment of resistance.
  Let us start, however, with one of his best-known poems, "Dirge,"
that delightfully ironic lament for the kind of life Max Horkheimer
describes so well in the passage I cited. In "Dirge" the boring rhythms
and habits, not of factory work, but of white-collar drudgery, seem

to determine the entire robotic life of the poem's man in the gray tweed suit:

> Just the same he wore one gray tweed suit, bought one straw hat,
>   drank one straight Scotch, walked one short step, took one long
>   look, drew one deep breath,
> Just one too many,
>
> And wow he died as wow he lived,
> Going whop to the office and blooie home to sleep and biff got married
>   and bam had children and oof got fired,
> Zowie did he live and zowie did he die.
> . . . .
> Very much missed by the circulation staff of the New York Evening
>   Post; deeply, deeply mourned by the B.M.T.,
>
> Wham, Mr. Roosevelt; pow, Sears Roebuck; awk, big dipper; bop,
>   summer rain;
> Bong, Mr., bong, Mr., bong, Mr., bong. (CP, 109–110)[6]

Like so many of Fearing's deliberately unlyrical poems, "Dirge" has the quality of a struggling or failed narrative; it is an ironic biography demonstrating the impossibility of a significant life story in a mechanical and yet threateningly unpredictable mass society.[7] The poem's disintegration into the impersonal and nonsensical reiterations of the final lines mocks the worker's initial certainty, his "personal pride in the certain, certain way he lived his own, private life," referred to earlier in the text. The comic-strip sound effects, which gradually seem to invade and take over the poem, are appropriate and expressive, and not only in the humorous deflation they effect: the life described in "Dirge" is constituted by a series of atomistic, discontinuous moments rather like the comic strip, with its sequence of separate frozen-action frames and its characteristically violent and undignified reversals. Fearing's poem suggests that a life made up entirely of *Erlebnissen* – of repeated motions and purchases that, in the end, add up to nothing – can have no distinctive personal character; it is, moreover, ideally expressed by the fragments and "shocks" of mass-reproducible art, supplied here by the various biffs, whams, and pows that punctuate every act.

One could hardly wish for a better gloss of this poem than that suggested in another passage from Horkheimer, which adduces not the comics but the movies as a central metaphor:

> You will remember those terrible scenes in the movies when some
>   years of a hero's life are pictured in a series of shots which take about
>   one or two minutes, just to show how he grew up or old, how a war
>   started and passed by, a[nd] so o[n]. This trimming of an existence
>   into some futile moments which can be characterized schematically

symbolizes the dissolution of humanity into elements of administration. Mass culture in its different branches reflects the fact that the human being is cheated out of his own entity which Bergson so justly called "durée."[8]

"Dirge" is a poem about precisely such fragmented and futile "moments," about an individual life that shrivels or dissolves amid the institutions and forces that govern contemporary life: Sears Roebuck, Mr. Roosevelt, the *New York Evening Post* – all as vast, remote, and fateful as the summer rain and the stars. It is, in short, about the loss of personal experience in the world of mass culture.

The connection between Fearing's work and the conventions of the comic strip, suggested in "Dirge," is one that earlier critics have also emphasized: Weldon Kees once remarked, rather acidly, that Fearing's view of life was at one time limited to that of a *New Masses* cartoon.[9] Stripped of its disparaging implications, the observation actually suggests an interesting line of investigation. It is not necessarily a bad thing, I think, for a poem to resemble a *New Masses* cartoon; these were often quite fascinating examples of American political art. William Gropper's cartoons, in particular, taking their inspiration from Grosz and Berlin Dada, combined strong modernist designs with a sharp demystificatory humor and an acute sense of the way in which the very form of the cartoon or comic strip, its stylizations and visual repetitions, might capture the more sinister rhythms of modern life. His cartoon "The Great American Individualist" (see illustration, page 114) is a classic of its kind.[10] Its stylization not only captures perfectly the danger of mechanical conformity, but also suggests the homologous function of such apparently diverse ideological institutions as the factory, the church, the school, the advertising industry, the stock market, the newspaper: all become devices – exercise machines, as it were – training the worker for that powerless moment of (oof!) being fired.

To recognize the thematic continuities between a poem like "Dirge" and Gropper's cartoons is to grasp something about the interactive character of artistic production on the left during the decade. It also emphasizes the pervasive erosion during the Depression of one of the nation's fondest myths. Both "Dirge" and "The Great American Individualist" challenge that old American parable about work: Horatio Alger's rags-to-riches story, according to which personal intitiative, perseverance, and thrift must ultimately be rewarded with material success – or, as Fearing once phrased it in a witty attack on the *Saturday Evening Post,* "Industry, plus a little love (. . . the true romance formula with a little English on the ball), inevitably surmount[s] all obstacles."[11] The classic Alger story met with bitter criticism and ridicule during the Depression, and understandably so. Even if we set aside the fact that the

dream of success and of class mobility was rendered more tenuous than ever before by the economic crisis, this favorite myth of a producer-capitalist culture also became problematic in that it represented work as a *career,* in which success could be won through the gradual accumulation of experience and the development of one's character. Corny and formulaic though the Alger novel may be, it remains a *Bildungsroman* of sorts: a narrative of personal development. But in the turbulent and unstable world of the Depression, this very narrative premise came to seem inapplicable: the two essential ingredients of such an exemplary biography, development and opportunity (and we might as well say *Erfahrung*), seemed to have disappeared. Individual diligence had already been rendered irrelevant by the standardization of the pace and nature of work on the assembly line, and the economic crisis added the huge difficulty of landing a job in the first place. Moreover, whether in the factory or the office, the working life of the employee, constantly threatened by layoffs, was reduced to a series of "shocks," of discrete gestures.[12] Ironically, this loss of the necessary lived continuities was evident even in the *Saturday Evening Post,* which tried so strenuously to keep the rags-to-riches parable alive. The magazine's choicest stories about the shaping of a personality, as Fearing suggests in his article on the *Post,* had come to assume that quality of frozen moments, of repeated images: they are "schoolbook legend[s] in which, every week, Abraham Lincoln [does] his arithmetic lesson on a shovel beside the flickering hearth and Washington [cannot] tell a lie." Opportunity, which once seemed to be a democratic birthright and which the *Post* still ritually conjured up during the Depression, stalked its pages like a ghostly platitude: "half individual liberty, and half," Fearing believed, "cigar-store Indian."[13]

One can find empirical support for Fearing's intuitions about the decay of the Alger story and the loss of *Erfahrung* in Leo Lowenthal's research on popular biographies from the *Post* and *Collier's.* According to Lowenthal, the "idols of consumption" that, after 1929, came to dominate the magazine biographies were essentially presented as lucky automatons, as "the static image of a human being to whom a number of things happen, culminating in a success which seems to be none of his doing."[14] Opportunity, he notes, appears in these biographies as a freakish and unexpected "break," the result perhaps of "being discovered" or being in "the right place at the right time."

This lucky coincidence, essential to the threadbare ideology of success in the thirties, was a constant motif, not only in the magazine biographies but also in other popular forms. We could again bring to mind Chaplin's *Modern Times,* which in this respect, as in so many others, is a rich parable for the age. In the film the plucky little waif is noticed quite by chance, as she dances in the street; then, from one shot to the next, she is transformed from a tattered urchin to a sequined show girl. We may see in this almost magical transformation the paradigm of a new kind of success story, of which the thirties produced a few, much-trumpeted "real life" examples: think of Lana Turner, for instance, who was catapulted into fame after being noticed by the right person as she unsuspectingly sat drinking a milkshake in a tight sweater, without (as Alan Jenkins coyly phrases it) "any visible means of support."[15]

The curious thing about such typical stories of luck and fame is that they are simultaneously (as Adorno and Horkheimer have also noted) stories of powerlessness. There is nothing much one can do if one did not happen to be around at that unpredictable instant when the doors to success, or, more humbly, to employment, opened. Success thus becomes a matter not of acquired excellence or developed skills but of an uncontrollable fate – a long shot.[16]

LONG SHOTS: GAMBLING AS IDEOLOGY

In such a context, the world of work becomes homomorphous with what one might at first think of as its opposite: gambling. This parallel is also suggested in Benjamin's Baudelaire essay. At the game of chance, as at the assembly line, he notes, there is no possibility of *Erfahrung* or development. The past counts for nothing: "Each operation at the machine is just as screened off from the preceding operation as a *coup* in the game of chance is from the one that preceded it." Benjamin even meditates, rather fancifully, on the similarly abrupt and jerky gestures of the card players and machine operators (and we might now add to this list of sensory jolts the abrupt montage by which Chaplin illustrates his heroine's fragile, and as it turns out short-lived, success story).[17]

In the light of these observations, it seems almost uncannily appropriate that the era of U.S. history we are concerned with derives its name from a game of cards: the New Deal. Historians of the period frequently comment on the proliferation of games of chance, betting and gambling. While the stock market crash abruptly brought an end to the nation's dream of making a killing on Wall Street, one could still do so in the Parker Brothers' new and fantastically popular game of Monopoly. Americans bought hundreds of thousands of tickets for the Irish Sweepstakes, and the stories of the lucky winners became front-page news. Slot machines and pinball machines became ubiquitous. In 1939 these devices swallowed up as much money (between 10 and 15 billion nickels) as Americans spent that year in shoe stores. Bingo games flourished, and in the worst years of the Depression, the movie industry managed to win back its audiences by staging bank nights, games of Kino or Screeno, with prizes of cash or colorful Fiesta tableware.[18] Such leisure activities were no mere forms of escape – as Ralph Ellison's 1944 story "The King of the Bingo Game" illustrates so well. Rather, they functioned, as Warren Susman has observed, as "alternative (if socially marginal) patterns duplicating in structure what institutionalized society demanded and normally assumed it could provide."[19] Their "educational" function, more pessimistically read, has much in common with that of the funfair with its Big Dipper roller coaster and Dodgem cars: of keeping a person powerless and "off center" in a world of unpredictable fortunes.

Fearing's poetry – homing in once again on a characteristic structure of feeling in Depression culture – repeatedly explores the experience and ideology of gambling. The many references to betting in his poems (among which we find titles like "Longshot Blues," "Jackpot," and "Winner Take All") should be understood in the light of the historical circumstances I have just described, where gambling functions as a spectacular representation of the capitalist system: political economy is made to appear as a competitive game where a few lucky winners may draw aces, but where everybody is essentially paralyzed, at the mercy of the fall of a die. The failed biography in "Dirge" is thus appropriately introduced by the following lines:

> 1–2–3 was the number he played but today the number came 3–2–1;
> Bought his Carbide at 30 and it went to 29; had the favorite at Bowie but the track was slow –
>
> O executive type, would you like to drive a floating-power, knee-action, silk-upholstered six? Wed a Hollywood star? Shoot the course in 58? Draw to the ace, king, jack?
> O fellow with a will who won't take no, watch out for three cigarettes on the same, single match; O democratic voter born in August under Mars, beware of liquidated rails –
>
> Denouement to denouement, he took a personal pride in the certain, certain way he lived his own, private life,
> But nevertheless, they shut off his gas; nevertheless, the bank foreclosed; nevertheless, the landlord called; nevertheless, the radio broke,
>
> And twelve o'clock arrived just once too often. (CP, 109)

Fearing's poem places the life of the modern flunky in the unstable contemporary world of "liquidated rails," a context in which the distance between what an individual (even a "fellow with a will") may do and the powers that determine his life has become unbridgeable: so unbridgeable that the social system assumes the threatening inscrutability of fate.[20] At the end of the second stanza, the poet thus briefly assumes the sinister voice of a soothsayer ("O democratic voter born in August under Mars, beware . . ."), a role he would adopt more frequently with the advent of the McCarthy era, as American society became more akin to the occult, replete with buried secrets, oracular denunciations, and rigid controls.[21] Here the astrologer's ominous intonations help to create the suggestion that the mundane business of economic survival (paying the gas and the rent, listening to the radio, making it through another day) has become as uncontrollable as the near-hit, near-miss gambles at the lottery, the stock market, and the racetrack described in the first two lines. And while the individual's actions seem completely irrelevant and impotent, the minutest matters of chance (such as the order of digits) or the most unremarkable of actions (such as lighting three cigarettes with one match) become imbued with an entirely disproportionate power. Indeed, the adjective "floating-power," if we detach it from its specific denotations in the advertising slogan ("would you like to drive a floating-power, knee-action, silk-upholstered six?"), offers a particularly accurate description of the mystifying operations of the system. Prestige, success, and control over one's life become matters of attaining an indefinable "floating power," which unfortunately only comes randomly to any one individual, commodity, or event.[22]

"Longshot Blues" presents Fearing's most extended meditation on this theme of capitalist society as a vast lottery. The poem emphasizes the paradoxical combination of utter randomness and minute precision that determine the game of chance:

> What if all the money is bet on the odd;
> Maybe the even wins,
> What if the odd wins, but wins too late,
>
> Whoever, wherever,
> Ever knows who will be just the very one
> This identical day at just this very, very, very, very hour,
>
> Whose whole life falls between roto-press wheels moving quicker than
>   light, to reappear, gorgeous and calm, on page eighteen –
> Who reads all about it: *Prize-winning beauty trapped, accused,*
>
> Who rides, and rides, and rides the big bright limited south, or is
>   found, instead, on the bedroom floor with a stranger's bullet through
>   the middle of his heart,
> Clutching at a railroad table of trains to the south while the curtains
>   blow wild and the radio plays and the sun shines on, and on, and on,
>   and on,
> Never having dreamed, at 9 o'clock, it would ever, at 10 o'clock, end
>   this way,
>
> Forever feeling certain, but never quite guessing just exactly right,
> As no man, anywhere, ever, ever, ever, ever, ever, knows for sure –
>
> Who wins the limousine, who wins the shaving cup, who nearly wins
>   the million-dollar sweeps,
> Who sails, and sails, and sails the seven seas,
> Who returns safe from the fight at the mill gates, or wins, and wins,
>   and wins, and wins the plain pine coffin and a union cortege to a
>   joblot grave? – (CP, 129–30)

The insistent repetitions of "Longshot Blues" capture something of the dreariness of such unstable, risky, fragmented lives. When temporal development is lost (*Erfahrung* in life itself, or narrative continuity in the representations of that life), we are left essentially with parallelisms, reiterations, or enumerations of standardized options. The limousine, the shaving cup, the millon-dollar sweeps, and even the pine coffin, though paradigmatically distinct, are still functionally, or syntagmatically, identical: they are the things you get, not the things you make, deserve, or necessarily even wish for. A wish, after all, as Benjamin suggests, is an experience of sorts, since it implies a projection into the future.[23] These various "prizes" represent, on the contrary, the reification of wishes. They are the symbolic or spectacular crystallizations of the outcome and meaning of a life: a commodified stand-in for what once had a temporal dynamic.

The same could be said of the list of desirable "denouements" in "Dirge" ("O executive type, would you like to drive a floating power, knee-action, silk-upholstered six? Wed a Hollywood star? Shoot the course in 58? Draw to the ace, king, jack?") or of the corny finales that are mocked in the poem "If Money" – the title of which already suggests a trivialized kind of dreaming:

> What rainbow waits, especially, for you,
> Who will call your number, that angel chorales will float across the
>   wire,
> What magic score do you hope to make,
> What final sweeps do you expect to win that the sky will drop clusters
>   of stars in your hair and rain them at your feet. (CP, 163)

These are mass-produced, technicolor dreams, as Fearing's saccharine imitation of commercial language indicates. The phrase "especially, for you" is particularly ironic; applied to such prefabricated prizes it can only mean "for all of you." It is, of course, itself a cliché: a rhetorical gadget of pseudoindividualization that is so often stamped on the promises of advertising.[24]

The series of blandly optimistic assertions that conclude "Longshot Blues" provide a similar mockery of official optimism. Indeed, since the poem has shown the chances of success (and even survival) to be entirely unpredictable, this list of "perfect denouement[s]" (CP, 115) reads as a tally not of wishes, but of pure illusions:

> With that long black midnight hour at last exploding into rockets
>   of gold,
> With every single cloud in the sky forever white and every white cloud
>   always the winner in its race with death,
> With every pair of eyes burning brighter than the diamonds that burn
>   on every throat,
> With every single inch of the morning all yours and every single inch
>   of the evening yours alone, and all of it always, always, altogether
>   new. (CP, 130)

In these inanely happy endings, everything and everybody is presented as being, after all, a winner. It is telling, however, that these lines come right after the mention of the possible death of the striker at the mill gate, a fate that is blithely (and, of course, ironically) applauded: the dead striker too "wins, and wins, and wins, and wins the plain pine coffin and a union cortege to a joblot grave." The poem's representation of life as a game where everybody will "win" thus operates as a kind of social euphemism or decoy. The ironic celebration of "that long midnight hour at last exploding into rockets of gold" in "Longshot Blues" serves the same function as the shimmering display of "Rockets, rockets, Roman candles, flares" in "American Rhapsody (4)": they are ideological cover-ups, which serve, in the metaphor of that poem, to "veil . . . the nothingness" into which we would otherwise fall (CP, 146). To phrase the idea in more concretely political terms, one might say that the poem draws our attention to the kind of red herring implicit in, say, Ronald Reagan's optimistic pronouncement that he could not bear to think of an America in which it was no longer possible for somebody to get rich: a celebratory dream that served to defend and hide the dog-eat-dog laissez-faire of his socioeconomic policies insofar as they applied to the many who did not get rich.

Fearing's America (as Kenneth Burke once put it) is a place "where many are asked to face the emptiness of failure in order that a few may face the emptiness of success."[25] For him the important issue is not, finally, what has been won, but what has been lost; not whether one person hit the jackpot, but how many people's lives were proven by this exception to be utterly mundane and undistinguished. Thence the pressing questions of his "Twentieth-Century Blues," questions that unmask the ideology of the long shot:

> And what is gone soldier, soldier, step-and-a-half marine who saw the whole world; hot-tip addict, what is always just missed; picker of crumbs, how much has been lost, denied, what are the things destroyed,
> Question mark, question mark, question mark, question mark.
>
> (CP, 124–25)

In "Longshot Blues," however, as in so many other instances, he chooses to work ironically. While the poem's sinister contents would seem to move us toward negation, its deliberately inappropriate happy endings imitate, and thus expose, the blindness, denial, and deceit at work in the culture.

"LOSS-PROOF PACKAGES": MASS CULTURE AS EVASION

Fearing's poem "Yes, the Agency Can Handle That," which I referred to briefly in Chapter 3, explicitly associates the denial of negativity and social ills with mass-mediated culture. The poem describes the process of manufacturing a story for a big magazine:

> You recommend that the motive, in Chapter 8, should be changed from ambition to a desire, on the heroine's part for doing good; yes that can be done.
> Installment 9 could be more optimistic, as you point out . . .
> Script 11 may have, as you say, too much political intrigue of the sordid type; perhaps a diamond-in-the-rough approach would take care of this. And 12 has a reference to war, that as you suggest, had better be removed; yes.
>
> .   .   .   .
>
> And script 600 brings us to the millennium, with all the fiends of hell singing Bach chorales.
>
> .   .   .   .
>
> And there is no mortal ill that cannot be cured by a little money, or lots of love, or by a friendly smile; no.
> And few human hopes go unrealized; no.
> And the rain does not ever, anywhere, fall upon corroded monuments and the graves of the forgotten dead. (CP, 183)

The poem's cynical view of the homogenizing operations of the culture industry concurs with a principle laid down by Bernard Rosenberg in his introduction to an influential early collection of essays on mass culture, namely that in mass culture "everything is remediable."[26] Though clearly marked by the Cold War intellectuals' antipathy to mass culture, the idea still carries a certain demystifying force and is certainly basic to Fearing's (and also Nathanael West's) satirical representations of the media. In *The Day of the Locust,* to cite but one choice instance, Tod Hackett wonders if the producer Mr. Grotenstein may have decided to remedy Napoleon's historic defeat at Waterloo by changing the script of his film version of the battle. And West's satire here, we must bear in mind, is not all that exaggerated: in the thirties, after all, Hollywood did come up with such astonishingly "remedied" products as a version of *Moby-Dick* in which Ahab not only kills the whale, but gets the girl![27]

The ironic insistence in "Longshot Blues" that every cloud must be a "winner in its race with death" and that everything must be "always, altogether new" also mimics the logic of Rosenberg's axiom. In fact, as early as his 1927 essay on Lindbergh, Fearing had noted a compulsion that he felt was becoming characteristic of American cultural production: a refusal to admit any loss, to let anything die.[28] This denial of death not only represents the most absurd extreme of the insistence that everything must be remediable. It is also the logical extreme of the fragmentation of experience and the elimination of human development expressed in the game of chance and personified in the automaton: modern man as robotized flunky or distracted gambler. Guy Debord's remark that the social absence of life is identical to the social absence of death seems exactly to the point: in a society where a person's life is considered in terms of identical and abstract working hours, or identical dollars expended, one cannot afford to be reminded of death – that final retreat of individuality and persistent proof of the irreversible continuity of history and biology, of the fact that living things can never be "altogether new."[29] Official and affirmative culture, of which Fearing's poems present so many parodic versions, can never admit such irredeemable loss.

These ideas inform one of Fearing's most humorous but also most theoretically explicit movie reviews: that of *Fury*, the 1936 antilynching film, starring Spencer Tracy.[30] The first part of the film, he felt, was powerful and realistic: "When flames leap up the old courthouse and encircle the caged victim, you actually smell the burning flesh." But the substantial theme is squandered and trivialized when the hero is saved from certain death by dint of a "simple miracle in the scenario." Fearing's response is both humorous and serious. First he adopts the voice of a reverential supplicant: "Saint Metro-Goldwyn-Mayer, be with me in my hour of need! You can avert famine, war and pestilence by a close-up of Garbo singing a presidential proclamation." Then he announces to the "movie hopheads taking the cure under Prof. Fearing" that he plans to account for such things as the film's contrived but deftly performed resuscitation in his serious six-volume treatise entitled "Evasion and Exposition: The Essential Methods of Each, with an Analysis of Their Relative Values, Purposes, Habits and Habitat." Among the principles he proposes to expound in these tomes is the notion that "evasion" (which he opposes to accurate "exposition") is "the essential element of any art in a society based on exploitation." Regardless of its degree of technical excellence (and a film like *Fury*, he felt, demonstrated remarkable technical ingenuity and skill in the way it managed to connect its constituent improbabilities), all art that is built on evasion, on ideological mystification, must in the end be stagnant. Despite Fearing's jokey tone, the point of the discussion is not only to make fun of the movies, but to suggest the real power of "Saint Metro-Goldwyn-Mayer" et al. regarding the magic of political containment and the imperative of the market: "Remember," he says, "we have to sell these pictures in the South." Unlike many contemporary commentators, Fearing does not think that the problem with the movie industry is one of artistic quality: "There's something wrong with the system," he says in an earlier review, something that technical improvements would only patch up more effectively.[31] The truth – the stark fact, for example, of a black man burned to death (the likely situation, as Fearing points out, in real life) – has to be evaded or sweetened; otherwise something might happen. "We might explode," Fearing suggests, or "there might even, as some say, be a revolution."[32]

In his poetry, as in his reading of *Fury,* the paradigmatic form of "evasion," and of the axiom that "everything is remediable," is the miraculous resurrection: the insistence in commercial texts that even death be turned into a "perfect denouement." His poems often show how merely rhetorical remedies are applied to absolutes and finalities like death and the loss of virginity, and illustrate how transcendent powers are claimed for the solutions offered in the soaps, the movies, and comic strips (the genre, par excellence, of bizarre transformations and miraculous recoveries). In "Sunday to Sunday," for example, one of the typical human tragedies of the Depression – the man who flings himself in front of a train so that his family may benefit from his life insurance policy – is instantly patched up and in the process deprived of human dignity: "Picked from the tracks, scraped from the wheels, identified, this happy ending restores the nation to its heritage: A Hearst cartoon" (CP, 103).

The same kind of scenario is given a more extended treatment in "Obituary," where death is again robbed of its finality. The poem could be read as an allegory of the evasive relationship of official culture and the life of the ordinary people during the Depression. A working man is flattened by a ten-ton truck – killed, as it were, by his "friends," the representatives of big business, mass culture, and the state. Then without much ado he is picked up, fed, shaved, and put to work again:

> Take him away, he's dead as they die,
> Hear that ambulance bell, his eyes are staring straight at death;
> Look at the fingers growing stiff, touch the face already cold, see the stars in the sky, look at the stains on the street,
>
> Look at the ten-ton truck that came rolling along fast and stretched him out cold,
>
> Then turn out his pockets and make the crowd move on.
> Sergeant, what was his name? What was the driver's name? What's your name, sergeant?
> Go through his clothes,
> Take out the cigars, the money, the papers, the keys, take everything there is,

And give a dollar and a half to the Standard Oil. It was his true-
blue friend.
Give the key of his flat to the D.A.R. They were friends of his, the
best a man ever had.
Take out the pawnticket, wrap it, seal it, send it along to the People's
Gas. They were life-long pals. It was more than his brother. They
were just like twins.

Give away his shoes,
Give his derby away. Donate his socks to the Guggenheim fund,
Let the Morgans hold the priceless bills, and leaflets, and racing tips
under lock and key,
And give Mr. Hoover the pint of gin,
Because they're all good men. And they were friends of his.

Don't forget Gene Tunney. Don't forget Will Hays. Don't forget Al
Capone. Don't forget the I.R.T.
Give them his matches to remember him by.
They lived with him, in the same old world. And they're good men,
too.

That's all, sergeant. There's nothing else, lieutenant. There's no more,
captain.
Pick up the body, feed it, shave it, find it another job.

Have a cigar, driver?
Take two cigars –
You were his true-blue pal. (CP, 84–85)

"Obituary" could be seen as a companion piece to "Dirge." Both poems
share a connection with the conventions of the comic strip: in one case
the language dissolves into the familiar sound effects of the genre and in
the other the narrative imitates its typical surreal recoveries. Both
poems, moreover, are in the final analysis political satires, resembling in
theme and method W. H. Auden's poem "The Unknown Citizen"
(written at the end of the decade). Like "The Unknown Citizen," "Obituary" evokes the increasingly intrusive power of the state and its institutions over the citizen's life, and its total disregard for the citizen's autonomy or happiness. The pitiful possessions of the victim in this poem –
the pawn ticket, the pint of gin, the dollar and a half, and the racing
tips – reveal a life of undistinguished poverty and exploitation; in life
and in death he belongs as much to his "friends" Mr. Hoover, Mr.
Morgan, and Standard Oil as does the Unknown Citizen to the bureaucracies that scrutinize and control his every act and habit. Yet in each
case the speaker elaborately denies any conflict of interest; as Auden's
official briskly puts it: "Had anything been wrong, we should certainly
have heard."[33] In these poems, as in "Dirge," the spokesmen for the
powers that be voice their respect, grief, or friendship for the deceased,

who was clearly no more than a number, flunky, or (in Horkheimer's phrase) "element of administration" – a cog whose life was as undistinguished as his end, which in "Obituary" lacks even the significance of finality: "Zowie did he live and zowie did he die" is an appropriately unruffled summary. These three poems are all, then, ironic elegies, affectless, clinical, postmortem-like dirges, peppered only with the ersatz grief of the mechanical announcements and praises of the institutions that count on the custom and good behavior of the deceased: "Very much missed by the circulation staff of the New York Evening Post; deeply, deeply mourned by the B.M.T." The "social absence of life" of these automatons precludes any true mourning.

In one of his most explicitly political poems, "1933," Fearing takes the implications of this social denial of death a few steps further. The historical events of this year, which marked not only the deepest slump of the Depression but also the fall of the Weimar Republic and Hitler's rise to power, certainly provided ample grounds for sinister fantasy. International events had undisputedly become more ominous, more conspiratorial, and more dominated by manipulative oratory; the "real" world was increasingly becoming a world of pseudoevents, of staged spectacles – with murderous consequences. The political scene in "1933" (CP, 94–96) resembles a bizarre cartoon in the style of, say, Georg Grosz and stars such grotesque but recognizable caricatures as "John D. Christ," "Little 'Safe for Democracy' Nell," and "Adolphe 'Safety of France and Society' Thiers," whose name Fearing (I think deliberately) misspells as "Adolf" in the 1940 version of the poem. Moreover, the events assume the evasive logic of mass culture, in which (as Fearing presents it) all ills are patched up and even death is stripped of its finality. From this it would follow that no statement, act, or conclusion is of any permanent consequence; we are thus left, in "1933," with a world of illusion, where violence and death are by no means eliminated, but constantly forgotten, repeated, and trivialized.

The poem is again enumerative and deliberately repetitive. It reiterates at different points variations on the theme presented in its opening section:

> You heard the gentleman, with automatic precision, speak the truth.
> Cheers. Triumph.
> And then mechanically it followed the gentleman lied.
> Deafening applause. Flashlights, cameras, microphones. Floral tribute.
>   Cheers. (CP, 94)

As always in Fearing's poetry, these praises and celebrations nicely serve the purposes of evasion: the media spectacle has already established the speaker as an institution, and therefore as a repeatable, and always superlative, commodity (irrespective of truth, an absolute that the poem in any case demands we put under erasure). Another redeemable absolute is "the lady's virginity," which is every now and again, reassuringly, restored. And death, as we might have expected, is continually annulled: by the mere sound of a senator's voice on the radio and a magic circle around the London cenotaph "ten million dead [are] returned to life, shot down again, again restored." Such mechanical, repetitive remediation seems, toward the end of the poem, to have virtually eliminated all possibility of authentic or critical response: a bayonet through the heart is met with laughter, and the creepiest necrophiliac escapades are met with only more celebrations:

> Heard once more the gentleman speak, with automatic precision, the
> final truth,
> Once more beheld the lady's virginity, the lady's decency, the lady's
> purity, the lady's innocence,
> Paid for, certified, and restored.
>
> Crawled amorously into bed. Felt among the maggots for the mould-
> ering lips. The crumbled arms. Found them.
> Tumult of cheers. Music and prayers by the YMCA. Horns, rockets.
> Spotlight. (CP, 95–96)

When the poem in the final lines turns on its readers ("these are the things you did, this is your record / You") it is to accuse each of us of sharing the state of Steve, the sideshow robot of "No Credit" – a limbo of mechanical contentment, mindless illusion.

"1933" with its disconnected, dreamlike incidents is Fearing's most obscure poem, and as such it may appear to be more in line with the conventions of high modernism than those of mass culture, of which I have argued it offers a parodic exaggeration. There are certainly moments when it is vaguely reminiscent of the gloomy imagery of Eliot's "Gerontion" (the "ashes, cinders, scrapiron, garbage" of the decayed metropolis and the sinister séance with a baroness in the sewers of Berlin) or of the gruesome surrealism of Salvador Dali (the image, for example, of a sirloin wrapped in papal documents). But one should bear in mind that clashing juxtapositions, logical leaps, and surrealist effects were not confined to the domain of high culture. As Warren Susman has pointed out, the popular art of the twenties and thirties frequently demonstrated surreal tendencies. He notes, for example, the prevalence of the dream theme and of magical transformations in the comics, sentimental ballads, advertising, and popular fiction of the day. Wizards (not least of which the immensely popular Wizard of Oz) abounded. Some of Fearing's poems could, I think, shed some light on this phenomenon: if as he suggests, the exploitative political situation demands an art in which all is to be remedied, such agents of magic would clearly come in handy.

While one could argue (as Susman does) that these fantasies reflect a sense of the new scientific wonders that were daily reshaping and redefining the patterns of life, they relate equally to the sense of powerlessness and the debased wishing that underlie the ideology and practice of gambling, where a stroke of luck, like the wave of a wand, can suddenly redeem everything without any recourse to the boring agency of time or labor.[34] The public's apparent delight in wizards, in instantaneous solutions and magical transformations, would to Fearing appear to be very dangerous symptoms, to be childish, wishful thinking of the kind he exposes in "American Rhapsody (3)." In the dreary world of pretense evoked in this poem, there is nothing left for the would-be lovers but to engage in an elaborate game of empty fiats: "You can be a princess and I'll be the beggar; no, you can be the beggar, and I'll be king," or even more cruelly, "Murder can be comic and hunger can be kind" (CP, 122). This kind of thinking can only postpone real solutions, if any remain. Without work and especially a continuous sense of time, personal identity is lost; life becomes at best a random game and wishes become delusory fantasies.

IMPERFECT DENOUEMENTS: THE POLITICS OF NEGATION

A brief recapitulation is, I think, in order. It seems to me that Fearing's poems from the thirties spell out the threat of a psychological robotization, resulting from a perceived fragmentation of experience, on the one hand, and a cultural evasion of negativity and critique, on the other. These phenomena are connected in his writing to the social insecurities of the Depression, to the nature of work, and, above all perhaps, to the optimistic character of mass culture, which perpetuates the paralyzing ideologies of luck and of instant transformation. If his reading of the culture of the thirties and the meaning of mass culture seems, from our perspective, unduly paranoid, we must recall that his poems also convey the historical circumstances that create such paranoia: the gaping contrast between the disastrous realities of economic crisis and the bland optimism of official discourse, and also (as "1933" suggests) the threat of murderous manipulation and deception presented by the specter of Fascism in Europe. These poems prefigure, as I have suggested, some of the positions we have come to associate with the theorists of the Frankfurt school: a pessimistic prognosis of a one-dimensional culture whose symptoms are evident in the perceived homologies between administered work, administered leisure, and administered culture in an increasingly fragmented and rationalized social space.

The line of argument set up so far in this chapter allows us now to read Fearing's single most ambitious poem, "Denouement," in a new light. Though almost all of Fearing's (few) critics have recognized the importance of this poem, they fail to understand its exact relation to his other poems, and thus miss the implications of its political project, a failure compounded by a tendency to conceive of "politics" largely in terms of party alignment. These critics thus either focus on the unflattering depiction of the strike organizers in the final section, as comforting proof that Fearing was not really a Communist (Santora), or read the positive moment where the dreams of "millions of hands that move as one" as an assertion of Communist collectivist ideals (Dahlberg).[35] It seems to me that this poem reveals and summarizes both Fearing's interpretation of the nature and function of mass culture and the possibilities of political resistance to it through a kind of negative dialectic. It is a move that only Charles Humboldt, in a retrospective appreciation, has described with precision: "In Fearing, the alien implies its opposite and the yearning for a better world is imbedded in the hard dark of the present like a seed in rock."[36]

The first part of "Denouement" (P, 57), which I compared earlier to Muriel Rukeyser's poem "Movie," indicates Fearing's wariness of any direct expression of this yearning. Such expression can assume, or so he seems to fear, an uncomfortable resemblance to the empty imperatives of "American Rhapsody (2)" – especially in an economy intent on the production of desire and dreams. Genuinely utopian impulses can easily be commodified, institutionalized, and transmuted into the passive magical thinking he associates with advertising and Hollywood. I cite again the lines in question:

> Sky, be blue, and more than blue; wind, be flesh and blood; flesh and
>   blood, be deathless;
>   walls, streets, be home;
>   desire of millions, become more real than warmth and breath and
>   strength and bread;
>   clock, point to the decisive hour and, hour without name when
>   stacked and waiting murder fades, dissolves, stay forever as the
>   world grows new;
>
> Truth, be known, be kept forever, let the letters, letters, souvenirs,
>   documents, snapshots, bills be found at last, be torn away from a
>   world of lies, be kept as final evidence, transformed forever into
>   more than truth. (P, 57)

As I argued in Chapter 4, the imagery of this opening section suggests how the potentially revolutionary hope that the social "desire of millions" may for once become real can change into the contrived and all too "perfect denouements" of the silver screen: into "South Sea music" and "a thunderbolt kiss." On closer reading, however, it appears that one cannot blame this failure entirely on the evasions of the dominant culture, but also in some measure on the kind of oppositional dreaming the poem imitates. If one looks carefully at the list of fiats with which the poem opens, it seems that they already lean toward the dangerous ground of an impossible technicolor hyperreality: the demand is not that the sky be blue, but "more than blue," not that the "desire of millions" become real, but "more real than warmth and breath and strength and bread." Even more important, the desire for a kind of messianic revolutionary moment partakes of the self-same impulse (albeit in the hope of social amelioration) to deny mortality and halt the flux of time, which Fearing's work associates with mass culture: the poem asks that "flesh and blood" be "deathless," that the "decisive hour when murder fades" stay forever, and that "the world grow[] new." No wonder, then, that for Fearing these desires appear to dissolve into the benumbed realm of the spectacle – of that "million mile screen."

The second section of "Denouement" (P, 58–60) immediately presents a challenge to the optimistic, technicolor fantasies of the opening movement. Even from the first line it is made brutally clear that flesh and blood are not and could never be deathless:

> But here is the body found lying face down in a burlap sack, strangled in the noose jerked shut by these trussed and twisted and frantic arms. (P, 58)

We might see Fearing's project in this part of the poem as an attempt to rewrite and complicate the cartoon-like postmortem of "Obituary." Here, too, the agents of the state come to deal with the pathetic effects of the deceased – the bed, in this case, and the vase holding saved-up cigar store coupons – and the poem takes the form of an official investigation into the victim's life and death.[37] But whereas in "Obituary" only the smug and efficient voice of the officer in charge is heard (leaving the reader to salvage, from telling details and silence, a sense of the painful truths that escape the officer's neat rhetorical wrap-up of the case), "Denouement" presents this voice in a debate of sorts with another voice. It is a voice that reveals some of the answers to the crucial question of which we spoke earlier: "how much has been lost, denied, what are all the things destroyed / Question mark, question mark, question mark, question mark" (CP, 124). While the poem provides no hard and fast indication of which lines belong to which of these two disembodied debaters, the sequence of statements, objections, and contradictions, and especially the political interests of each speaker, permit a fairly safe identification. In "Denouement" the voice of the powers that be, which I shall call (applying Fearing's own terminology) the voice of evasion, is explicitly identified with the mass media. It blandly denies any conflict of interest and, like the speaker in "Obituary," smugly and self-servingly refers to all parties as "friends." For a contemporary readership this voice must surely have been reminiscent of Franklin Roosevelt's reassuring fireside addresses: " 'My friends . . . my friends,' issues from the radio and thunders 'My friends' in newsreel close-ups, explodes across headlines, 'Both rich and poor, my friends, must sacrifice . . .' " (P, 58). As the postmortem proceeds, it appears that the string of questions fired by the voice of evasion constitutes an attempt to defuse the implications of the death by identifying the deceased as a media institution, or at least as a recognizable American type. Are you not, the voice asks, that Depression exemplar of enduring determination, the man "who started life again with three dependents and a pack of cigarettes?" Or at least "the senator's son," or "the beef king's daughter, married in a storm of perfume," or perhaps "the clubman who waves and nods and vanishes to Rio in a special plane?" (P, 58–59).

The other voice, which we may call the voice of exposition, counters the attempts to turn the victim into a safe "institution" by simply pointing to his scarred lungs and rickety bones: this is clearly no debonair clubman. It constantly draws our attention to the grim realities of the present, describing in clinical detail the corpse in the postmortem room, "the lips taped shut and the blue eyes cold, wide, still, blind, fixed beyond the steady glare of electric lights." It reminds us, furthermore, in some of the most moving and unironic lines Fearing ever wrote, of those who have died; those who are lost, forgotten, and poor; those, in short, who are not treated as "friends" though they may be addressed as such, who do not exist in the media and will never be recognized by a culture of evasion:

> but how will you know us, attentive, strained, before the director's
>   desk, or crowded in line in front of factory gates
> but how will you know us through ringed machinegun sights as we
>   run and fall in gasmask, steel helmet, flame-tunic, uniform, bayo-
>   net, pack,
> but how will you know us, crumbled into ashes, lost in air and water
>   and fire and stone,
> how will you know us, now or any time, who will ever know that we
>   have lived or died? (P, 60)

The voice of evasion at first protests against this unavoidable testimony, exchanging for the pleasing tones of a Roosevelt the accusations of a red-baiter and revealing in the process its true partisanship: "The witness is lying, lying, an enemy, my friends, of Union Gas and the home." But the section ends with the tenuous realization that the grim truths revealed by this postmortem might endanger such cherished and timeless ideals as "deathless hope" or "pride that was made of iron" or "the faith that nothing could destroy," a realization that nevertheless seems to fade into a drugged stupor, the final retreat of evasion: "Morphine. Veronal. Veronal. Morphine. Morphine. Morphine. Morphine" (P, 60).

In the third section of "Denouement" the scene shifts from the terrain of this allegorical postmortem to the realistically depicted headquarters of a strike committee:

> Leaflets, scraps, dust, match-stubs strew the linoleum that leads up-
> stairs to the union hall, the walls of the basement workers' club
> are dim and cracked and above the speaker's stand Vanzetti's face
> shows green, behind the closed doors the committeeroom is a fog
> of smoke. (P, 60)

Exposition, it would seem, now takes precedence, although the descriptions of the struggle are still met with (and partly revealed through) the uncomprehending voice of reaction: "Who are these people and what do they want, can't they be decent, can't they at least be calm and polite, / besides the time is not yet ripe. . . ." (P, 61).

The issues probed, however, remain the same; in fact, one could say that the final section of the poem presents a dialectical resolution of the problems posed in the earlier sections. "Denouement" starts out with fantasies of a timeless utopia, which then are challenged and negated by the unavoidable reality of death. Bearing in mind Charles Humboldt's remark about Fearing's oblique method, we should note that the very fact that the corpse of the second section does not conveniently arise – is not resurrected as a Hearst cartoon, for instance – already represents a political advance in its very negativity. The full implications of this moment of negation are still being explored in the third section. Fearing here starkly emphasizes the fact that in the real and very imperfect world of political struggle (evoked by such details as the messy committee room, scabs arriving in trucks, squabbling among the union members), the contrived solutions of mass culture simply do not apply: the victims of real struggles cannot, the poem explicitly points out, be resurrected:

> . . . they sink in clouds of poison gas and fall beneath clubs, hooves,
> rifles, fall and do not arise, arise, unite,
> never again these faces, arms, eyes, lips. (P, 61)

But for once Fearing does not leave us without a solution, a dialectical synthesis. Resurrection is indeed impossible, unless

> . . . we live, and live again,
> return, everywhere alive in the issue that returns, clear as light that still
> descends from a star long cold, again alive and everywhere visible
> through and through the scene that comes again, as light on moving
> water breaks and returns, heard only in the words, as millions of
> voices become one voice, seen only in millions of hands that move
> as one. (P, 61)

Impossible unless, in other words, we translate all hope of resurrection from the level of wishes to that of collective political commitment. The suggestion that issues and struggles may be transcendent and enduring is reinforced by the various political slogans cited in the poem, which all express a fight for survival, for life over death: "Bread not Bullets," "Red Front," "Arise," "Your party lives," and finally the motto reminding us of the fight for the lives of the Scottsboro Boys (and those of Sacco and Vanzetti before them): "They Shall Not Die." The poem thus posits that a resurrection of sorts is enacted in political struggle, in a struggle fully cognizant of the negative, of those who have died, and of the opposing bayonets of the troopers, which, as the final line reminds us, remain ever drawn and ready.

One further point must be made in conclusion. I have argued that Fearing, like Benjamin and the other members of the Frankfurt school I have referred to in this chapter, views the experience of the ordinary citizen as being shaped in identical ways by the organization of work and the structures of mass-produced leisure. Both spheres are characterized by a logic of fragmentation and repetition, which permits no development over time, no uniqueness, and no completion. But "Denouement" suggests an important difference between Fearing's position and that of the Frankfurt school, and even that of his onetime colleagues at the *Partisan Review:* high culture as a repository of ideals, or of an oppositional negativity, is not for him, finally, a privileged category. For Fearing the remedy for problems of society and subjectivity is not to be found in culture, but in struggle; the locus of the negative is not in art, but in the violent realities of life. The poem "Denouement," for all its ironies, *is* not a solution, but *describes* one: that of political action, of "liv[ing] again . . . in the issue that returns." It is at such moments that Fearing reveals the difference between himself and the pessimistic postwar theorists he often seems to resemble. Despite his recurrent fears of manipulation, of a one-dimensional culture of evasion, his work preserves that emphasis on politics and on historical agency that was still so alive in the culture of the thirties.

PART III

Nathanael West

6

"A Surfeit of Shoddy"
West and the Spectacle of Culture

. . . a photograph of a stoutly framed, neatly latticed billboard, foursheeted with a plump, fashionably-clad family smiling through the windshield of their shiny sedan, emblazoned with boxcar legends: "World's Highest Standard of Living – There's No Way Like the American Way." But beyond the billboard lies a rank weedpatch, a rubbish heap, a rotting shanty with a patched roof, and a brick back-wall which bears a sodawater advertisement.

George R. Leighton, Five Cities

Whoever [in history] has emerged victorious participates to this day in the triumphal procession in which the present rulers step over those who are lying prostrate. According to traditional practice, the spoils are carried along in this procession. They are called cultural treasures, and a historical materialist views them with cautious detachment. For without exception the cultural treasures he surveys have an origin which he cannot contemplate without horror. They owe their existence not only to the efforts of the great minds and talents who have created them, but also to the anonymous toil of their contemporaries. There is no document of civilization which is not at the same time a document of barbarism. . . . A historical materialist therefore dissociates himself from it as far as possible. He regards it as his task to brush history against the grain.

Walter Benjamin, "Theses on the Philosophy of History"

Walter Benjamin's often-quoted observation that "there is no document of civilization which is not at the same time a document of barbarism" emerges from his musings on Flaubert's re-creation of the fall of Carthage in *Salammbô* and evokes the archaic image of a Roman triumphal procession. Yet it applies equally to the culture of the twentieth century – and not only to high culture, but to any cultural product in which the power of the victors of history is symbolically invested.[1] The spoils of late capitalism are, of course, no longer displayed only in occasional military processions, or even in their rhetorical equivalents, such as Nixon's 1959 "Kitchen Debate" with Khrushchev, in which the vice-president proudly held up those millions of cars, TV sets, and radios as emblems of U.S. political superiority.[2] The spectacularization of power as "culture" enacted in the classical parade has become a constant feature of everyday life (indeed, according to some critics it is the most characteristic feature of contemporary culture); the show goes on incessantly on TV, in display windows, catalogues, museums, and so forth.

PROGRESS ON PARADE

Benjamin's famous thesis, written in 1940, has a special significance for the troubled decade from which it emerges. It was during the thirties, as Warren Susman has persuasively argued, that Americans discovered the notion of "culture," not only in the Arnoldian sense of the highest achievements of human intellect, but as a particular way of life: a way of life that increasingly came to be associated with commodities and consumption.[3] This self-consciousness about the meanings, patterns, and fashions of contemporary life, suggested in the keyword "lifestyle," was intertwined with scientific, technological, and institutional developments that made it possible to represent (whether to inculcate or merely reinforce) such "lifestyles" to the American masses: one thinks of radio, newsreels, opinion polls, cameras capable of taking candid photographs, and so forth. Culture could thus become more than ever a matter of display; and its commercial products, now designed with a view to "eye appeal," increasingly functioned as advertisements for the culture itself.[4]

It is not difficult to find specific manifestations of these developments. In 1934, for example, the Museum of Modern Art in New York held an important exhibition entitled "Machine Art," which, as the name would suggest, boldly erased the distinction between art and mass production. On display, as works of art, were common household objects: stoves, toasters, kitchenware, chairs, vacuum cleaners, cash registers, laboratory equipment. The show was followed the very next year by an Industrial Arts Exposition at the Rockefeller Center, which featured, in a series of model rooms, various new labor-saving devices and new styles of decoration.[5] These exhibitions indicate a self-conscious effort to aestheticize mass-produced material goods through the new arts of industrial design – an effort that, in view of the traditional separation of the utilitarian and the beautiful, must be seen as bearing distinctly utopian overtones. A little bit of "art" or at least of the "arty" now seemed to become available to everybody. But equally, such celebratory displays of commodities represent an objectification of the notion of culture and a veiling of the chaotic world of production through the magic of shows and appearances. The most striking examples of culture on parade were undoubtably the decade's series of great exhibitions, especially the Chicago World's Fair of 1933 and the New York World's Fair of 1939. All of these had the short-term aim of stimulating business and, in the long run, of propagating (especially through such displays as the various "homes of tomorrow," replete with brand-new gadgets and streamlined designs) the notion that consumer goods were the key to future happiness.

The ideological project of all the fairs – to reveal the gospel of inevitable progress and to celebrate the status quo in a triumphal parade of its products – was perhaps most overtly trumpeted by the organizers of the Chicago World's Fair, which was rather grandiosely entitled "A Century of Progress." The official guidebook to the fair proclaimed again and again the familiar but mythical message: that "the march of progress has not . . . swerved aside, nor even been seriously retarded, that so-called 'recessions' are temporary, like the receding wave that leaves the shore." "History," it asserted, "holds the evidence that this is true."[6] The delusory nature of such assertions, coming in the darkest year of the Great Depression, the year in which Hitler took power in Germany, was not lost on contemporary observers, nor was the dramatic contrast between the colorful modernist buildings on the Lake Shore and the "miles and miles of . . . dreary, sodden, utterly hope-destroying tenements" that lay at its doorstep.[7] In that year Chicago schools were in chaos, its teachers were unpaid, gang wars were continuing, the mayor was charged with corruption, unemployment was rife, and hundreds – those losers of history who get stomped on in the triumphal parade – fed daily on the garbage dumps.

Such jarring contrasts were frequently evoked in the literature and the visual arts of the thirties. Indeed, it is fair to say that Benjamin's detached and essentially oxymoronic perspective on the vaunted products of American "progress" became a characteristic stance in the expressive culture of the decade. The strategy I have in mind is perhaps most strikingly captured in a famous photograph taken by Margaret Bourke-White in 1937. In the upper half of the frame we see a billboard (the self-same poster that caught George Leighton's attention) showing a happy American family in their shiny car, capped by the slogan "The World's Highest Standard of Living"; below this celebratory image we see the breadline, the sad figures of those left behind in the triumphal procession of society's advance.[8] Bourke-White's camera angle, one might say, is identical to the point of view of Benjamin's historical materialist.

The photograph's strategy of bringing into focus not just the celebratory billboard, but the human cost of progress and consumption can also be found in the work of many American writers of the decade. Even if we confine ourselves to the early years of the New Deal, we can find a whole array of literary illustrations of the axiom that each document of consumer culture is a document of barbarism: scores of poems and novels were concerned to show the ugly underside of the pretty picture of consumerist dreams. There is, for instance, Nelson Algren's damning juxtaposition (in the final section of *Somebody in Boots*) of the technological boosterism of the Chicago World's Fair, its displays of new-fangled souvenirs and patents, with the hunger and poverty of the city's tenements.[9] Or there is Stephen Vincent Benét's bitter response (in his "Ode to Walt Whitman") to the question "'Is it well with these States?'" – a lament for a land in which things seem more important than people:

> "We have made many, fine new toys.
>
> . . . .
>
> These are your tan-faced children, the parched young,
>
> . . . .
>
> With the toys of plenty about them,
> The shiny toys making ice and music and light,
> But no price for the shiny toys and the last can empty.
>
> . . . .
>
> The walkers upon nothing, the four million.
> These are your tan-faced children."[10]

Or there is the more specific protest in Tillie Olsen's "I Want You Women up North to Know," a "worker correspondence" poem, which contrasts the pretty stuff in the department stores with the ugly, hidden story of their production:

> i want you women up north to know
> how those dainty children's dresses you buy at macy's, wanamakers,
>   gimbels, marshall fields,
> are dyed in blood, are stitched in wasting flesh,
> down in San Antonio, "where sunshine spends the winter."
>
> I want you women up north to see
> the obsequious smile, the salesladies trill
>   "exquisite work, madame, exquisite pleats"
> vanish into a bloated face, ordering more dresses,
>   gouging the wages down,
> dissolve into maria, ambrosa, catalina,
>   stitching these dresses from dawn to night,
>   in blood, in wasting flesh.
>
> . . . .
>
> Women up north, I want you to know
> when you finger the exquisite hand made dresses

> what it means, this working from dawn to midnight,
> on what strange feet the feverish dawn must come
>   to maria, catalina, ambrosa . . .
> how the malignant fingers twitching over the pallid faces jerk them
>   to work,
> and the sun and the fever mounts with the day – long plodding hours,
>   the eyes burn like coals . . .[11]

Or there is that remarkable passage from *Tender Is the Night* in which Scott Fitzgerald, erstwhile celebrant of twenties glitz, documents (not without a touch of the Benjaminian "horror") the origins of his heroine's stylish splendor:

> Trains began their run at Chicago and traversed the round belly of the continent to California; chicle factories fumed and link belts grew link by link in factories; men mixed toothpaste in vats and drew mouthwash out of copper hogsheads; girls canned tomatoes quickly in August or worked rudely at the Five-and-Tens on Christmas Eve; half-breed Indians toiled on Brazilian coffee plantations and dreamers were muscled out of their patent rights on new tractors – these were some of the people who gave a tithe to Nicole.[12]

Though these examples differ in style and in degrees of writerly polish, their purpose and their ironic vision is constant: the authors strive to draw the eye away from the realm of spectacular consumption, away from those self-congratulatory commodities, to the human beings that produce them. This is, arguably, the classic demystificatory gesture – the classic form of protest – in the literature of the thirties. At the end of the decade, Halford A. Luccock observed that the "theme for a whole library of depression literature" can be found in the invitation (implicit, as he sees it, in Leighton's description of that classic advertising poster) to "Come behind the billboard!" And our examples suggest that what is discovered there, for the most part, is the counterimage of human suffering.[13]

IN THE AMERICAN JUNGLE: WEST'S COMMODITIES

It is in the context of this emergent consumer society, with its self-congratulatory displays of commodities, and in relation to the technique of humanistic demystification, that I would now like to examine the work of Nathanael West. West has always been seen as concerned with the fantasy texts of consumer culture: with the newspaper sob column and the comic strips, with Hollywood and the movies, and with the "mass-man" and the "mob." Indeed, his rediscovery by the literary establishment in the late fifties may have had much to do with the fact that his work seems to support the Cold War intellectuals' conflation of mass culture and "totalitarianism."[14] There is some support for this kind of reading: West certainly seemed to despise the former underwear and fur merchants that ran Hollywood, despaired over the lack of any grounding truths in a world of proliferating and standardized fantasies, was above all deeply concerned by the threat of fascism and the possible manipulation of the masses through the media. But in the readings of West that follow I am not interested to repeat the standard arguments that show how West's "art" successfully trounces the inane fantasies of mass culture. The fact is that West's writing (as I shall argue more fully in later chapters) holds out very little hope for art as a panacea for social or spiritual ills. Indeed, it seems to me quite incorrect to impose retroactively the rigid and hierarchical oppositions of the Great Divide, the line between "avant-garde" and "kitsch," onto a writer whose connections with Dada and Surrealism are still quite patent and whose politics were quite different from the "apolitical" cultural politics of the fifties that dominates a good deal of West criticism.

In the following three chapters I treat West's critique of mass culture as inseparable from a critique of consumer society, a critique of the "culture of abundance." Mass-mediated culture in these chapters must therefore be understood not only as a matter of clichéd style or hackneyed plot lines. It is a matter of what we buy: of our clothing and interior design; it is to be found not only in the movie theater, but in the department store, in the curio shop, and at the World's Fair. It is not just a matter of texts (unless, of course, we understand this notion to refer to all manner of social coding). West, I am convinced, shared this understanding. It seems to me telling, for instance, that his Hollywood novel has precious little to do with movies per se, but is fascinated by the social meaning of the city, its architecture, its cults, and its fashions.[15] And if West understood "mass culture" in this sense, he must have understood also that any challenge to it could not be victorious on a purely discursive or textual level, by simply exorcizing the "disorder of Hollywood," or the "diseases" of fantasy or poor taste, in a work of art. Therefore, instead of validating his novels along these lines, as many earlier critics have done, we need to examine the implicit cultural politics of West's novels more carefully, and to read his work not by automatically assuming the validity of the hierarchical oppositions of the Great Divide, but by placing it in the context of the commercial discourses and the cultural politics of his time, as well as the contemporary critical writings of Walter Benjamin (that have already proved illuminating with regard to Fearing's work).

West understood all too well the Benjaminian notion that "culture" and consumer goods could serve as a kind of ideological spectacle. Yet unlike the artists I have mentioned, he seldom if ever deploys the technique of juxtaposing this kind of consumerist display with the shocking or moving image of suffering humanity. His characters, in contrast, are often not fully human, but resemble ventriloquist's dummies, party dresses, mechanical toys, poorly made automatons: machines whose fate is unlikely to inspire any of that pathos on which much of the decade's protest art so often relies.[16] His descriptions of *things,* on the other hand, are charged with a peculiar intensity. In *The Day of the Locust,* for instance, we are made to note a collection of ornamental dogs in the curio cabinet of a whorehouse:

> There were glass pointers, silver beagles, porcelain schnauzers, stone dachshunds, aluminum bulldogs, onyx whippets, china bassets, wooden spaniels. Every recognized breed was represented and almost every material that could be sculpted, cast or carved. (DL, 76)

Or we are asked to attend to details one would think could interest only a prospective consumer studying a catalogue: chairs "covered with rose and gray, glazed chintz bound in violet piping," "pale gray" wall paper with a "tiny, widely spaced flower design in violet," trousers in "reddish Harris tweed with a hound tooth check" (DL, 74, 69). The precision seems almost gratuitous, even fetishistic.

In his personal life, West was equally concerned with styles and objects. The deliberate image that he cultivated during his years at Brown University, for example, suggests a preoccupation with styles and brand names that surely verges on the self-parodic: he wore, as his biographer Martin Jay reports, "Brooks Brothers suits, argyle socks, Whitehouse and Hardy brogues, Brooks shirts and ties, and Herbert Johnson or Lock and Co. hats." He drove a red Stutz Bearcat and played the banjo. Later in life he became an avid collector of duck decoys and hunting paraphernalia and meticulously decorated his home in a colonial style with touches of the old Southwest in the draped serapes, carved chairs, and ironwork.[17] Clearly commodities were to West a significant part of the "American jungle."[18] And whatever function they may have played in his "lifestyle" – self-expression, masquerade, camouflage, or joke – he had very clear ideas about their valence as elements of his literary style. Attention to such objects had to do with writing "in the American grain," with that unflinching focus on local particularities of language and things that William Carlos Williams advocated, in opposition to the more symbolically resonant and more European "objective correlatives" of T. S. Eliot.

But West was not exactly Williams's disciple: in the early thirties he presumed to lecture the poet on the need to work "not only in but against the American grain and yet idiomatic in pain."[19] The remark (which I would like to associate with Benjamin's advice to "read history against the grain") is crucial for an understanding of West's attitude toward commodity culture. Let me explain by way of speculation: when West and Williams were coediting the second issue of *Contact* (a gathering of what they called "American Primitives"), they intended for a time to print an excerpt from an old Sears, Roebuck catalogue as though it were a poem.[20] Now, when read "in the American grain," this "poem" could be seen as a piece of proto Pop Art, an unlyrical but nevertheless celebratory enumeration of the "pure products of America." It is conceivable that Williams, who could find delight in unprepossessing sources, may have perceived such an experiment in this light; and a few years earlier, Matthew Josephson might have praised such a poem along with his admired "Great American Billposter."[21] But it seems doubtful that West would have intended the catalogue as a paean or even a neutral pastiche: read against the grain, the very form of the catalogue – its endless enumeration, the absurd enticements of "useful" and attractive details, its banal sameness and banal variety – could be read as a satire on the senseless proliferation of things. The Sears catalogue, read antagonistically, thus comes to resemble the whorehouse curio cabinet: both become unlyrical poems on the theme of production and reproduction run amok.

This technique of (potentially) parodic citation is also evident in West's novels, where he frequently plagiarizes or imitates scraps of commercial texts: the platitudes of the agony columns ("Do not let life overwhelm you"), the blandishments of advertising slogans ("smoke a 3 B pipe"), or the blare of headlines ("Mother slays five"). And for *A Cool Million* he ransacked Horatio Alger's boy books: at least one-fifth of the text is cribbed from Alger with only the slightest variation.[22] Often West tries to give the sense that he has reproduced documents, signs, and placards in his text. The following business-card-cum-catalogue from *A Cool Million* is, as it were, glued into the text like a subway ticket in a Dadaist collage:

EZRA SILVERBLATT

Official Tailor
to the

NATIONAL REVOLUTIONARY PARTY

Coonskin hats with extra long tails, deerskin shirts with or without fringes, blue jeans, moccasins, squirrel rifles, everything for the American Fascist at rock bottom prices. 30% off for Cash. (CM, 113)

Most important, West's lists of commodities are also, as I have already suggested, parodic citations of sorts. They are best seen as antiadvertisements, which use the same heightened, meticulous descriptions we would find in commercials to achieve the opposite aim: not to produce desire, but to attack the whole practice of the mass production of desire.

Though West claimed that he was not interested in "the Frenchified symbolist stuff" and later in his life insisted that he was not, properly speaking, a "surrealist writer," his intention and methods are certainly related, for instance, to those of Marcel Duchamps, whose moustachioed Mona Lisa mockingly quotes Leonardo's "masterpiece" in order to challenge the hallowed institution of art.[23] The difference, if indeed there is a difference, may be contextual: for the French avant-garde, bourgeois art is the prime target; for West, in America, it is bourgeois commerce. The British critic Jonathan Raban is therefore right when he observes, in a perceptive but hostile essay, that West's Surrealism is "the home-town Surrealism of the neighbourhood supermarket"; but he reveals a misunderstanding of the Surrealist project when he reads this small-time tackiness and the taint of commerce as a sign of West's inferiority to his European counterparts.[24] After all, as Walter Benjamin argued, the mother of Surrealism was the shopping arcades of Paris. For Breton and his disciples, Dada and Surrealism were precisely a matter of using local scraps and commercial waste – a matter of petty bricolage, even of being sickening and tasteless.[25] Besides, West knew very well that his "American super-realism" was a technique shared by the managers of supermarkets, where, as West describes it in The Day of the Locust, "colored spotlights played on the showcases and counters, heightening the natural hues of the different foods. The oranges were bathed in red, the lemons in yellow, the fish in pale green, the steaks in rose and the eggs in ivory" (DL, 87–88). In the heyday of American social realism, with its focus on poverty and scarcity, such a passage must at least be credited with a measure of prescience: it looks forward not only to the postwar society of affluence, but to the postmodern realization that (as one of Norman Mailer's characters puts it) "reality is no longer realistic."[26]

Raban's essay, however, addresses other more important charges against West, which ultimately concern the political implications of his artistic strategies. West's obsession with things remains to Raban problematic and distasteful, both in spite and because of the oppositional negativity of his catalogues. They seem to him symptomatic of the "shrill, high-pitched nausea" with which this "surfeited realist" regards the social scene, an attitude entirely devoid of that dialectical perspective – of that "wonderful doubleness of vision" – which allowed Fitzgerald to acknowledge simultaneously the promises and the deceit of the consumerist dream. Since they lack that humanizing touch of which I spoke earlier, West's novels appear to this critic to replicate rather than critique the reifying processes of commodity production: *The Day of the Locust,* for example, works like a production line: "It takes the scattered ingredients of a recognizably real Hollywood and turns them into the hard, bright patterns of cheap industrial design." West's writing, to Raban, is finally as much symptom as diagnosis of reification – an example rather than a critique of commodity fetishism.[27]

These accusations merit serious consideration, especially since they identify so clearly the occupational hazards of the parodist: producing mere clones of the object of parody, losing a critical edge and sliding into pastiche. (We may recall that Kenneth Fearing too suffered such charges, when Alexander Bergman condemned his *Collected Poems* as "a surrender and a contribution to the propaganda of the press and radio.")[28] Any response to such accusations is complicated by the fact that the meaning of a "cited" text is not readily resolved by looking at the text itself, which often remains silent in its facticity as verbal or visual object – smiling mysteriously, perhaps like Warhol's multiple Mona Lisas. Whatever political edge such a text has cannot be stated overtly and remains inseparable from the bricoleur's intentions, as well as its audience's strategies of interpretation. In West's case both of the latter are problematic: he tended to be secretive, jokey, and evasive, while most of his critics have felt compelled to depoliticize him in order to praise his talent and universality.

Insofar as Raban's charges are ad hominem, as when he takes West's sickened outrage at the excess and cheapness of mass production as an indication of "parochial, mean, and hysterical talent," they are easily set aside.[29] The fact that one can find several similarly "nauseous" enumerations of objects in other texts from the thirties suggests that West's affliction cannot only be a personal foible, but must be in some measure a response to contemporary cultural trends. West's catalogue of the incongruous jumble of historical reproductions in a studio junkyard – "the skeleton of a Zeppelin, a bamboo stockade, an adobe fort, the wooden horse of Troy, a flight of baroque palace stairs that started in a bed of weeds and ended against the branches of an oak, part of the Fourteenth street elevated station, a Dutch windmill, the bones of a dinosaur, the upper half of the Merrimac, a corner of a Mayan temple" (DL, 131) – is surely no more hysterical or "nauseous" than Nelson Algren's description of the Chicago World's Fair in *Somebody in Boots.* In fact, as Algren describes it, the Century of Progress (which, incidentally, did feature a reproduction of a Mayan temple) bears an uncanny resemblance to West's Hollywood:

> On either side [of South Street] hawkers sold patent medicines, World's Fair flags and World's Fair flowers, World's Fair souvenirs and

World's Fair balloons, patent cork screws, patent razor blades, patent cameras, patent ties, patent hose, beach balls, pocket-knives, patent salves of diverse cures . . . and inside the gates was chaos. Nude dancers, wind-tunnels, Indians, Byrd's South-Pole ship. Dante's Inferno, Miss America, alligator-wrestlers, Lincoln's cabin, flame-divers, a five-legged cow beside the House of David, *pigs ships temples villages gorillas clocks artillery cats dogs camps* – a zigzag riot of fakery, a hash of hot-dog stands and shimmy shows lapped by the lake.[30]

Even the movies offer a case in point. The final scenes of Orson Welles's 1940 film, *Citizen Kane* (where the camera pans over the leavings of Kane's gargantuan possessiveness, rooms crammed with thousands of joyless collectibles), reveals a similar revulsion at an absurd surfeit of commodities. These scenes, with their melodramatic lighting, cavernous spaces, and Gothic atmosphere, are arguably also overwrought; but the point is surely that the excess of the visual description matches the accumulative hysteria of Kane himself and, indirectly, of the culture he represents. Thus juxtaposed, these texts emerge perhaps more clearly as early diagnoses – and not mere symptoms – of the *horror vacui* of that America of simulacra described in Umberto Eco's *Travels in Hyperreality,* where a frenzied passion for fakery, replication, and collection comes to seem the key national characteristic.[31]

It is more difficult to defend West against the implication that his negativity is undialectical and even inhuman. I would maintain, however, that even if nothing of Fitzgerald's sense of romance and interest in character remains in his work, West nevertheless specializes in a peculiar double vision of his own. It is often a look frozen at that horrible moment of realization when displays in which we still see traces of utopian desire reveal themselves as cheap seconds or fakes: ugly, monstrous, but above all sad. One of West's unpublished short stories, written around 1933, hinges precisely on this kind of double take. In "The Sun, the Lady and the Gas Station" West describes two choice spectacles of commodity culture in the thirties: a visit to the "Streets of Paris" exhibit at the Chicago Century of Progess and a drive down Hollywood's "Miracle Mile."[32] The locations are crucial: the Century of Progress was, as we have seen, designed to serve as a manifestation of an inspiring and utopian vision of a bright tomorrow; and Hollywood, in the dictionary of received ideas, is "a paradise on earth" (DL, 138). But in each vignette the sun comes out and reveals the tawdriness of the show. This cheap phoniness is universal. Hollywood is just a copy of yet another fake: Asbury Park, New Jersey. And even the real Paris, the narrator supposes, would be no different from its seedy simulacrum at the fair. The concluding image of the story adds a sense of grotesque horror to these nasty revelations: a smooth seductive face melts in the sun and gradually reveals itself as the sagging visage of an old crone. This Westian double take strikes me as strongly reminiscent of the experience captured in James Ensor's paintings (to which Josephine Herbst compares his work) where the smiling masks of the merrymakers blend into the leers of skeletons, and the carnival parade becomes the dance of death.[33]

"BUY AMERICAN": THE BORDELLO AS MUSEUM

"The Sun, the Lady and the Gas Station," however, is perhaps still open to Raban's charge that West's attitude toward commodity culture is undialectical and inhuman: it is fair to say that his "double vision" remains concerned with things and that the moment of horror clearly depends not so much on moral indignation or human sympathy as on an aesthetic outrage, or perhaps a nostalgia for some lost authenticity. But elsewhere in West's work moral and political indignation emerges more strongly. There is a sharp satirical sting, for example, in the fact that his most lavish examples of conspicuous consumption are to be found in houses of ill repute: Mrs. Jenning's establishment in *The Day of the Locust* and Wu Fong's in *A Cool Million*. The former, meticulously described in language that I compared earlier to that of a sales catalogue, is the single "triumph of industrial design" (DL, 72) in West's otherwise monstrously tacky Hollywood; the latter, decorated by the interior designer Asa Goldstein, specialist in colonial interiors and exteriors, presents the visitor with a full array of antiquarian and contemporary styles in its "Pennsylvania Dutch, Old South, Log Cabin Pioneer, Victorian New York, Western Cattle Days, California Monterey, Indian, and Modern Girl series of interiors" (CM, 126). Indeed, as the prosaic and entirely unsexy catalogue of the various prostitutes suggests, it is nothing short of a parodic museum of American regional cultures and artifacts:

> Lena Haubengrauer from Perkiomen Creek, Bucks County, Pennsylvania. Her rooms were filled with painted pine furniture and decorated with slip ware, spatter ware, chalk ware and "Gaudy Dutch." Her simple farm dress was fashioned of bright gingham. . . .
> Mary Judkins from Jugtown Hill, Arkansas. Her walls were lined with oak puncheons chinked with mud. Her mattress was stuffed with field corn and covered by a buffalo robe. There was real dirt on her floors. She was dressed in homespun, butternut stained, and wore a pair of men's boots.
> Patricia Van Riis from Gramercy Park, Manhattan, New York City. Her suite was done in the style known as Biedermeier. The windows were draped with thirty yards of white velvet apiece and the chandelier in her sitting room had over eight hundred crystal pendants attached to it. She was dressed like an early "Gibson Girl."

> Powder River Rose from Carson's Store, Wyoming. Her apartment was the replica of a ranch bunkhouse. Strewn around it in well-calculated confusion were such miscellaneous articles as spurs, saddle blankets, straw, guitars, quirts, pearl-handled revolvers, hayforks and playing cards. She wore goatskin chaps, a silk blouse and a five-gallon hat with a rattlesnake band. (CM, 126–27)

The object of the satire is not the age-old matter of debased sexual mores, but the specifically contemporary one of national culture turned into spectacle. It is significant, I think, that in Alice Sweethorne's "Old South" suite visitors "gasp with pleasure," not at her sexual ministrations, but at the sight of the beautiful worksmanship on the Charleston iron grillwork displayed in her room. The whores are not described as examples of iniquity, but rather as mannequins modeling the various styles – or, more exactly, as actresses in period costume at some more comprehensive, all-American Williamsburg.

Though scarcely reminiscent of William Carlos Williams, the whorehouse passage from *A Cool Million* is an example of writing that is both in and against the American grain: observant of American products, critical of the objectification and fetishism they imply. This critique emerges quite clearly not despite, but because of, West's affectation of worldly admiration for these establishments. His praise of Wu Fong and Mrs. Jennings as shrewd and tasteful students of fashion or models of refinement and high culture sharpens rather than mutes the satirical point: these panders, charging their well-earned "brokerage fee," are model American entrepreneurs brushed against the grain. Especially wicked is West's praise of the "crafty oriental" Wu Fong's nationalism. Inspired by Hearst's "Buy American" campaign to sponsor home products and talent, Wu Fong turns his exotically styled "House of all Nations" into "a hundred per centum American place" (CM, 126). The cutting insinuation is of course that, in the case of this entrepreneur, "Buying American" carries a sinisterly literal meaning.

West's brothels therefore present a "double vision" with strongly political implications: they are simultaneously places of exploitation and degradation and display cases of contemporary style. They suggest, moreover, a further comparison between West and his more orthodox Marxist contemporaries, who typically (and rather puritanically) associated consumerism with prostitution. This association was by no means a Depression coinage (Mike Gold, for instance, described the *Saturday Evening Post* of the early twenties as being "putrid with prosperity like the bulky, diamonded duenna of a bawdy-house"), but almost any issue of the *New Masses* during the late twenties and early thirties offers evidence of its currency.[34] Herman Spector's "Night in New York" is a typical example:

the city is a chaos;
confusion of stone and steel,
the spawn of anarchic capitalism

. . . .

pornographic offerings,
eruptions on the skin of streets
from the tainted blood of commerce,
are electrically alight and lewd.

signs flash bargain messages.
with a twinkling of legs a whore passes

. . . .

taxis slide softly.[35]

Nelson Algren's chapters on the Chicago World's Fair in *Somebody in Boots* again provide a case in point, and even share West's sense of the spectacular quality of both commodified sex and consumer culture. Algren undercuts the boosting speeches at the opening of the fair with the patter of a sideshow barker for a tawdry burlesque peep show (*"hottest woman-show off the grounds. . . . Yo' can put ever'thin' she wears on a letter behind a two-cent stamp!"*), thus equating the fair (which turns Chicago into "a whore, selling a tin souvenir") and the mayor's "pimp [ing] for Big Business" with the pornographic titillation purveyed by smaller fry.[36]

But West's peculiar comic rhetoric, which, like that of Claude Estee in *The Day of the Locust*, "permit[s] him to express his moral indignation and still keep his reputation for worldliness and wit" (DL, 172), keeps him from delivering the straightforward (and somewhat ham-fisted) denunciations of Spector and Algren. His dandified worldliness and genuine fascination with the products of consumer culture give the flat enumerations of his satire a certain precision and topicality that are lacking in the two proletarian writers' blanket condemnations of the culture of abundance. In noting Wu Fong's change to a more patriotic packaging of his whorehouse, for instance, West captures and satirizes what was a very prevalent design trend of the Depression decade. (In fact, West's Wu Fong in some sense predicts the general tendency toward an "Americanism" that was to grow in strength with the Popular Front and the various New Deal cultural programs.) The historian Lary May has described the self-same change of style in the design of movie theaters of the time: while the movie palaces of the twenties were built in lavishly exotic Moorish, Baroque, or Chinese styles, those from the mid-thirties were done in local styles and materials: the Ute Theater in Colorado Springs, for instance, was built in adobe, and incorporated Indian and Mission styles. Names like the Tivoli, Alhambra, and Rialto made way for the Roosevelt, the Lincoln, the Pocahontas, the Will

Rogers, and the Colonial.[37] Moreover, even a casual glance at the language of magazines from the period would suggest that West was shrewdly picking up on a new kind of popular discourse in which identity and personality were cast as a matter of preconceived and premarketed styles of consumption. *Hollywood Magazine,* for example, reported in August 1931 that the actress Dolores del Rio had, after marrying an art director, changed from the "El Rancho Mexicana" look to the "Ultra-Art Moderne Vamp."[38] The article featured photographs of Dolores in her new matching "Hollywood Bauhaus" abode, in which she displayed in rich profusion the kind of "stream-lined" accoutrements that Asa Goldstein might have scattered around the suite of Wu Fong's "Modern Girl."

I am suggesting that if we historicize rather than lament West's focus on things, his work can be valued for addressing squarely that key twentieth-century transition from a producer-capitalist economy to a consumption-oriented "culture of abundance" – a transition that the predominant social realist mode, with its focus on scarcity and struggle, inevitably tends to ignore. *A Cool Million,* which critics usually dismiss as a tasteless and inaccurate satire on the rise of an American fascism, can then (as the whorehouse catalogue suggests) be read profitably as a satire on the commodification of American culture. In this narrative of an American Candide's journey to dissolution and martyrdom, we witness not only how regional customs and crafts are transformed into the stock-in-trade of a whorehouse, but how homes are ransacked by interior designers or given over to museums, how political life is turned into a fascist costume parade: how experience, in short, retreats into representations, clichés, costumes, and souvenirs.

THE WORLD'S FAIR AND THE CHAMBER OF HORRORS

In such a reading, Mr. Shagpoke Whipple, West's savage caricature of a Calvin Coolidge turned fascist, emerges as representing a somewhat more ambiguous set of values than one might expect. From the first encounter, where we see Whipple communing with his picture of Lincoln, the plowboy president, he is the advocate of that old American dream, the Horatio Alger rags-to-riches story: the master parable for the producer-capitalist culture of work, delayed gratification, and private enterprise. But he is also the ideologue of a culture of spectacles and commodities: celebrating American technology, holding forth on the marvelous inventions (such as the safety pin and four-wheel brakes [CM, 97–98]), and turning the "dismantled" young hero, Lemuel Pitkin, into a sideshow exhibit and then into a rallying symbol for his very fashion-conscious party.

And, indeed, there is a close connection between these two aspects of

the Whipple ideology: the success story is, one might say, the individualist – and therefore all the more American – version of the myth of
historical progress. It is thus uncannily appropriate, in view of our
earlier discussion, that Whipple should at one point in the novel urge his
company to visit that grand spectacle, the Chicago Century of Progress
(CM, 140). Though A Cool Million tells us nothing about this sightsee-
ing trip (the narrative is at this point again interrupted by yet another
dastardly plot of "Jewish" bankers and Communists), the explicit allusion to the World's Fair underlines the novel's satirical engagement with
the products and ideology of a self-congratulatory "American tradition."

It is significant, in this regard, that Nathanael West visited the Chicago World's Fair in preparation for writing A Cool Million and took a
specific interest in an exhibition of American schoolbooks.[39] From my
study of the guidebooks and photographs of the fair, I would guess this
was the exhibition by Ginn and Company of educational books from the
sixteenth to the nineteenth century, displayed in a colonial schoolroom in
the so-called Hall of Social Science. To visit this booth, West would
have had to pass some of the more egregiously ideological demonstrations of progress (which is, of course, much easier to prove in the
domain of the technological than in society). He would have seen, for
instance, a series of dioramas presenting changes in the life of the family.
Here, according to one disgruntled visitor, progress in all fields of social
life was demonstrated in the most absurd and unconvincing spectacles:

> Progress in affection [was shown by] a family group of Colonial days
> over against a couple alighted from an automobile and linked in a close
> embrace – to the edification of passers-by; [progress] in religion, by a
> family gathering singing hymns versus a nearly empty church in which
> a servant of God addressed the microphone; [and progress] in recre-
> ation, by outdoor games on the one hand, and on the other, a movie
> audience absorbed in a scene of osculation on the screen.[40]

A Cool Million certainly gives us a general sense of what West's reaction
to such a sight would have been. The official culture's cynical insistence
on social and historical optimism – so blatantly evident in this exhibit –
comes under a relentless attack in the narrative of the plucky, hard-
working "American Boy," who, ever faithful to the belief that he can
make it in the "land of opportunity," loses his home, his body parts,
and his life. But the fair's relevance to the book becomes even clearer
when, shortly after their visit to Chicago, West's motley crew of adven-
turers run into a traveling exhibition advertised by the following billboard:

FREE   FREE   FREE

Chamber of American Horrors
Animate and Inanimate
Hideosities

also

Chief Jake Raven

COME ONE   COME ALL

S. Snodgrasse

Mgr.

FREE   FREE   FREE

(CM, 160)

The "Chamber of American Horrors" must, I think, be understood as the exact antitype to the Century of Progress and its political agenda. The objects displayed in the "inanimate" part of the exhibition offer a surrealistically distorted version of the kind of thing one might have encountered in the medical exhibitions at the Century of Progress's Hall of Science or the displays of new commodities and new production processes (suggesting a strange "combination of Hollywood and Houdini," as one visitor complained) in the various manufacturer's pavilions.[41] West describes the collection of "Hideosities" as follows:

> The hall which led to the main room of the "inanimate" exhibit was lined with sculptures in plaster. Among the most striking of these was a Venus de Milo with a clock in her abdomen, a copy of Power's "Greek Slave" with elastic bandages on all her joints, a Hercules wearing a small, compact truss.
>
> In the center of the principal salon was a gigantic hemorrhoid that was lit from within by electric lights. To give the effect of throbbing pain, these lights went on and off.
>
> All was not medical, however. Along the walls were tables on which were displayed collections of objects whose distinction lay in the great skill with which their materials had been disguised. Paper had been made to look like wood, wood like rubber, rubber like steel, steel like cheese, cheese like glass, and, finally, glass like paper.
>
> Other tables carried instruments whose purposes were dual and sometimes triple or even sextuple. Among the most ingenious were pencil sharpeners that could also be used as earpicks, can openers as hair brushes. Then, too, there was a large variety of objects whose real uses had been cleverly camouflaged. The visitor saw flower pots that were really victrolas, revolvers that held candy, candy that held collar buttons and so forth. (CM, 163)

Though depicted in a monstrously satirical light, these unpleasant but intriguing objects remain recognizable as the trophies of Western art and the inventions of American technology: a world's fair brushed against the grain, where archaic forms of beauty merge tastelessly with promises of medical and therapeutic relief; where the infinite plasticity of kitschy novelties mocks, even as it reveals, the transformative powers of technology.

The passage deploys a peculiarly Westian grotesque that one is tempted to call Surrealist, until one recalls that such objects – candy revolvers, ashtrays in the shape of classical and not so classical nudes – might very well be for sale at Woolworth's. Yet this particular sample of West's "American superrealism" does bring to mind the earlier work of Max Ernst in whose collages (some of which West purchased in 1926) figures in strange harnesses combine incongruously with all manner of fauna, flora, and machines.[42] But the passage should not be seen only in terms of West's artistic experimentation or as making a simple point about the tastelessness of modern production. In condensed symbolic fashion the description of the exhibition homes in on several recurrent themes that have come to characterize subsequent analyses of late capitalist culture.

The Chamber of American Horrors hints, through the plaster copies of classical sculptures, at the loss of value suffered by high art in an age of proliferating reproduction. These grotesquely transmuted and adapted classical figures function as signs of cultural decay. The other details of the exhibit, however, evoke more than this general lament. The Venus with the clock in her abdomen not only offers, like Duchamps's moustachioed Mona Lisa, a mockery of the solemn institution of artistic beauty, but suggests the merger of the once-separate realm of the aesthetic with that of mass-produced commodities. (We should remember that kitsch, the artsy clock or cute cigarette lighter, represents not a simple debasement of high art, but the incorporation of aesthetics, of style, into the objects of everyday use.) Likewise, the bandaged Greek slave and the Hercules wearing a truss, while sounding again the familiar mock-heroic themes of the loss of cultural grandeur and power, reveal something more specific about the nature of consumer culture. Like the figures in Ernst's collages these patched statues resemble nothing so much as the solemnly ridiculous people depicted in late-nineteeth-century medical advertisements for prosthetic contraptions; and the electric hemorrhoid is clearly a more recent and more tasteless example of this kind of commercial art. These items may serve also as symbolic reminders of the origins of modern advertising in the promotion of patent medicines, and perhaps more generally of what Jackson Lears has called the "therapeutic origins" of consumer culture, which locates all salvation in a secular realm of things.[43] The medical exhibits are thus emblematic of the "aspirin" culture of commodified cures that West's Miss Lonelyhearts so violently rejects (ML, 13).

Finally, the collection of gimmicks along the walls indicates that West discerns behind the triumphs of contemporary chemical engineering – the invention of colorful and protean materials out of which the brand-new consumer products of the twenties and thirties were produced – an impulse toward a cheap and delusive cleverness. Moreover, these objects, fashioned out of disguised substances, serving multiple but entirely elusive and camouflaged uses, hint at the emergence of a culture of illusion, misleading appearances, and fabricated needs, a culture that, as Henri Lefebvre phrases it, has suffered a "decline of referentials."[44] The "real" becomes quite elusive when appearances become so infinitely metamorphic and (in all senses of the word) plastic. This parodic world's fair thus looks ahead to the synthetic masquerade of his superreal Hollywood, where all original materials are transmuted and even plainness becomes an elaborately contrived style – as in Homer Simpson's house, where the doors are of gumwood painted like fumed oak, the hinges factory-stamped to appear hand-forged, and the Governor Winthrop dresser painted to look like unpainted pine (DL, 80–81). West, in other words, foresees the now-familiar postmodern dystopia where even the natural is elaborately produced; and the crude bizarrerie of this passage thus offers a more pointed and even prophetic critique of American material culture than one might at first think.

But it is in the "animate" half of the exhibition that West comes closest to articulating something like the Benjaminian idea of culture – and I would here have us recall the image of the triumphal procession discussed at the opening of this chapter. The live "Hideosities" announced on the billboard turn out to be a pageant entitled *The Curse of Columbus,* which enacts the more shameful aspects of U.S. history: the fate, one might say (though the performance is presented quite comically), of those who are trampled underfoot in the course of that inevitable progress. In the show, West tells us, Quakers are "branded, Indians brutalized and cheated, Negroes sold, children sweated to death" (CM, 163). The performance culminates with a little play on more recent history, of which West gives us the full text. The opening scene takes place in 1928. A white-haired old grandmother, sitting in her comfortable parlor, hears on the radio an advertisement for the Indefatigable Investment Company of Wall Street. Soon she is visited by the company's smooth-talking salesman and is persuaded to invest all of her savings in Iguanian Gold Bonds, so that her grandsons can have fur coats and Brooks Brothers suits and banjos like the other boys. After a curtain and a scene change, the second act takes us to a busy street during the Depression. We see the grandmother and her grandchildren dying of starvation. Two millionaires enter. They chuckle smugly at the thought of their profits from the Iguanian bonds, proceed to trip over the four pitiful bodies and exit cursing the streetcleaning department for its negligence. We are clearly not intended to take this stuff piously: the text even tells us (ironizing the irony) that the show is nothing but Communist propaganda. But even so, I would argue that the sketch presents us with something quite like the parade of history "in which the present rulers step over those who are lying prostrate" while holding up, as their spoils, the ridiculous treasures collected in the "inanimate" part of the show. It is, needless to say, a farcical rendition of the idea implicit in Benjamin's famous thesis – or, more precisely, a comic-strip version, to judge by the visual stereotyping of the silk-hatted capitalists with dollar signs embroidered on their vests. But this humorous flattening out of the image does not finally minimize the seriousness of West's critique of the notion of history – and the spectacle of abundant commodities – as progress.

AGAINST THE GRAIN: COMMUNIST AND ETHNOGRAPHIC CRITIQUES

Unlike his more conscientiously Communist contemporaries (whom he liked to refer to as "Western Union boys" and "boy scouts"), West was reluctant to spell out, unironically, the tale of oppression that might elaborate the link between the cultural parade and those bodies that lie prostrate in its wake.[45] And perhaps we should concede that such hesitation might indicate a kind of intellectual honesty: unless one accepts the simple formula that a decadent capitalist system must perforce produce a debased culture (as did many of the New Masses writers discussed earlier), the exact relationship between the economic forces and the forms of cultural production is in fact difficult to specify. My reading of the objects in the Chamber of Horrors as the treasures of an exploitative system, it must be said, goes against the explicit assertions of West's almost universally debunking satire: A Cool Million certainly pokes fun at such "politically correct" interpretations. The traveling show described earlier also includes a little lecture by the Communist poet Sylvanus Snodgrasse in which he tries to prove the causal relationship between the oppressive hideosities of the "animate" tableaux and the aesthetic horror of the "inanimate" display; but the narrator assures us that these arguments are "not very convincing" (CM, 164). The fact that Snodgrasse is a former con man who becomes a Communist because his poems don't sell clearly extends the satire to the literary Left.

Yet this is not to say that my reading is incorrect or that West did not share, at least to some degree, the convictions and commitment of his many friends on the left. The arguments by which Mr. Whipple tries to discredit the American horror show are so ludicrous and offensive as to make the jokes on Snodgrasse seem rather mild. West has the ex-president explain that the grandmother in the play didn't have to buy the bonds unless she wanted to, that the authorities won't allow any one to die in the streets, and that a distinction should be made between good (i.e., American), and bad (i.e., Jewish) capitalists. Moreover, the narrative voice in which Snodgrasse is condemned consistently represents the ideological platitudes of the Hearst press and echoes the stupidities of Whipple: we can hardly credit the same speaker who can assert quite blandly that "the inferior races greatly desire the women of their superiors" and endorse the rights of Americans to sell "their children's labor without restrictions as to either price or hours" (CM, 93, 110, 166). West's parodic strategy, in short, involves a dual and evasive gesture. He avoids the standard harangue about the evils of the capitalist mode of production, but he nevertheless flags the reader's attention to the existence of such arguments and demonstrates the utter ludicrousness of the nationalist and protofascist counterarguments.

This characteristic ironic shiftiness has perhaps too often been taken as an indication that West was not really sympathetic to leftist positions or that he was fundamentally apolitical. To illustrate this point we might examine another case of such evasiveness: a 1934 review of Gene Fowler's biography of Mack Sennett, entitled "Soft Soap for the Barber" – one of West's two or three surviving nonfictional commentaries on mass culture. In this piece, he refuses to offer any explanations of or excuses for the poor taste of the archetypal consumer of mass entertainment – the barber in Purdue.[46] Rather, West simply asserts that the barber can be defended and that he would rather leave the task to the Marxist, Mike Gold, than to the uncritical celebrator of the "popular" arts, Gilbert Seldes: again a gesture toward a Marxist argument that West declines to recapitulate. Jay Martin, West's biographer, feels that the article leaves us with a hint of irony regarding both views of the masses. But there is some evidence to suggest that West was actually quite serious in his endorsement of Gold's position and that he backed away from expounding it himself not for reasons of political conviction, but because he was conscious of the undermining effects of his own "promiscuous irony," aware that his professions of sentiment and conviction came out sounding (as Raban points out) as though they should be in quotation marks.[47] After all, when he finally does venture an explanation of the mental state of the masses in *The Day of the Locust*, West mentions, as Mike Gold might have done, how these haunted and frustrated middle Americans have been dehumanized through work and cheated by the promises of leisure and abundance:

> All their lives they had slaved at some kind of dull, heavy labor, behind
> desks and counters, in the fields and at tedious machines of all sorts,
> saving their pennies and dreaming of the leisure that would be theirs
> when they had enough. Finally that day came. They could draw a
> weekly income of ten or fifteen dollars. Where else should they go but
> California, the land of sunshine and oranges?
>
> Once there, they discover that sunshine isn't enough. They get tired
> of oranges, even of avocado pears and passion fruit. Nothing happens.
> They don't know what to do with their time. They haven't the mental
> equipment for leisure, the money nor the physical equipment for plea-
> sure. . . . They have been cheated and betrayed. They have slaved and
> saved for nothing. (DL, 177–78)

Gold, for his part, felt sure that West was "fundamentally on the side of
the people" – though still afflicted by such lamentable bourgeois diseases
as indirection and an addiction to symbolism.[48] The judgment is predictable, given Gold's literary criteria; but what strikes me as surprising is
the extent to which West, at least toward the end of his life, appears to
have shared it. In an important letter to Malcolm Cowley written in
September 1939, West casts himself as something of a proletarian writer
manqué, and laments that very skeptical worldliness which he always
seems so overanxious to maintain:

> [I] write out of hope for a new and better world – But I'm a comic
> writer and it seems impossible for me to handle any of the "big things"
> without seeming to laugh or at least smile. Is it possible to contrive a
> right-about face with one's writing because of a conviction based on a
> theory? I doubt it. What I mean is that out here we have a strong
> progressive movement and I devote a great deal of time to it. Yet
> although this new novel is about Hollywood, I found it impossible to
> include any of those activities in it. . . . Take the "mother" in
> Steinbeck's swell novel – I want to believe in her and yet inside myself
> I honestly can't. When not writing a novel – say at a meeting of a
> committee we have out here to help the migratory worker – I do
> believe it and try to act on that belief. But at the typewriter by myself
> I can't. I suppose middle-class upbringing, skeptical schooling, etc. are
> too powerful a burden for me to throw off – certainly not by an act of
> will alone. ALAS!
>
> I hope all this doesn't seem silly to you – to me it is an ever-present
> worry and what, in a way, is worse – an enormous temptation to
> forget the bitter, tedious novels and to spend that time on committees
> which act on hope and faith without a smile. (It was even a struggle
> this time for me to leave off the quotation marks.)[49]

If the political edge to West's nauseated perspective on consumer culture
does not necessarily reveal itself explicitly, we cannot assume that it is

nonexistent, or that he has no affinities with the literary Communists of the thirties. And it certainly is not fair to say, as Raban does at one point, that West's disaffection is no more profound than "being sickened by the excess of an overstocked refrigerator or a sweaty crowd on a Christmas-shopping spree."[50] As West himself explained to William Carlos Williams, the act of reading against the American grain was "idiomatic in pain": and this pain is caused not only by random violence or neurotic self-torment, but also by social ills.

West's interest in the fate of Native Americans, to which his critics have paid surprisingly little attention, suggests a further angle on his social criticism. According to his brother-in-law, S. J. Perelman, West was "much impressed with the Indian and the bad deal he had received." As late as 1939, West had hopes of writing a screenplay on the Seminole leader Osceola, who had all the qualities of an American hero, "yet, in the end, lost everything."[51] West's fascination with such topics was shared by many intellectuals of the thirties. Jay Martin has noted that the popularity of Oliver La Farge's 1930 novel, *Laughing Boy,* did much to spark renewed interest in Native American matters; but this interest was also in some sense an inevitable concomitant of the decade's fascination with the idea of "culture" – and of an authentic American culture in particular. The Depression decade was a time when cultural anthropology rose to greater prominence. The important and popular work of Margaret Mead, Ruth Benedict, and Robert Redfield laid down what George Marcus and Michael Fischer have termed the "ethnographic paradigm" of their discipline, a paradigm that carries as part of its very raison d'être, "a submerged and unrelenting critique of Western civilization as capitalism."[52] Like the more pessimistic Marxist theory of Benjamin and the Frankfurt school, this ethnographic critique challenges the idea of Western civilization as a narrative of progress: from the point of view of non-Western cultures, especially, in the United States, of Native Americans, the benefits of the machine, of technology, and of abundant commodities may appear rather negligible in relation to what they might destroy – or might already have destroyed. It is no accident, for instance, that Stuart Chase, the author of the best-selling ethnographic text *Mexico: A Study of Two Americas* should first have emerged as a fierce critic of consumer culture, who in his book, *Your Money's Worth,* describes the U.S. as a "Wonderland" of deceptive salesmanship, through which the consumer wanders like a lost and gullible Alice.[53] The critique of mass culture, the critique of the commodity, and the study of anthropology were plainly interwoven in the culture of the thirties.

While the ethnographic critique relied on different principles (a validation of nature, spiritual vision, and organic communities) than thirties Marxism, there are certainly ways in which these two lines of critique could also be seen as contiguous rather than simply antithetical. Despite its emphasis on technology and optimistic teleology, American Marxism in the thirties retained, as I have argued, elements of what Raymond Williams has termed a residual critique, insofar as it opposed the emergent culture of abundance from the point of view of an earlier, more Spartan culture of production. (And we might recall that William Empson categorized proletarian literature as a version of the pastoral.) Moreover, the "ethnographic critique" held a certain emotional appeal that was by no means lost on American Communists. Mike Gold again emerges as an interesting figure: while he was quite orthodox in the hope he held out for the transformative power of modern factories (under a more just system of ownership, of course), his own work was not unaffected by the idea of the natural and pastoral, and he certainly did not ignore the critical potency of the figure of the Native American.[54] One of his "Worker's Correspondence" poems uses such a figure quite effectively:

> Arrested as a picket in a recent strike
> I have found my cellmate here an Indian Chief
> His name John Thunder of the Ottawas
> Once his father owned America.[55]

There is, then, a resonant context for West's use (both in *A Cool Million* and in *The Day of the Locust*) of the figure of the American Indian – the most obvious victim of the march of "civilization" – to denounce the absurdity and triviality of American material culture. I would argue that the very presence of his strange Indian chiefs brings to bear something of the ethnographic critique and suggests that in West's mind also the culture of abundant commodities was based, finally, on injustice and dispossession.

His take on this critique, however, is wonderfully twisted – and no less ironic than his take on the more orthodox Marxist analysis. The character of Chief Israel Satinpenny in *A Cool Million* seems designed to avoid any easy contrast between the authentic culture of the primitive man, in touch with nature, and the artificial civilization of the machine man. Satinpenny is a Harvard man, who can explicitly deny his own noble savagery by his sophisticated invocation of Spengler and Valéry and their gloomy view of modernity. Even so, his call to arms stands as a powerful plaint against the gigantic absurdity of a system of production responsible not only for that vaunted profusion of marvelous commodities, but also for such disasters as the Great Depression:

"In our father's memory this was a fair, sweet land, where a man could hear his heart beat without wondering if what he heard wasn't an alarm clock, where a man could fill his nose with pleasant odors without finding that they came from a bottle. Need I speak of springs that had never known the tyranny of iron pipes? Of deer that had never tasted hay? Of wild ducks that had never been banded by the U.S. Department of Conservation?

"In return for the loss of these things, we accepted the white man's civilization, syphilis and the radio, tuberculosis and the cinema. We accepted his civilization because he himself believed in it. But now that he has begun to doubt, why should we continue to accept? His final gift to us is doubt, a soul-corroding doubt. He rotted this land in the name of progress, and now it is he himself who is rotting. The stench of his fear stinks in the nostrils of the great god Manitou.

"In what way is the white man wiser than the red? We lived here from time immemorial and everything was sweet and fresh. The pale-face came and in his wisdom filled the sky with smoke and the rivers with refuse. What, in his wisdom, was he doing? I'll tell you. He was making clever cigarette lighters. He was making superb fountain pens. He was making paper bags, doorknobs, leatherette satchels. All the powers of water, air and earth he made to turn his wheels within wheels within wheels. They turned, sure enough, and the land was flooded with toilet paper, painted boxes to keep pins in, key rings, watch fobs, leatherette satchels.

"When the paleface controlled the things he manufactured, we red men could only wonder at and praise his ability to hide his vomit. But now all the secret places of the earth are full. Now even the Grand Canyon will no longer hold razor blades. Now the dam, O warriors, has broken and he is up to his neck in the articles of his manufacture.

"He has loused the continent up good. But is he trying to de-louse it? No, all his efforts go to keep on lousing up the joint. All that worries him is how he can go on making little painted boxes for pins, watch fobs, leatherette satchels . . . he is dying of a surfeit of shoddy."
(CM, 156–57)

There is no pathos here: none of that humanistic criticism-through-pity evoked, for instance, by the equally apocalyptic denunciation of poverty amid plenty in *The Grapes of Wrath*, where Steinbeck decries the injustice of a situation in which children must die of pellagra while "golden mountains" of oranges are set ablaze for the sake of profits.[56] Indeed, the overheated and somewhat comic bombast of the passage is a sign that Satinpenny does not escape West's parodic humor. But the humor should not necessarily be read as a distancing effect; indeed, the deliberately incongruous references to Valéry and Spengler (like the silly references to banjos and Brooks Brothers suits in *The Curse of Columbus* playlet) may be a curious sign of the author's identification with Satinpenny: West specifically cited the ideas of Valéry and Spengler as important influences on himself and his generation.[57] And as in the case of "Chamber of American Horrors," the element of comedy does not invalidate the social criticism. The speech presents one of the rare occasions in which West asks, "What has been lost?" (the question that Kenneth Fearing asks so urgently), and actually answers it in direct, even rather romantic and pastoral terms: "a fair, sweet land" – nature unproduced, undefiled, authentic. West's critique, moreover, works, characteristically, through *things*: objects which emblematize an economic system that ignores real need and use. The list of the products that the "paleface" continues to churn out absurdly and to his own demise are not just random or silly. They are all, significantly, what I would call metacommodities, things that you "need" only because you have other things: cigarette lighters, little painted boxes for pins, watch fobs, paper bags, key rings, leatherette satchels. West's Indian chief leaves us with a frightening image, perhaps surreal, perhaps postmodern, of nature "produced": the Grand Canyon itself as metacommodity, a massive receptacle for razor blades.

The Indian in *The Day of the Locust* offers an even sharper indictment of consumer culture, precisely because of the fact that, unlike the blustering Chief Satinpenny, he seems bereft of authentic speech. He mouths received opinions (such as the view that "greasers" are good with horses) and old gags (such as the signature line from an old vaudeville act that he does in a Yiddish accent: "Vas you dere, Sharley?"). Like Chief Jack Raven in *A Cool Million* (and the real Sitting Bull before him), who ends up as an exhibit in a traveling show, this man, ignominiously referred to as Chief Kiss-my-Towkus, has become part of the commodity spectacle. When Tod Hackett encounters him outside the Sunset Boulevard saddlery store, he is wearing a sandwich board that reads

TUTTLE'S TRADING POST

for

GENUINE RELICS OF THE OLD WEST

Beads, Silver, Jewelry, Moccasins,

Dolls, Toys, Rare Books, Postcards,

TAKE BACK A SOUVENIR

from

TUTTLE'S TRADING POST

(DL, 172)

In terms of his social function this "chief" is indistinguishable from a cigar store Indian. He has been turned into an advertisement and announces for us that the history of the West has been reduced to curios, relics, and souvenirs – curios, however, that are "idiomatic in pain," bearing the features of a history of violence and dispossession. The Hollywood saddlery store (the hangout of formerly real cowboys and Indians now turned into movieland simulacra of themselves) displays, among its fancy boots and saddles, a large collection of torture instruments: "fancy braided quirts, spurs with great spiked wheels and double bits that looked as though they could break a horse's jaw without trouble" (DL, 108). These Western accoutrements are, to use the phrase from *Miss Lonelyhearts*, "the paraphernalia of suffering": signs of the loss not only of "a fair sweet land" but of authentic experience.

"THE REVOLUTIONARY ENERGIES OF THE OUTMODED"

His brief description of the Hollywood Indian offers, perhaps, a symbolic summation of West's critique of commodity culture. This image, along with West's displays of evocative objects, helps us define the political strategy implicit in his work. Let us for a moment juxtapose the image of the Indian in the sandwich board, of the dispossessed *as* a billboard, with the image described at the beginning of this chapter: Bourke-White's photograph of the advertising poster and the bread-line – the image of the dispossessed *under* the billboard. The comparison could perhaps elicit the same complaints against West that I have already raised in this chapter: the Hollywood Indian is clearly a grotesque, not sufficiently human to evoke any pathos or sympathy. He fades in interest compared with the list of things inscribed on his person. Whereas Bourke-White's picture creates a dialectical tension between the official optimism of consumer culture and the human lives which expose that optimism, West seems to offer us an image of one-dimensional negativity: human beings can no longer serve as truth tellers since they have themselves become things, or advertisements of things; they too are drawn into the world of the commodity spectacle. (And, in case I seem to be making too much of the unfortunate Kiss-My-Towkus, we should recall that his fate is not singular in West's novels: Miss Lonelyhearts's problem, for instance, is precisely the fact that he must operate as an advertisement for his newspaper, and Lemuel Pitkin's melancholy fate is to become an advertisement for the American fascists.) West's image, while itself still imbued with critical irony, alerts us to the potential elimination and assimilation of opposition and critique in a world of commodities – or at least the elimination of the kind of critique that depends on our pity for the unfortunate or on the demystifying potential of the proletariat and the poor.

In this sense it is fair to say that West epitomizes the danger of the spectacularization of culture in a way that Bourke-White's documentary truth telling cannot. Her famous photograph, after all, has become something of a cultural souvenir itself: it is collected in *The Best of Life* and treasured as an icon of the period. The juxtaposition, in short, does not necessarily favor Bourke-White's picture with its accessible moral and emotional statement; it also reveals, particularly from our historical perspective, the prophetic strengths of West's discomfiting method. It suggests, moreover, the signal respect in which the social realist techniques of the thirties are suspect (and here we must include not only Bourke-White's photograph, or the related texts I have cited in this chapter, but also the widespread attempts of both the cultural "proletarians" and the artists and writers of the Popular Front to represent the sufferings of the marginalized). Such techniques court what Walter Benjamin has described as the "old and fatal confusion – perhaps it begins with Rousseau – of glorification of the simplicity of life of those in bondage," a shortsighted attempt to "touch the flesh of reality."[58] In its appeal to the true life of those who suffer, the documentary art of the period attempts to claim for itself the sanction of reality, of anti-ideology; but as the example of the Bourke-White photograph suggests, this claim cannot ultimately prevent the art object's ideological reincorporation into the parade of culture, its becoming just another period image.

West, however, avoids this "fatal confusion" of too easily invoking the "flesh of reality." His work suggests that not only the human face and figure can provide a dialectical and potentially revolutionary reading of culture. We might see his focus on things, his curious representation and imitation of social reification, in the light of the metaphor Benjamin applies to the practice of the Surrealists: they do not, he argues, attempt to humanize a world of objects, but "exchange . . . the play of human features for the face of an alarm clock that in each minute rings for sixty seconds."[59] One could say, in other words, that West shares Benjamin's own historiographic and critical practice (suggested in part by his reading of the Surrealists): he focuses not on the sphere of production, but on the sphere of consumption and exchange, and devises ways in which "cultural commodities" can be transformed into "dialectical images."[60]

The concept of the "dialectical image" is not easily defined; but I would venture a description that suggests all manner of interpretive applications to West's work. The creation of dialectical images involves the discovery and representation of a historical document, object, sample, or text, of a peculiar ambiguity: an ambiguity that allows us to see both the denial and the possiblity of a revolutionary utopia. It is an image which, as Jackson Lears phrases it, would "call into question the given facticity of the existing social world and promote the hope of transcending it."[61] Or in Benjamin's own words, it is an image in which "we begin to recognize the monuments of the bourgeoisie as ruins even before they have crumbled."[62] This definition would include, for instance, those moments I have described as the "double takes" of West's unpublished short stories. And it suggests grounds on which Jonathan Raban's descriptions of West's novels as assembly lines, grinding out objects and objectified human beings, can be turned into a positive rather than a negative judgment.[63] It is only as a maker of dialectical images (or so Benjamin would argue) that West could identify with the proletariat not as a mere well-wisher or ideological patron, but as a producer running an assembly line of skewed, distorted, secondhand, outmoded versions of the prized commodities of American culture: tarnished objects in hock that mimic the brand-new arrays of its department stores, whorehouses that rival its museums, painted facades that mock its monuments.

Just as for Benjamin the privileged source of dialectical images was the arcades of Paris, the source for West was the streets of Hollywood, that papier-mâché "paradise on earth" which is simultaneously a hell of desire and thwarted dreams, a city whose plenitude and variety are figured as "conflagration" of all known historical styles and artifacts, and of bourgeois civilization itself. New, but already crumbling and always immediately obsolete, the capital of the media moguls is made up of what Benjamin might call a series of "wish-symbols" turned "into rubble."[64] It is perhaps not entirely coincidental, therefore, that West's ruinous and seedy Hollywood in fact resembles Benjamin's descriptions of the decayed arcades of the twentieth century (the present moment that Benjamin's history of the nineteenth-century arcades addresses, in the same way that West's Hollywood now speaks to the postmodern scene of television images, shopping malls, and theme parks). These latter-day arcades had become a place, just like West's Hollywood, where one could buy pictures, postcards, and souvenirs, where one could see films, pornography, and freak exhibits. They were, as Benjamin's friend Siegfried Kracauer noted, a space where "desires, geographical excesses . . . images ripped out of sleep," all those things that are banned elsewhere, were made manifest, and where, in their very grotesquerie, humiliation, and exile, these things present a kind of "protest action" against the somewhat more tasteful "facade-culture outside."[65] This idea of seediness and perversity as a "protest action" is readily applied to *The Day of the Locust* and allows us to perceive a critical dimension in West's superannuated grotesques and their off-color activities, which are clearly presented as mockeries of mainstream culture. For instance, Abe Kusich, the dwarf and Hollywood bookkeeper, compares himself to Morgan and Lloyds; Harry Greener, vaude-villian and charlatan, dresses like a cheap imitation of a banker; Miss Jennings, the madam, runs a brothel just as other cultured ladies might run a lending library (DL, 62, 77, 73). No wonder West felt that a character like Steinbeck's Ma Joad, the sturdy, stoic heroine of produc-tion, would throw his "peculiar half-world" – the dialectical image of the bourgeois world in decay – completely out of whack.

Perhaps West's most interesting dialectical image, and the one with which I would like to conclude this discussion of West and the spectacle of culture, is the souvenir – the object Benjamin describes as "the sure harbinger of the beginning of death."[66] While ostensibly serving as the token of personal inclusion in some moment of lived pleasure or authen-tic culture, the souvenir is also in West the sign of absence and exclusion. An unpublished story, "The Adventurer," describes a collection of such objects: "fans, perfume bottles, an embroidered slipper, a gilt dance card, theatre programs, elaborate menus."[67] What makes this collection so compelling is that these are the mementos of the pleasure of others, picked out of a dumbwaiter by the janitor. The wider implications of this image, as symbolic of the souvenir-like nature of the culture at large, are quite explicitly suggested. As the story progresses, the protag-onist suddenly comes to see the library, the site of his own vicarious adventures, as no different from this pathetic collection: it is, he realizes, "the Apocalypse of the Second Hand!"[68]

This intriguing phrase, which seems to me very similar in its implica-tions to Benjamin's equally oracular phrase, "the revolutionary ener-gies" of the "outmoded," resonates far beyond the context of this curi-ous little text.[69] Its explosive suggestions, however, are given dramatic and narrative form only in the very last scene of West's last novel. It is a mesmerizing scene, and I shall return to discuss its meaning more fully in the next chapter. But we might note for the moment that the curious sense of relief that accompanies this outburst of violence is at least partly explained by the frustration instilled by a culture of souvenirs: it is with the mob riot which concludes *The Day of the Locust* that those who have been doomed to a life of marginality, of spectator status, take their revenge. The mob is, significantly, a mob of souvenir hunters on the rampage: "Individually," West comments, "the purpose of its members might simply be to get a souvenir, but collectively it would grab and rend" (DL, 176).[70] The event (which Tod Hackett's painting, *The Burn-ing of Los Angeles*, depicts as the fall of civilization) could be understood as West's imagination of the "revolutionary energies" of the secondhand: the moment when the pent-up oppositional forces of the outmoded, the excluded, and the superannuated are explosively released. The city, pasted together out of all of history like some world's fair, is set ablaze by a mob of new barbarians in a carnival mood. West's art, one might finally say, replaces the archaic image of the triumphal march of culture with the counterimage, anarchic and frightening, but certainly also liberatory, of the sacking of civilization.

7

"When You Wish upon a Star"
Fantasy, Experience, and Mass Culture

Wishes were everywhere: the speculative desires for wealth typical of the late twenties – fed by bond salesmen, Old Counselors on the radio, and newspaper hucksters – exploded into uncontrolled wishing on all levels of life in the thirties; for now a gulf wider than ever before, an unbridgeable gulf perhaps, lay between the ideals of society and the possibilities of fulfilling them.

Jay Martin, *Nathanael West: The Art of His Life*

As things lose their use value, they are hollowed out in their alienation and, as ciphers, draw meanings in. Subjectivity takes control of them, by loading them with intentions of wish and anxiety.

Theodor Adorno, letter to Walter Benjamin,
5 August 1935

Nathanael West's distinctive contribution to the literature and social criticism of the thirties lies in his recognition of the importance of collective dreams and desires, in his understanding that the Depression was a matter not only of people wanting food and shelter, but also of people wanting "to add inches to the biceps and to develop the bust . . . to write and live the life of an artist . . . to be an engineer and wear leather puttees . . . to develop a grip that would impress the boss" (ML, 22).[1] Most remarkable, perhaps, is his sense that collective dreams are not just evidenced in movies or soaps or advertisements, but that they also saturate the very objects circulated in his culture: that mass-produced *things,* in short, can be wishes of sorts. (What strange desire, one wonders, is wrapped up in those "leather puttees"?) This materialization of wishing is, I would argue, the central preoccupation of West's Hollywood novel, *The Day of the Locust.* In Hollywood even the fashions sported by the "masqueraders" on the street are imbued with dreams of instant change:

166

> The fat lady in the yachting cap was going shopping, not boating; the man in the Norfolk jacket and Tyrolean hat was returning, not from a mountain, but an insurance office; and the girl in slacks and sneaks with a bandanna around her head had just left a switchboard, not a tennis court. (DL, 60)

The city's architecture, likewise, is described as a catalogue of escapist daydreams: "Mexican ranch houses, Samoan huts, Mediterranean villas, Egyptian and Japanese temples, Swiss chalets, Tudor cottages, and every possible combination of these styles" line the slopes of its canyons (DL, 61). This mishmash of exotic styles – all those turrets, minarets, and columns – is explicitly identified as the material embodiment of a "builder's fancy" or a movie mogul's whim (DL, 61, 175).

West's descriptions of Hollywood in the thirties (which, he felt, were so accurate they could be backed up with a photographic study for *Look* or *Life*) are illuminated by Walter Benjamin's observation that in Paris of the nineteenth century – Paris in the time of the arcades – the new possibilities of iron-and-glass construction allowed architecture to occupy the role of the unconscious.[2] The same claim, it seems to me, could be made with regard to West's city, constructed, as it is, out of even more plastic substances. West's protagonist, Tod Hackett, notices that the buildings are "all out of plaster, lath and paper," but he charitably "blame[s] their shape on the materials used":

> Steel, stone and brick curb a builder's fancy a little, forcing him to distribute his stresses and weights and to keep his corners plumb, but plaster and paper know no law, not even that of gravity. (DL, 61)

Despite the brand-new possibilities offered by these cheap but protean materials, the architectural "wish-images" take their shapes (as Benjamin might have predicted) from utopian forms of the past – specifically from fairy tales: "a miniature Rhine castle with tarpaper turrets pierced for archers" (DL, 61) and "domes and minarets out of the *Arabian Nights*" (DL, 159). West's Hollywood is, in short, not simply the city where the fantasies of the silver screen are produced, it is itself such a fantasy: a place that one of West's critics has called "the Land of Wish."[3]

In this chapter, I extend that epithet to West's fictional world at large. My contention is not only that the wish is key to our understanding of the phantasmagoric imagery of his novels, but that West's theory of wishing, if I may call it that, implies a theory of mass culture – the social and institutional guise of the wish. Again it seems to me that this implicit theory resonates with the work of the Frankfurt school – with that of Benjamin, of course, but also with some of the gloomily revolutionary moments in the work of Adorno. For both these critics (and indeed for Marx, who insisted on its mysterious nature) the commodity is not an inert *thing*, but a *text:* a text that bears a surprisingly contradictory and complicated message. Mass-produced objects, as Adorno observed, can become "controlled" by subjectivity, by wishes and fears.[4] This "subjectivity," moreover, is not just the meaning imposed by the producers, but the meaning attached to the object by the potential, current, or even (as in the important case of the secondhand object) the *former* owner – by the consumer, in short. In this respect, one could argue that the formal interests of the Frankfurt school critics – their analyses of mass-produced texts – are more open to contested meanings than is often supposed. The very form of such a text may register a struggle between the purely functional, profit-oriented intentions of the "culture industry" and the utopian desires of ordinary people.[5] It is possible, in other words, to discover in Critical Theory a space for the "Land of Wish," which may prove to be nothing other than the landscape of the political unconscious.

WEST'S DISEASE

The importance of the wish in West's work was perhaps first emphasized by W. H. Auden, who declared (in one of the "Interludes" from *The Dyer's Hand*) that West's novels were essentially "parables about a Kingdom of Hell whose ruler is not so much the Father of Lies as the Father of Wishes." West's nearly exclusive fixation on a condition of terminal wishfulness led Auden to compare him to a physician specializing in a single ailment, which the poet, in honor of its discoverer, named "West's Disease." He describes the symptoms as follows:

> This is a disease of the consciousness which renders it incapable of converting wishes into desires. A lie is false; what it asserts is not the case. A wish is fantastic; it knows what is the case but refuses to accept it. All wishes, whatever their apparent content, have the same and unvarying meaning: "I refuse to be what I am." A wish, therefore, is either innocent or frivolous, a kind of play, or a serious expression of guilt and despair, a hatred of oneself and every being one holds responsible for oneself.
>
> Our subconscious life is a world ruled by wish but, since it is not a world of action, this is harmless; even nightmare is playful, but it is the task of consciousness to translate wish into desire. If, for whatever reason, self-hatred or self-pity, it fails to do this, it dooms a human being to a peculiar and horrid fate. To begin with, he cannot desire anything, for the present state of the self is the ground of every desire, and that is precisely what the wisher rejects. Nor can he believe anything, for a wish is not a belief; whatever he wishes he cannot help knowing that he could have wished something else.[6]

The metaphor of "disease" already marks the Auden essay as participating in the characteristic Cold War rhetoric about mass culture and politics: a rhetoric of germophobia, abounding in words like "virulence," "hygiene," "contamination," and "ooze," which as Andrew Ross has noted all too often makes the period's cultural pronouncements sound like lessons in immunology.[7] The reading of West's work implicit in the Auden "diagnosis" is thus (inevitably) ideologically fraught and marked by its own historical moment.[8] But it nevertheless has moments of insight, and I would like briefly to test its validity, not to praise or bury Auden, but to establish certain preliminary requirements for a theory of wishing that would best illuminate and account for West's cultural politics and artistic practice.

Auden's diagnosis remains useful in that it homes in on the key issue in West's work and alerts us to what still makes West seem so relevant: his novels' deep concern with the production of desire in an era of mass-mediated culture, and their prophetic grasp, even in the decade of the Great Depression, of "the psychopathology of affluence" that is to come.[9] One can detect in Auden's description of the eternal second-guessing of the compulsive wisher, who knows that he or she could always have wished for something else, the signs of that peculiarly postmodern shape of neurosis: the Lacanian desire to desire.

But in other respects the "West's Disease" essay is misleading, especially since it elides the sociopolitical dimension of West's work. We should perhaps note, first of all, that the medical metaphor might not have pleased West: after all, he has Miss Lonelyhearts launch a vehement attack on the "no morality, only medicine mentality" – the habit of describing all social ills in terms of disease, as abnormalities susceptible to the therapy of a "damned aspirin" (ML, 12–13). But as problematic as the metaphor itself is the fact that Auden locates the pathology within the individual consciousness; he blames the failure to translate wishes into desire, and thence into the "world of action," on personal morbidities like self-hate or resentment. Such psychologizing, of course, ignores the fact that West wrote at a time when a global depression stymied the dreams and ambitions of millions and when hopes and plans for one's life had per force to assume the character of wishing, to manifest themselves in gambling, betting, and games of chance.[10] Auden's assumption of an uncontingent subjectivity, and of the ability to determine one's own fate, is ahistorical to a degree that is disconcerting, even if we take into account his apostasy from the Marxist position he held in the thirties. Indeed, toward the end of the essay, when Auden does extend the blame for "West's Disease" beyond the individual psyche, he implies that democracy itself, with its greater equality of opportunity, generates the resentment of the mediocre who in the static societies of the past would simply have accepted their fate:

> There have, no doubt, always been cases of West's Disease, but the chances of infection in a democratic and mechanized society like our own are much greater than in the more static and poorer societies of earlier times.
>
> When, for most people, their work, their company, even their marriages were determined, not by personal choice or ability, but by the class into which they were born, the individual was less tempted to develop a personal grudge against Fate; his fate was not his own but that of everyone around him.
>
> But the greater the equality of opportunity in a society becomes, the more obvious becomes the inequality of the talent and character among individuals, and the more bitter and personal it must be to fail, particularly for those who have some talent but not enough to win them second or third place.[11]

Auden's theory of wishing devolves, in other words, into a reactionary theory of mass culture, corresponding to that presented, for example, in Ortega's *Revolt of the Masses:* a theory suspicious of the accession of the masses to the privilege of choice, antidemocratic, ascetic, and dangerously nostalgic. It is, curiously, not an unusual position among postwar liberal intellectuals. Since Clement Greenberg's seminal essay of 1939, "Avant-Garde and Kitsch," the mass culture debate had been marked by the (understandable) fear of totalitarianism; but this barbarism tended (unjustifiably) to be associated with an "excess of democracy, welling up from the apocalyptic moment, as Greenberg describes it, when 'every man, from the Tammany alderman to the Austrian house-painter, finds that he is entitled to his opinion.' "[12]

West's work does not coincide with such idealist and ultimately reactionary thinking. To accept Auden's analysis, one must ignore, for example, the picture presented in *A Cool Million,* where West's starry-eyed American Boy, despite his conscious decision to work his way up the ladder of success, is buffeted by the realities of the Depression until he joins a host of other American boys in the breadlines, in packing crate homes, and in the ranks of the fascists: a demise West figures quite brutally as physical mutilation or, as the subtitle would have it, as the "dismantling" of Lemuel Pitkin. Though not all of West's doomed characters are undone in this obvious a fashion, they are nevertheless clearly conceived as victims, betrayed by something much less metaphysical than Auden's "Father of Wishes."

But setting aside for the moment these overtly political considerations, it is fair to say that the "West's Disease" diagnosis tends to suppress some of the more uncomfortable – more postmodern – implications of West's work. Auden's notion of the wish depends on certain essentialist concepts that are constantly challenged and undermined in West's fiction. The essay assumes (commonsensically perhaps) that one can speak unproblematically of the self. The category of "what I am" – much as the fantasist might refuse it – still functions as a stable norm; the paralysis induced by "West's Disease" could, it would seem, be overcome if the wisher were to accept the "present state of self." Such a reading of West's work is problematized by the deliberately unconvincing theatricality of his "characters." It is impossible to think of most of these figures as representations of "selves" with any depth, stability, or capacity for change. Shrike in *Miss Lonelyhearts*, Shagpoke Whipple in *A Cool Million*, and Faye Greener in *The Day of the Locust* are most accurately described as conglomerations of speeches, platitudes, and gestures. In the case of characters who do not immediately strike one as grotesques or caricatures, such as Tod Hackett, the artist figure in *The Day of the Locust*, West seems to set out deliberately to destroy their credibility as personalities with "selves," "subconscious minds," or any other such profundities. Hackett, for instance, is described as having "a whole set of personalities, one inside the other like a nest of Chinese boxes" (DL, 60) – an infinite regress of containers opening to reveal further containers that entirely contradicts the notion of the "inner self."

This emptiness, flatness, and theatricality are entirely in keeping with West's announcement in his "Some Notes on Miss L." that a novelist can learn nothing about "reality" from Freud, though he may still be important as a kind of "Bulfinch," an encyclopedist of old mythologies.[13] Even though this remark emerges in the context of West's comments on his novelistic innovations in *Miss Lonelyhearts*, the suggestion that psychology has moved into the shady realms of myth should not be seen primarily as a matter of antimimetic modernist technique. West's rejection (or, perhaps more precisely, flattening out) of Freud, depth psychology, and character seems, on the contrary, to serve a representational purpose. He seems to have discerned in contemporary circumstances a challenge to the very nature and existence of the autonomous self. It is a threat that came to haunt the theorists of the Frankfurt school (although they might still explain the phenomenon in Freudian terms). It also concerned American observers even earlier in the decade. As I noted in Chapter 2, the sociologist Robert Lynd wrote with great urgency (in 1933, the same year *Miss Lonelyhearts* appeared) about the challenge that the accelerating production of needs in consumer society presented to the stable, rational personality of classical economics, a phenomenon that threatened to change the subject of old into "bundles of impulses and habits shaped in response to an unsynchronized environment."[14] Similarly, West suggests, in his unpublished story "The Adventurer," that character is haphazardly constituted of worthless odds and ends:

> Buttons, string, bits of leather, a great deal of soiled paper, a few shouts, a way of clasping the hands, of going up steps, of smoothing a lapel, some prejudices, a reoccurring dream, a distaste for bananas, a few key words repeated endlessly. With time . . . memories pile up, hindering action, covering everything, making everything second-hand, rubbed, frayed, soiled. The gestures and the prejudices, the dislikes, all become one and that one not itself but once removed, a dull echo.[15]

This remarkable passage suggests that a life that feeds on wish and fantasy (like that of Joe Rucker, the story's vicarious "adventurer") challenges any easy assumption of the continuity of personal experience, or the integrity of "what I am." One cannot help but notice how the language West uses here to suggest the dismantling of the subject foreshadows several key deconstructive tropes. He speaks of repetitions, recurrences, echoes without origin, of the one that is "not itself but always once removed": all hinting at the constant deferral of the ground-ing signifier or, to use West's own image, at the Chinese box one opens to find yet another Chinese box. But this groundlessness, whereby nothing is itself or original, is for West not the bliss of "free play," but a fearful dystopia: the whole world becomes the domain of the always already seen, heard, felt. As West phrases it in "The Adventurer," it is "The Apocalypse of the Second Hand!"[16] This undermining of authen-ticity throughout the social body is the real focus of West's special obsession. Wishing, in short, is not for West a matter of the denial of "the present state of self," but rather a general deferral of presence – of what Kenneth Fearing would have called "bona-fide life" – into memo-ries, habits, echoes.[17]

The distinction between fantasy and reality, or between the playful "world ruled by wish" and the "world of action," on which the diagno-sis of "West's Disease" depends, also strikes me as inapplicable to West's fictive world – and, for that matter, to the social formation it addresses. This distinction is, of course, sanctioned by common sense and repro-duced in the conventional oppositions between, say, the world of art and the "real" world or the "vulgar Marxist" opposition between the solid economic base and the ephemeral ideological superstructure. But perhaps the most troubling insight suggested in West's work is that wishes and dreams are no longer so easily confined to what Auden chooses to see as the "harmless" realm of the dream or the unconscious. The point is neatly brought home by the (formerly) oxymoronic phrase "the business of dreams" (ML, 22), which seems to resonate throughout

Miss Lonelyhearts; and it is reiterated by the description of the jumble of sets in the Hollywood studio backlot, where every wish that ever troubled an individual is reproduced in "plaster, canvas, lath and paint" (DL, 132) on what West calls a "dream dump." Dreams and illusions, West implies, have been brought under the sway of the political economy and have solidified into the obsolescent materiality of buildings and commodities – from the old vaudevillean Harry Greener's fraudulent "Miracle Solvent" to the successful screenwriter's imitation Old South mansion (DL, 91, 68).

Such material wishes are left out of the diagnostic picture of "West's Disease," and necessarily so, since they would challenge the idealist – or, indeed, wishful – notion that the consciousness must translate wishes into desires and thence into actions. On the streets of Hollywood, wishes are conscious, concrete, and even profitable, but people are still passive, frustrated "starers," hating those who seem to live that "bona-fide life." There is little chance that this kind of wish could be redeemed or transformed by an act of will: "Only dynamite," Tod Hackett muses, "would be of any use" against the architectural excesses he observes (DL, 61). Nor is this Hollywood dreamland adequately theorized as a "refusal of what is the case." Though permeated with make-believe, it clearly is there; it is "the case."

We should be cautious, however, not to confuse the solidity of the commodified wishes that we encounter in West's fiction with any comfortable notion of "reality." Wishes are not made "real" at the Hollywood "dream dump" (which functions as an apocalyptic figure for mass-mediated culture in general), but they are made "photographic" (DL, 132): two-dimensional rather than three-dimensional. It is thus no accident that all the Hollywood dreams have the aspect of the facade, the masquerade, and the movie set. They are perfect examples of Daniel Boorstin's "pseudo-events": simulations that can no longer be defined in contradistinction to the norm of "what is the case," since they cumulatively undermine the very category of the real.[18] Or, perhaps more exactly, West's conception of wishes seems to prefigure Guy Debord's conception of the society of the spectacle. For West, as for Debord, the disintegration of the real into the image, the mock-up, and the seedy facade is correlated with the domination of the commodity form. It is at the moment when even dreams become a business that all the common-sense categories of which I spoke earlier are absorbed and erased in the totality of the spectacle: illusion as reality, reality as illusion.[19]

This deconstruction is illustrated perfectly in an unpublished short story by West from the early thirties, "Mr. Potts of Pottstown." This story could easily serve as a parable illustrating Debord's nightmare of the total invasion of the social space by the spectacle, turning the world into a museum or an amusement park and rendering us all tourists and spectators: permanent fantasists.[20] Mr. Potts, a kind of southern Don Quixote, full of heroic dreams, runs a hunt club in Pottstown, Tennessee, in spite of the fact that there is no game in the local woods. All is well, until the townsfolk abandon Mr. Potts's pet dream and sign up with a rival fantasy, an alpine club. Mr. Potts now sets out to confront the Real – the actual Alps, symbol for all the Romantic poets of the sublime and irreducible power of nature, of the unproduced. He orders climbing gear in the latest mode, "down to ice glasses and spiked shoes," from Abercrombie and Fitch, and sets out to ascend the Jungfrau. But on the slopes, he encounters a Swiss goatherd yodeling a familiar tune from under a luxuriant moustache and, to his great astonishment, recognizes the yodeler as Jimmy Larkin – a boy from Pottstown. Jimmy confesses that he is hired to provide local color: Switzerland, with its Alps, avalanches and crevasses, and all, is a gigantic fake, "an amusement park owned by a very wealthy company. The whole show is put on for the tourist trade – lakes, forests, glaciers, yodlers [sic], peasants, goats, milkmaids, mountains and the rest of it. It's all scenery. . . . It's like the opera."[21] And there, at the Magic Mountain of a universal Disneyland, the unpublished story leaves us. There is no unmediated reality for the wisher to confront, no cure for the individual sufferer. Just as the notion of the personality, of "what I am," becomes a problem in West's work, so too does the notion of "what is the case" become indistinguishable from the spectacular, from the profitable trade in the fantastic.

West's social criticism, then, goes beyond the identification of psychological aberrations, beyond fixed identities, and rigid differences between the real and the wishful. To understand the social imaginary of what West himself described as the "peculiar half world" of his fiction, we need to think rather more contradictorily, or dialectically; we need, in short, to find a more social and materialist conception of the wish.[22]

REIFIED WISHES

In the 1939 essay "On Some Motifs in Baudelaire" (an essay I have discussed briefly in relation to the fragmentary character of modern lives represented in Kenneth Fearing's work), Walter Benjamin offers a brief meditation on the idea of wishing. These observations offer suggestions for a fresh, and, I think, more accurate, reading of West's work. Like Auden, Benjamin distinguishes between wishing and desire – but seems to reverse the latter's terms. For Benjamin a wish, far from being sealed off from action in the frivolous realm of the subconscious, amounts to "a kind of experience." This somewhat paradoxical observation is developed in a discussion of Goethe's dictum that "what one wishes for in one's youth, one has in abundance in old age":

> The earlier in life one makes a wish, the greater one's chances that it will be fulfilled. The further a wish reaches out in time, the greater the hopes for its fulfillment. But it is experience that accompanies one to the far reaches of time, that fills and divides time. Thus a wish fulfilled is the crowning of experience. In folk symbolism, distance in space can take the place of distance in time; that is why the shooting star, which plunges into the infinite distance of space, has become the symbol of a fulfilled wish.[23]

In other words, the wish functions as something of a roadmap, a pattern, or a thread for a life story. As such it is akin to Auden's conception of "desire," which (though it remains undefined in his essay) seems to have the character of a decision, to have a shaping influence on a person's life. Benjamin's rather fanciful definition is best understood as a hypothetical antithesis to a different kind of dreaming, and one that, as we have already seen, was particularly prevalent in the American thirties: the gambler's "desire to win and make money." Gambling, as Benjamin sees it, is entirely sealed off from the kind of continuous and shaping experience he associates with the wish: with each hand or each roll of the die the game starts all over again, canceling out whatever went before.[24] The gambler's desire, ever identical, ever repetitive, thus resembles Auden's "wishes," those dreams of instant transformation that can never extend into commitment or belief.

But whereas Auden's oppositions are placed in the static and judgmental relationship implicit in his medical metaphor (whereby "desire" is somehow normal and mere wishing an illness), Benjamin implicitly places his oppositions in a historical perspective: the images of the falling star and the roulette wheel represent modes of dreaming characteristic of different historical moments and produced by different material conditions. The reference to folk symbolism (and possibly even the mention of Goethe) suggests that the wish – along with the continuous, cumulative experience that could bring it to fulfillment – belongs to an earlier time. This explains why Benjamin's evocation of the wish does not strike a contemporary reader as "true." The passage I cited really makes sense only as a touchstone, an imagined positive, in the broader context of Benjamin's materialist history of experience: a history that includes a theory of mass culture and traces a process of irreversible fragmentation of the self, of time, space, and narrative.

This history is explicitly invoked in the description of the short-lived but repetitive passion of the gambler. Despite the mirage of hope and the atmosphere of reckless adventure associated with the game of chance, it remains, for Benjamin, the mirror image of industrial production – which is equally futile and empty, and in which experience also counts for nothing. Like the victims of "West's Disease" evoked in Auden's essay, the gambler is doomed to a hell of passivity, but it is a material hell, defined as "the province of those who are not allowed to complete anything they have started."[25] This hell is not the doom of freakish caricatures in a metaphysical parable, or of an aberrant group afflicted by a disease, but the life of the gambler, of the factory worker, of the cog in the bureacratic machine, of the fellow who lost his job: of most people living and working under capitalism. For Benjamin, the Baudelairean gambler, accompanied by his eternal partner "La Seconde" (the secondhand), is the quintessential modern man, the man who has been "cheated out of his experience."[26]

As such, the gambler tells us much about West's California dreamers, embittered by their boring lives at machines, desks, and cash registers, who inspired the original title of *The Day of the Locust:* "The Cheated."[27] Indeed, there is a moment in the novel when West seems to provide, in a single visual image, a perfect encapsulation of Benjamin's meditations on the fragmentation of wishes into the mechanical repetitiveness of gambling. He describes the dwarf Abe Kusich, with his Tyrolean hat of "the proper magic green color," as a figure straight out of the fairy tale – the traditional home of the wish. But West duly notes a change: instead of the "crooked thorn stick," the Hollywood midget carries a rolled copy of the *Daily Running Horse* (DL, 64). The magic potency of the dwarf's staff, West seems to say, has shrunk into the modern hopes for a lucky break – the stock-in-trade of the Hollywood bookie.[28]

West's description of Faye Greener's daydreaming is likewise illuminated by Benjamin's meditation. Her fantasies (variations of the plots of B movies, inspired, or so it seems to Tod Hackett, by the Tarzan poster on her wall) are clearly not wishes or stories in the Benjaminian sense. The very size of her collection of dreams, which West describes as a thick pack of cards, makes it unlikely that any one of them would ever be cherished for long or become authenticated by a life's experience. As West's image suggests, they are standardized – interchangeable with each other or with the ice-cream soda that Faye sometimes settles for when she can't choose between the prefabricated alternatives. Whatever the exotic and fanciful details that might go into them – Russian counts, South Sea islands, modern Cinderellas – they all express the same impulse: to succeed, to marry a rich man, and especially to "make loads and loads of money" (DL, 105). West's depiction of Faye's dreaming, in short, allows us to make a connection between the passivity of the Hollywood extra, lolling on her bed as she waits for a lucky break, and the gambler slouched at roulette, hoping his number will come up. While West, of course, did not necessarily intend this association, he does explicitly compare Faye's fantasies with industrial production, the mirror image of gambling: Faye's technique is "mechanical," her dreams "manufactur[ed]" (DL, 104–5). No wonder, then, that she thinks of them not as experiences, but as commodities: the key dream in her collection is the one in which a Hollywood studio buys her stories – and she (again) makes loads and loads of money.

One could argue, I suppose, that these particular connections between West's novel and Benjamin's conception of wishing are only interesting coincidences. However, another more consistently developed link – indicative of substantial common ground between their understanding of mass-mediated culture – is suggested by the thematics of distance in both writers' work. It may at first strike one as odd that Benjamin should hit upon the category of distance to distinguish between the true wish and the gambler's desire: "The ivory ball which rolls into the *next* compartment, the *next* card which lies on top are the very antithesis of a falling star," which plunges through the vastness of outer space.[29] But in fact distance is an important concept in Benjamin's theoretical work. In his seminal essay "The Work of Art in the Age of Mechanical Reproduction" (1936), he describes the historical changes in the reception of the work of art (from the contemplative awe of the privileged viewer in front of the ritual artwork, to the amused distraction of the mass audience watching a film) in terms of the shriveling of "aura."[30] While "aura" functions as a multipurpose term for Benjamin and is variously identified with authority, awe, originality, and personal experience, it is in all contexts associated with spatial or temporal remoteness. As Benjamin notes in the Baudelaire essay, the concept of the aura comprises a "unique manifestation of a distance." This definition applies to Benjamin's most notable instances of the auratic: the inapproachability of the ceremonial object (as opposed to the mechanically reproduced object, brought into the homes of ordinary men and women), the evanescence of the Proustian *mémoire involontaire* (as opposed to readily available photographic memories), and the storyteller's "lore of faraway places" or "lore of the past" (as opposed to the information in the newspaper that equates a fire in a local attic with a distant revolution).[31] Moreover, all these examples, read the other way around, imply another key definition: mass culture, the social counterpart to the gambler's desire, is always characterized by the abolition of distance. It is available anywhere, anytime.

Whether West could have expressed this theoretical insight in explanatory prose must remain a matter of speculation and is finally beside the point. The idea constantly finds symbolic expression in the descriptive details and incidents of his novels. We need not search far for examples. The very first paragraph of *The Day of the Locust* juxtaposes the heroics of military history with the bureaucratized time and space of the present: "Around quitting time," Tod Hackett looks out of his office window to witness a routed army, in the glorious regalia of the Napoleonic era, fleeing past in disarray and disappearing behind a Mississippi steamboat. As it turns out, the mob – complete with dolmans and shakos, sabre-taches and muskets – is a bunch of extras from *Waterloo,* the movie. They are followed by "a little fat man, wearing a cork sun-helmet, polo shirt and knickers," yelling, "Stage Nine – you bastards – Stage Nine!" (DL, 59) through a megaphone. The humor is to some degree mock-heroic, relying on deflationary anachronism, on the incongruity of the archaic language and references. But the intention of the passage, unlike that of, say, Pope's mock-heroic, is not to valorize the past, but to suggest that in Hollywood the remoteness and uniqueness of past events and distant places have been abolished: Waterloo can happen, and happen again, right outside one's window. It is, moreover, likely to be a rather silly affair, since Hollywood's tendency is to render everything "remediable" (and here West would seem to agree with Bernard Rosenberg and Ernest van den Haag's generalization about mass culture).[32] As a result of its "technical reproducibility," the historical event loses its seriousness and authority: Hollywood's Battle of Waterloo holds no more terrors than the crevasses of Mr. Potts's Alpine amusement park; a military disaster means nothing more than a reshoot the next day and a larger bill from the costume company. West clearly delights in playing with the mock-heroic effects of Hollywood's repetition of history as farce, as one can see from deflationary jokes like "The French killed General Picton with a ball through the head and he returned to his dressing room. . . . The Scotch Greys were destroyed and went to change into another uniform" (DL, 133–34). But more important, this comic-strip-like abolition of historical finality is clearly linked to the loss of aura. West's Waterloo scene suggests that even death – the one event that should be singular and original – can become multiple, mass-produced, eternally repeatable. Tod Hackett watches, for example, how, again and again, a horse guard shouts "Vive l'Empereur!" clutches his bosom and dies. The scene raises, in short, the same ideas we discussed in connection with Fearing's poem "1933," where a supposedly irrevocable event like the loss of life or loss of virginity is likewise remedied, and repeated.

The idea of the vicinity of all styles, all places, and all of history is central to another piece of Westian bravura: the description of Tod Hackett's wanderings through the studio backlot (DL, 130–32). In pursuit of Faye Greener, Tod crosses a desert, complete with looming

sphinx, turns right to find himself on a cow town street with a plank
sidewalk, from which he can see a jungle compound with huts and
water buffalo, then steps through the doors of the "Last Chance Saloon"
onto a Parisian boulevard and Romanesque courtyard. From there incongruous details accumulate even more rapidly: Tod has to pass "the
skeleton of a Zeppelin, a bamboo stockade, an adobe fort, the wooden
horse of Troy, a flight of baroque palace stairs . . . part of the Fourteenth Street elevated station, a Dutch windmill, the bones of a dinosaur, the upper half of the Merrimac, a corner of a Mayan temple"
before he reaches the road he is heading for: an abbreviated odyssey that
adds nothing to his stock of experience. It is a passage that, as I noted
earlier, bears a fascinating resemblance to contemporary descriptions of
the Chicago World's Fair of 1933. Indeed, several items in this list can
be traced back to specific exhibits at the fair: the reproduction of the
Mayan temple, the stockade and fort (a reconstruction of Fort Dear-
born), the dinosaur (reproduced in the Sinclair Grotto of moving and
growling prehistoric monsters), and the zeppelin (the familiar blimp of
the Goodyear Company) were all on display in Chicago. One of the
most popular exhibitions, moreover, was called "Hollywood."[33] This
connection between Hollywood's "history of civilization" in the form
of a dream dump and the optimistic and much-touted message of the
Chicago Century of Progress is, of course, deeply ironic. The suggestion is that history can no longer be seen as the proud procession of
civilization – no longer as something that spans the distance of years –
but as the collapse and ruin of human wishes.

The implications of the "dream dump" passage are further illuminated
when we consider it in juxtaposition to a passage from Balzac's novel
La peau de chagrin – a description that Benjamin collected and annotated
as part of his research for the Arcades Project. The Balzac passage parallels
almost exactly West's allegorical vision of the Hollywood backlot as a
kind of a historical junkyard, as the "final" and ever-growing "dumping
ground" where every kind of human dream meets its simulacral end.
Balzac's young hero ventures into the overwhelmingly vast warehouse
of a four-story magazin d'antiquités:

> The young stranger first compared . . . three rooms stuffed with civili-
> zation, with sects, with divinities, with masterpieces, with royalties,
> with debaucheries, with reason and with madness to a mirror of many
> facets, each one representing a world. . . . The sight of so many na-
> tional or individual existences, attested by these human tokens which
> had survived them, in the end altogether numbed the young man's
> senses. . . . The ocean of furniture, of inventions, of fashions, of
> works, of ruins, composed an endless poem for him. . . . He clung to
> every joy, seized on every pain, took hold of every formula of exis-

tence and generously scattered his life and his emotions among the
simulacra of this plastic and empty world. . . . He was suffocating
under the debris of fifty vanished centuries, he was sick with all these
human thoughts, done in by all the luxury and art. . . . If modern
chemistry boils creation down to a gas, does not the soul just as
capriciously concoct terrible poisons by the rapid concentration of its
pleasures. . . . or its ideas? Do not men perish under the devastating
effect of some moral acid which has suddenly spread throughout their
inner being?

Both the warehouse and the Hollywood "dream dump" reveal what
Benjamin calls the "pathological aspect of the notion of 'Culture,' "
something far more vast and ruinous than the "disease" of individual
wishfulness.[34] If the studio backlot is, as Tod Hackett muses, a "history
of civilization in the form of . . . a dream dump," it is a paradoxical
history in which time and distance have no place: a history where the
extensiveness of narrative is replaced by the flatness of juxtaposition and
a history that relentlessly boils down, concentrates, and homogenizes all
the dreams and wonders of the world. Their presence in reproduction in
this "Sargasso of the imagination" is in fact a sign of their absence: the
loss of their uniqueness and authenticity.

What applies to the historical past also goes for the even more evasive
realm of story and legend. Much of the Hollywood kitsch in *The Day of
the Locust* simulates the traditional trappings of fairy tale and romance.
One can find, for instance, the dwarf's "magic green" Tyrolean hat, or
the turrets of Rhine castles straight out of the Brothers Grimm, or the
"domes and minarets out of the *Arabian Nights*," or the "Cinderella Bar"
in the shape of a slipper (DL, 64, 61, 143). These details reveal West's
understanding of the utopian dimension of consumer culture: that elusive promise of transformative magic of which even Harry Greener's
"Miracle Solvent" bears the trace. But simultaneously, the desperate
obviousness of these materialized fantasies has the effect of abolishing
the "uniqueness of distance." The remote and evanescent "once upon a
time" becomes the solid here-and-now of Hollywood Boulevard and in
the process loses all its auratic potency.

West's description of Kahn's Persian Palace makes this point particularly well. With its profusion of rosy minarets and columns, streaked
with violet searchlights, the building clearly solidifies a fantasy of oriental luxury – which, indeed, a huge electric sign identifies as Coleridge's
"Kubla Khan": "MR. KAHN," it spells out in letters ten feet high, "A
PLEASURE DOME DECREED" (DL, 175). One could, of course,
simply read the allusion as a neat deflation of the Hollywood mogul
who presumes to compare himself to the legendary warlord. But if one
recalls the details of Coleridge's poem, it seems that the implications of

the reference go beyond this supercilious (and anti-Semitic) mock-heroic. "Kubla Khan" offers a perfect encapsulation of all that Benjamin associates with the auratic. The mythical Xanadu, with its sacred river and measureless caverns, remote in time and space, is made even more distant by the fact that it is but a vaguely remembered fragment of a vision in a dream. The pleasure dome itself is an evanescent miracle: a momentary reconciliation of sun and ice, seen as a reflection "float[ing] on the waves." But the unique intensity of the lost experience is empowering, testimony to a magical presence, and the poem concludes at a pitch of romantic "awe" with the incantatory description of the intoxicated poet. The poem, one might say, is a true wish (as the plea "Could I revive within me . . . " suggests): a wish, born of a sense of loss, that would find fulfillment in a life devoted to the achievement of poetic craft.

The utopian fantasy embodied in Mr. Kahn's Persian Palace Theater, on the other hand, is perfectly accessible, offering luxury and an exotic "experience" to all comers at a small price. We might recall that, historically, the lavish picture palaces were indeed bearers of the utopian message of the culture of abundance (a message nicely debunked in Fearing's "Ballad of the Salvation Army," with its references to the "movies at night," the "one big bed," and the "big gold dome").[35] But the taste of luxury the "pleasure dome" offers is short-lived and the experience vicarious – as evidenced by the frustrated violence of the crowd that gathers outside the theater to catch a glimpse of the stars arriving for a world premiere. This horde of "starers" and "torchbearers" feels resentful and betrayed – and bored, West tells us, since they "don't know what to do with their time" (DL, 178). They are, in short, the exact antithesis of Benjamin's wisher, who is precisely the individual who knows the trajectory of his or her life. The fantasy materialized in Mr. Kahn's palace can never be their own, in the way that Coleridge's lost vision is indisputably his own.

All the spectacular assertions of the presence of utopia – the electric sign, the searchlight, the lavishness of the building, the impending arrival of the stars – finally amount to the artificial repackaging of "aura": they are the present signs of the absence of magic, or religious awe. West, significantly, describes the radio announcer, who provides a live commentary on the gala event, as a "a revivalist preacher whipping his congregation towards the ecstasy of fits" (DL, 176): this media preacher's task is to galvanize the crowd into an auratic response. But paradoxically, as the riot scene that closes the novel reveals, the fans are likely to respond only with a fiercer and more anarchic desire to bring things closer than the producers of mass-mediated culture have bargained for: crossing the barriers "to get a souvenir," to "grab and rend"

(DL, 176). It would seem, then, that for West the artificial reproduction of distance is a precarious and dangerous business (we might recall, for instance, the hysterical quality of the attempts by Miss Lonelyhearts to invoke and revivify Christ in the modern wasteland); and it is associated for him – as for Benjamin – with the fascist manipulation of the masses.[36]

THE DIALECTIC OF THE DREAM DUMP

Some final comparative comments are necessary if we are to understand the political implications of West's theory of the wish, and of mass culture, its institutional and material guise. For Benjamin, the abolition of the auratic has both positive and negative implications. The unique distance and awe that characterize the reception of the auratic artwork have, historically, reproduced the authoritarian relations of a hierarchical society. The shriveling of aura should therefore not be theorized undialectically as a pure loss. Mass-reproducible culture, conversely, represents a democratic impulse, a "sense of the universal equality of things." Its increasing importance is an index of the ascendancy of the modern masses and expressive of their "desire . . . to bring things 'closer' spatially and humanly, which is just as ardent as their bent towards overcoming the uniqueness of every reality by accepting its reproduction."[37] These theoretical speculations, which perhaps now seem all too familiar to us, can be rendered fresh and concrete again if we try to imagine the experience of an early radio listener (recorded by Alice Marquis in her cultural history of the thirties): a man who, after tuning in to the live coverage of a 1931 naval conference in London, was moved to write a letter commending "this marvellous new enterprise that permits ordinary men to button up their underwear to the accompaniment of an address by a European monarch."[38]

It is hard not to delight in this irreverently democratic juxtaposition. But it is also hard to ignore (especially after a discussion of West's curiously violent and painful work) the dystopian aspects of the same techniques of mass production and mass communication: universal standardization, loss of individuality, and even that characteristically postmodern specter, the "museumification" and "Disneyfication" of world history and geography. Indeed, we should note that after his 1936 essay, "The Work of Art in an Age of Mechanical Reproduction," Benjamin's conception of mass culture also became much less optimistic: the liberatory possibilities of the new mode of perception seemed to fade from view as he considered, in various forms, the menace of the modern fragmentation of experience. The "universal equality of things" (which Benjamin connects with the new antihumanist science of statistics) suggests, after all, not only democratic political possibilities, but also the totalitarian uniformity of fascism.[39]

West, on the other hand, never credited mass culture with the debunking capacities that Benjamin (if only for a while) regarded as inherent in the new media's very techniques of reproduction. Even in *Miss Lonelyhearts,* the mass-mediated solace of the newspaper advice column is figured as a kind of sham religion. Mass-mediated culture, the novel suggests, is not merely a matter of the reproduction of images, but a practice of simulation: the reproduction of lost aura in the form of the commodity. It is not, for West, a demystifying agent – at least not inherently and immediately so. The Hollywood we see in *The Day of the Locust* clearly represents a monstrous invasion of inauthenticity, reminiscent of the exhibition of American "Hideosities" and fakes from *A Cool Million:* the studio-lot sphinx is, after all, made of papier-mâché, the soldier's armor of cardboard, the waterfall of cellophane. One could easily be tempted, therefore, to define West as yet another practitioner of what Patrick Brantlinger has termed "negative classicism" (the habit of theorizing mass culture as social decay).[40] There are even moments when he seems to resemble those "positive classicists," Pound and Eliot. The Hollywood temple of Eros, in which the "god himself [lies] face downward in a pile of old newspapers and bottles" (DL, 131), reminds one of such Poundian images as the "Beer-bottle on the statue's pediment!" from Canto VII; and the desolation of the studio lot strongly recalls the gloomy symbolism of *The Waste Land,* with its "partially demolished buildings and broken monuments, half hidden by great, tortured trees, whose exposed roots writhed dramatically in the arid ground, and by shrubs that carried, not flowers or berries, but armories of spikes, hooks and swords" (DL, 132).

But while, from Eliot's point of view, the "immense panorama of futility and anarchy" can and should be ordered by a "mythic structure" and "made possible [again] for art," the waste land of West's fiction problematizes any such redemptive possibility.[41] It does not automatically follow from West's powerful critique of mass culture that he would endorse the promises and authority of high culture. This is not to say, of course, that critics have not tried to find redeeming artistic order in *The Day of the Locust.*[42] Even in the most nuanced and theoretically self-conscious reading of the novel to date, Thomas Strychacz discovers in it significant moments when West seems to endorse the "authoritative" and "privileged context" of art. For instance, when Tod Hackett compares the peculiar landscapes of Hollywood to the work of the painters of "Decay and Mystery" (Rosa, Guardi, and Desiderio), the association, Strychacz feels, "allows Tod to form chaos into composition"; the artistic order of the "old masters" frames the incoherent contemporary jumble, just as later on Tod's painting, "The Burning of Los Angeles" – and the language in which West describes the painting – "give structure to the chaos they describe."[43] Apart from the fact that this kind of ordering and redemption is primarily textual and aesthetic, there remains another (perhaps insuperable) difficulty with any assertion about cultural hierarchies in the novel. If the kitsch-scape of Hollywood resembles these paintings, the paintings in turn, with their "bridges which bridged nothing, . . . palaces that seemed of marble until a whole stone portico began to flap in the light breeze," and so forth, resemble the great historical dumping ground of Hollywood facades. It is only an *a priori* validation of them as "art" that gives them any interpretative privilege. Or to use another case in point: when West compares Homer Simpson, his utterly passive man of the crowd, to "one of Picasso's great sterile athletes, who brood hopelessly on pink sand, staring at veined marble waves" (DL, 83), Homer is not necessarily thereby transformed. His sterility and passivity could equally be transferred to the Picasso, and be read as a comment on the sterility and social impotence of the masterwork.

For West, in short, high culture is no more valuable, no more transformative, than what has been thought of as its mass-mediated antagonist. On the contrary, there are many suggestions in his work that high art shares the dissembling, facade-like aspect of mass-produced dreams. *The Day of the Locust,* for instance, records a snippet of Hollywood shoptalk, which suggests that West saw clearly that "art" could very well serve the same ideological interests as the mass media – indeed, that it could give the culture industry an appearance of respectability. A party guest remarks that the Hollywood moguls "ought to put some of the millions they make back into the business again":

> Like Rockefeller does with his Foundation. People used to hate the Rockefellers, but now instead of hollering about their ill-gotten oil dough, everybody praises them for what the Foundation does. It's a swell stunt and pictures could do the same thing. Have a Cinema Foundation and make contributions to Science and Art. You know, give the racket a front. (DL, 71)

Give the racket a front: this cutting bit of satire should not surprise us. From the very opening scene of his first novella, West associates the revered tradition of Western culture with an age-old image of deceit: the Trojan horse. And he strategically places the same beast in the rubble of the studio backlot, side by side with the dinosaur bones, the Mayan temple, and the Fourteenth Street el. On the "dream dump," the ruin of all wishes, of all received ideas of happiness, there is no distinction between high and low; high culture therefore offers no redemption.

West's utter negativity about art is one reason we cannot equate his cultural politics with Pound's and Eliot's elitist brand of cultural melancholy or with the Cold War liberals' vision of a Western tradition of high art, threatened by the germs of Communism and kitsch. We might also consider, in this regard, the observation that concludes the first chapter of *The Day of the Locust*. In response to Hollywood's parade of fashions and its smorgasbord of architectural styles, Tod Hackett, or perhaps the author himself, comments: "It is hard to laugh at the need for beauty and romance, no matter how tasteless, even horrible, the results. . . . Few things are sadder than the truly monstrous" (DL, 61). The remark, though mandarin in its revulsion at the ugliness of mass-produced dreams, demands sympathy for the dreamers. It expresses an attitude toward the mass audience that corresponds not so much to the disdain felt by the advocates of high culture as to, say, the emotions felt by Charlie Chaplin for his fans:

> What kind of a filthy world is this – that makes people lead such wretched lives that if anybody makes 'em laugh they want to kneel down and touch his overcoat, as though he was Jesus Christ raising 'em from the dead. There's a comment on life. There's a pretty world to live in. When those crowds come round me like that – sweet as it is to me personally – it makes me sick spiritually, because I know what's behind it. Such drabness, such ugliness, such utter misery that simply because someone makes 'em laugh and helps 'em to forget, they ask God to bless him.[44]

For West as well, mass culture is not a regrettable sign of the demise of culture, but a sign of need: of what is lacking at the hotel desk, at the switchboard, in the insurance office. The meaning of the Westian wish is not, as Auden would have it, "I refuse to be what I am," but rather "Things are not what they should be." To say this is not only to shift the debate from the psychological and cultural to the social and political. It also means that West's Hollywood, with its kitschy wishes and fake religions, does offer, after all, a moment of truth. It suggests, I think, that his novels (especially *Miss Lonelyhearts* and *The Day of the Locust*) can be read in light of Marx's dialectical insight that religion, though the pinnacle of illusion, is also the bearer of a diagnostic truth, an accurate index of intolerable conditions.

This dialectical turn should not strike literary scholars as extraordinary: the same kind of reading is, after all, brought into play by the indirection of irony and satire (and West is nothing if not a satirist), where human follies are exhibited and forced to speak wisely against their own nature. In its very effort at mystification and fantasy, the culture represented in *The Day of the Locust* gives the lie to the utopian claims of the American Dream and the national myth of California as the land of milk and honey. But to read West in a Marxian fashion raises the tricky question of whether yet another dialectical move is possible: Could one discover in West's very negativity, his peculiarly bleak case of *Kulturpessimismus,* a positive moment? Could one see in his refusal to offer a vision of cultural "health" an insistence on a revolutionary solution? This is terrain we should tread cautiously, since such negative dialectics could easily be no more than a kind of wishful thinking: a last-ditch effort to retrieve the possibility of a redemptive reading (though with the important distinction that it would at least be a redemptive reading of the social rather than the literary text).

This caution notwithstanding, it seems to me that West's work does indeed offer us something closely akin to those "dialectical images," which I also discussed at the end of the preceding chapter. We may certainly find such an image in the description of "The Burning of Los Angeles" (the large painting that absorbs Tod Hackett's imagination throughout *The Day of the Locust*):

> He was going to show the city burning at high noon, so that the flames would have to compete with the desert sun and thereby appear less fearful, more like bright flags flying from roofs and windows than a terrible holocaust. He wanted the city to have quite a gala air as it burned, to appear almost gay. And the people who set it on fire would be a holiday crowd. (DL, 118)

West's juxtaposition of the "holocaust" and the "holiday" scarcely needs underscoring. Here, and in the riot scene at end of the novel (when the apocalyptic painting is again evoked in festive terms as a "bonfire" of all known architectural styles), West forces us to take up a peculiarly ambiguous position. We cannot see the painting, or the riot itself, as "happy" or "good," but what is there to mourn in the culture that is being consumed? Why grieve as the flames lick at the "corinthian column" holding up the fake-exotic "palmleaf roof of a nutburger stand?" (DL, 184–85.)

West's "positive moment," then, is as uncomfortable as the gloomy vision of revolution that Theodor Adorno (in a very Benjaminian moment) offers us at the end of his essay on Spengler: "That which stands against the decline of the west," he observes, "is not the surviving culture but the Utopia that is silently embodied in the image of decline."[45] In its paradoxical assertion that dystopian impulses represent, in their very negativity, the only utopia possible in the present cultural context, the remark perhaps strains common sense. But such a dark hint at a kind of revolutionary nihilism is all we get from West: the studio backlot (figured as both world's fair and ruin) and the "Burning of Los Angeles" (figured as both carnival and riot) offer us as much of a positive as we can find in his work. And yet if for West, as for Marx, "the abolition of the illusory happiness of people is a demand for their true happiness," then the ruinous aspect of the Hollywood dream is not only a sign of decay, or cause for cultural despair, but a sign of hope.[46] The destruction of these materialized wishes, which in *The Day of the Locust* seems already under way, is the precondition for change, the precondition for an as yet unimaginable redemption.

8

The Storyteller, the Novelist, and the Advice Columnist

"Dear Miss Dix:

"How can I make myself more popular? I am fairly pretty and not a dumb-bell, but I am so timid and self-conscious with people, men especially. . . . I'm always sure they're not going to like me. . . .

Joan G____"

ANSWER: "Poor Joan – you *have* an inferiority complex haven't you? Yet no woman need feel inferior. . . . *Feel* that you're charming, Joan, and others will find you so!

"Pretty clothes will help you tremendously. . . . [And] if you use that wonderful product, Lux, you'll keep your dainty garments COLOR FRESH and NEW a long, long, time. . . . Your surroundings, too, can help you win self-confidence and poise. Pretty curtains, gay sofa cushions, table linens – all can form part of the magic spell if kept lovely with Lux."

Dorothy Dix, *Ladies Home Journal* (March 1931)

The storyteller is a man who has counsel for his readers. But if today "having counsel" is beginning to have an old-fashioned ring, this is because the communicability of experience is decreasing. In consequence we have no counsel either for ourselves or for others. After all, counsel is less an answer to a question than a proposal concerning the continuation of a story which is just unfolding. To seek this counsel one would first have to be able to tell the story.

Walter Benjamin, "The Storyteller: Reflections on the Works of Nikolai Leskov"

It is folly to suppose that a society which reads a daily paper, sees a news reel weekly, and hears the radio every other hour, is going to be novelized successfully by the old-time story teller.

Henry Seidel Canby, *Seven Years Harvest*

In 1931 (the same year West's first novel, *The Dream Life of Balso Snell,* was published), one of the very first Gallup polls discovered what at the time seemed to be shocking information about the interests and tastes of the mass audience. The survey found that the vast majority of newspaper subscribers preferred the comics to the lead news stories and that the "advice to the lovelorn" column was more popular than any item of foreign news, by a margin of 2 to 1.[1] This was the kind of evidence that social prophets could take as a gloomy omen of cultural decay and of the distressing shallowness of what was then called the "tabloid mind." But the information was also of great interest to advertising agencies; and from these quarters there soon emerged what I am tempted to call a new narrative genre: advertisements in the form of comic strips. The idea quickly caught on, to the extent that the early thirties to mid-thirties came to be known, among some in the advertising trade, as "the balloon talk period."[2]

The 1934 strip "Mother Minds Her Business" (see illustration, page 190) is a typical example of the genre and captures one of the dominant characteristics of Depression advertising generally: an emphasis on the familiar, the traditional, and the folksy – an invocation of the old-timey family values of the "Mom knows best" sort.[3] These now-familiar "mini-dramas of love-lost-and-regained through the conquest of B.O.," of marriages saved by Wonder Bread, and of academic success ensured by the energizing powers of Ovaltine became, one might argue, the paradigmatic mass cultural form of the early thirties (just as MTV – with its combination of popular music, video, advertising, fashion spreads, and tropes from any number of fictional or cinematic genres – would seem to be today). The comic strip itself, the historian Roland Marchand observes, was already a compendium of the characteristic formal devices of all the mass media:

> From the movies came the ideas of continuity of action, quick-cutting from scene to scene, and focusing attention through the occasional close-up. From the confession magazines came the power of personal testimony and the intimate drama. From the tabloids came an emphasis on brevity and pictorial imagery. And from the radio came the persuasiveness of a conversational style and the seductiveness of eavesdropping.[4]

To all these features, the "continuity series" ads, as they were called in the trade, added the ready-made solutions of advertising, the form that so many critics (most notably Adorno and Horkheimer) have regarded as the quintessence of mass culture.[5] The "plots" of the comic-strip ads were thus even more unvaried than those of another of the decade's

generic inventions, the soap opera (for which Herta Herzog, in one of
the early studies of the form, defined the formula: "getting into trouble
and out again").[6] They always delivered the same message: that a solution can be purchased, neatly packaged, in the form of a commodity. If
only for their typicality, the comic-strip ads of the early thirties are
historical documents of great interest, in both their form and content –
in their amalgam of mass cultural trends and in their peculiarly concentrated "psychic compromise or horse-trading" between utopian desires
and commercialized solutions.[7] They deserve attention as symptoms and
clues of a particular moment in a materialist history of experience.

Moreover, and specifically to our purpose, this undignified new addi-
tion to the genealogy of epic forms could not have failed to impinge on
Nathanael West's thinking as he worked on *Miss Lonelyhearts,* the novel
he considered giving the subtitle "a novel in the form of a comic strip."[8]
West was always an aficionado of mass culture, and between 1929 and
1933 this interest started to take a more serious, investigative, even
anthropological turn. Inspired perhaps by William Carlos Williams's use
of nonliterary documents in his book *In the American Grain,* by the
reportorial impulse of much American writing of the time, and by the
experiments of the Dadaists and Surrealists, West (as his biographer Jay
Martin observes) consciously "interested himself in entertainments in
which the masses were interested, and now reassessed movies, cartoons,
popular literature, and jazz as expressions of collective yearning." His
friend John Sanford recalls specifically how he and West amused themselves by reading the advertisements from magazines aloud to each
other; and one can easily imagine them delighting in those speech-
balloon dialogues crafted by the copy writers for Post Bran Flakes,
Lifebuoy, and Listerine.[9]

The textual evidence of an influence or a parodic response to the
comic-strip ads is certainly suggestive. Many of West's critics have felt
that although he eventually gave up his idea of actually treating the
chapters like the conventional frames of the cartoon strip and of placing
the dialogue in speech balloons, traces of his original concept of "a novel
in the form of a comic strip" are still evident. They note, for instance,
the novel's episodic structure, its rapid tempo, its caricature-like descriptions, its comically excessive violence, and its "primary colored locations."[10] But the thematic and ideological content of the comic-strip
ad – the easy solutions of advertising, combined with the pseudopersonal solace of the advice letter – is even more clearly inscribed in the
novel, albeit in ironic form. It is instructive to compare the language of
some of the advertisements of the time with that of the sad letters sent
to Miss Lonelyhearts's advice column. Copywriters did not hesitate to

insert the solutions offered by their products into emotional situations only slightly less violent and embarrassing than those described by his desperate clients. Take, for instance, the following sample from the *Saturday Evening Post* of October 1935:

> "No, Dickie boy . . . Mommy hasn't got an ear ache . . . she's just trying to shut out Daddy's grumblings! And don't cry . . . you'll get another little wagon . . . Daddy didn't mean to kick it so viciously." Poor Dickie – and poor mother. . . but hasn't anybody got a kind word for father . . . dear old father who almost goes crazy every time he shaves? There is a solution – if father will only listen: switch to the Valet AutoStrop Razor.[11]

While Miss Lonelyhearts is much less confident that "there is a solution" than the makers of Valet AutoStrop Razor, the text is certainly saturated with the language of commercial hype, descriptions of advertising posters, parodic slogans, and so forth. Shrike, the cynical newspaper editor, advocates the escape provided by high art and religion in the terms of advertisements: he advocates the delights of Bach, Beethoven, and Brahms with the line "Smoke a 3 B pipe" and recommends "Christ Dentist" as being, rather like Listerine, the "Preventer of Decay" (ML, 35). In the context of his monologues, even the biblical question "When the salt has lost its savour, who shall savour it again?" (ML, 35) comes to resemble a household hint, a letter to Betty Crocker or Dorothy Dix. Indeed, toward the end of the novel when Miss Lonelyhearts pretends to offer himself as the solution to all of his fiancée Betty's problems, he is described in words that, to my ear at least, have the unmistakable tone of advertising copy. Miss Lonelyhearts presents himself as something that would go "with strawberry sodas and farms in Connecticut" – a new brand of aftershave, one is tempted to suggest on the strength of the adjectives: "simple and sweet, whimsical and poetic, a trifle collegiate, yet very masculine" (ML, 56).

Beyond these details, it is fair to say that the entire thrust of the novel is to demolish all of society's received ideas of redemption – including the comic strip ads' typical messages of everyday salvation. But even if the influence is not direct, if *Miss Lonelyhearts* is marked by advertising only in the general way in which *all* literature in the twentieth century is, arguably, marked by a discursive struggle with advertising, the connection remains of interest.[12] The comic-strip ads of the thirties, with their symbolic representation of actual and intimate speech, their straightforward narrative, and their happy ending resulting from friendly advice, offer an interesting critical perspective on the issues I would like to raise in this chapter. At stake, once again, is West's understanding of mass culture and, specifically, its relation to what he himself understood as the historically determined forms and possibilities of narrative.

NARRATIVE IN THE AGE OF MECHANICAL REPRODUCTION

The question of narrative was implicit in the preceding chapter in the discussion of mass culture and wishing in the work of Benjamin and West. It is evident that Benjamin, following Goethe, regards the true wish as a narrative of sorts: conceived in childhood and fulfilled by the experience of a lifetime, the wish reveals the meaning, shape, or "theme" of an individual's development.[13] It renders a life significant and communicable. In other words, Benjamin's brief comments on wishing relate directly to one of the central concerns of his critical work from the thirties: an investigation of the material history of experience and of the way in which the structure of experience is related to artistic forms. The passage on wishing (from his 1939 essay on Baudelaire) harkens back to the 1936 essay "The Storyteller: Reflections on the Works of Nikolai Leskov," his ambitious attempt to spin a three-ply history of narrative forms, modes of production, and forms of experience. The story, as Benjamin defines it in this context, closely resembles the wish. Both are (or both are products of) a particular "kind of experience." Just as the true wish is figured by the distance in space traversed by the falling star and is fulfilled by the continuous pattern traced by an individual life, so the story gains its authority from the distance of its origins in the "lore of faraway places" or "the lore of the past"; it is authenticated by the acquired wisdom of the experience of the storyteller, the imprint of whose life it bears.[14] And just as, in an age of mechanical production, the wish loses its connection with individual lives and shrinks into the repetitive and short-lived desire of the gambler at the wheel, so narrative too loses both the authority of lived experience and the awe of distance. In the age of mass culture, the story fragments into the short-lived bits of information that are splattered on the pages of the newspaper – evidence, for Benjamin, of a decay of experience and of a new menace to older narrative modes of "producing" that experience. Given this perspective, incidentally, it is easy to imagine how Benjamin might have read another kind of typical advertisement from the thirties, those for products that recommend themselves as timesavers to the inexperienced housewife: "GRANDMOTHER AMAZED AT FRUITCAKE MADE IN TWO MINUTES." Dromedary Dixie-Mix would be, for him, another example of the idea that modernity is characterized by an "increasing aversion to sustained effort" – an aversion with profound effects on all cultural forms.[15]

Nathanael West was no less preoccupied with the structure and quality of contemporary experience and was, as a novelist, inevitably engaged with the problem of devising narrative forms that might adequately express and critique that experience. His preoccupation with narrative was also implicit in our discussion of the wish in Chapter 7. Faye Greener's trashy dreams, the prime example of Westian wishing, are after all a collection of stories: plots of B movies in which an heiress is saved by a handsome sailor or a chorus girl rises to stardom. Moreover, the startling fashions and architecture of Hollywood, which I described earlier as material wishes, are also congealed stories or, more accurately perhaps, fragmentary, synecdochic indices of stories – of Grimm's fairy tales, Arabian nights, and so forth.

While West never formulated his thoughts on narrative in any extended or theoretical fashion, some of his critical comments do suggest that, in the course of writing *Miss Lonelyhearts,* he was radically questioning the form and, indeed, the possibility of narrative in the contemporary cultural context. In "Some Notes on Violence," which he published in *Contact* in 1932, West suggests that the structures of experience in contemporary America have rendered older forms of narrative problematic.[16] In America, West announces, "violence is idiomatic" (and the ambiguous phrase fittingly conflates the experience and the expression or linguistic production of that experience). The newpapers provide a case in point:

> To make the front page a murderer has to use his imagination, he also has to use a particularly hideous instrument. Take this morning's paper: FATHER CUTS SON'S THROAT IN BASEBALL ARGUMENT. It appears on an inside page. To make the first page he should have killed three sons and with a baseball bat instead of a knife. Only liberality and symmetry could have made this daily occurrence interesting.[17]

Among the casualties of this sensational processing of violent experience are the received conventions of the novel: "Artistic truth," West suggests, no longer requires "the naturalism of Zola" or "the realism of Flaubert." The idiom of the mass media and the idiom of everyday life have made the psychological verisimilitude and the emotional descriptions of the nineteenth-century European novel appear overwrought. An American, drilled in the shock of contemporary living by the daily assault of headlines, would respond to such writing (or so West imagines) as inaccurate and inappropriate ("'What's all the excitement about'") or as belonging to a purely aesthetic category – as a matter of style without any referential urgency (" 'By God, that's a mighty fine piece of writing, that's art' ").[18] These insights, I think, show a remarkable similarity to Benjamin's argument that contemporary "experience

has fallen in value" and no longer lends itself to older forms of narrative
and that, conversely, our very capacity for experience is undermined by
the mass-produced forms of narrative that confront us daily in the
newspapers and on the billboards.

Such considerations must have influenced West's original plan to write
Miss Lonelyhearts in the form of a comic strip; indeed, even as it stands,
Miss Lonelyhearts remains a kind of antinovel that explores (as Jonathan
Raban has astutely observed) "the possibility that the conventions of the
Novel . . . have been made unworkable by the urban industrial world
of pulp media and cheapjack commodities."[19] For the time being, however, I would like to postpone discussion of West's technical experiments and his cultural and novelistic politics and first consider how his
novel – directly and thematically – confronts the problems raised by
Benjamin's "Storyteller" essay: the decay of the subjective significance
of life, the resulting loss of the ability to tell stories, and therefore also
the ability to give advice.

These problems are dramatically implicit in the very situation *Miss
Lonelyhearts* depicts: the agonies of the agony columnist who has no
counsel for his confused readers, or even for himself. They are also
raised quite explicitly at several points in the novel. Shrike, for instance,
announces to Miss Lonelyhearts in tones of mock pathos: "My good
friend, I want to have a heart-to-heart talk with you. I adore heart-to-
heart talks and nowadays there are so few people with whom one can
really talk. Everybody is so hard-boiled" (ML, 21).[20] While this lament
for the decay of conversational exchange is offered with elaborate irony,
its validity is borne out by any number of the novel's intensely metaphorical evocations of the prevailing social relations. The ugly urban
waste land in which it is set is, in every detail, the antithesis of the older
organic community that Benjamin associates with storytelling: that lost
social space where things are made by hand and where experience can
be related by word of mouth. The "multiple" chaos of the city street resists interpretation and permits only those fragmentary, desultory, dis-
jointed experiences that Benjamin elsewhere describes as "urban shock":

> Broken groups of people hurried past, forming neither stars nor
> squares. The lamp-posts were badly spaced and the flagging was of
> different sizes. Nor could he do anything with the harsh clanging
> sound of street cars and the raw shouts of hucksters. No repeated
> group of words would fit their rhythm and no scale could give them
> meaning. (ML, 11)

This sensory assault offers no material for narrative, no continuity, no
distance, no aura. The city is therefore appropriately figured as a "world
of doorknobs," replete with depersonalized, mass-produced objects

(ML, 9). It is a "dead world," from which any trace of the magic and miracle that empower the storyteller's craft has fled – displaced perhaps (as a telling passage suggests) by the newspaper:

> The gray sky looked as if it had been rubbed with a soiled eraser. It held no angels, flaming crosses, olive-bearing doves, wheels within wheels. Only a newspaper struggling in the air like a kite with a broken spine. (ML, 5)

In such descriptive moments, *Miss Lonelyhearts* reiterates the idea from "Some Notes on Violence" that the newspaper is both cause and effect of the general decay of experience and narrative. In another of Miss Lonelyhearts's gloomy observations of the urban scene, the sensational "events of the day" seem to produce not stories, but headlines emblazoned on posters: "Mother slays five with ax, slays seven, slays nine. . . . Babe slams two, slams three. . . . " (ML, 25). The repetitive phrases suggest that even these big-time events are no different from those frustratingly banal "doorknobs": standardized, fungible, infinitely replicable. News, in other words, resembles mass-produced goods, not the handcrafted items to which Benjamin compares the story: the clay pot to which the handprint of the potter still clings.[21] It is thus appropriate that the newsmen in the novel (who could be seen as the modern counterparts of the storyteller) are described as machines, which relentlessly destroy the individual qualities of whatever experiences come their way. As Miss Lonelyhearts observes, the cynical journalists are "machines for making jokes": "A button machine makes buttons, no matter what the power used, foot, steam, or electricity. They, no matter what the motivating force, death, love or God, made jokes" (ML, 15). And though Miss Lonelyhearts himself no longer willingly participates in this manufacture (realizing that his own life has also been reduced to a punch line), he cannot, as it were, change the whole mode of narrative production.

Of all the newsmen in the novel, it is Miss Lonelyhearts himself who invites the most sustained comparison with the storyteller; indeed, the antithesis is so exact as to make Miss Lonelyhearts almost the photographic negative of Benjamin's exemplary and nostalgic figure. The storyteller (to recapitulate his attributes) is "a man who has counsel for his readers," the man whose ability to articulate the unity of his own life imbues experience with unique meaning and authenticity and gives it a public usefulness and relevance. Like so many characters in Nikolai Leskov's stories (the occasion for Benjamin's meditation), he is a kind of a secular saint: "the righteous man" who can reach into the "depths of inanimate nature" and perceive the "natural prophecy" and order of the created world. He is a man of "incomparable aura," the imagined positive and touchstone in Benjamin's critique of modern life.[22] In short, the storyteller is everything that West's confused advice columnist strives, and fails, to be. Miss Lonelyhearts is the quintessential modern man, who (not unlike Benjamin's novelist) can record only the "profound perplexity of the living."[23] He has no identity, other than the generic, commercial, and, significantly, female name his job forces him to assume. His life, as presented in West's jagged narrative, is episodic; and he can find no words, can offer no advice that has not already been mass-produced and trivialized. However much he might search for a "sincere answer" (ML, 1) his position at the *New York Post Dispatch* dooms him to be an impostor: he is, ironically, employed to provide counsel by the very institution that menaces the ability to give counsel, to "produce" experience in anything other than the fragmentary standardized form of information (or, as West suggests, the joke). Worse yet, while his "stories" are expected to be of practical use to the column's readers, they must finally be useful in the way the Dorothy Dix letter of our epigraph is useful – as a promotion for a commodity, not as a genuine benefit to the personal life of the recipient. The point is illustrated only too well by the grounds on which Shrike objects to Miss Lonelyhearts's recommendation in one of his columns that a reader commit suicide: the problem is not that this advice might be unwise, but that it might reduce the circulation of the paper (ML, 18).

It is important to remember that "having counsel," as Benjamin conceives of it, is not simply a matter of an individual's efforts and talents. The master storyteller can operate only in a context where everybody tells stories, since his advice is really a proposition concerning a life story related to him by somebody else.[24] But as both Benjamin and West seem to suggest, experience in mass society is, at best, private in character and relevance; it has forfeited any universal applicability. Miss Lonelyhearts's hard-boiled colleagues in the speakeasy are thus quite correct when they observe that "the trouble with him, the trouble with all of us," is that there is no longer any "outer life, only an inner one, and that by necessity"; thus, even if Miss Lonelyhearts were to have "a genuine religious experience," it would be "personal, and so meaningless, except to a psychologist" (ML, 15). Exchangeable meaning, like language, cannot be invented by an individual.

When Miss Lonelyhearts, then, feels his tongue sitting in his mouth like a "fat thumb," his plight is in good measure due to the fact that the letters from his clients – the materials from which he is supposed to shape his wise proposals – do not present the kind of problems that could ever be resolved by counsel. The very fact that they are *letters*, written in isolation and confusion, already signifies the disappearance of the kind of community of tellers and interpreters in which advice is possible. One cannot (Benjamin suggests) draw out the "moral of the story" when the whole issue of the "the meaning of life" has become problematic, when people want (as one of Miss Lonelyhearts correspondents puts it) "to no . . . what is the whole stinking business for" (ML, 47). Moreover, though the awkward language and misspelling may seem to indicate a certain individuality (at least compared with the callous brevity of the newspaper headlines or with Shrike's eloquent recitations of the cliches of culture), West's description of them suggests that they too are mass-produced: the letters are "all of them alike, stamped from the dough of suffering with a heart-shaped cookie knife" (ML, 1). These "heart-shaped" letters are, one might say, the symbolic stand-in for the "heart-to-heart" exchange – just as the speech balloon of the comic strip is the symbolic stand-in for the conversational voice.

The same mass-produced quality, the same loss of a truly personal life and direct speech, is evident also in the people Miss Lonelyhearts observes or encounters in person. The crowds, who walk like zombies "with a dreamlike violence," stumble into movie theaters, and grab love-story magazines from the garbage cans, have "torn mouths" – a detail as much symbolic as visual, emphasizing the alienation of the city dwellers from any expressive capacity (ML, 38–39). Equally symbolic is West's description of the cripple Peter Doyle, who "looked like one of those composite photographs used by screen magazines in guessing contests" (ML, 45). Constructed out of the fragments of mass culture, Doyle proves, not surprisingly, incapable of telling his story, of unifying the fragments of his life into a unique and meaningful narrative. At his meeting with Miss Lonelyhearts in the speakeasy (and the word comes to seem ironically significant), he struggles to give "birth to groups of words that lived inside him as things" (ML, 45–46). He resorts to narrating his predicament pictorially, like a cartoon figure, through frantic gesture and wild motion, and eventually just hands Miss Lonelyhearts another agony column letter. Even in a face-to-face situation it is impossible for him to tell his story.

Another case in point is Miss Lonelyhearts's coy mistress, Mary Shrike. Though less grotesque and inarticulate than Peter Doyle, her identity is also pieced together from the commodities and commodified language that surrounds her: she "talk[s] in headlines" (ML, 20). In the El Gaucho restaurant, amid the fake gaiety of "guitars, bright shawls, exotic foods, and outlandish constumes," Mary becomes "Spanish," "languorous and full of abandon" (ML, 22). Ironically, Mary is one of the most avid confessors and storytellers in the novel. But her endless stories about her tragic childhood are really only arbitrary signs of the personal, of the "heart-to-heart," without any necessary connection to her actual life; it is *talk,* something to say when one wants to be "poetic" or discuss "something besides clothing or business or movies" (ML, 23). Mary confesses, for instance, that her "father was a portrait painter, a man of genius"; but as Miss Lonelyhearts muses, she might equally well have said, "My father was a Russian prince, my father was a Piute Indian Chief, my father was an Australian sheep baron, father lost all his money in Wall Street," or (to come full circle) "my father was a portrait painter" (ML, 23). West's list of options is particularly corrosive in suggesting that even parents, whom one would think of as the indisputable guarantee of an individual's uniqueness and "originality," have also in a sense become manufactured goods, standardized functions in the "business of dreams." Mary Shrike is, in short, a kind of true-story machine, as her consistent association with technological imagery seems to emphasize: her dress resembles "glass-covered steel"; her "pantomime" behavior strikes Miss Lonelyhearts as "cleanly mechanical" (ML, 22). No wonder that Miss Lonelyhearts finds himself incapable of offering a "proposition" concerning the "unfolding" of her life: the "life" of this Betty Boop–like confession machine is unlikely to do anything as organic, or conventionally novelistic, as to unfold.[25]

This emphasis on the social dimension of storytelling helps us make sense of some of the more violent and vicious passages in the novel. In the "Clean Old Man" chapter, for instance, Miss Lonelyhearts discovers an old man lurking in the stalls of the men's room and tries to force him to produce some kind of narrative, some kind of confession. The dialogue at the end of the chapter is, I think, peculiarly resonant in the light of our current discussion:

> Miss Lonelyhearts put his arm around the old man. "Tell us the story of your life," he said, loading his voice with sympathy.
> "I have no story."
> "You must have. Every one has a life story."
> The old man began to sob.
> "Yes, I know, your tale is a sad one. Tell it, damn you, tell it."
> When the old man remained silent, he took his arm and twisted it.
> . . . He was twisting the arms of all the sick and miserable, broken and betrayed, inarticulate and impotent. He was twisting the arm of Desperate, Broken-hearted, Sick-of-it-all, Disillusioned-with-tubercular-husband. (ML, 18)

What Miss Lonelyhearts is, in effect, trying to do in this scene is to restore by force the community of narrative exchange in which his archaic role would no longer amount to fraud. His failure is thus evident not only in the old man's silence, but in the fact that in his effort to extract a life story where there is none, he assumes another fake identity. He masquerades as Havelock Ellis, the psychologist: therapeutic culture's institutionalized stand-in for what the older community of the storyteller "naturally" provided.[26] It is not only in their relation to people that one can trace the ironic connection between West's advice columnist and Benjamin's storyteller, but also in their relation to the inanimate world. Miss Lonelyhearts's hysterical obsession with the jumbled objects of the modern city, and his frustration at their trashy irrelevance and mute facticity, are (like his assault on the Clean Old Man) the result of a desperate attempt to restore some significant order, some sense of aura to the dead world. But whereas the storyteller effortlessly stands, as Benjamin puts it, at the "apex" of the "hierarchy of the world of created things," the things in Miss Lonelyhearts's world submit to no such hierarchy or order.[27] At one point in the novel, they even "take the field" against their would-be redeemer:

> When he touched something, it spilled or rolled to the floor. The collar buttons disappeared under the bed, the point of the pencil broke, the handle of the razor fell off, the window shade refused to stay down. [Miss Lonelyhearts] fought back, but with too much violence, and was decisively defeated by the spring of the alarm clock. (ML, 11)

One. of Miss Lonelyhearts's dreams is particularly evocative in this regard. In it he imagines himself to be "a magician who [does] tricks with doorknobs" and commands them to bleed, flower, and speak (ML, 9). The dream is reminiscent of a passage in *The Dream Life of Balso Snell* where Beagle Darwin imagines himself performing a juggling act with "an Ivory Tower, a Still White Bird, the Holy Grail, the Nails, the Scourge, the Thorns, and a piece of the True Cross" (BS, 56). It symbolically expresses a desire to reinvest the world of mass-produced commodities with aura, to turn the most banal of everyday objects into relics, into mystical objects that bring to the world a message of redemption and transformation. But, again like the Clean Old Man episode, the dream also hints at the failure of these efforts. The mystical metamorphosis occurs on the stage of a crowded theater; the redemption is show biz, a matter of "tricks," a magician's sleight of hand.

Like Benjamin, then, West is concerned with the social, interpersonal, and even material aspects of narrative and counsel, as (among other things) his minute, even obsessive interest in the bric-a-brac of the urban world would suggest. Miss Lonelyhearts's doorknobs, for instance, are not only metaphorical (as in the phrase "dead as a doorknob [or door-nail]," which may be suggested here); nor are they exactly "objective correlatives," expressive of a certain state of mind. They also synecdochically stand for modern *things,* objects and commodities manufactured and related to in a certain way – and in a different way from the items of handicraft that Benjamin invokes in the "Storyteller" essay. As such they are signs of the resistant facticity of the contemporary world and reminders that not everything – not all kinds of narrative or all kinds of redemption – is possible at any given moment in history. No matter, then, how intense Miss Lonelyhearts's desire to be sincere, and no matter how genuine his personal religious experience, the storyteller's world cannot be reinvented (or so his dream tells us) except by a kind of social prestidigitation, and on the level of appearance.

DEPRESSION CULTURE AND THE "VOICE OF EXPERIENCE"

The comparative analysis of our two texts is already suggestive for what I have been calling a materialist history of experience. But to assess their respective explanatory and critical power fully, we need to consider also their representational accuracy or (to put the notion in a somewhat less problematic fashion) to consider to what extent Benjamin's theoretical hypotheses and West's fictional representations correspond to the cultural diagnosis offered by historical texts. It is in this context that the shrewdness of West's response and of his cultural politics becomes most evident.

The work of certain American social historians offers both empirical and subjective support for Benjamin's sense that "having counsel is beginning to have an old-fashioned ring."[28] Roland Marchand has listed several broad social and demographic changes (all relating to the demise of smaller communities under the impact of a consolidating national market) that, by the twenties and thirties, had created what he calls an "advice vacuum": greater mobility, generational discontinuity, more complex forms of social interaction, the proliferation of mass-produced goods, and (I would add) the isolation and shrinking of households in the new apartments and suburbia. All of these trends tended to sever city dwellers from the shared forms of knowledge of smaller communities and "disrupted informal, intrafamily, and intracommunity channels of advice." Ideological factors augmented these demographic effects. In the irreverent and debunking twenties (when it became perhaps more important than ever before to seem "up-to-date"), "the acids of modernity" also helped devalue the authority of small-town experience and handed-down social wisdom.[29] Urbanized Americans increasingly felt themselves to be engulfed by a society of crowds, in which old ties, individual identity, and individual experience seemed to be irrelevant if not erased by the scale and impersonality of mass society. The advent of the Depression, with its gigantic statistics and its vast yet incomprehensible ravages on the old certainties, extended this disconcerting experience also to smaller and rural communities. The Austrian economist

Peter Drucker, in an analysis often cited by U.S. critics and memoirists of the period, described the emotional and subjective effects of the economic crisis as follows:

> Like the forces of war, depression shows man as a senseless cog in a senselessly whirling machine which is beyond human understanding and has ceased to serve any purpose but its own.
> [The individual] can no longer explain or understand his existence as rationally correlated and co-ordinated to the world in which he lives; nor can he co-ordinate the world and the social reality to his existence. The function of the individual in society has become entirely irrational and senseless. Man is isolated within a tremendous machine, the purpose and meaning of which he does not accept and cannot translate into terms of his experience.[30]

The implication of these observations strikes me as very similar to that of Benjamin's memorable evocation of the individual's bafflement on the battlefields of Flanders:

> A generation that had gone to school on a horse-drawn streetcar now stood under the open sky in a countryside in which nothing remained unchanged but the clouds, and beneath these clouds, in a field of force of destructive torrents and explosions, was the tiny, fragile human body.[31]

The illogical enormities of modernity, implicit in such things as mechanical warfare and rampant inflation, utterly defy the interpretative and communicative equipment of the individual and powerfully attest to Benjamin's proposition that personal "experience had fallen in value."[32]

But it is here that the cartoon-strip ads, which I discussed at the beginning of this chapter, come back to plague us. For it is also possible to argue, if we look at the United States in the early thirties, that Benjamin was dead wrong: that advice, stories, and the speaking voice – far from being on the decline – had become a growth industry. To historicize the essay and novella we are concerned with here, one would have to juxtapose them with such forgotten historical documents as the "balloon-talking" advice strips, or perhaps the radio program entitled the "Voice of Experience" (which offered advice to listeners on intimate matters, and on a single day in 1933 received 6,500 letters from its listeners).[33] One would have to consider the hundreds of "useful" promotional stories in the magazines and the hours of conversation one could tune in to on the radio. One would have to recall the folksy tone and the atmosphere of *Gemeinschaft* evoked by advertisements; how the homey Betty Crocker, for instance, was invented to answer those "questions that in more neighborly communities had been asked over the back fence"; or how Sears, Roebuck and Co. asked their rural radio audience if they could "pull up a chair and talk things over. . . . The main idea is just to . . . *visit*. Are you going to be home?"[34]

The recent work of Lawrence Levine on the popular culture of the thirties does exactly this, and in a way that challenges the sense of rupture and loss implicit in Benjamin's and Marchand's accounts of urban industrial society. Levine records, for instance, the fact that people would retell the stories they heard on the radio to each other, that they found solace and companionship in the voices of broadcasters, and that they consumed mass-mediated popular forms not as atomized individuals but as social groups. By this argument, the mere presence of the marketplace and new technologies of mass communication did not radically alter cultural forms or erode interaction and people's capacity for community. Levine questions, in short, the rigid distinction between "organic" and industrial societies that seems to mark "The Storyteller," as well as a number of influential sociological and ethnographic studies from the time (such as Stuart Chase's *Mexico: A Study of Two Americas*).[35] From Levine's more optimistic perspective, the comic-strip ad, with its speech balloons, its reassuring advice, and family values, might offer further evidence that mass culture is not necessarily the antithesis to older traditions – that it could perhaps be seen as the "folk culture" of industrial society.[36]

In citing this optimistic reading, I am to some extent playing the devil's advocate. I am personally far from believing, for instance, that the invention of radio actually restores the storyteller's voice or a traditional community of exchange (though many versions of this wishful position – notably McLuhan's celebration of the "global village" – have been proposed very seriously). There is a danger, in Levine's democratically minded approach, in his highly attractive effort to represent the people as active agents even in mass society, of simply patching over the difference between orality and technically mediated voices and of simplifying the possible contradiction between the social implications and the surface forms of mass-mediated texts.[37] The presence of symbolic representations of and commodified substitutions for the traditional advice giver's role and the lost neighborliness of older communities are also signs of their social absence, just as (to take a parallel from Benjamin) the novel's attempt to discover "the meaning of life" is a sign of the *lack* of immanent meaning in a fragmented daily life. The growth of an advice *industry*, controlled and designed from above, is not the same as the "handcrafted" counsel of the experienced storyteller; the speech balloon is not the same as the spoken voice; the "just for you" address of the advertisement is not, finally, personal or intimate. Nor, to return to the question of narrative forms, is the catchy advertising slogan identical to the "moral of the story." After all, the story, as

Benjamin describes it, is primarily a heuristic construct, a device in a revolutionary pedagogy: it represents an ideal of authenticity and a lived totality, a narrative form so connected to daily labor, so "woven into the fabric of real life" that it can hardly be thought of as ideological.[38] The reinvention of homey advice and *Gemeinschaft* in the American media must, by contrast, appear as a matter of ideology, even of "false consciousness." (One hesitates to use this phrase, but this is where the essay's perspective leads us.) This reinvention is based, finally, on the nostalgic pretense that in the vast enterprise of industrial modernity, nothing has been lost. And while "The Storyteller" has also been criticized as overly nostalgic, its nostalgia is clearly intended to serve a different purpose: to *emphasize* what has been lost; to offer critique, not consolation or a way to "cope."[39]

But even so, the arguments brought forward by Levine must be taken seriously, since they do indicate a weakness in the "Storyteller" essay's history of experience insofar as it applies to the American scene. The problem could perhaps be traced back to the fact that in this essay Benjamin takes the newspaper as the paradigmatic form of mass culture and reads its fragments of information as both symptom and cause of the decay of experience in mass society.[40] The truth is not quite so simple. The value of exchanged experience does not fall straight into "bottomlessness," nor does the idea of community or the useful story disappear; but they undergo, one might say, one of those "false sublations" in which capitalism seems to specialize: advice and speech are, as it were, recalled to a second, symbolic life in such forms as the comic-strip ad. There is, of course, a certain historical irony, as Marchand has pointed out, in the fact that the language most favored by the culture industry, the language that served to promote and maintain a complex system of standardized mass distribution, was everything but abstract and mechanical, and relied, on the contrary, on a "person-to-person, conversational tone of voice that belied the very nature of mass communications."[41] "The world of radio and popular music," Marchand adds, "had a word for this fusion of apparent intimacy with mass appeal; it was called crooning."[42] Both Marchand's synecdoche of "crooning" and my own of the comic-strip ad, warn us that mass culture cannot be accounted for simply in terms of fragmentation and loss of aura: we need to consider also the culture industry's "simulation of authenticity" and the commercialized survival of traditional forms in an age of crowds.[43]

WEST, MASS CULTURE, AND THE NOVEL

Miss Lonelyhearts confronts these issues squarely, as indeed its central focus on the figure of the advice columnist – the simulation of the "old-time story teller," or the priest – would seem to require. The central idea that the agony columnists have become the "priests of twentieth-century America" (ML, 4) implies that, for West, the old rituals of confession and prayer, and the old community of face-to-face or heart-to-heart speech, have not been lost, exactly, but reinstituted. The novella both exposes and parodies this process. Moreover, the constant association of the good news of advertising and the solace of the sob column with the good news of the Christian gospel suggests that West saw mass culture essentially as a kind of mystification: as the "material reconstruction of the religious illusion," in Guy Debord's phrase.[44] This is not to deny the fact that *Miss Lonelyhearts* also presents us with the kind of fragmentary, machine-like experience associated with the loss of aura, or that it depicts modernity in terms of a kind of Weberian rationalization and "demagicization." (One need only bring to mind the loss of auratic distance implicit in Shrike's debunking remarks about the "Passion in the Luncheonette" and the "Agony in the Soda Fountain" [ML, 7].) But *Miss Lonelyhearts* is at least equally concerned with a process of remystification, with the culture industry's tendency to recirculate traditional forms of meaning – often the very meanings that it has undermined and replaced.

It is important not to overemphasize the notion that religion has become debased by this modern substitution – not to read West as though he were T. S. Eliot, so to speak. For West mass culture is certainly a sham, but so is religion: both gospels are equally mendacious. Indeed, the authority of religion and the authority of the mass media are shown to be inextricably confounded. Even in his final moments of ecstacy and resolve, Miss Lonelyhearts can think of his success only in terms of a transcendental mass culture: he would submit drafts of his column to God, and God, like an editor on high, would approve them and bestow a numinous authority upon his advice (ML, 57). One of Shrike's comments casts Miss Lonelyhearts's religious impulse in a particularly sinister light (and one suspects that his view here bears authorial sanction). He implicitly associates Miss Lonelyhearts's efforts to reinstate a mystical order with fascism – a political order that Benjamin, for one, regarded as a particularly toxic reinvention of the auratic. Miss Lonelyhearts, Shrike announces, is the "swollen Mussolini of the soul" (ML, 52); and the implication is that his attempts to, as it were, make the spiritual and cultural trains run on time, to take on the role of a kind of cultural Superman or a press agent for God, are both archaic and arrogant.

The world West evokes in *Miss Lonelyhearts,* in short, is not simply a world of fragmented narratives and lost meanings, but one of proliferating images, pseudotruths, and slogans. It is a world replete with clichéd solutions evoked in a wide range of rhetorics, equivalent only in their optimistic and rather fatuous affirmation. There is, for instance, the advice columnist's cheap aestheticism (in a style we might call Walter Pater Lite): "Life *is* worth while, for it is full of dreams and peace, gentleness and ecstasy, and faith that burns like a clear white flame on a grim dark altar" (ML, 1). There is the feature editor's mock primitivism (we might call it William Wordsworth Lite): "You are fed up with the city and its teeming millions. The ways and means of men, as getting and lending and spending, you lay waste your inner world, are too much with you. . . . So you buy a farm and walk behind your horse's moist behind, no collar or tie, plowing your broad swift acres. As you turn up the rich black soil" (ML, 33). There are consumer culture's smaller promises of mundane transformation: the "advertisements offering to teach writing, cartooning, engineering, to add inches to the biceps, and to develop the bust" (ML, 22). And there is, finally, that grand panacea, offering solace to all sufferers from dental problems, acne, poverty, and hunger:

> Art! Be an artist or a writer. When you are cold, warm yourself before the flaming tints of Titian, when you are hungry, nourish yourself with great spiritual foods by listening to the noble periods of Bach, the harmonies of Brahms and the thunder of Beethoven. . . . For you *l'art vivant,* the living art, as you call it. Tell them that you know that your shoes are broken and that there are pimples on your face, yes, and that you have buck teeth and a club foot, but that you don't care, for tomorrow they are playing Beethoven's last quartets in Carnegie Hall and at home you have Shakespeare's plays in one volume. (ML, 34–35)

These proliferating discourses of redemption make any kind of "true" redemption far harder to imagine. Most important, they drown out the hope of cultural salvation that still may have seemed viable to an earlier generation of modernists (artists whose work, in the world of *Miss Lonelyhearts,* is reduced to the status of a classy decoration): the American hedonist can now evade life's woes by "fornicat[ing] under pictures by Matisse and Picasso" or "spend[ing] an evening at home with Proust and an apple" (ML, 34).

The culture of simulations evoked in *Miss Lonelyhearts,* in short, places the artist in a quandary no less intransigent than that of the advice columnist. It is fair to say, moreover, that the novel, the form that most concerns West (and which also stands at the center of the "Storyteller" essay) is perhaps the most vulnerable of all art forms to this kind of critique.[45] It is not just the case that, as a physical object, the novel remains sealed, amid the headlines, billboards, and movies, in what Benjamin once called the "archaic stillness of the book."[46] The inner form of its narrative (at least according to the Lukácsian conception put forward in "The Storyteller") consciously aspires to a sense of unity and significance: the novel assumes the responsibility of reinventing a "substitute totality" in the modern world.[47] Its focus on the problem of "the meaning of life" places on the novel the increasingly difficult task of delivering (often through the auratic agencies of memory) an ineffable meaning from the recalcitrant and fragmentary materials of isolated lives. And while this totalizing effort is, for Lukács, both progressive and positive, the novel's heroic efforts at meaning and unity can also be seen as falsely utopian: an ideological contrivance, simulating a coherence that is in fact lacking in everyday life.

Both Benjamin and West emphasize the latter view. Their work implies that the "substitute totality" of the novel is no longer tenable – no longer, as Shrike might have put it, "a Way Out." Benjamin's comments on the ideological alibi represented by the novelistic character are precisely to the point: "By integrating the social process with the development of a person, it bestows the most frangible justification on the order determining it. The legitimacy it provides stands in direct opposition to reality. Particularly in the *Bildungsroman,* it is this inadequacy that is actualized."[48] West shows even less patience with the notion of *Bildung;* the very idea of a character's education and spiritual growth is subjected to a scornful parody in Shrike's corny and mendacious narrative about Miss Lonelyhearts's rise through the "University of Hard Knocks":

> And then, the man, the man Miss Lonelyhearts – struggling valiantly to realize a high ideal, his course shaped by a proud aim. But alas! cold and scornful, the world heaps obstacle after obstacle in his path. Deems he the goal at hand, a voice of thunder bids him "Halt!" "Let each hindrance be thy ladder, thinks he. Higher and higher, mount! And so he climbs. . ." (ML, 54)

It is curious to note, therefore, that the Lukácsian view of the redemptive novel and of the novelist as a kind of superhero "whose very creation stands as that momentary reconciliation of matter and spirit toward which his hero strives in vain," has exerted a certain residual power over West criticism.[49] Despite *Miss Lonelyhearts*'s profound skepticism about the transformative possibilities of art, critics have often defended the view that (as John Keyes puts it) "as an artist . . . West can succeed where Miss Lonelyhearts must fail."[50] They have tended, one might say, to read West's work via that persistent and surely hackneyed axiom that "Art orders Life." We might consider here, as a typical instance, an essay that has been kept in circulation by virtue of its inclusion in two of Harold Bloom's recent collections of critical essays on West. After an appropriately negative assessment of the "disorder of language" in the modern world, the critic in question announces with surprising confidence that West was, "as an artist, a practising idealist":

> Miss Lonelyhearts looks at a gray sky, and empiricist that he is, sees only a dirty tabula rasa. Against that he sees the most referential and hence the most ephemeral of all literature, a newspaper, failing (naturally) to soar. But West's words lift nicely, bearing for the space of our imagination all the significance Miss Lonelyhearts misses in his, not in the form of crosses and doves, to be sure, but in the form of figures, of ideas, of words, touched with life and touching us with the same.[51]

This kind of interpretation minimizes West's discomfiting profundity as a cultural critic in the very same gesture that it celebrates him as an artist. It refuses to take seriously the novella's persistent assertion that literature is not enough, that, though it might come "in one volume" rather than in a can, literature has become another commodity, another ready-made pseudosolution.

Both Benjamin and West, by contrast, place an implicit embargo on this kind of easily affirmative reading of the novel: the kind in which the heroic reader, one might say, abets the heroic novelist in his efforts. By a curious and intriguing coincidence, both "The Storyteller" and *Miss Lonelyhearts* contain telling descriptions of a person reading a novel. These scenes of reading, it seems to me, provide cautionary images for future readers and critics, and therefore merit our close attention.

In Section XV of his essay, Benjamin draws a picture of a reader whose "burning interest," fanned by the effect of suspense, feeds on the novel as a fire feeds on "logs in the fireplace."[52] It is not an unsympathetic description (indeed, one cannot help thinking of this avid reader as Benjamin himself). Yet the metaphor with which he expresses the novel's power of absorbing the mind – that of "a dry material" for the readerly flame – is clearly double-edged. The novel, the image suggests, is fascinating, but no longer vital; in fact, the whole scene of reading is somewhat desolate. In contrast to the men or women who make up the audience of the storyteller (figures we are clearly intended to picture in the company of others – spinning and weaving, perhaps, with other spinners and weavers as they listen), the reader of the novel sits alone. He seems cold, as he devours his book, trying to warm his "shivering life" by the inevitably self-consuming flame of his reading. The futility of this readerly pleasure recalls something of the ridiculous passion of the suffering art lover in Shrike's caricature, who tries to warm himself before the "flaming tints of Titian." Moreover, Benjamin's description even gives the act of reading a certain antisocial ghoulishness: the "meaning of life," he posits, emerges only at the moment of death; it is only with the retrospective wisdom provided by the *finis* – the death of a character or the end of a narrative – that the total significance of fictional life can be seen at all. What the reader of the novel seeks, therefore, is to draw from the death of another "the warmth which we never draw from our own fate."[53] The novel, the product of the solitary bourgeois subject, thus appears doomed to produce further fragmentation: it can only increase the lonely individuality that has made it difficult to share experiences, to tell stories, in the first place. It is with this idea that the "Storyteller" essay's discussion of the novel comes to a rather abrupt end; from this point on, Benjamin's meditations turn exclusively to the decaying craft of the story.

This shift in direction is, I think, critically significant. It suggests that the novel – the novel as substitute totality, that is – has become an aesthetic and political dead end. It may even represent, if we attend to the logic of Benjamin's thought, a certain danger. For Benjamin, as Jürgen Habermas once observed, held the strangely mystical and pessimistic view that "the semantic potential on which human beings draw in order to invest the world with meaning and make it accessible to experience" is not infinite; this potential, deposited in the earliest cultural forms, "cannot be expanded but only transformed."[54] It would therefore seem particularly troubling that the "meaning of life," so heroically synthesized by the novelist's backward glance, is "jealously" seized upon and recklessly "swallow[ed]" by the solitary reader – who cannot relay this experience to others.[55] Benjamin's critical efforts, in this essay and elsewhere, therefore tend to privilege marginal and nonaffirmative forms: forms in which the "semantic potential" is not given in such a readily consumable package as the novel, or forms where meaning is in even greater danger of being lost forever. These forms might be literary (as in the case of the Baroque allegorists and the Surrealists) or mass-produced (as in the case of the fascinating detritus of the early forms of commercial culture – dioramas, fashions, expositions, advertisements – studied in the *Arcades Project*). And they might also be archaic, outmoded, like the story: rendered obsolescent by the forces of modernity and marginalized to the very point of extinction, the story yields not a remembered and synthesized meaning, but one that is virtually forgotten – though once experienced from day to day. Benjamin tries to preserve, in the fragmentary meditations of his essay, the memory-trace of an earlier unity still legible in this dying form. He therefore places, at the end of the essay, a counterimage to the novel's destructive and scarcely warming fire: "the gentle flame" of the story, which (like the metaphor of the still-germinative seeds from the ancient pyramids he uses earlier in the essay) suggests a more productive albeit parsimonious illumination.[56] In this sense, Benjamin's "conservative revolutionary" criticism can ultimately be regarded as redemptive; it intends to transform rather than destroy the promises of culture – high culture and mass culture alike.[57]

The scene of reading in *Miss Lonelyhearts* is at first glance a happier scene than the one from "The Storyteller." It is placed, perhaps strategically, quite early in the text. In his austere room, Miss Lonelyhearts pores over *The Brothers Karamazov* – the passage where Father Zossima preaches the necessity of learning "to perceive the divine mystery in things" and striving "to love the world with an all-embracing love" (ML, 8). Miss Lonelyhearts reads with appreciation. But West slyly suggests that this act of reading is little different from someone reading a sob column, or a comic-strip ad: Miss Lonelyhearts finds Father Zossima's words to be "excellent advice" and believes quite readily that, if he followed it, the "Kingdom of Heaven would arrive" and "his column would be syndicated" (ML, 8). The utopian promises of literature, religion, and mass culture are again sinisterly intertwined; and Miss Lonelyhearts's rather cheap and self-serving idealism makes us all the more suspicious of false solutions, of a "spiritual liniment" (ML, 53), that can all too easily become a "damned aspirin" (ML, 13). Shortly afterward, when one of his nastier colleagues salutes Miss Lonelyhearts with a mocking "How now, Dostoievski?" his hopes for cultural salvation, or even a useful lesson, seem idle indeed (ML, 25).

West, in short, seems set to discourage any effort at affirmative reading – or writing. The very first pages of *Miss Lonelyhearts* already debunk the notion that art can discover the meaning of life or (as André Breton puts it) can present "the public with the literary precipitate of a certain form of existence."[58] Shrike here suggests that Miss Lonelyhearts responds to his agony letters with lines like "*Art Is One of Life's Richest Offerings*" or "Art is distilled from suffering" (ML, 4). But these platitudes, so often replicated in the critical formula that art orders and interprets life, seem utterly empty in the face of the simultaneous vacuity and horror of the lives described in the letters. Such moments suggest that in *Miss Lonelyhearts* West was grappling with the disconcerting sense that the only untainted, "unsimulated" possibility left open for a writer was not the creation but the critique of culture. His original idea of writing "a novel in the form of a comic strip" should then perhaps be grasped as a way of avoiding the invention of yet another false utopia or false totality – a refusal to bring a "cultural" solution to bear on lived problems. My sense is that West's position can be glossed quite accurately by Greil Marcus's comments on the subversive practice of the Situationist International in the sixties:

To make art would be to betray the common, buried wishes art once spoke for, but to practice détournement – to write new speech balloons for newspaper comic strips, or for that matter old masters, to insist simultaneously on "devaluation" of art and its "reinvestment" in a new kind of social speech, a "communication containing its own criticism," a technique that could not mystify because its very form was demystification.[59]

The problem with this suggestion is, of course, that *Miss Lonelyhearts* is not, in fact, "a novel in the form of a comic strip" – though, as I have noted, certain traces of the original idea remain. For a more rigorously citational practice we need to wait for the Situationists' own "detourned" cartoon strips, or for such postmodern borrowings as the paintings of Roy Lichtenstein, or the art of Barbara Kruger, or perhaps Martin Rowson's comic-book version of *The Waste Land*. Even Kenneth Fearing's poems, with their phony resurrections and their deliberately vacuous imitations of the "perfect denouements" of mass culture, are perhaps closer to the parodic subversion Marcus describes; and so is West's second novel, *A Cool Million*, stripped of any sign of high literary style, brutally comic in its sadistic violence, and deliberately vacuous in its optimistic clichés. *Miss Lonelyhearts*, in comparison, still seems "literary": it is still a novel. At its conclusion, Miss Lonelyhearts dies, unlike the cartoon characters who rebound from under the path of the steamroller and unlike Fearing's depression victims who are casually scraped from the tracks, to be resurrected as a "Hearst cartoon" (CP, 56). It is a denouement that seems to invite the stock taking of "the meaning of life" that the end of a novel implicitly announces.

But, in fact, such stock taking is not so easily done; and West's rather open-ended and deflationary final sentence seems to work against a traditional sense of closure: "They both rolled *part of the way* down the stairs" (ML, 58, my emphasis). West's work, as he himself puts it, leaves us "nothing to root for," not even, in good conscience, the artistic value of the novel itself.[60] The very question of the meaning of life (which, as Benjamin sees it, energizes the novel) seems trite after it has been asked so many times and has been so very patently and so very flatly thematized. *Miss Lonelyhearts*'s answer to this question, moreover, has been made abundantly clear: there is no meaning in the lives people are now doomed to lead. It seems to insist that, as long as the world remains unchanged, all cultural promises will be the merest hype and the difference between novels and mass culture will be irrelevant. In other words, if a solution is to be found (and West makes no claim that it will), it will be found not in culture, but in a transformed way of life. I say this cautiously, since the extreme negativity of *Miss Lonelyhearts* does not exactly sanction this final and desperate hope. But it is significant that in "Burn the Cities," a poem published in the same year, West presents an image that forecasts the ending of *The Day of the Locust* and that we might juxtapose to the nostalgic "gentle flame" of Benjamin's storyteller; it is the image of the destructive flames of social revolution.

> The Eastern star calls with its hundred knives
> Burn the cities
> Burn the cities
>
> . . . . . .
>
> Burn the cities
> Burn Paris
> City of light
> Twice-burned city
> Warehouse of the arts
> The spread hand is a star with points
> The fist a torch
> Burn the cities
> Burn Paris
> City of light
> Twice-burned City
> Warehouse of the arts
>
> The spread hand is a star
> The first a torch
> Workers of the World
> Unite
> Burn Paris . . .[61]

In the rubble of the great cities of culture, West places, startlingly, the figure of Karl Marx, who "performs" the very trick Miss Lonelyhearts could never pull off: "the miracle of loaves and fishes," of giving the masses not the "stones" that Shrike always urges him to deliver in his column, but bread.

I would propose, in conclusion, the following formula: if the novel traditionally problematizes and explores the meaning of life, West's "novel in the form of a comic strip" problematizes and explores the meaning of the novel. In this sense we could say that *Miss Lonelyhearts* is, indeed, "a communication containing its own criticism"; if not fully demystifying in its *form,* it is so in the subversive *relation* between its form and thematic content. Moreover, for all its "negative classicism," its disdain for mass culture, West's work still seems to challenge the postwar rigidities of the Great Divide. It refuses to celebrate high culture as a repository of value and recognizes that a critique of the times must take its cue from the commercial language of the times. It is bold enough to hold that disorder and negation might offer the only hope for significance and to confront the possibility that outdated artistic pieties might be inadequate – just as inadequate as the good country life advocated by Miss Lonelyhearts's sentimental fiancée, or the pleasures of the 3 B pipe, or salvation by Mother's Lifebuoy, or even the magic of Lux.

Epilogue
"Happy Ending"

In 1952, the first issue of *Discovery* magazine, edited by John Aldridge and Vance Bourjaily, contained a strange new story by Kenneth Fearing, entitled "Happy Ending."[1] It is not a story that is easy to like, exactly. One gets the sense that Fearing's barbed satire, which in the thirties ranged so boldly, had become confined, against its nature, to a suburban cocktail party. The story – really a satirical allegory of sorts – concerns a gossipy coterie of the kind of people Fearing most despised: a "healthy, normal, reasonably prosperous group of people" from those professions most responsible for the creation of a well-adjusted, homogeneous culture of consumption: a designer of jewelry and accessories, a manufacturer of household appliances, a doctor, and a personnel statistician for a large corporation.[2] What happens, essentially, is this: a few members of the group suffer a series of not-so-accidental injuries; these events soon escalate into a spate of deliberate acts of self-mutilation – a perverse kind of keeping-up-with-the-Joneses, which all the characters are gradually drawn into. They first lose joints from their fingers, then whole digits, then ears, eyes, and limbs.

But this "preventive surgery," as they decide to call it, is cast as no loss at all; the "sacrifices," everyone blithely asserts, are really "improvements."[3] The lost fingers are replaced with admirable little commodities: attractively decorated lipsticks, miniature flashlights, tiny cigarette lighters, little phials for saccharine tablets, gilt tubes of solid cologne, cute little pencils, and even car keys. Two of the women replace their earlobes with permanent decorations of silver and sapphire, or gold and ruby (who needs to worry about piercing any longer?); and one man exchanges his ear for a little speaker, so that "ghostly radio voices" sound permanently in his head. Another's eye is replaced with a thin beam of light, which also serves as a kind of high-tech fashion accessory: it "could be changed to any shade desired, and to illuminate different

214

designs, or words." The doctor, not to be outdone, remodels his entire face below the eyes in shiny aluminum, adding a built-in attachment for his physician's reflector. The climax of the story involves the festive sacrifice of the handsome Blane Hewett's severed leg plus the "simple announcement" by his wife that she is expecting a child: a strange and, I think, deliberately nasty juxtaposition of the corny and the horrific, which Fearing's narrator blandly describes as a "cheerful climax."[4]

"Happy Ending" can be read as a summary of and a last word on Fearing's poetic themes of the thirties. It also has obvious connections with Nathanael West's satire, *A Cool Million*. While West did not live to see the affluent postwar America, which is the immediate object of Fearing's satire, his work seems to gesture toward the same frightening loss of humanity. The bland optimism and grotesquerie of "Happy Ending" is prefigured by West's "dismantling of Lemuel Pitkin," who loses his teeth, his eye, his leg, his scalp, and his life – all without losing faith in the "American Way." The only difference, in West's satire, is that the objects that replace these missing parts are less opulent and shiny: Lem, the Depression boy, must make do with false teeth, a glass eye, a wooden leg, a shabby wig, and the like.

These satirical allegories express a threat that haunted both West and Fearing: a fear that human beings might come to lose even the capacity to feel pain and, indeed, loss. "Happy Ending," moreover, can be read as a fantastic enactment of the abstract and abstracting process of reification. The narrative literalizes the process by which the commodity (as Lukács describes it) stamps its impression on human consciousness, on individuals' qualities and abilities.[5] It captures, in its horrific grotesque, the nightmare that ultimately underlies all cultural criticism based on reification: the fear that human beings will be turned into mass-produced things.

This fear is a recurrent motif in twentieth-century expressive culture. Fearing's image, for instance, of the doctor with his high-tech aluminum jaws and his functional, built-in physician's reflector, looks back to similar images in the work of the historical avant-garde. (The invasion of the body by the commodity is, after all, an idea that is readily expressed by collage or assemblage, the favored forms of Dada and Surrealism.) But such fantasies are also omnipresent in postmodern culture, which (at least in Fredric Jameson's influential description of it) has become a culture of "cyborgs with amnesia, where human relations are not even relations between things but relations between images of things."[6] William Gibson's novel, *Neuromancer*, for example, deploys the same motif of the invaded and dismantled body, though no longer in the form of grotesque, but in the form of a kind of noir science fiction. In his postapocalyptic world, there is a thriving black market in body parts, and nervous systems are routinely hooked into vast computer networks. There is also a choice example of the "improved" body: a sexy female killer with retractable scalpel blades instead of nails and silver lenses with "microchannel image-amps" built right into her cheekbones – permanent fashion accessories that are now also permanent weapons.[7] Similarly modified humanoids also stalk such popular texts as *Robocop* and the *Terminator* films, though here the reification (which in Fearing's curiously disturbing story is criticized via the very inanity and conventionality of the characters) tends to be eroticized and glamorized. We are asked, in such texts, to accept these cyborgs as "improved."

The persistence of such images of the merger of the human and the commodified suggests that there is still a certain power in the critique of reification. It is this kind of critique, finally, that makes the work of Fearing and West seem current and that allowed their work of the thirties to cut across the division between high and mass culture: to record the material forces to which all cultural products, whether noble or tacky, were increasingly subject. But a cultural criticism based on the commodity form presents a problem when it comes to the question of political practice: how does one, exactly, resist the vast and abstract and deadening forces of reification? It is no accident, I think, that the popular texts about the "improved body" so often involve fantasies about power – about the ability to actually go out and change the world by force. This study has suggested ways in which Fearing, West, and other writers of the thirties tried to address this problem, whether by an art of negation and irony, or by sacrifice to an ongoing political struggle, or by a search for the "real thing," or by the creation of "dialectical images," or by an attempt to create an alternative culture. But the question of what transformative practice might emerge from this kind of critique is still a living and urgent one. It is not a question to which our scholarship on literature and mass culture will find any easy answers, but it is also not one we can afford to forget.

Notes

1   Susan Buck-Morss, *The Dialectics of Seeing: Walter Benjamin and the "Arcades Project"* (Cambridge, Mass.: MIT Press, 1989), 347.
2   The phrase "political dynamite" is Theodor Adorno's, from a 1934 letter to Benjamin. Cited in Buck-Morss, *The Dialectics of Seeing*, 4.
3   For an account of the emergence of the "Great Divide" in these early years see Lawrence W. Levine, *Highbrow/Lowbrow: The Emergence of Cultural Hierarchy in America* (Cambridge, Mass.: Harvard University Press, 1988); see also Paul R. Gorman's extremely useful overview, "The Development of an American Mass Culture Critique" (Ph.D. diss., University of California, Berkeley, 1990).
4   See Andreas Huyssen, *After the Great Divide: Modernism, Mass Culture, Postmodernism* (Bloomington: Indiana University Press, 1986). Greil Marcus has recently subjected the high, if not desperate, seriousness of these Cold War debates to a bit of ridicule: "With the world governed by what Harold Rosenberg called 'the power trance,' art was put forward as the last redoubt of creativity and critical will, the note sounded with echoes of Thermopylae or the Charge of the Light Brigade: 'What can fifty do,' Clement Greenberg wrote in 1947 of the New York abstract painters, 'against a hundred and forty million?' " *Lipstick Traces: A Secret History of the Twentieth Century* (Cambridge, Mass.: Harvard University Press, 1989), 168.
5   Michael Denning, "The End of Mass Culture," *International Labor and Working-Class History* 37 (Spring 1990): 7, 9.
6   Ibid., 8–9.
7   Andrew Ross, *No Respect: Intellectuals and Popular Culture* (New York: Routledge, 1989).
8   Fredric Jameson, "Reification and Utopia in Mass Culture," *Social Text* 1 (Winter 1979): 133–34.
9   Stuart Hall, "Notes on Deconstructing 'The Popular,' " in *People's History and Socialist Theory*, ed. Raphael Samuel (London: Routledge & Kegan Paul,

1981), 227–40. Michael Denning offers a valuable comparative reading of these two influential essays in "The End of Mass Culture," 4–6.

10   While noting the importance of Van Wyck Brooks's 1915 essay, "Highbrow and Lowbrow," the British critic Richard King suggests that the modernism/mass culture debate really *originates* in the late thirties. Although I think the "origins" of the issue have been pushed back rather significantly by Levine's work, King is right insofar as the thirties do indeed seem to mark a new and crucial phase in the debate. See King's "Modernism and Mass Culture: The Origins of the Debate," in *The Thirties: Politics and Culture in a Time of Broken Dreams,* ed. Heinz Ickstadt, Rob Kroes, and Brian Lee (Amsterdam: Free University Press, 1987), 120–42.

11   Patrick Brantlinger, *Bread and Circuses: Theories of Mass Culture as Social Decay* (Ithaca, N.Y.: Cornell University Press, 1983), 30. Gorman has listed some of the early instances of the term – e.g., Rose Strunsky's translation of Leon Trotsky's *Literature and Revolution* (1925); F. R. Leavis's *Mass Civilization and Minority Culture* (1930); and a number of essays from the *New Masses* in the early thirties, when the term seems to acquire some currency. The *Oxford English Dictionary,* as Gorman notes, lists a 1939 article as the first occurrence ("The Development of an American Mass Culture Critique," 10n).

12   Robert Warshow, "The Legacy of the Thirties," in *The Immediate Experience: Movies, Comics, Theater and Other Aspects of Popular Culture* (New York: Doubleday, 1964); Dwight Macdonald, "A Theory of Mass Culture," in *Mass Culture: The Popular Arts in America,* ed. Bernard Rosenberg and David Manning White (New York: Free Press, 1957), 59–73. This "scandal of the middle-brow" has been studied and challenged by Janice Radway. See her essays, "The Scandal of the Middlebrow: The Book-of-the-Month Club, Class Fracture and Cultural Authority," *South Atlantic Quarterly* 89 (Fall 1990): 703–36, and "The Book-of-the-Month Club and the General Reader," *Critical Inquiry* 14 (Spring 1988), 516–38.

13   Eric Homberger, *American Writers and Radical Politics, 1900–39: Equivocal Commitments* (London: Macmillan, 1986), 128–29. See also Utz Riese, "Neither High nor Low: Michael Gold's Concept of a Proletarian Literature," in *The Thirties,* ed. Ickstadt et al., 143–66.

14   I am thinking, for instance, of Dwight Macdonald's dismay at the very notion of Bauhaus toasters in the home or Eliot plays on Broadway, in "A Theory of Mass Culture," 64.

15   Alice G. Marquis, *Hopes and Ashes: The Birth of Modern Times, 1929–1939* (New York: Macmillan, 1986), 164–68.

16   James Agee and Walker Evans, *Let Us Now Praise Famous Men* (Boston: Houghton Mifflin, 1969), 14.

17   We might perhaps think of Agee's fascination with the authenticity of scarcity as an instance of the "anorexic" response to consumer culture that Susan Willis describes in *A Primer for Daily Life* (New York: Routledge, 1991), 20.

18   Agee and Evans, *Let Us Now Praise Famous Men,* 15.

19 Matthew Josephson, "The Great American Billposter," *Broom* 3 (1922): 310.

20 Alfred Kreymborg, "THE LATEST HEADLINES," *New Masses* 4 (June 1928): 16.

21 See, e.g., Paul Buhle, *Marxism in the United States: Remapping the History of the American Left* (London: Verso, 1987), 157; and for a more detailed study of popular music and the Old Left, Robbie Lieberman, *"My Song Is My Weapon": People's Songs, American Communism and the Politics of Culture, 1930–1950* (Urbana: University of Illinois Press, 1989).

22 Letter from Theodor Adorno to Walter Benjamin, 18 March 1936, in *Aesthetics and Politics: Theodor Adorno, Walter Benjamin, Ernest Bloch, Bertolt Brecht, Georg Lukacs,* ed. Perry Anderson et al. (London: Verso, 1977), 123.

23 Raymond Williams, *Marxism and Literature* (Oxford: Oxford University Press, 1977), 122–23.

24 Denning, "The End of Mass Culture," 4.

25 Ross, *No Respect,* 233–34.

26 See Robert Christgau, "Theory of the Pleasure Class: Pop Culture Without Tears," review of *No Respect* by Andrew Ross, *Village Voice Literary Supplement* 80 (November 1989): 27.

27 T. J. Jackson Lears, "Making Fun of Popular Culture," *American Historical Review* 97 (December 1992): 1421. There have recently been attempts to redress certain simplistic and received ideas about Critical Theory. In the essay just cited, Lears refutes the all too pervasive notion that the Frankfurt school failed to recognize the dialectical and self-contradictory nature of popular texts. In "The Frankfurt School in the Development of the Mass Culture Debate," Eugene Lunn defends the Frankfurt school against the equally common charges of antidemocratic elitism and regressive nostalgia (in *The Aesthetics of the Critical Theorists: Studies on Benjamin, Adorno, Marcuse, and Habermas* [Lewiston, N.Y.: Edwin Mellen Press, 1990]: 26–84).

28 Jackson Lears also emphasizes this problem in "Making Fun of Popular Culture," his response to Lawrence Levine's essay "The Folklore of Industrial Society: Popular Culture and Its Audiences," *American Historical Review* 97 (December 1992): 1369–99. Picking up on the metaphor of *renting,* which De Certeau uses to describe the audience's relatively autonomous *use* of cultural products, Lears observes: "Certainly, 'we all know' that people can put their individual stamp on even the most poorly made tract house; but they are still stuck with the tacky vinyl siding and the widening cracks in the 'pressure-treated' lumber on the deck. The house, built swiftly from the bottom line up, creates an inescapable set of constraints on their choices" (1423). While I hate to belabor Lears's witty reference to the "bottom *line,*" it seems worth underscoring that *capital,* and not merely symbolic capital, remains determinant, even if not absolutely so.

29 Robert Lynd, "The People as Consumers," in *Recent Social Trends in the United States: Report of the President's Research Committee on Social Trends,* one volume edition (New York: McGraw-Hill, 1932), 857.

30 Willis, *A Primer for Daily Life,* 12–13.

31 Denning, "The End of Mass Culture," 7–8.

2 HARD TIMES, MODERN TIMES

1   Alfred Kazin, *Starting Out in the Thirties* (Boston: Little, Brown, 1965), 165.

2   Jean Baudrillard, *The Mirror of Production* (St. Louis, Mo.: Telos Press, 1975), 144. The passage resembles the similarly dystopian economic history traced by Guy Debord (though Debord does not assign any firm date to the shift he describes): "Whereas in the primitive phase of capitalist accumulation, 'political economy sees in the *proletarian* only the *worker*,' who must receive the minimum indispensable for the conservation of his labor power without ever considering him 'in his leisure, in his humanity,' these ideas of the dominant class are reversed as soon as the production of commodities reaches a level of abundance which requires a surplus of collaboration from the worker. The worker, suddenly redeemed from the total contempt which is clearly shown him by all the varieties of organization and supervision of production, finds himself every day, outside of production and in the guise of the consumer, seemingly treated as an adult, with zealous politeness. At this point the *humanism of the commodity* takes charge of the worker's 'leisure and humanity,' simply because now political economy can and must dominate these spheres as *political economy*. Thus the 'perfect denial of man' has taken charge of the totality of human existence." See Debord, *Society of the Spectacle* (Detroit: Black & Red, 1983), proposition 43.

3   Warren I. Susman, *Culture as History: The Transformation of American Society in the Twentieth Century* (New York: Pantheon, 1984), xx.

4   Richard Wightman Fox, "Epitaph for Middletown: Robert S. Lynd and the Analysis of Consumer Culture" in *The Culture of Consumption: Critical Essays in American History, 1880–1980*, ed. R. W. Fox and T. J. Jackson Lears (New York: Pantheon, 1983), 103.

5   Several authors have noted the importance of 1927: see Susman, *Culture as History*, 187; Robert A. M. Stern, *George Howe: Towards a Modern American Architecture* (New Haven, Conn.: Yale University Press, 1975), 71–78, and "The Relevance of the Decade," *Journal of the Society of Architectural Historians* 24 (1965): 6–10; Allen Churchill, *The Year the World Went Mad* (New York: Crowell, 1960); Joseph J. Corn, ed., *Imagining Tomorrow: History, Technology and the American Future* (Cambridge, Mass.: MIT Press, 1986), 82–89; and Robert Heide and John Gilman, *Dime-Store Dream Parade: Popular Culture, 1925–1955* (New York: Dutton, 1979), 33.

6   Lizabeth Cohen, "The Class Experience of Mass Consumption: Workers as Consumers in Interwar America," in *The Power of Culture: Critical Essays in American History*, ed. Richard Wightman Fox and T. J. Jackson Lears (Chicago: University of Chicago Press, 1993), 137.

7   For Baudrillard's use of the term, see "Marxism and the System of Political Economy," in *The Mirror of Production*, 114–41.

8   Lawrence W. Levine, "The Folklore of Industrial Society: Popular Culture and Its Audiences," *American Historical Review* 97 (December 1992): 1369–99. The essay is part of a forum discussion including responses to Levine by Natalie Zemon Davis, Robin D. G. Kelley, and T. J. Jackson Lears; I

discuss this important debate somewhat more fully in Chapter 8. Though I have some problems with Levine's approach to popular culture, he seems to me quite correct when he argues that while the general shift from a production-oriented to a consumption-oriented culture "took place not suddenly but cumulatively, as all such changes do, the Great Depression unquestionably expedited it." See Levine, "American Culture and the Great Depression," *Yale Review* 7 (Winter 1985): 213.

9   This point becomes only too clear when one notes the similarities between the ideological cornerstones of the "Reagan revolution" and those of the "Middletown Spirit" (which already struck Robert Lynd as positively antediluvian in 1935). These include, for example, the hoary old notion that we need " 'more business in government and less government in business' "; " 'that it undermines a man's character for him to get what he doesn't earn' "; " 'that Americans are the freest people in the world' "; " 'that the family is a sacred institution' "; and " 'that the chance to grow rich is necessary to keep initiative alive.' " Robert S. Lynd and Helen Merrell Lynd, *Middletown in Transition: A Study in Cultural Conflicts* (New York: Harcourt, Brace, 1937), 402–18.

10   Boyden Sparkes, "Horatio Alger at the Bridge," *Saturday Evening Post*, 2 May 1936, 20–21, 69–72, 74. The absurdities asserted in this article approach those of West's Shagpoke Whipple. The successful magazine editor S. S. McClure, interviewed for the piece, puts forward the unlikely view that hardship is an advantage, *tout court*: "Anyone who is in easy circumstances – I don't mean rich at all, but with sufficient income for comfort – has to overcome a great handicap to get on equal terms in the world with a man who has to make his way entirely" (69).

11   Levine, "American Culture and the Great Depression," 212.

12   Charles Eckert, "Shirley Temple and the House of Rockefeller," in *American Media and Mass Culture: Left Perspectives,* ed. Donald Lazere (Berkeley: University of California Press, 1987), 167.

13   For a discussion of the "turn to Gramsci" see, e.g., Tony Bennett's useful introduction to Bennett, Colin Mercer, and Janet Woollacott, eds., *Popular Culture and Social Relations* (London: Open University Press, 1986).

14   Greil Marcus, *Lipstick Traces: A Secret History of the Twentieth Century* (Cambridge, Mass.: Harvard University Press, 1989), 105.

15   Kenneth Fearing, "American Rhapsody (4)," *Complete Poems,* ed. Robert M. Ryley (Orono, Me.: National Poetry Foundation, 1994), 146.

16   Susman, *Culture as History,* xxix–xxx.

17   A Redstocking Sister, "Consumerism and Women," in *Woman in Sexist Society: Studies in Power and Powerlessness,* ed. Vivian Gornick and Barbara K. Moran (New York: Basic Books, 1971), 659–60.

18   Fredric Jameson, "Reification and Utopia in Mass Culture," *Social Text* 1 (1979): 144; see also Stuart Hall, "Notes on Deconstructing 'The Popular,' " in *People's History and Socialist Theory,* ed. Raphael Samuel (London: Routledge & Kegan Paul, 1981), 229: "If the forms of provided commercial popular culture are not purely manipulative, then it is because, alongside the false appeals, the foreshortenings, the trivialisation and short-circuits,

there are also elements of recognition and identification, something approaching a recreation of recognisable experiences and attitudes to which people are responding."

19   Michel de Certeau, *The Practice of Everyday Life* (Berkeley: University of California Press, 1984), esp. xii, 18, 30–32.

20   Cited in Patrick Renshaw, "Organized Labour and the Keynesian Revolution," in *Nothing Else to Fear: New Perspectives on America in the Thirties,* ed. Stephen Baskerville and Ralph Willett (Manchester: Manchester University Press, 1985), 230.

21   Mike Davis, *Prisoners of the American Dream: Politics and Economy in the History of the American Working Class* (London: Verso, 1986), 51.

22   Stanley Aronowitz (for one) has noted that the theory of revolution as the outcome of the inevitable economic crisis of capitalism must be reexamined: "There is absolutely no evidence that depressions in themselves lead to a rise of revolutionary activity, much less revolutionary consciousness among workers. On the contrary, workers tend to become profoundly conservative under conditions of increasing material deprivation. . . . The economic crisis of the 1930s resulted in a strengthening of the capitalist state, rather than the development of a large revolutionary workers' movement." *False Promises: The Shaping of American Working Class Consciousness* (New York: McGraw-Hill, 1973), 53–54.

23   The phrase is from the German sociologist Werner Sombart (1906), cited in Lizabeth Cohen, "The Class Experience of Mass Consumption," 136.

24   Cohen, "The Class Experience of Mass-Consumption," 152–60. See also Levine, "The Folklore of Industrial Society," 1372–73, 1376, 1378–80.

25   Cited in Robert S. McElvaine, *The Great Depression: America, 1929–1941* (New York: Times Books, 1984), 175, 180.

26   Studs Terkel, *Hard Times: An Oral History of the Great Depression* (New York: Washington Square Press, 1978); Alice G. Marquis, *Hopes and Ashes: The Birth of Modern Times, 1929–1939* (New York: Macmillan, 1986); Roland Marchand, *Advertising the American Dream: Making Way for Modernity, 1920–1940* (Berkeley: University of California Press, 1985); and Heide and Gilman, *Dime-Store Dream Parade.*

27   Cited in Halford E. Luccock, *American Mirror: Social, Ethical and Religious Aspects of American Literature, 1930–1940* (New York: Macmillan, 1941), 247–248.

28   In his essay, "Advertising and the Development of Consumer Society," in *Cultural Politics in Contemporary America,* ed. Ian Angus and Sut Jhally (New York: Routledge, 1989), Stuart Ewen argues that *Modern Times* is utopian and visionary, in the sense that it places against "the robotic rhythms of factory life . . . a politics of spontaneity, a manifesto for sensuality and positive disorder" (86–87). He points out that the use of the Chaplinesque tramp in the IBM advertising campaigns of a few years ago is therefore particularly ironic: the film tries to find a way out of the Taylorized efficiency of modern progress, whereas the ads instruct us to accept and adapt to it. Ewen's remarks suggest that my reading is a little dour and fails to take the disruptiveness of the film's humor and playfulness into account.

But there is good reason to see in *Modern Times* a promotion of that other, less spontaneous utopia: the utopia of consumption. Apart from the textual evidence I have cited, there is the fact that Chaplin himself explicitly advocated a Keynesian rather than a revolutionary solution to the economic crisis: "If America is to have sustained prosperity," he commented in a 1931 interview, "the American people must have sustained ability to spend." Cited in David Robinson, *Chaplin: His Life and Art* (New York: McGraw-Hill, 1985), 457.

29 Allen Jenkins, *The Thirties* (London: Heinemann, 1976), 14; Susman, *Culture as History*, 154.

30 Jenkins, *The Thirties*, 15; see also Frederick Lewis Allen, *Only Yesterday and Since Yesterday: A Popular History of the 20s and 30s* (New York: McGraw-Hill, 1973), 276.

31 See, e.g., Terkel's interview with Clifford Burke (*Hard Times*, 104): "The Negro was born in depression. It didn't mean too much to him, The Great American Depression, as you call it. There was no such thing. The best he could be is a janitor or a porter or a shoeshine boy. It only became official when it hit the white man." Or consider the blues tune that black workers in the South sang during the thirties: "De raggedy man see de hahd time, . . . when his money is gone / Now you an' me see de hahd time . . . Sence we wuz bawn." Cited in Levine, "American Culture and the Great Depression," 198.

32 Daniel Horowitz, *The Morality of Spending: Attitudes towards Consumer Society in America, 1875–1940* (Baltimore: Johns Hopkins University Press, 1985), 135, 153–54.

33 Lynd and Lynd, *Middletown in Transition*, 46.

34 Fox and Lears, in their introduction to *The Culture of Consumption*, express a similar view: "To discover how consumption became a cultural ideal, a hegemonic 'way of seeing' in twentieth-century America, requires looking at powerful individuals and institutions who conceived, formulated, and preached that ideal or way of seeing. Most recent social history has focused on the cultures of the common people, a previously neglected subject. But it is impossible to understand the cultures of ordinary Americans without appreciating the ways those cultures are influenced and delimited by the ideals, plans, and needs of the powerful. The study of dominant elites – white, male, educated, affluent – is a critically important part of social history" (x–xi).

35 Cited in Charles W. Wood, "Can It Be Solved?" *Forbes* (15 April 1927), 11. See also Stuart Ewen, *Captains of Consciousness: Advertising and the Social Roots of the Consumer Culture* (New York: MacGraw-Hill, 1976), 52.

36 Mrs. Christine Frederick, *Selling Mrs. Consumer* (New York: Business Bourse, 1929), 4–5. The book's curious epigraphs ("Happy are the people whose annals are blank in history books" and "The silence of the people is a lesson for kings") and the dedication (to Herbert Hoover) suggest a surprisingly overt – and rather troubling – ideological and political agenda.

37 Advertisement for Young & Rubicam, Inc., *Fortune* (September 1931). Reprinted in Marchand, *Advertising the American Dream*, 301.

38 Horowitz, *The Morality of Spending*, 153–58.

39 Ibid., 155.

40 Baudrillard, *Mirror of Production*, 129.

41 Horowitz, *The Morality of Spending*, 153. One should, I think, be careful of the claim that the elusiveness of use-value is a purely contemporary phenomenon. The prime commodities of mercantile capitalism (such as coffee, chocolate, and tobacco) were frequently frivolous, fashionable items. As W. F. Haug has pointed out, the creation and control of a need for luxury is not restricted to late capitalism – it has always been part of the history of commodities and their use. See his *Critique of Commodity Aesthetics: Appearance, Sexuality and Advertising in Capitalist Society* (Minneapolis: University of Minnesota Press, 1986), 21.

42 Horowitz, *The Morality of Spending*, 161–68.

43 Fox, "Epitaph for Middletown," 104.

44 Robert Lynd, "The People as Consumers," *Recent Social Trends in the United States: Report of the President's Research Committee on Social Trends*, one-volume ed. (New York: McGraw-Hill, 1932), 857; Mark C. Smith, "Robert Lynd and Consumerism in the 1930s," *Journal of the History of Sociology* 2 (Fall-Winter, 1979–80): 100.

45 Lynd, "The People as Consumers," 866–67, 857.

46 Max Horkheimer, "The End of Reason," *Studies in Philosophy and Social Science* 9 (1941): 384.

47 Lynd and Lynd, *Middletown in Transition*, 509–10.

48 Robert S. Lynd and Helen Merrell Lynd, *Middletown: A Study in Contemporary American Culture* (New York: Harcourt, Brace, 1929), 82n.

49 Lynd and Lynd, *Middletown in Transition*, 46.

50 This often-cited figure, based on the Hays Commission calculations, may also, in fact, be inflated: Lary May has argued that since the source for these figures was the film producers, they were likely to have been optimistic in order to get bank loans for the construction of new movie houses. A Gallup poll of 1940 suggests that weekly attendance may actually have been around 54,275,000. See May, "Making the American Way: Moderne Theaters, Audiences, and the Film Industry, 1929–1945," *Prospects* 12 (1987): 108–9.

51 Allen, *Since Yesterday*, 279–80.

52 The phrase is Fredric Jameson's. See his "Reification and Utopia in Mass Culture," *Social Text* 1 (Winter 1979): 141.

53 The public had surely not forgotten Chaplin's much-publicized divorce settlement in the late twenties, when Lita Chaplin collected a tidy sum of $825,000. For an interesting historical analysis of the economic dimension to the appeal of movie stars, see Charles Eckert's essay on Shirley Temple cited in note 12 above. Eckert suggests that while Temple appealed to audiences because of her childish cuteness, she was even more fascinating in that she seemed to make millions of dollars without any effort. For Shirley, work was like play – and yet was immensely lucrative. That was what people were obsessed with, to the point that women wrote to Mr. George Temple to ask him if he would assist in the conception of a second little tap-dancing gold mine. As Eckert notes, "Shirley, orphaned, often in poor clothes, with noth-

ing to give but her love, was paradoxically spectacular with the idea of money. And the paradox could as easily be perceived as an oxymoron in which the terms *need* and *abundance* were indissolubly fused" ("Shirley Temple and the House of Rockefeller," 174). The same paradoxical appeal may well have been operative in the case of Chaplin's forlorn tramp.

54 On the advice books of the thirties, see Levine, "American Culture and the Great Depression," 214–15; Susman, *Culture as History*, 164–65; Allen, *Only Yesterday*, 256; and Charles R. Hearne, *The American Dream and the Great Depression* (Westport, Conn.: Greenwood Press, 1977), 138–64.

55 Leo Lowenthal, "The Triumph of Mass Idols," in *Literature, Popular Culture, and Society* (Palo Alto, Calif.: Pacific, 1961), 109–40.

56 Ibid., 127. I discuss this idea in relation to Kenneth Fearing's work in Chapter 5.

57 Ibid., 126.

58 Warren Susman, "Personality and the Making of Twentieth Century Culture," in *Culture and History*, 222–86; David Riesman et al., *The Lonely Crowd: A Study of the Changing American Character* (New Haven, Conn.: Yale University Press, 1969).

59 Lowenthal, "The Triumph of Mass Idols," 123. See also the comments at the conclusion of the essay: "It is some comfort for the little man who has become expelled from the Horatio Alger dream, who despairs of penetrating the thicket of grand strategy in politics and business, to see his heroes as a lot of guys who like or dislike highballs, cigarettes, tomato juice, golf, and social gatherings – just like himself" (135).

60 Marchand, *Advertising the American Dream*, 217–22, 288–95.

61 Warren Susman, for one, has argued that twentieth-century Marxist analyses of culture have frequently ended up "extolling the values and institutions of the older capitalist order of the nineteenth century" (*Culture as History*, xxix); Chapter 5 of Susman's book, "Socialism and Americanism," offers a fuller discussion of his views.

62 Cited in Daniel Aaron, *Writers on the Left: Episodes in American Literary Communism* (New York: Columbia University Press, 1992), 94.

63 *The Essential Marx*, ed. Ernst Fischer in collaboration with Franz Marek, trans. Anna Bostock (New York: Herder & Herder, 1970), 118.

64 Malcolm Cowley, *Exile's Return* (New York: Viking, 1956), 61–62. Warren Susman and Jonathan Arac have also commented on this intriguing passage; see Susman, *Culture as History*, 80, and Arac, ed., *Postmodernism and Politics*, Theory and History of Literature, vol. 28 (Minneapolis: University of Minnesota Press, 1986), xxxi.

65 The phrase is from Robert E. Dunbar's 1925 piece in the *Daily Worker*, entitled "Mammonart and Communist Art." Cited in Eric Homberger, *American Writers and Radical Politics, 1900–39: Equivocal Commitments* (London: Macmillan, 1986), 125.

66 Marcus Klein, *Foreigners: The Making of American Literature, 1900–1940* (Chicago: University of Chicago Press, 1981), 99.

67 William Empson, *Some Versions of the Pastoral* (London: Chatto & Windus, 1950), 6.

68   Raymond Williams, *Marxism and Literature* (Oxford: Oxford University Press, 1977), 122–123.

69   On Gold and Dell, see Klein, *Foreigners*, 79–81. Gold's most notoriously homophobic piece is "Wilder: Prophet of the Genteel Christ," in *Mike Gold: A Literary Anthology*, ed. Michael Folsom (New York: International, 1972), 197–202. Another virulent example of the mysogynistic and homophobic tendency of American Communists is Robert Forsythe's "Mae West: A Treatise on Decay," in *New Masses: An Anthology of the Rebel Thirties*, ed. Joseph North (New York: International, 1969), 311–14.

70   On the idea of "weightlessness," see T. J. Jackson Lears, "From Salvation to Self-Realization," in *The Culture of Consumption*, ed. Fox and Lears, 9–10, 16.

71   Marchand, *Advertising the American Dream*, 66–69; see also Andreas Huyssen, "Mass Culture as Woman: Modernism's Other," in *After the Great Divide: Modernism, Mass Culture, Postmodernism* (Bloomington: Indiana University Press, 1986), 47–53.

72   Helen Woodward, *Through Many Windows* (New York: Harpers, 1926), 298.

73   Cited in Marchand, *Advertising the American Dream*, 300.

74   The label "Capitalist Realism" is Michael Schudson's in *Advertising, the Uneasy Persuasion: Its Dubious Impact on American Society* (New York: Basic Books, 1984), 214–218.

75   Marchand, *Advertising the American Dream*, 74.

76   See James Rorty, *Where Life Is Better: An Unsentimental Journey* (New York: John Day, 1936), especially the incident Andrew Ross describes as a "symptomatic meeting between the 'missionary' of proletarian culture and the 'slavetrader' in commercial popular culture": Rorty gives a ride to a subscription salesman for the McFadden journals, and, distressed to learn how popular these *"Blue Romances"* are, and how reactionary the man's positions seem to be, dumps him in the middle of nowhere (96). Ross observes, correctly I think, that "Rorty's lack of fraternity could be seen as a displacement of his own frustrated mission to convert the masses, a frustration that pervades his and many other likeminded narratives." *No Respect: Intellectuals and Popular Culture* (New York: Routledge, 1989), 49–50.

77   Kenneth Burke, *Attitudes Towards History* (Berkeley: University of California Press, 1984), 103–4.

78   Gold, "America Needs a Critic," in *Mike Gold: A Literary Anthology*, ed. Folsom, 139.

79   Cited in Homberger, *American Writers and Radical Politics*, 233.

80   Kenneth Burke, "Revolutionary Symbolism in America," in *American Writers' Congress*, ed. Henry Hart (New York: International, 1935), 89.

81   Susman, "Socialism and Americanism," in *Culture as History*, 80.

82   Ibid., 82.

83   Back cover of *New Masses* 19 (27 September, 1938); cited in Paul Buhle, *Marxism in the United States: Remapping the History of the American Left* (London: Verso, 1987), 179.

84   Gold, "America needs a Critic," 139. The University of Wisconsin YCL

pamphlet is cited in Irving Howe and Lewis Coser, *The American Communist Party: A Critical History* (New York: Praeger, 1962), 338, and is discussed in Susman, *Culture as History*, 81.

85 Susman, *Culture as History*, 80–81.

86 For a discussion of this connection, see Leonard Quart, "Frank Capra and the Popular Front," in *American Media and Mass Culture*, ed. Lazere, 178–83.

87 Stanley Aronowitz puts forward the same judgment in his useful overview, "Culture and Politics," *Politics & Society* 6 (1976): 363.

88 Fox and Lears, eds., *The Culture of Consumption*, ix.

89 Both Horowitz, *The Morality of Spending*, 164, and Fox, "Epitaph for Middletown," 103, concur.

90 I am influenced here by Susan Buck-Morss's account of Walter Benjamin's revolutionary hermeneutics, "Walter Benjamin – Revolutionary Writer (I)," *New Left Review* (September 1982): 97.

91 See, e.g., R. W. B. Lewis, "Days of Wrath and Laughter: West," in *Nathanael West: Modern Critical Views*, ed. Harold Bloom (New York: Chelsea House, 1986), esp. 72–75; Jeffrey Duncan, "The Problem of Language in *Miss Lonelyhearts*," in ibid., esp. 153–56; and John Keyes, "Nathanael West's 'New Art Form': Metamorphoses of Detective Fiction in *Miss Lonelyhearts*," *English Studies in Canada* 8 (March 1982), esp. 84–85. Keyes offers a characteristic formulation: "West's accomplishments in this novel thus transcend and transform the mass culture upon which it is based" (84).

92 Buck-Morss, "Walter Benjamin – Revolutionary Writer (I)," 97–98.

3 THE POLITICS OF LITERARY FAILURE: FEARING, MASS CULTURE, AND THE CANON

1 See, e.g., Kenneth Burke's judgment that "there is no contemporary poet who is neater at noting with ironic corrosion the grotesque injustices of our ailing economic structure" ("Recent Poetry," *Southern Review* 1 [1935–36]: 177, or Robert Cantwell's observation that "more than any other writer Fearing sums up the attitude of his generation" (cited in Jack Salzman and Leo Zanderer, eds., *Social Poetry of the 1930s: A Selection* [New York: Burt Franklin, 1978], 322, or Weldon Kees's comment on the topicality of his subject matter: "Fearing . . . gathers up-to-the-minute horrors with all the eager thoroughness of a bibliophile cackling over pagination errors" ("Fearing's Collected Poems," *Poetry* 57 [January 1941]: 264).

2 Kenneth Fearing, "Beyond Estheticism," review of *Returning to Emotion* and *The King of Spain* by Maxwell Bodenheim, *Menorah Journal* 15 (September 1928): 283.

3 My citations from Fearing's poems are for the most part from *Kenneth Fearing: Complete Poems*, ed. Robert M. Ryley (Orono, Me: National Poetry Foundation, 1994) and from *New and Selected Poems* (Bloomington: Indiana University Press, 1956). The page references will henceforth be cited parenthetically following the abbreviations CP and NS respectively. However, in a few cases where Fearing's later revisions seem to me to have signifi-

cantly muted the topical interest of the original versions, I cite from the following earlier volumes: *Poems* (New York: Dynamo, 1935) and *Dead Reckoning* (New York, Random House, 1938). These titles are abbreviated P and DR respectively. For comments on Fearing's "corrections" of earlier versions, see Kees, "Fearing's Collected Poems," 267–68n.

4   Warren I. Susman, *Culture as History: The Transformation of American Society in the Twentieth Century* (New York: Pantheon, 1983), 101.

5   Cited in Kees, "Fearing's Collected Poems," 266.

6   Susman, *Culture as History,* 103.

7   To date there are only two published biographical essays on Kenneth Fearing. The first is Patricia B. Santora's "The Life of Kenneth Flexner Fearing (1902–1961)," *College Language Association Journal* 32 (1989): 309–22. This article is taken from her Ph.D. dissertation, "The Poetry and Prose of Kenneth Flexner Fearing" (University of Maryland, 1982). Santora has done some primary research, and has corresponded with surviving family members, friends, editors, and others. I use and gratefully acknowledge this work. However, her biography – indeed her whole dissertation – entirely fails to relate Fearing to the literary and historical context in which he worked and seems largely aimed at purging him of the taint of his Communist associations. The second and most recent essay is Robert Ryley's fine biographical introduction to the National Poetry Foundation's new edition of the *Complete Poems* (ix–xxvii). Ryley's detailed research will give the reader a greater sense of Fearing's personal life and relationships, especially in his later years, than the present brief and polemical sketch.

8   Santora, "Poetry and Prose," 3–6, 21; Horace Gregory and Marya Zaturenska, *A History of American Poetry, 1900–1940* (New York: Harcourt, Brace, 1942).

9   See, e.g., Lionel Abel, *The Intellectual Follies: A Memoir of the Literary Venture in New York and Paris* (New York: Norton, 1984), 14–15; Albert Halper, *Goodbye, Union Square: A Writer's Memoirs of the Thirties* (Chicago: Quadrangle Books, 1970), 43, 92, 102; Horace Gregory, *The House on Jefferson Street: A Cycle of Memories* (New York: Holt, Rinehart & Winston, 1971), 120–21, 163.

10   Kenneth Rexroth, *American Poetry in the Twentieth Century* (New York: Herder & Herder, 1971), 114–115; Halper, *Goodbye, Union Square,* 92; Santora, "Poetry and Prose," 7.

11   Kenneth Burke, "Fearing's New Poems," *New Masses,* 30 (21 February 1939): 27.

12   See Guy Debord, *Society of the Spectacle* (Detroit: Black & Red, 1983), propositions 204–10. One might think of Fearing's style in terms of Debord's definition of "détournement" as the "language of anti-ideology."

13   William Rose Benét, "Contemporary Poetry," *Saturday Review* 12 (15 June 1935): 18; Kees, "Fearing's Collected Poems," 267.

14   Santora, "Poetry and Prose," 5. According to Robert Ryley, Fearing had apparently failed, retaken, and passed a course in calculus in 1924, but the university had never officially acknowledged his completion of the degree

(letter to the author, 14 July 1993). S. J. Kunitz and H. Haycraft, eds., *Twentieth Century Authors: A Biographical Dictionary of Modern Literature* (New York: H. W. Wilson, 1942), 444.

15 Kenneth Fearing, "Another Ghetto Novel," review of *The Mother* by Scholom Asch, *Menorah Journal* 19 (March 1931): 328–29; Halper, *Goodbye, Union Square,* 92; Kenneth Fearing, "Hoboken Blues," *New Masses* 3 (April 1928), 27; Kenneth Fearing, "Symbols of Survival," *Partisan Review* 2 (May-June 1935): 89–91; Santora, "Poetry and Prose," iii–iv, 10–11.

16 Albert Halper, *Union Square* (New York: Literary Guild, 1933), 10–13, 27, 167, 294; Gregory, *The House on Jefferson Street,* 120–21. The line I am referring to is from "Dirge": "O executive type, would you like to drive a floating-power, knee-action, silk-upholstered six?" (*CP,* 109).

17 Horace Gregory, "Revolution and the Individual Writer," *Partisan Review* 2 (April-May 1935): 53; C. Cudworth Flint, "Two Party Poets," *Kenyon Review* 1 (Spring 1939): 223–26.

18 Santora, "Poetry and Prose," 12–13. For a more considered and balanced assessment of Fearing's relationship to the Communist Party, see Robert Ryley's biographical essay (*CP,* xviii–xx).

19 Ibid., 12; Kunitz and Haycraft, eds., *Twentieth Century Authors,* 444.

20 One of the pieces that might have led to the judgment that the Communists disapproved of Fearing is Alexander F. Bergman's review of Fearing's *Collected Poems.* It offers quite a harsh assessment of his pessimistic poems: "They are a surrender and a contribution to the propaganda of the press and radio, to their deliberately cultivated fatalism designed to rob the people of the spirit of resistance against the fascist offensive. They constitute a cancellation of his identification with the progressive forces among the people."

Since Fearing's poetry was always pessimistic, it is tempting to read between the lines here a difference of opinion on other matters, such as the Moscow trials. Yet I see little evidence for Walter Kalaidjian's claim that the disapproval of the Party contributed to Fearing's subsequent obscurity – rather the contrary: publications connected to the Party put him on the map in the twenties and thirties. See Bergman, "Fearing's Poems" *New Masses* 37 (19 November 1940): 25; Walter Kalaidjian, "Transpersonal Poetics: Language Writing and the Historical Avant-Gardes in Postmodern Culture," *American Literary History* 3 (Summer 1991): 331.

21 Kunitz and Haycraft, eds., *Twentieth Century Authors,* 444; Rexroth, *American Poetry in the Twentieth Century,* 114.

22 See, e.g., Edward Dahlberg, "Kenneth Fearing: A Poet for Workers," review of *Poems* by Fearing, *New Masses* 15 (21 May 1935): 24–25.

23 Halper, *Union Square,* 286–93, 63.

24 Kunitz and Haycraft, eds., *Twentieth Century Authors,* 444. For some Russian-inspired poems, see Lewis's "The Man from Moscow," "Just Propaganda," and "Star Ride," in *Social Poetry of the 1930s,* ed. Salzman and Zanderer, 144–47; as well as Funaroff's (Charles Henry Newman's) "Uprooted" and Bodenheim's "To a Revolutionary Girl," in *Proletarian Literature in the United States: An Anthology,* ed. Granville Hicks et al. (New York:

International, 1935), 178, 147. The last two poems use the image of Russian women as the antithesis to the unemployed American man and to the sentimental, consumption-oriented American girl.

25 I am thinking here of Burke's address, "Revolutionary Symbolism in America," in *American Writers' Congress,* ed. Henry Hart (New York International, 1935), 89−90.

26 Estelle Gershgoren Novak, "The *Dynamo* School of Poets," *Contemporary Literature* 11 (Autumn 1970): 527−28; Fearing, "Hoboken Blues," 27.

27 Gold could be seen as representing a strong version of this belief: for him, Left politics were essential for great creative efforts; bourgeois artists might be technically skilled, but they "cannot create a great art" ("Two Critics in a Bar-Room," *Liberator* 4 [September 1921]: 30). A more moderate version can be found in Cowley's essay "What the Revolutionary Movement Can Do for a Writer," collected in *Think Back on Us . . . : A Contemporary Chronicle of the 1930s* (Carbondale: Southern Illinois University Press, 1972), 88−93.

28 Kenneth Fearing et al., "The Situation in American Writing: Seven Questions," *Partisan Review* 6 (1939): 34.

29 Stanley Burnshaw, for instance, proclaimed that a "Marxist poet has no reason to be obscure" ("Notes on Revolutionary Poetry," *New Masses* 10 [February 1936]: 13). See also Kees, "Fearing's Collected Poems," 266; and Fearing, "Hoboken Blues," 27.

30 Fearing, "The Situation in American Writing," 35.

31 Fearing, "U.S. Writers in War," *Poetry* 56 (September 1940): 318−22.

32 Cited in Bettina Drew, *Nelson Algren: A Life on the Wild Side* (New York: Putnam's, 1989), 253.

33 Anon., "Kenneth Fearing, 1902−1961," *Mainstream* 14 (August 1961): 26.

34 Gregory and Zaturenska, *A History of American Poetry,* 465; Santora, "Poetry and Prose," 16; Anon., "Kenneth Fearing, Author, Was 59," *New York Times,* 27 June 1961, 33, col. 3.

35 James Ashbrook Perkins, "An American Rhapsody: The Poetry and Prose of Kenneth Fearing" (Ph.D. diss., University of Tennessee, 1972), 143−48; Santora, "Poetry and Prose," 170, 16.

36 Charles Humboldt, "The Voice Persisted Until Death: An Appreciation," *Trace* 46 (Summer 1962): 220−21.

37 Allen Guttman, "The Brief Embattled Course of Proletarian Poetry," in *Proletarian Literature of the Thirties,* ed. David Madden (Carbondale: Southern Illinois University Press, 1968), 256; Eric Mottram, "The Hostile Environment and the Survival Artist: A Note on the Twenties," in *The American Novel and the Nineteen-Twenties,* ed. Malcolm Bradbury and David Palmer (London: Edward Arnold, 1971), 235−36. Fearing's work also appears in four important anthologies of writing from the 1930s: Louis Filler, ed., *The Anxious Years: America in the Nineteen Thirties − A Collection of Contemporary Writings* (New York: Putnam's, 1963), 220−22; Harvey Swados, ed., *The American Writer and the Great Depression* (Indianapolis, Ind.: Bobbs-Merrill, 1966), 443−44; Jack Salzman, ed., *Years of Protest: A Collection of American Writings of the 1930's* (Indianapolis, Ind.: Bobbs-Merrill, 1970), 182−86; and

Joseph North, ed., *New Masses: An Anthology of the Rebel Thirties* (New York: International, 1969), 40–42.

38 Walter Lowenfels, ed., *The Writing on the Wall: 108 American Poems of Protest* (Garden City, N.Y.: Doubleday, 1969), 116; George Quasha and Jerome Rothenberg, eds., *America: A Prophecy – A New Reading of American Poetry from Pre-Colombian Times to the Present* (New York: Random House, 1973), 272–74; Sy Kahn, "Kenneth Fearing and the Twentieth Century Blues," *The Thirties: Fiction, Poetry Drama,* ed. Warren French (Deland, Fla.: Everett Edwards, 1967), 133–40; M. L. Rosenthal, "The Meaning of Kenneth Fearing's Poetry," *Poetry* 64 (July 1944): 208–23; Daniel Aaron, "Late Thoughts on Nathanael West," in *Nathanael West,* ed. Jay Martin (Englewood Cliffs, N.J.: Prentice-Hall, 1971), 161–70.

39 Cary Nelson, *Repression and Recovery: Modern American Poetry and the Politics of Cultural Memory, 1910–1945* (Madison: University of Wisconsin Press, 1989), 109–10, 166, 285–86; Alan M. Wald, *The Revolutionary Imagination: The Poetry and Politics of John Wheelwright and Sherry Mangan* (Chapel Hill: University of North Carolina Press, 1983), 13; and Walter Kalaidjian, "Transpersonal Poetics," 319–36. Nelson's book not only offers new readings of the political poetry of the thirties, but examines the way in which the established literary histories of this period have served to erase a long tradition of political poetry from our memory and have radically restricted our notions of American modernism. Wald's book counters the long-held assumption that all Communist-inspired poetry was intellectually unchallenging and artistically worthless and rediscovers, especially in the work of Wheelwright, some of the interesting negotiations between Marxism and modernism that went on in the literature of the thirties. Walter Kalaidjian's essay concurs in many ways with my own work: his project is also, one might say, to reread the literary history of the thirties as telescoped through the present.

40 David Rosenthal, "Save These Books," review of Kenneth Fearing, *Collected Poems* and *The Hospital, Village Voice Literary Supplement* (4 March 1987): 53.

41 Bruce Fearing, "letter to kenneth/epistle to pop," *boundary 2* 12 (Fall 1983): 69.

42 Ibid., 71.

43 M. L. Rosenthal, *Our Life in Poetry: Selected Essays and Reviews* (New York: Persea Books, 1992), 161.

44 Nelson, *Repression and Recovery,* 38–39.

45 Ibid., 57.

46 Barbara Herrnstein Smith, "Contingencies of Value," *Critical Inquiry* 10 (September 1983): 11–19.

47 Nelson, *Repression and Recovery,* 69.

48 Fearing, "Beyond Estheticism," 283.

49 Robert Penn Warren, "The Present State of Poetry in the United States," *Kenyon Review* 1 (1939): 385–86.

50 Debord, *Society of the Spectacle,* proposition 24.

51 Ibid., proposition 12.

52   Nelson, *Repression and Recovery*, 244.

53   Ibid., 4.

54   Kenneth Fearing, "Literary Gelding," *New Masses* 3 (September 1927): 9; Kenneth Fearing, "A Teacup Revolutionist," rev. of *East Wind* by Amy Lowell, *New Masses* 2 (November, 1926): 26.

55   Fearing, "Literary Gelding," 26.

56   Jane Tompkins, *Sensational Designs: The Cultural Work of American Fiction, 1790–1860* (New York: Oxford University Press, 1985), 191–92. For further evidence to support Fearing's sense of a radical restriction of literary possibilities, see, e.g., Rexroth, *American Poetry in the Twentieth Century*, 124–25; Nelson, *Repression and Recovery*, 35–37; and Richard Ohmann, *Politics of Letters* (Middletown, Conn.: Wesleyan University Press, 1987), 45–91. Nelson notes how several poets from the fifties perceived the terrain of modern poetry as dominated by a few gigantic talents, titans or dinosaurs fighting for supremacy – a vision he ascribes to a retrospective illusion, imposed on the wild diversity of modernist writing by subsequent critics and canon makers. This hypostasized view of literary activity as a battle for greatness mirrors, he argues, the simplistic political views of the Cold War: "It resembles the ideological strategy of those who promoted a vision of a world contest between freedom and communism, the United States and the Soviet Union, with most of the world's diverse cultures simply invisible to us" (37). Fearing's essay makes the connection between the Cold War and the narrowing of cultural space for poetry seem even closer.

Ohmann's work also seems to me to coincide strikingly with Fearing's position. He argues that at a time when discussable political ideas "reached only from corporate liberalism to welfare-state liberalism," a shrinkage that many Americans experienced as "the end of ideology" (82), American literature also seemed to have suffered a loss of political responsibility. Moreover, viewed from middle distance, almost all the novels that gained canonical or precanonical status seem uncannily alike: from *The Catcher in the Rye* to *Herzog* to *The Bell Jar* to *One Flew over the Cuckoo's Nest*, they are all variations on what Ohmann calls "the illness story." In all of these novels the alienation of a character confronted with a bureacratic or shallow or hypocritical social order is figured as the problem of the individual – as madness, disease, or personal crisis; and the story inevitably concludes with the individual's slight recovery: acceptance, adjustment, or mature resignation. Granted, these novels offer more than Fearing's anecdotes about elderly relatives, but they equally rule out of order (or at least beyond the bounds of that highly ideological category of "verisimilitude") any kind of social resolution to problems that are still identifiable as social. They remain, in other words, safe and risk-proof.

Finally, Ohmann notes that the route by which canonical or precanonical status is achieved is almost suspiciously invariable: all these novels were likely to have been reviewed in the *New York Times Book Review* and the *New York Review of Books,* and were likely to have been published by Random House (which just happens to be the proprietor of the *New York Review of Books*). This argument seems to corroborate Fearing's sense that the channels of communication have become increasingly centralized, and therefore more amenable to control and surveillance.

57   Cary Nelson discusses the "interesting failure" of Vachel Lindsay in *Repression and Recovery*, 69–70. The most sympathetic discussions of Gold are by the German scholar Utz Riese, "Neither High nor Low: Michael Gold's Concept of a Proletarian Literature," in *The Thirties: Politics and Culture in a Time of Broken Dreams*, ed. Heinz Ickstadt, Rob Kroes, and Brian Lee (Amsterdam: Free University Press, 1987), 143–66; by James D. Bloom, *Left Letters: The Culture Wars of Mike Gold and Joseph Freeman* (New York: Columbia University Press, 1992); and by Marcus Klein, *Foreigners: The Making of American Literature, 1900–1940* (Chicago: University of Chicago Press, 1981), 231–48.

58   Peter Bürger, *Theory of the Avant-Garde* (Minneapolis: University of Minnesota Press, 1984), 24–27 and throughout the text.

59   Cited in Stanley Edgar Hyman, "Ideals, Dangers, and Limitations of Mass Culture," in *Culture for the Millions? Mass Media in Modern Society*, ed. Norman Jacobs (Princeton, N.J.: Van Nostrand, 1961), 139.

60   This was during the mid-seventies at the University of Stellenbosch, South Africa. The comfortable formalism I recall here was very soon to meet an important and, ultimately, irresistible challenge in the highly political and antiaesthetic writings of the emerging Soweto poets.

61   Andreas Huyssen, *After the Great Divide: Modernism, Mass Culture, Postmodernism* (Bloomington: Indiana University Press, 1986), vii–viii, 1–15.

62   Dahlberg, "Kenneth Fearing: A Poet for Workers," 24.

63   Fredric Jameson, "Reification and Utopia in Mass Culture," *Social Text* 1 (Winter 1979): 135–36.

64   Thomas Strychacz, *Modernism, Mass Culture, and Professionalism* (Cambridge University Press, 1993), 6–9 and throughout the text.

65   Strychacz, I should note, is entirely aware of the importance of readerly strategies: indeed, his approach in *Modernism, Mass Culture, and Professionalism* is especially innovative with regard to its rigorous insistence that the dialectic between modernism and mass culture cannot be understood without also taking into account the contemporaneous rise of professional literary critics. The cultural authority of modernist literature, he argues, is dependent on the prestige of literary academicians who can validate obscure and experimental texts (and, of course, in the same act validate themselves as expert interpreters). It is a powerful argument, and one that would seem to disarm my own efforts at an antiliterary, antiauthoritarian, and materialist reading. "All writers within the university," Strychacz posits, "even those who seem to attack its purpose and rationale, perpetuate a 'cultural endowment' that confers authority on those able to speak knowledgeably about it" (44). But this argument is also claustrophobic, as powerful arguments often are; it is rather depressing to learn that "our context is the 'museum world' of the academy," and that any testing of its limits will only confirm their existence and power (206). It is precisely in the hope of thinking beyond our museumized moment that I have turned in this project to writers from the thirties – writers for whom an eventuality that Stry-

chacz instantly rules out was by no means unimaginable: "a nationwide economic collapse severe enough to restructure the entire socioeconomic fabric of the United States" (37).

66 Kees, "Fearing's Collected Poems," 266. Walter Kalaidjian has also taken this position, and has noted how even a respected theorist of the avant-garde like Andreas Huyssen has ignored the presence of an "indigenous American avant-garde in the classical European sense." Huyssen's comment underscores, as Kalaidjian observes, the repression of this avant-garde in subsequent critical reception ("Transpersonal Poetics," 321).

67 Julian Gumperz, "Georg Grosz – Up Out of Dada," New Masses 3 (April 1927): 18; Fearing, "Another Ghetto Novel," 329.

68 Greil Marcus, Lipstick Traces: A Secret History of the Twentieth Century (Cambridge, Mass.: Harvard University Press, 1989), 195.

69 Walter Benjamin, Illuminations: Essays and Reflections, trans. Harry Zorn (New York: Schocken, 1969), 172–73, 238, 249–51.

70 Cited in Benjamin, Illuminations, 192.

71 Lionel Abel recounts in his memoir how Fearing recited the poem on the way to a speakeasy (The Intellectual Follies, 15).

72 See Huyssen, After the Great Divide, 9–11.

73 Guttman, "The Brief Embattled Course of Proletarian Poetry," 256.

74 Kalaidjian has underscored a significant irony in the reception of twentieth-century poetry: while celebrated modernists like Joyce and Eliot characteristically deployed a kind of textual collage, the identical technique could be invoked by the New Critics as cause to dismiss a writer like Fearing, who deployed his irreverent collages for politically progressive ends ("Transpersonal Poetics," 330–31).

75 See, e.g., Peter Ackroyd, T. S. Eliot: A Life (New York: Simon & Schuster, 1984); The Letters of T. S. Eliot, ed. Valerie Eliot (New York: Harcourt, Brace, Jovanovich, 1988); "Tradition and the Individual Talent," in Critical Theory Since Plato, ed. Hazard Adams (New York: Harcourt, Brace, Jovanovich, 1981), 787. My reading of Eliot is most influenced by Franco Moretti's essay "From the Waste Land to the Artificial Paradise," in Signs Taken As Wonders (London: Verso, 1983), 208–39; and Cairns Craig, Yeats, Eliot, Pound and the Politics of Poetry: Riches to the Richest (Pittsburg: University of Pittsburg Press, 1982).

76 Indeed, Walter Kalaidjian has preferred to speak of a "transpersonal" rather than an "impersonal" poetics in the case of Fearing, thus linking the more populist aesthetics of the poets of the thirties with the postmodern and poststructuralist understanding of language, subjectivity, and the ideology of discursive forms – with the idea that the poet does not so much create a language, as language creates the poet ("Transpersonal Poetics," 319 and throughout the essay).

77 Benjamin, Illuminations, 195.

78 Garland Greever and John M. Bachelor, eds., The Soul of the City: An Urban Anthology (Boston: Houghton Mifflin, 1923). Fearing's poem "The Drinkers" (CP, 59), which starts out by comparing four men in a Village speakeasy to a painting by Franz Hals, and then proceeds to undermine the

comparison, seems to be a response to Marguerite Wilkerson's poem "In a Certain Restaurant," which begins, "These diners should have sat for old Franz Hals . . ." (78).

79   Ezra Pound, *The Collected Early Poems* (New York: New Directions, 1982), 34.

80   Fearing's strange image of classical art as "stuffed serpents" finds a curious parallel, some years later, in Isidor Schneider's "Stuffed Bird" (*New Masses* 18 [April 2, 1935]: 31). In what now seems a comically ponderous conceit, Schneider compares traditional bourgeois poets to the stuffed birds that, years ago, were displayed on parlor mantelpieces:

> We are the stuffed birds. We are stood on the mantels,
> dumb and dusty, in the little poets' corners in the journals –
> the daily, the weekly, the monthly stuffed poets.
>
> In the bookshelves of the best homes we have little niches
> and regularly, by more careful maids, are picked up and dusted.
> Who stuffed these birds? A miracle! They stuffed themselves.
> They ate a sawdust known as Unconcerned-with-Politics,
> and drank embalming fluid labelled pure-hundred-poetry,
> and shuddered, choked, and had convulsions;
> but gentle critics, running to their aid, were pecked.

The poem (which I have cited only in part) must count among the worst ever to have appeared in the *New Masses,* but it certainly suggests the persistence and prominence of the attack on the institution of art by the literary Left.

81   Debord, *Society of the Spectacle,* proposition 180.

82   Roland Barthes, *S/Z* (New York: Hill & Wang, 1974), 4.

83   See, e.g., Kalaidjian's interesting juxtaposition of Fearing's poem "Ad" and Perelman's "Seduced by Analogy," in "Transpersonal Poetics," 332–33.

4 THE UNDERCOVER AGENT AND THE CULTURE OF THE SPECTACLE

1   Kenneth Fearing, "The Screen," *New Masses* 18 (24 March 1936): 27.

2   Matthew Josephson, *Life Among the Surrealists: A Memoir* (New York: Holt, Rinehart & Winston, 1962), 274.

3   As is always the case with bold generalizations, the argument may be somewhat reductive; yet Lears cites some persuasive examples that suggest an increasing conservatism and standardization in popular culture: "This change is clear in the drift away from what film historians call 'the cinema of attraction,' which was part of a vaudeville-style entertainment mix and delighted in artifice for its own sake, and toward the classic Hollywood cinema of extended 'real life' drama. The syndication of comic strips followed the same pattern, as the ferment of the turn of the century cooled and surrealist fantasy (such as Winsor McCay's Little Nemo) gave way to wooden adventure stories. The rise of literalism affected advertising as well: rebus-like trade cards and exotic patent medicine brochures yielded to the story-and-photo realism of J. Walter Thompson's 'editorial style.' " T. J.

Jackson Lears, "Making Fun of Popular Culture," *American Historical Review* 97 (December 1992): 1423.

4   Hadley Cantril's *The Invasion from Mars: A Study in the Psychology of Panic* (Princeton, N.J.: Princeton University Press, 1940) offered an influential commentary on the 1938 *War of the Worlds* scare, interpreting the event as a demonstration of the manipulability of the mass audience. But as Lawrence Levine has recently argued, the interpretations that people actually brought to bear on the show are indicative not so much of the audience's gullibility as of a state of political anxiety (well justified by the subsequent course of history) and of the audience's tendency to translate what they heard into something they found credible. The following is a good example: "'I knew it was some Germans trying to gas all of us. When the announcer kept calling them people from Mars I just thought he was ignorant and didn't know yet that Hitler had sent them all.'" See Levine, "The Folklore of Industrial Society: Popular Culture and Its Audiences," *American Historical Review* 97 (December 1992): 1384.

5   Fearing, "The Screen," 27.

6   Kenneth Fearing, "Nevertheless It Moves," *Partisan Review* 3 (1936): 30.

7   Ibid., 30; and "The Screen," 27.

8   Kenneth Fearing, "Artists in Last Year's Uniforms," *New Masses* 18 (11 February 1936): 29; Fearing, "Nevertheless It Moves," 30.

9   I owe the phrase to Janice Radway's work on the debates surrounding the Book-of-the-Month Club. See her essay, "The Scandal of the Middlebrow: The Book-of-the-Month Club, Class Fracture and Cultural Authority," *South Atlantic Quarterly* 89 (Fall 1990): 703–36.

10 I am thinking here of the writers Daniel Horowitz includes in his term "modern moralists" (the Lynds, Stuart Chase, and Alfred M. Bingham), all of whom were opposed to consumer culture, not from the point of view of a residual puritanical self-restraint, but from the ideal of a more organic, enriching, communal experience than that offered in a mechanized, homogenized civilization. See *The Morality of Spending: Attitudes toward the Consumer Society in America, 1875–1940* (Baltimore: Johns Hopkins University Press, 1985), 162. These writers are also briefly discussed in Chapter 2, this volume.

11 Kenneth Fearing, "A Voice from the Past," *New Masses* (5 May 1936): 27.

12 See Lewis Erensberger, "From New York to Middletown: Repeal and the Legitimation of Nightlife in the Great Depression," *American Quarterly* 38 (Winter 1986): 761–78. The rise of such forms of commercial entertainment in the twenties and thirties was the subject of much debate and must be considered in a general evaluation of mass culture criticism during the period. The positions range from moralistic jeremiads about the sexual permissiveness encouraged by dance halls and lamentations about "the threat of leisure"; to sociological studies, which regarded commercial leisure as a "city problem" produced by the need to escape boring occupations; to more anthropological approaches, which criticized the mechanization and commodification of entertainment and the ousting of more communal, "folk" practices. See Paul R. Gorman, "The Development of an American

Mass Culture Criticism" (Ph.D. diss., University of California, Berkeley, 1990), 167–212, for a detailed overview of this body of criticism.

13 Jean Baudrillard, *La societé de consommation: Ses mythes, ses structures* (Paris: Denoël, 1970), 28–30. Baudrillard explains the connection between the Melanesians and modern consumers as follows: "La masse des consommateurs ne vit-elle pas la profusion comme *un effet de nature,* environée qu'elle est par les phantasmes du pays de Cocagne et persuadée par la litanie publicitaire que tout lui sera donné d'avance, et qu'elle a sur la profusion un droit légitime et inaliénable?" (29).

14 Erensberger, "From New York to Middletown," 761–78; Lary May, *Screening out the Past: The Birth of Mass Culture and the Motion Picture Industry* (New York: Oxford University Press, 1980) and "Making the American Way: Moderne Theaters, Audiences, and the Film Industry, 1929–1945," *Prospects* 12 (1987): 89–124. The last essay makes the interesting discovery that, by the mid-thirties, the design of theaters had in fact changed both for practical and for ideological reasons: the new, more streamlined buildings appealed to nationalistic, vernacular, and republican sentiments, and as such, May argues, they announced "a new national vision for popular culture and the country" (90).

15 Kenneth Fearing, "It Was All a Mistake" *New Masses* 2 (April 1927): 8.

16 Vachel Lindsay, *Collected Poems* (New York: Macmillan, 1941), 123–25. Alfred Tennyson, "Songs from *The Princess,*" in *A Collection of Poems,* ed. Christopher Ricks (Garden City, N.Y.: Doubleday, 1977), 292–93.

17 I owe the phrase "dime-store dream parade," which is to me very expressive of the emergent culture of abundance in the thirties, to Robert Heide and John Gilman's book, *Dime-Store Dream Parade: Popular Culture, 1925–1955* (New York: Dutton, 1979).

18 Fearing, "It Was All a Mistake," 8.

19 Raymond Williams, *Marxism and Literature* (Oxford: Oxford University Press, 1977), 121–27.

20 Richard H. Pells, *Radical Visions, American Dreams: Culture and Social Thought in the Depression Years* (Middletown, Conn.: Wesleyan University Press, 1973), 174–75.

21 Robert Forsythe, "Mae West: A Treatise on Decay," in *New Masses: An Anthology of the Rebel Thirties,* ed. Joseph North (New York: International, 1980), 313–14. The piece first appeared in the 9 October, 1934 issue of the *New Masses.*

22 For the term "negative classicism," see Patrick Brantlinger, *Bread and Circuses: Theories of Mass Culture as Social Decay* (Ithaca, N.Y.: Cornell University Press, 1983), 17–18.

23 Michael Gold, "Faster, America, Faster! A Movie in Ten Reels," *New Masses* 2 (November 1926): 7–8. Another early example is his essay "Two Critics in a Bar-Room," in which he claims that the *Saturday Evening Post*'s writers "feed the masses the opium of a cheap romanticism, and turn their thoughts from the concrete to the impossible. They gild the filth in which we live; they make heroes out of slave-drivers, and saints out of vultures. But they cannot create great art" (*Liberator,* 4 [September 1921]: 30). The

remark is characteristic both in its use of the metaphor of addiction and in its suggestion that Communism is the necessary source of new "great art."

24 Muriel Rukeyser, "Movie," *New Masses* 11 (12 June 1934), 28; a somewhat revised version appears in Rukeyser's *Collected Poems* (New York: McGraw-Hill, 1982), 58–59. To get a sense of the poem's quality, we might compare "Movie" with another contemporary poem about film, "Evening Cinema" by Lawrence Lee:

> Here are the meadows where we may forget.
> Wake not the faces lifted to a dream,
> For of the world we bear some likeness yet,
> Shadow beside shadows let the heart take root,
> The fallow mind send up its tendril wish
> The body be of air from head to foot.
>
> The passing to Elysium is swift:
> For two starred hours the lotus holds the soul;
> Then, in the light, the soft illusions lift,
> And with some look of dream still in their eyes
> The wakers stand upon real streets and see
> Toward what dark rooms the homeward turning lies.

(Cited in Halford E. Luccock, *American Mirror: Social, Ethical and Religious Aspects of American Literature, 1930–1940* [New York: Macmillan, 1941], 55.) The greater intellectual complexity of Rukeyser's metaphors and the intensity brought to the poem by her sense of the political stakes involved are, I think, strikingly evident in contrast. While Lee is obviously more tolerant of the "escape" function of the movies (and in this respect more in tune with current defenses of the legitimacy of popular culture), there is very little to this poem's cultural analysis other than the rather hackneyed appearance/reality opposition, which in effect assimilates the movies to something very like the genteel tradition's notion of the "poetic."

25 Rukeyser is probably alluding here to a specific film: the MGM production *Hallelujah!*, which was much criticized in the *New Masses* for its sweetening of social realities – its portrayal, for instance, of prosperous-looking blacks in the cotton fields. Her evocation of the idealized and "movie-made" America concurs in many respects with the views presented a few years earlier in a *Daily Worker* article: an essay in which Myra Page lambasted the flattering image sold in popular literature of America as "the land of democracy, where peace and harmony of interests reigns between the classes," and criticized the way in which adventure magazines romanticized imperial adventures and military posturing. See Myra Page, "Dope – For the Workers," *Daily Worker*, 17 January 1931, 4.

26 Michael Schudson, *Advertising, the Uneasy Persuasion: Its Dubious Impact on American Society* (New York, 1984), 214–18. This matter is also discussed in Chapter 2, this volume.

27 *New Masses* 2 (March 1927): 2.

28 Michael Gold, "Towards an American Revolutionary Culture," *New Masses* 7 (July 1931): 12.

29 Ibid., 12.

30 Cited in Pells, *Radical Visions, American Dreams*, 264.

31 See, e.g., Isidor Schneider's article, "Mass Writers Wanted," *New Masses* 19 (12 May 1936): 24–25, which I described in the introductory chapter, and the many discussions at the Third American Writers' Congress about how writers might use the mass media – whether popular magazine stories, radio dramas, or Hollywood screenplays – to progressive ends (reported in Donald Ogden Stewart, *Fighting Words* [New York: International, 1940], esp. 43–47, 79–90, 106–20).

32 For a sense of this relationship, see Lawrence H. Schwartz, *Marxism and Culture: The C.P.U.S.A. in the 1930s* (Port Washington, N.Y.: Kennikat Press, 1980), and Harvey Klehr, *The Heyday of American Communism: The Depression Decade* (New York: Basic Books, 1984).

33 Utz Riese, "Neither High nor Low: Michael Gold's Concept of a Proletarian Literature," in *The Thirties: Politics and Culture in a Time of Broken Dreams*, ed. Heinz Ickstadt, Rob Kroes, and Brian Lee (Amsterdam: Free University Press, 1987), 143–66.

34 See, e.g., Levine, "The Folklore of Industrial Society," 1369–99, and Gorman, "The Development of an American Mass Culture Critique," 221–23, 235–36, 272.

35 See in this regard Raymond Williams's caveat: "It can be persuasively argued that all or nearly all initiatives and contributions, even when they take on manifestly alternative or oppositional forms, are in practice tied to the hegemonic: that the dominant culture, so to say, at once produces and limits its own forms of counter-culture. There is more evidence for this view (for example in the case of the Romantic critique of industrial civilization) than we usually admit." *Marxism and Literature*, 114.

36 Guy Debord, *Society of the Spectacle* (Detroit: Black & Red, 1983), proposition 42.

37 "Have you a little fairy in your home?" tops the list of totally uninformative but memorable slogans listed by Stuart Chase and F. J. Schink in *Your Money's Worth: A Study in the Waste of the Consumer's Dollar* (New York: Macmillan, 1927), 13–14. I have so far not discovered what product was advertised by the phrase, though it would seem to refer to one of the new timesaving electric appliances (my guess would be a vacuum cleaner). The fantastic, magical associations evoked by the line are common in the advertisements for domestic appliances discussed by Roland Marchand in *Advertising the American Dream: Making Way for Modernity, 1920–1940* (Berkeley: University of California Press, 1985), 267–74. Indeed, as Marchand points out, the typical postures and expressions of the women in these ads (such as the 1930 advertisement for a new Hoover reproduced on 273) are nothing less than worshipful: the vacuum cleaner seems to stand at the center of an adoration scene.

38 Kenneth Fearing, "Have You a Fairy in Your Home?" *New Masses* 3 (April 1928): 15.

39 The designation of the celebrity as "human pseudo-event" is from Daniel J. Boorstin's *The Image: A Guide to Pseudo-Events in America* (New York: Atheneum, 1987), 66. See also his discussion of Lindbergh as one of the first

and best examples of this notion (66–73)'. Debord, *Society of the Spectacle*, proposition 1.

40   One can hardly resist adding to this list of examples the 1933 tabloid sensation concerning the kidnapping of the Lindbergh baby, whose demise is uncannily prefigured in Fearing's essay by his hope that the much-publicized aviator received an "adequate ransom from the kidnappers." The famous scandals mentioned in this essay are described with considerable verve in Allen Churchill's book on 1927, *The Year the World Went Mad* (New York: Crowell, 1960).

41   Debord, *Society of the Spectacle*, 49.

42   Ariel Dorfman, *The Empire's Old Clothes: What the Lone Ranger, Babar, and Other Innocent Heroes Do to Our Minds* (New York: Pantheon, 1983), 201.

43   In "The Legacy of the 30's," Warshow articulates a position that could be seen as a fairly typical anti-Stalinist rereading of the cultural history of the thirties; yet its resonances with the Fearing material from the decade are clear: Warshow observes that "the most important effect of the intellectual life of the 30's and the culture that grew out of it has been to distort and eventually destroy the emotional and moral content of experience. . . . In fact, the chief function of mass culture is to relieve one of the necessity of experiencing one's life directly." *The Immediate Experience: Movies, Comics, Theatre and Other Aspects of Popular Culture* (New York: Doubleday, 1964), 7.

44   The worst of them is Steve Hagen, the true villain of *The Big Clock;* but there are other threatening Steves in "How Do I Feel?" (DR, 56) and in Fearing's story, "Happy Ending," *Discovery* 1 (1953): 142–53, which I discuss in the Epilogue.

45   The first TVs were displayed in department stores in 1938, and some of the first programs were screened at the New York World's Fair the following year. James L. Baughman's essay "The Promise of American Television, 1929–1952," *Prospects* 11 (1986): 119–34, argues that quite a few writers who speculated on what television might bring were "strikingly prescient in describing the medium's 'promise.' " Fearing's forecast for the medium was more grisly than most, but not completely anomalous. It would seem that, by the end of the thirties, after seeing developments in commercial radio, the public had become rather more jaded about yet another techno-logical miracle.

46   Walter Benjamin, "N [Theoretics of Knowledge; Theory of Progress]," trans. Leigh Hafrey and Richard Sieburth, *Philosophical Forum* 15 (Fall-Winter 1983–84): 18.

47   Fredric Jameson, "Postmodernism and Consumer Society," in *The Anti-Aesthetic: Essays on Postmodern Culture,* ed. Hal Foster (Seattle: Bay Press, 1983), 125, and "Postmodernism, or, The Cultural Logic of Late Capital-ism," *New Left Review* 146 (July-August 1984): 58.

48   Jameson, "Postmodernism, or the Cultural Logic of Late Capitalism," 65–77.

49   Ibid., 64.

50   Walter Benjamin, *Illuminations: Essays and Reflections,* trans. Harry Zorn (New York, Schocken, 1969), 88–9, 158–59.

51 Jameson, "Postmodernism and Consumer Society," 125.

52 Benjamin, *Illuminations*, 184.

53 The lines can also be glossed quite accurately by Guy Debord's comments on how the memory of each event is lost in what he calls the "inflation of their hurried replacement at every throb of the spectacular machinery" (*Society of the Spectacle*, proposition 157). Regarding this theme, there is clearly a kind of continuity between Benjamin and Fearing in the thirties, Debord in the sixties, and Jameson in the seventies and eighties: that continuity resides ultimately in the importance of the thematics of reification in each of these critics' approach to capitalist culture.

54 Kenneth Fearing, "*Fury* – Anti-Lynch Film," *New Masses* 19 (16 June 1936): 28. I also discuss this interview and its treatment of the lynching in Chapter 5.

55 Fearing, "Nevertheless It Moves," 30.

56 Ibid., 30.

57 The phrase "hieroglyphic civilization" is Vachel Lindsay's, cited in Warren I. Susman, *Culture as History: The Transformation of American Society in the Twentieth Century* (New York: Pantheon, 1984), xvii.

58 Miles Orvell, *The Real Thing: Imitation and Authenticity in American Culture, 1880–1940* (Chapel Hill: University of North Carolina Press, 1989).

59 We have already seen a similar position in Fearing's analysis of people's response to Charles Lindbergh. See "Have You a Fairy in Your Home?" 27.

60 I am thinking here, for instance, of advertisements from the period by such companies as Paige-Jewett cars, Pepperell sheets, and Arden lipsticks which propagated the idea of the "mood ensemble," of commodities in colors that might (as the latter claimed) "change your personality to suit your mood – or your gown." These ads are reproduced in Marchand's *Advertising the American Dream*, 139–40.

61 *Saturday Evening Post* advertisement cited in Robert S. Lynd and Helen Merrell Lynd, *Middletown: A Study in American Culture* (New York: Harcourt, Brace & World, 1929), 265.

62 Marchand, *Advertising the American Dream*, 356.

63 One of Debord's theses in the *Society of the Spectacle* suggests an excellent explanation of these lines: "This society which eliminates geographical distance reproduces distance internally as spectacular separation" (proposition 167).

64 Jameson, "Postmodernism, or the Cultural Logic of Late Capitalism," 65.

65 In a recent essay, "Parataxis and Narrative: The New Sentence in Theory and Practice," *American Literature* 65 (June 1993), 313–24, the Language poet Bob Perelman has challenged Jameson's version of postmodernism (at least insofar as poetry is concerned), arguing that the practice of the Language poets is not, as Jameson would have it, "the rubble of snapped signifying chains," but an effort at a new and politically conscious renarrativization. For a definition of the term "structure of feeling," see Williams, *Marxism and Literature*, 128–35. Fred Pfeil's essay "Postmodernism as a 'Structure of Feeling,' " in *Marxism and the Interpretation of Culture*, ed. Cary Nelson and Lawrence Grossberg (Urbana: University of Illinois Press,

1988), 381–403, is an excellent example of a periodization and definition of postmodernism based on these questions of "feeling" and "tone" and on the way these subjective qualities are rooted in a particular historical and class experience.

66 Andy Warhol, interview with G. R. Swenson, in John Russell and Suzi Gablik, *Pop Art Redefined* (London: Thames & Hudson, 1969), 116.

67 Debord, *Society of the Spectacle*, proposition 59.

5 "ZOWIE DID HE LIVE AND ZOWIE DID HE DIE": MASS CULTURE AND THE FRAGMENTATION OF EXPERIENCE

1 Walter Benjamin, *Illuminations: Essays and Reflections*, trans. Harry Zorn (New York: Schocken, 1969), 155–200.

2 Maurice R. Davie, *Problems of City Life: A Study in Urban Sociology* (New York: Wiley, 1932), 603. Warren Susman's description of pinball strikes me as evoking something quite similar to Benjamin's Dodgem cars: "The pinball machine was the ideal toy of the machine age, with its spinning balls passing through a series of obstacle pins that meant points for the player if they met, although at the same time the solemn injunction 'Do Not Tilt' severely limited the player's opportunity to interfere with the chance movement of the balls." The game captures the essence of the kind of experience I sense both in Fearing's poetry and more generally in the culture of the thirties: sudden jolts, lucky hits, uncontrollable misses. See *Culture as History: The Transformation of American Society in the Twentieth Century* (New York: Pantheon, 1984), 197.

3 Benjamin, *Illuminations*, 176.

4 Letter from Max Horkheimer to Leo Lowenthal, cited in Martin Jay, *The Dialectical Imagination: A History of the Frankfurt School and the Institute for Social Research, 1923–1950* (Boston: Little, Brown, 1973), 213–14.

5 Kenneth Fearing, *The Big Clock* (New York: Mysterious Book Club, 1987), 5–6.

6 One detail in the poem seems to me almost uncannily in accord with Benjamin's ideas about the political meaning of "shock" in both work and leisure. At the end of the poem, Fearing invokes the "big dipper," which refers, of course, to the constellation (and suggests an uncontrollable fate in the stars) but may also be a reference to a well-known roller coaster ride of the day.

7 The poem "Model for a Biography," from Fearing's 1943 volume, *Afternoon of a Pawnbroker* (CP, 231), is perhaps the most self-conscious in the way it addresses this idea of a failed biography, of the incalculable ups and downs of a rather undistinguished but therefore representative life. (It is perhaps for this reason rather less interesting and rhetorically inventive than "Dirge.")

8 Jay, *The Dialectical Imagination*, 214.

9 Weldon Kees, "Fearing's Collected Poems," *Poetry: A Magazine of Verse* 57 (January 1941): 269.

10 *New Masses* 5 (April 1930): 10–11.

11 Kenneth Fearing, "Crowther and the Cherry Tree," *New Masses* 18 (3 March 1936): 19. The "Crowther" of whom Fearing speaks here enters into the literary history of the thirties in another curious and intriguing way. He is Samuel Crowther, the author of *The Romance and Rise of the American Tropics,* an offensively partisan and jingoistic story of the role of U.S. corporations in the Caribbean – including the history of Minor C. Keith's rise from necktie salesman to railroad builder. It is this account that Dos Passos uses, even to the point of borrowing the wording, in his bitterly ironic biography of Keith, entitled "Emperor of the Caribbean": one of the ugliest portraits in *U.S.A.*'s gallery of American villains. See Barry Maine, "Representative Men in Dos Passos's *The 42nd Parallel,*" *Clio* 12 (1982): 37.

12 In various thirties texts, the lives of the unemployed are also described as fragmentary, patched up out of disconnected experiences. Alfred Hayes's poem "In a Coffee Pot," for instance, describes the bitter disappointment of promising young men, erstwhile candidates for success, who go on the fritz and end up sitting in an all-night coffee joint, where they vacantly note every irrelevant, atomized action:

> The Greek's awakened from his dream. The dead cigar
> Drops ash. He wipes the coffee bar.
> He goes to fill the boiler once again.
> The clock hand moves. A fly soars down
> And stalks the sugar bowl's bright rim.
>
> . . . .
> He crawls head downwards down a peeling wall
> And I crawl after him.

(Collected in *Proletarian Literature in the United States: An Anthology,* ed. Granville Hicks et al. [New York: International, 1935], 164.) Tom Kromer's *Waiting for Nothing* is another excellent example of a text whose "narrative" fragments never cohere, never develop. See *Waiting for Nothing and Other Writings,* ed. Arthur D. Casciato and James L. W. West III (Athens: University of Georgia Press, 1986).

13 Fearing, "Crowther and the Cherry Tree," 19.

14 Leo Lowenthal, "The Triumph of Mass Idols," in *Literature, Popular Culture, and Society* (Palo Alto, Calif.: Pacific Books, 1961), 118, 126–27. I also discuss this study in Chapter 1, this volume.

15 Alan Jenkins, *The Thirties* (London: Heineman, 1976), 28. It is interesting that comic-strip advertisements of the time (of which I shall have more to say in Chapter 8) adopted the form of this story as well: in "How Betty Found Romance in Hollywood," Betty is advised to use Yeast Foam Tablets, is noticed by a producer, and, in the space of a few panels, turns from an ordinary girl with bad skin to a beautiful star engaged to her leading man (*Saturday Evening Post,* 20 January 1934, 83).

16 Horkheimer and Adorno describe the ideology of luck at some length in the "Culture Industry" essay: "Ideology conceals itself in the calculation of probabilities. . . . The girls in the audience not only feel that they could be on the screen, but realize the great gulf separating them from it. Only one girl can draw the lucky ticket, only one man can win the prize, and if,

mathematically, all have the same chance, yet this is so infinitesimal for each one that he or she will do best to write it off and rejoice in the other's success, which might just as well have been his or hers, and somehow never is." (*Dialectic of Enlightenment,* trans. John Cumming [New York: Continuum, 1991], 145).

17   Benjamin, *Illuminations,* 177. Benjamin's connection between the motions of the gambler and the worker may appear a bit fanciful to some readers; yet his comment may help us retrieve and reimagine something of the shocking novelty that Taylorism still carried in the twenties and thirties. Consider the following striking reminiscence of a visitor to one of Ford's assembling plants in 1932:

> Every employee seemed to be restricted to a well-defined jerk, twist, spasm or quiver resulting in a fliver. I never thought it possible that human beings could be reduced to such perfect automats.
>
> I looked constantly for the wire or belt concealed about their bodies which kept them in motion with such marvelous clock-like precision. I failed to discover how the motive power is transmitted to these people and as it don't seem reasonable that human beings would willingly consent to being simplified into jerks, I assume that their wives wind them up while asleep.

(Cited in Stuart Ewen, *Captains of Consciousness: Advertising and the Social Roots of Consumer Culture* [New York: McGraw-Hill, 1977], 11–12.)

18   Susman, *Culture as History,* 161–63; Fredrik Lewis Allen, *Only Yesterday and Since Yesterday: A Popular History of the 20's and 30's* (New York: Bonanza, 1986), 151–54; Jay Martin, *Nathanael West: The Art of His Life* (New York: Carol & Graf, 1984), 162–63. One need only read Lionel Abel's description (*The Intellectual Follies: A Memoir of the Literary Venture in New York and Paris* [New York: Norton, 1984]) of his mother's dutiful attendance and nervous expectation on the lottery nights, to get some sense of the ideological training that goes on in "everyday life" and leisure: "I discovered this in the thirties: Ordinary life remains quite as ordinary even when there is pain in it. As to ordinary life: Almost everyone went to the movies at least once a week, and admissions were generally no more than twenty-five cents. . . . Now, as to the pain: Most people went to the movies not just to pass the time, but to win some money in the lotteries and bingo games that were regularly part of the show. As I remember, my mother, who went to the movies then exclusively for this purpose, never became absorbed in the films shown, and generally waited – tense, apprehensive, and hopeful – for the announcement of a winning number. But once, in despair at not having won on other occasions, and at having spent money uselessly, since she had not even watched the film, she left just before the announcement of a winner, and was not present to hear her own number called. Had she remained, she would have been awarded the sum of one hundred dollars. From this sad event she learned a lesson in patience, and from then on, no matter how boring the film – though, in fact, films were most often not boring in those days – she would stay to the very end, and was indeed repaid twice with one-hundred-dollar awards" (33–34).

19   Susman, *Culture as History,* 162.

20   This point is later emphasized by Adorno in his study "The Stars Down to Earth: The *Los Angeles Times* Astrology Column," *Telos* 19 (Spring 1974): 20.

21   See, e.g., "End of the Seers Convention" (CP, 235–36).

22   The term "floating-power" seems to have held a special significance for Fearing. Readers might recall that Jason Wheeler, the character modeled after Fearing in Albert Halper's *Union Square,* is obsessed with an advertisement in which this phrase appears: "But just because I'm not famous myself is no reason why I shouldn't drive a famous car. I *do.* I drive a Chrysler — with that patented Floating Power everybody is talking about." Though the novel does not develop the point, the quotation clearly offers a humorous comment on the absurdities of an increasingly reified world. In a society where social status no longer has anything to do with production, where celebrities are themselves turned into commodities, it seems hardly surprising that an object should be more famous, more potent, than its owner. And since Wheeler, like Fearing, is an unsuccessful "ex-Communist" poet who turns to writing sexy potboilers, the ad seems also to suggest a rueful comment on the problems of achieving literary fame: when literature becomes a vast cultural and political insitution, it becomes impossible to figure out why (in the words of the poem "Q & A") "this one is cherished by the gods, and that one not" (CP, 156). See Albert Halper, *Union Square* (New York: Literary Guild, 1933), 13.

23   Benjamin, *Illuminations,* 179. I shall discuss this idea in more detail as it pertains to Nathanael West's work in Chapter 7.

24   See Lowenthal, "The Triumph of Mass Idols," 133–34.

25   Kenneth Burke, "Fearing's New Poems," *New Masses* 30 (21 February 1939): 28.

26   Bernard Rosenberg and David Manning White, eds., *Mass Culture: The Popular Arts in America* (New York: Free Press, 1964), 5. The idea was first formulated by the sociologist Ernest van den Haag, whom Rosenberg acknowledges here.

27   I am thinking here of the 1930 version of *Moby-Dick,* directed by Lloyd Bacon and starring John Barrymore as Captain Ahab.

28   Kenneth Fearing, "Have You a Fairy in Your Home?" *New Masses* 3 (April 1928): 15.

29   Guy Debord, *Society of the Spectacle* (Detroit: Black & Red, 1983), proposition 160.

30   Kenneth Fearing, "*Fury* – Anti-Lynch Film," *New Masses* 19 (16 June 1936): 28.

31   Fearing attacks the apolitical approach to mass culture of his more conservative contemporaries in a review of the 1936 symposium, *The Movies on Trial:*

> Reading this book, which is full of hearty damns for Hollywood's box-office standard but practically bare of any reference to the class line-up on which it rests, is like reading a lot of last year's newspaper editorials:

. . . the motion-picture industry has degenerated into the mere demoralizing depicturization of debased events

states Congressman Raymond J. Cannon, with no originality but swell alliteration.

("Artists in Last Year's Uniforms," *New Masses* 18 [11 February 1936]: 29).

32 Fearing, "Fury – Anti-Lynch Film," 28.

33 W. H. Auden, *Collected Poems* (New York: Random House, 1976), 201.

34 Susman, *Culture as History*, xxvii.

35 Patricia B. Santora, "The Poetry and Prose of Kenneth Flexner Fearing" (Ph.D. diss., University of Maryland, 1982), 93–96. Dahlberg writes, rather melodramatically, in his review of Fearing's *Poems*, "Kenneth Fearing: A Poet for Workers": "Fearing is relentlessly tortured and for a moment it would seem as if despair were in the ascendancy. . . . But in "Denouement," a poem which, were it extended, would be a major piece of our times, the poet, looking beyond the horizon toward a socialist civilization, a Vita Nuova of the workers, sings out . . . and as the poems in their chronological progression become more incisive and attain Marxian lucidity, the caustic comments rise; expand into an affirmative Marxist statement" (*New Masses* 15 [21 May 1935]: 24–25). Dahlberg's piece was also used as the introduction to Fearing's *Poems* (New York: Dynamo, 1935).

36 Charles Humboldt, "The Voice Persisted Until Death: An Appreciation," *Trace* 46 (Summer 1962): 222.

37 Halford A. Luccock has suggested that Fearing here presents "a trial of laborers framed in a case practically the same as that which gives the theme to [Meyer] Levin's novel, *Citizens,* exhibiting the hopeless struggle of workers equipped with 'three dependents and a package of cigarettes,' against the alliance of owners, police and law courts" (*American Mirror: Social, Ethical and Religious Aspects of American Literature, 1930–1940* [New York: Macmillan, 1941], 228). The suggestion is an interesting one, though my own inclination is to read the interrogation rather more allegorically.

6 "A SURFEIT OF SHODDY": WEST AND THE SPECTACLE OF CULTURE

1 Walter Benjamin, *Illuminations: Essays and Reflections,* trans. Harry Zorn (New York: Schocken, 1985), 256.

2 Richard Wightman Fox and T. J. Jackson Lears, eds., *The Culture of Consumption, 1880–1980* (New York: Pantheon, 1983), ix–x.

3 Warren I. Susman, "The Culture of the Thirties," in *Culture as History: The Transformation of American Society in the Twentieth Century* (New York: Pantheon, 1985), 153.

4 Ibid., xxiv.

5 Ibid., 220–29, 189–90. See also Robert Heide and John Gilman, *Dime-Store Dream Parade: Popular Culture, 1925–1955* (New York: Dutton, 1979), 90.

6 *The Official Guide Book of the Fair* (Chicago: A Century of Progress, 1933), 10.

7 Paul Hutchinson, "Progress on Parade: Is the World's Fair an Empty Gesture?" *Forum* 89 (June 1933): 373. Hutchinson makes the interesting obser-

vation, in line with my present argument, that "the fair is, all ballyhoo aside, the most gigantic experiment in adult education this country has known" (371).

8   The reading of the photograph I offer here is, I think, a standard one − in accordance, for instance, with the ironic theme suggested in Leighton's description. But as is often the case with documentary photographs there is a slight element of distortion, or let us say emblematic generalization, here (whether in the picture itself or in my interpretation it is hard to tell): I find it difficult not to read the photograph as an indictment of the economic system, but the fact is that this particular breadline was not one of unemployed people but of flood victims.

9   Nelson Algren, *Somebody in Boots: A Novel* (New York: Thunder's Mouth Press, 1987), 235−36.

10 *Selected Works of Stephen Vincent Benét* (New York: Rinehart, 1942), 442−43.

11 Collected in Charlotte Nekola and Paula Rabinowitz, eds., *Writing Red: An Anthology of American Women Writers, 1930−1940* (New York: Feminist Press, 1987). The poem orginally appeared in the West Coast John Reed Club's magazine *Partisan* and included a headnote identifying it as based on a letter from Felipe Ibarro in the *New Masses* (9 January 1934).

12 F. Scott Fitzgerald, *Tender Is the Night* (New York: Scribner's, 1934), 55. Jonathan Raban's essay "A Surfeit of Commodities: The Novels of Nathanael West," in *The Novel and the Nineteen Twenties,* ed. Malcolm Bradbury and David Palmer (London: Edward Arnold, 1971), 231, first drew my attention to this passage.

13 Halford E. Luccock, *American Mirror: Social, Ethical and Religious Aspects of American Literature, 1930−1940* (New York: Macmillan, 1941), 118.

14 See Andrew Ross's chapter "Containing Culture in the Cold War," in *No Respect: Intellectuals and Popular Culture* (New York: Routledge, 1989), 42−64, for a discussion of this conflation.

15 West originally intended to give the novel an epigraph from Lewis Mumford: "From the form of a city, the style of its architecture, and the economic functions and social groupings it shelters and encourages, one can derive most of the essential elements of a civilization." Cited in Jay Martin, *Nathanael West: The Art of His Life* (New York: Carrol & Graf, 1970), 309. The quotation is to me very suggestive, confirming my sense that West's cultural analysis has certain connections with Benjamin's attempt (especially in the *Arcades Project*) to write a history of the nineteenth century using the objects and architecture of Paris, its motley array of products, artistic and commercial, as significant historical documents.

16 See, e.g., Nathanael West, *Miss Lonelyhearts & The Day of the Locust* (New York, New Directions, 1969), 54−55, 92, 171. Subsequent citations from West's novels are from this text and from *Two Volumes by Nathanael West: The Dream Life of Balso Snell & A Cool Million* (New York: Farrar, Strauss & Giroux, 1985). Page references to these editions will henceforth be incorporated parenthetically using the following abbreviations: BS (*The Dream Life of Balso Snell,* ML (*Miss Lonelyhearts*), CM (*A Cool Million*), and DL (*The Day of the Locust*).

17   Martin, *Nathanael West: The Art of His Life,* 53, 54, 56, 382.
18   The phrase comes from the editorial announcement by West and William Carlos Williams on the title page of the first number of *Contact:* "*Contact* will attempt to cut a trail through the American jungle without the use of a European compass" (ibid., 146).
19   Ibid., 146.
20   Ibid., 147.
21   See the piece (in *Broom* [November 1922]: 24) Josephson calls his "sketchy contribution to the theory of the popular arts." Josephson later revised such "unconsidered and over-optimistic pronouncements on the culture of the Machine Age, which ignored its human costs." See his memoir, *Life Among the Surrealists* (New York: Rinehart & Winston, 1962), 189–91.
22   Douglas H. Shepard, "Nathanael West Rewrites Horatio Alger Jr.," *Satire Newsletter* (Fall 1965): 13–28; Gary Scharnhorst, "From Rags to Patches, or *A Cool Million* as Alter-Alger," *Ball State University Forum* 21 (1980): 58–65.
23   Martin, *Nathanael West: The Art of His Life,* 146.
24   Raban, "A Surfeit of Commodities," 216, 230.
25   West's friend Josephine Herbst homes in on this bricolage-like quality of Surrealism when she describes Breton's formula "Changez la vie!" as "homemade." See "Nathanael West," in *Twentieth Century Interpretations of "Miss Lonelyhearts": A Collection of Critical Essays,* ed. Thomas H. Jackson (Englewood Cliffs, N.J.: Prentice-Hall, 1971), 40.
26   Norman Mailer, "The Man Who Studied Yoga," in *The Short Fiction of Norman Mailer* (New York: Howard Fertig, 1980), 279.
27   Raban, "A Surfeit of Commodities," 228.
28   Alexander Bergman, review of Kenneth Fearing's *Collected Poems, New Masses* 37 (19 November 1940): 25.
29   Raban, "A Surfeit of Commodities," 231.
30   Algren, *Somebody in Boots,* 219, 235. I suggest in the next chapter that some of the items strewn about in West's Hollywood backlot resemble exhibits at the world's fair.
31   Umberto Eco, *Travels in Hyperreality* (New York: Harcourt, Brace, Jovanovich, 1986), 23 and the entire first chapter. Eco's description of "that poor man's Hearst Castle," the Madonna Inn at San Luis Obispo, evokes exactly the same indiscriminate jumble of reproduced styles we see in these texts from the thirties: "Then there are the bedrooms, about two hundred of them, each with a different theme: for a reasonable price (which includes an enormous bed – King or Queen size – if you are on your honeymoon) you can have the Prehistoric Room, all cavern and stalactites, the Safari Room (zebra walls and bed shaped like a Bantu idol), the Kona Rock Room (Hawaiian), the California Poppy, the Old-Fashioned Honeymoon, the Irish Hills, the William Tell, the Tall and Short, for mates of different lengths, with the bed in an irregular polygon form, the Imperial Family, the Old Mill" (25). The Westian "bonfire of styles" is clearly still a feature of American culture.
32   Martin, *Nathanael West: The Art of His Life,* 171–72.
33   Ibid., 316.

34 Michael Gold, "Thoughts of a Great Thinker," *Liberator* 5 (March 1922): 24.

35 Herman Spector, "Night in New York," *New Masses* 4 (October 1928): 27.

36 Algren, *Somebody in Boots*, 235, 219, 237.

37 Lary May, "Making the American Way: Moderne Theatres, Audiences, and the Film Industry 1929–1945," *Prospects* 12 (1987): 104.

38 Heide and Gilman, *Dime-Store Dream Parade*, 108.

39 Martin, *Nathanael West: The Art of His Life*, 235.

40 Robert Morss Lovett, "Progress – Chicago Style," *Current History* 39 (1934): 435.

41 Hutchinson, "Progress on Parade," 372. Hutchinson's point is that "elements of 'showmanship' " seem to have entered into "modern scientific practice."

42 Martin, *Nathanael West: The Art of His Life*, 84.

43 See T. J. Jackson Lears's essay "From Salvation to Self-Realization: Advertising and the Therapeutic Roots of Consumer Culture, 1880–1930" in Fox and Lears, eds., *The Culture of Consumption*, 1–38.

44 Henri Lefebvre, *Everyday Life in the Modern World* (New Brunswick, N.J.: Transaction Books, 1984), 110–23.

45 Martin, *Nathanael West: The Art of His Life*, 216.

46 Nathanael West, "Soft Soap for the Barber," reprinted in William White, *Nathanael West: A Comprehensive Bibliography* (Kent, Ohio: Kent State University Press, 1975), 71–72. This review originally appeared in the *New Republic* 81 (14 November 1934): 23.

47 Raban, "A Surfeit of Commodities," 226.

48 Cited in Martin, *Nathanael West: The Art of His Life*, 257.

49 Ibid., 335–36.

50 Raban, "A Surfeit of Commodities," 230.

51 Martin, *Nathanael West: The Art of His Life*, 281.

52 George E. Marcus and Michael J. Fischer, *Anthropology as Cultural Critique* (Chicago: University of Chicago Press, 1985), 155–56. Paul R. Gorman offers an extremely helpful overview of this literature and its implications for American mass culture criticism in "The Development of an American Mass Culture Critique, 1910–1960" (Ph.D. diss., University of California, Berkeley, 1990), 191–212.

53 Stuart Chase and F. J. Schlink, *Your Money's Worth: A Study in the Waste of the Consumer's Dollar* (New York: Macmillan, 1927), 1–27.

54 On Gold's pastoral impulse, or the "residual" dimension to his critique, see James D. Bloom, *Left Letters: The Culture Wars of Mike Gold and Joseph Freeman* (New York: Columbia University Press, 1992), 118–19, and 127–28.

55 Cited in Cary Nelson, *Repression and Recovery: Modern American Poetry and the Politics of Cultural Memory, 1910–1945* (Madison: University of Wisconsin Press, 1989), 104. For another poetic treatment of the fate of Native Americans, see the first four stanzas of Joy Davidman's "Twentieth-Century Americanism," in Nekola and Rabinowitz, eds., *Writing Red*, 175–77.

56 John Steinbeck, *The Grapes of Wrath* (New York: Penguin, 1987), 449.

57 Martin, *Nathanael West: The Art of His Life*, 253.

58   Cited in Susan Buck-Morss, "Walter Benjamin – Revolutionary Writer (I)," *New Left Review* (September 1982): 61.

59   Walter Benjamin, "Surrealism: Snapshot of the Last European Intelligentsia," in *Reflections: Essays, Aphorisms, Autobiographical Writings* (New York: Schocken, 1986), 192.

60   Buck-Morss, "Walter Benjamin – Revolutionary Writer (I)," 82.

61   Jackson Lears, "Uneasy Courtship: Modern Art and Modern Advertising," *American Quarterly* (Spring 1987): 145.

62   Walter Benjamin, *Charles Baudelaire: A Lyric Poet in the Era of High Capitalism,* trans. Harry Zorn (London: NLB, 1973), 176. One humorous example of the dialectical image seems to me curiously Westian. Following Baudelaire, Benjamin observes that the very appearance of bourgeois businessmen could be seen dialectically: their sober business suits, the emblems of their status and power, simultaneously give them the appearance of "an immense cortege of undertakers" observing their own solemn funeral (77). Thus (as Susan Buck-Morss puts it in her excellent gloss of this passage) Baudelaire's image provides us with the power to dislodge the conventional association of fashionable dress with prestige and power; the bourgeois gentlemen are marked by their clothes as "allegorical signals of the revolutionary event for which they are their own grave-diggers" (see "Walter Benjamin – Revolutionary Writer [I]," 70–71). West seemed to intuit all too well the deathlike quality of fashion: one of his contemporaries at Brown University thought that West and his companion, Brae Rafferty, who affected exaggeratedly formal outfits from Brooks Brothers, topped with funereal homburgs, always looked like a pair of "well-heeled mortuary assistants." Quoted in James Light, *Nathanael West: An Interpretive Study* (Evanston, Ill.: Northwestern University Press, 1961), 10.

63   I am thinking of his comment on *Balso Snell*'s "runaway rhetoric, as repetitive as the flow of identical articles off an assembly line," or on the way that *The Day of the Locust* "works like a production line; it takes the scattered ingredients of a recognizably real Hollywood and turns them into the hard, bright patterns of cheap industrial design." Raban, "A Surfeit of Commodities," 220, 228.

64   Buck-Morss, "Walter Benjamin – Revolutionary Writer (I)," 101.

65   Cited in ibid., 74–75.

66   Ibid., 74.

67   Martin, *Nathanael West: The Art of His Life,* 167.

68   Ibid., 168.

69   Benjamin, *Reflections,* 181.

70   It has always been my suspicion that West's final scene was inspired by an incident that occurred at the close of the Chicago World's Fair in 1934. Sally Rand (whose fan dance at the "Streets of Paris" exhibit turned out to be the main attraction of the fair) described the event as follows to Studs Terkel: "On the eleventh of November, 1934, mass hysteria took over. They completely demolished the Century of Progress. They tore down flags, they tore down street lights, they tore down the walls. It started out being

souvenir hunters, but it became mass vandalism. Anybody who witnessed it had this terribly frightening feeling." See *Hard Times: An Oral History of the Great Depression* (New York: Washington Square Press, 1978), 204.

7 "WHEN YOU WISH UPON A STAR": FANTASY, EXPERIENCE, AND MASS CULTURE

1   My sense that the thirties were a time of peculiarly intense collective dreaming is reinforced by the titles of several books on the period. See, e.g., Malcolm Cowley, *The Dream of Golden Mountains: Remembering the Thirties* (New York: Viking, 1980); Jerre Mangione, *The Dream and the Deal: The Federal Writers' Project, 1935–1943* (Philadephia: University of Pennsylvania Press, 1983); Richard Pells, *Radical Visions, American Dreams: Cultural and Social Thought in the Depression Years* (Middletown, Conn.: Wesleyan University Press, 1989); and Robert Heide and John Gilman, *Dime-Store Dream Parade: Popular Culture, 1925–1955* (New York: Dutton, 1979).

2   Jay Martin, *Nathanael West: The Art of His Life* (New York: Carol & Graf, 1984), 340; Walter Benjamin, *Charles Baudelaire: A Lyric Poet in the Era of High Capitalism* (London: NLB, 1973), 158–59.

3   John Keyes, "Personality in the Land of Wish: Popular Motifs in Nathanael West's *The Day of the Locust*," in *Nathanael West: Modern Critical Views*, ed. Harold Bloom (New York: Chelsea House, 1986), 165–74.

4   See Walter Benjamin, "N [Theoretics of Knowledge; Theory of Progress]," trans. Leigh Hafrey and Richard Sieburth, *Philosophical Forum* 15 (Fall-Winter 1983–84): 12.

5   In his contribution to a recent debate in the *American Historical Review* on the study of popular culture, Jackson Lears makes a similar point, citing the following interesting observation from Adorno's 1966 essay, "Transparencies on Film": "The ideology provided by the [film] industry, its officially intended models, may by no means automatically correspond to those that affect the spectators. . . . Overlapping the official models are a number of inofficial [sic] ones which supply the attraction yet are intended to be neutralized by the former. In order to capture the consumers and provide them with substitute satisfaction, the unofficial, if you will, heterodox ideology must be depicted in much broader and juicier fashion than suits the moral of the story; the tabloid newspapers furnish weekly examples of such excess" ("Making Fun of Popular Culture," *American Historical Review* 97 [December 1992]: 1421). Adorno here asserts exactly the same position articulated by Fredric Jameson in his "Reification and Utopia" essay, which has been read, and to a degree presents itself, as a challenge to the Frankfurt school's theories of mass culture (*Social Text* 1 [1979]: 141). In the *Political Unconscious* the same model is applied to the symbolic operations of modernist narratives.

6   W. H. Auden, "Interlude: West's Disease," in *The Dyer's Hand and Other Essays* (New York: Random House, 1962), 241–42. The essay, which was probably written around 1957, has been collected in two of the subsequent

anthologies of West criticism: Jay Martin, ed., *Nathanael West: A Collection of Critical Essays* (Englewood Cliffs, N.J.: Prentice-Hall, 1971), 147–53, and Harold Bloom, ed., *Nathanael West*, 41–48.

7   Andrew Ross, *No Respect: Intellectuals and Popular Culture* (London: Routledge, 1989), 47. Ross provides a fascinating sampling of this rhetoric: "Harold Rosenberg, for example, would conclude that 'there is only one way to quarantine kitsch: by being too busy with art.' Louis Kronenberger speculated about 'how to avoid contamination without avoiding contact.' Irving Howe contended that 'the vast culture industries are parasites on the body of art, letting it neither live nor die,' and that 'direct criticism [of them] . . . is a necessity of hygiene.' [Dwight] Macdonald was quite unequivocal about the need for 'a staying power . . . against the spreading ooze of Mass Culture,' and David Riesman declared his fellow intellectuals' reluctance to 'give the patient a clean bill of health lest some other doctor find a hidden flaw' " (45).

8   We might bear in mind that Auden was an associate of the *Partisan Review* intellectuals at the very time when they were polemicizing vigorously against the incipient "totalitarian" threat of mass culture. Only a few years before Auden's meditation on West, the editors of the review addressed the following question to a group of writers: "Do you believe that a democratic society necessarily leads to a leveling of culture, to a mass culture which will overrun intellectual and aesthetic values traditional to Western civilization?" The terms in which the question is cast give a sense of how the mass culture debate had become linked to Cold War anxieties about the very survival of Western culture. See "Our Country and Our Culture" (editorial statement), *Partisan Review* (May-June 1952): 286.

9   The phrase, again one with rather medical resonances, is Susan Sontag's. See "Notes on Camp," in *Against Interpretation and Other Essays* (New York: Dell, 1966), 289.

10 See the discussion of gambling and betting in the thirties in Chapter 5, this volume.

11 Auden, "Interlude: West's Disease," 245.

12 Ross, *No Respect*, 45.

13 In Martin, ed., *Nathanael West: A Collection of Critical Essays*, 66–67. Some readers take these remarks as less dismissive of Freudian psychology than I do, and West does in fact call the "Bulfinch" role it can now play "important." But it should be noted that West dubs Horatio Alger, whom he parodies so mercilessly, the "Bulfinch of American Fable" (Martin, *Nathanael West: The Art of His Life*, 218). The connection certainly does not suggest that West would attach much truth-value to psychoanalysis.

14 Robert S. Lynd, "The People as Consumers," in *Recent Social Trends in the United States: Report of the President's Research Committee on Social Trends*, one-volume ed. (New York: McGraw-Hill, 1932), 866.

15 Martin, *Nathanael West: The Art of His Life*, 167.

16 Ibid., 168.

17 "American Rhapsody (3)" (CP, 92).

18 Daniel Boorstin, *The Image: A Guide to Pseudo-Events in America* (New York: Atheneum, 1987), 9–12, 36.

19 Guy Debord, *Society of the Spectacle* (Detroit: Black & Red, 1983), propositions 8 and 9.

20 Ibid., propositions 2 and 165–68.

21 Martin, *Nathanael West: The Art of His Life,* 168–70.

22 Ibid., 336.

23 Walter Benjamin, *Illuminations: Essays and Reflections* (New York: Schocken, 1985), 179. It is interesting that, throughout his life, Benjamin took the symbolism and forms of the folktale seriously, as the memory-trace of a more organic life and preserver of certain transformative possibilities, while for Auden folktales were mere "wish games." See Auden, "Interlude: The Wish Game," in *The Dyer's Hand,* 209–17.

24 Benjamin, *Illuminations,* 177–78.

25 Ibid., 179.

26 Ibid., 180. For Theodor Adorno and Max Horkheimer, the "culture industry" represents an extention of this principle of repetition and postponement, which cheats the individual of the experience of significant work, into the domain of leisure: "The culture industry perpetually cheats its consumers of what it perpetually promises. The promissory note which, with its plots and staging, it draws on pleasure is endlessly prolonged; the promise, which is actually all the spectacle really consists of, is illusory: all it actually confirms is that the real point will never be reached, that the diner must be satisfied with the menu." (*Dialectic of Enlightenment,* trans. John Cumming [New York: Continuum, 1991], 139).

27 Martin, *Nathanael West: The Art of His Life,* 312.

28 The fact that it is specifically a *newspaper* that replaces the "magic" of the fairy tales is also interesting, particularly in the light of Benjamin's hypothesis in the "Storyteller" essay (*Illuminations,* 83–110) that newspapers present a menace to older forms of narrative, such as storytelling. This idea will be discussed in further detail in Chapter 8.

29 Benjamin, *Illuminations,* 179.

30 Ibid., 220–25.

31 Ibid., 188, 84–85, 88–89.

32 See Bernard Rosenberg and David Manning White, *Mass Culture: The Popular Arts in America* (New York: Free Press, 1957), 5. This idea is discussed more fully in Chapter 5, this volume.

33 For information on the exhibits see, e.g., *The Official Guide Book of the Fair* (Chicago: Century of Progress, 1933), and James Weber Linn, ed., *The Official Pictures of A Century of Progress Exhibition, Chicago, 1933* (Chicago: Donnelley, 1933).

34 Benjamin, "N [Theoretics of Knowledge; Theory of Progress]," 38. The horrified glances that West's and Balzac's protagonists direct at the studio lot and at the warehouse respectively resemble exactly that of Benjamin's famous Angel of History from the "Theses on the Philosophy of History": looking backward from the present, as these figures do, any narrative or

temporal dimension seems to have been elided and to have collapsed; the past appears as a "pile of debris . . . grow[ing] skyward": "wreckage upon wreckage" (*Illuminations*, 257–58).

35 See the discussion of these theaters in Chapter 4, this volume.

36 Benjamin, *Illuminations*, 241–42.

37 Ibid., 223.

38 Alice Marquis, *Hopes and Ashes: The Birth of Modern Times, 1929–1939* (New York: Macmillan, 1986), 30.

39 Benjamin, *Illuminations*, 223.

40 Patrick Brantlinger, *Bread and Circuses: Theories of Mass Culture as Social Decay* (Ithaca, N.Y.: Cornell University Press, 1983), 18. The terms "positive classicism" and "negative classicism" are developed throughout the book, especially in the first two chapters (9–81).

41 T. S. Eliot, "Ulysses, Order and Myth," reprinted as "Myth and Literary Classicism" in *The Modern Tradition: Background of Modern Literature*, ed. Richard Ellmann and Charles Feidelson, Jr. (New York: Oxford University Press, 1965), 681.

42 R. W. B. Lewis's comments on the novel illustrate this impulse: "Against [the] tremendous force of hatred . . . West poses the allied powers of art and comedy. . . . superimposed in thought above the actual disorders, [Tod Hackett's] painting – it will be called 'The Burning of Los Angeles' – will eventually explain and comment upon the apocalypse it describes by the patterned juxtaposition of its elements" ("Days of Wrath and Laughter: West," in *Nathanael West: Modern Critical Views*, ed. Harold Bloom [New York: Chelsea House, 1986], 72–73).

43 Thomas Strychacz, *Modernism, Mass Culture, and Professionalism* (Cambridge University Press, 1993), 196–97, 199. Strychacz, it must be said, is fully aware that his attempts to emphasize the narrative organization of the novel and to show "legitimate, definable, stable points of difference" between the novel and the products of Hollywood may in effect impose a certain cultural hierarchy on a text that is curiously resistant to any such hierarchy and order.

44 From a 1931 letter from Charlie Chaplin to Thomas Burke, quoted in David Robinson, *Chaplin: His Life and Art* (London: Collins, 1985), 455–56.

45 T. W. Adorno, "Spengler Today," *Studies in Philosophy and Social Science* 9 (1941): 325. The line recalls for me Benjamin's long-standing fascination with ruins (dating back to his meditations on allegory in *The Origin of German Tragic Drama*). This aspect of Benjamin's thought is explored by Susan Buck-Morss in the chapter "Historical Nature: Ruin," in *The Dialectics of Seeing: Walter Benjamin and the Arcades Project* (Cambridge, Mass.: MIT Press, 1989). She notes, for instance, that for Benjamin "the debris of industrial culture teaches us not the necessity of submitting to historical catastrophe, but the fragility of the social order that tells us this catastrophe is necessary. The crumbling of the monuments that were built to signify the immortality of civilization becomes proof, rather, of its transiency. And the fleetingness of temporal power does not cause sadness; it informs political practice" (170).

46 Karl Marx, *Critique of Hegel's Philosophy of Right* (Cambridge University Press, 1970), 131.

8 THE STORYTELLER, THE NOVELIST, AND THE ADVICE COLUMNIST

1   Roland Marchand, *Advertising the American Dream: Making Way for Modernity, 1920–1940* (Berkeley: University of California Press, 1986), 110–11.
2   Ibid., 110, 304.
3   *Saturday Evening Post,* 27 January 1934, 46. The work of Roland Marchand and of T. J. Jackson Lears suggests that two tendencies predominate in thirties advertising: one is a hard-sell, screaming, tabloid style (which they both suggest reflects the pressure on copywriters, who were desperately trying to hold onto their jobs at a time when agencies competed tooth and nail for clients); the second is a folksy, slightly corny evocation of the old-fashioned and rural, of traditional virtues and values. See Lears, "Packaging the Folk: Tradition and Amnesia in American Advertising, 1880–1940," in *Folk Roots, New Roots: Folklore in American Life,* ed. Jane S. Becker and Barbara Franco (Lexington, Mass.: Museum of Our National Heritage, 1988), 123; and Marchand, *Advertising the American Dream,* 286–87.
4   Marchand, *Advertising the American Dream,* 111–12.
5   Ibid., 304. In "The Culture Industry: Enlightenment as Mass Deception," Theodor Adorno and Max Horkheimer assert that "advertising and the culture industry merge technically as well as economically" (in *Dialectic of Enlightenment,* trans. John Cumming [New York, Continuum, 1991], 163). For comparable views of American writers in the thirties see, e.g., James Rorty's use of the term "advertising business" to mean the "total apparatus of newspaper and magazine publishing in America, plus radio broadcasting and, with important qualifications, the movies" (*Our Master's Voice: Advertising* [New York: John Day, 1936], ix), or R. Peters's judgment that "American radio is advertising. All else is sugarcoating" ("Radio and Its Public," *New Masses* 19 [May 5, 1936]: 29).
6   Herta Herzog, "On Borrowed Experience: An Analysis of Listening to Daytime Sketches," *Studies in Philosophy and Social Science* 9 (1941): 66.
7   Fredric Jameson, "Reification and Utopia in Mass Culture," *Social Text* 1 (Winter 1979): 141.
8   Nathanael West, "Some Notes on Miss L," in *Nathanael West: A Collection of Critical Essays,* ed. Jay Martin (Englewood Cliffs, N.J.: Prentice-Hall, 1971), 66.
9   Jay Martin, *Nathanael West: The Art of His Life* (New York: Caroll & Graf, 1970), 165, 141.
10 See, e.g., *Nathanael West: The Art of His Life,* 179; Randall Reid, *The Fiction of Nathanael West: No Redeemer, No Promised Land* (Chicago: University of Chicago Press, 1971), 84–91; Joan Zlotnick, "The Medium Is the Message, Or Is It? A Study of Nathanael West's Comic Strip Novel," *Journal of Popular Culture* 5 (1971): 236–40; Jonathan Raban, "A Surfeit of Commodities: The Novels of Nathanael West," in *The American Novel and the Nineteen*

Twenties, ed. Malcolm Bradbury and David Palmer (London: Edward Arnold, 1971), 221; and Thomas Strychacz, *Modernism, Mass Culture, and Professionalism* (Cambridge University Press, 1993), 176–79.

11   "Children Never Understand," *Saturday Evening Post*, 5 October 1929, 104.

12   Two critics who put forward the idea of the general discursive contestation between literature and advertising, or literature and mass culture, are Jennifer Wicke and Fredric Jameson. The former argues that the "sudden profusion" of advertisements in the mid-twenties and after and the ideological pressure exerted by their collective social narrative "reshaped the reception of narrativity as a whole" (*Advertising Fictions: Literature, Advertisement, and Social Reading* [New York: Columbia University Press, 1988], 120.) Jameson argues, as we have seen, that the form and cultural meaning of modernist texts can be grasped fully only when they are seen in relation – indeed, in reaction – to mass culture, their dialectical Other ("Reification and Utopia in Mass Culture," 133–35).

13   Walter Benjamin, *Illuminations: Essays and Reflections* (New York: Schocken, 1985), 178–80.

14   Benjamin, "The Storyteller: Reflections on the Works of Nikolai Leskov," in *Illuminations*, 84–85, 91–92.

15   The advertisement in question dates from 1934 and is cited in Lears, "Packaging the Folk," 118; see also Benjamin, *Illuminations*, 93.

16   I would note here the parallel with Kenneth Fearing, who felt that poetry in modern America had to "discard the entire bag of conventions and codes usually associated with poetry and to create instead more exacting forms . . . based on the material being written about." Cited in Weldon Kees, "Fearing's Collected Poems," *Poetry: A Magazine of Verse* 57 (January 1941): 266.

17   West, "Some Notes on Violence," in Martin, ed., *Nathanael West: A Collection of Critical Essays*, 50.

18   Ibid., 51.

19   Jonathan Raban, "A Surfeit of Shoddy," 222.

20   Amusingly, the advertising men of the day seem to bear Shrike out here: a McCann-Erickson account executive announced in 1931 that "the day of the dilettante is gone. The hard-boiled boys who know the business from the bottom up are now in the front office" (Lears, "Packaging the Folk," 122–23). West is apparently picking up here on a characteristic "structure of feeling" among white-collar men in the grim years of the early thirties.

21   Benjamin, *Illuminations*, 92.

22   Ibid., 107–9.

23   Ibid., 87.

24   Ibid., 86.

25   Thomas Strychacz makes a similar argument with regard to Fay Doyle – another mechanical producer of "long, long stor[ies]" redolent of the movies or the true confession magazines. See *Modernism, Mass Culture, and Professionalism*, 168.

26   Warren Susman notes that the institutionalization and acceptance of psy-

chology – of the new professional experts in the "talking culture" – were also a legacy of the thirties. *Culture as History: The Transformation of American Society in the Twentieth Century* (New York: Pantheon Books, 1985), 210.

27 Benjamin, *Illuminations,* 104.

28 Ibid., 86.

29 Marchand, *Advertising the American Dream,* 342–47. The phrase "acids of modernity" is Walter Lippmann's, cited by Marchand.

30 Peter F. Drucker, *The End of Economic Man: A Study of the New Totalitarianism* (New York: John Day, 1939), 61, 55. These passages are cited in Alfred Kazin, *On Native Grounds* (New York: Reynal & Hitchcock, 1942), 365; and Frederick Lewis Allen, *Only Yesterday and Since Yesterday: A Popular History of the 20s and 30s* (New York: Bonanza, 1986), 55.

31 Benjamin, *Illuminations,* 84.

32 Ibid., 83–84.

33 Marchand, *Advertising the American Dream,* 356. The show "The Voice of Experience," understandably, attracted some sardonic criticism at the time. In his article "Radio and Its Public," R. Peters comments as follows: "It is a safe bet that Americans who will have faith in the Voice, as he calls himself in his moments of informality, for the solution of their intimate problems of living, will have similar faith in the recommended hair tonic for the salvation of hair. I have heard listeners wondering aloud what kind of people could possibly be interested in the Voice of Experience. The answer to that one is the kind of people who worry about thinning hair and are ready to try something in a bottle for that dread remedy" (29). With the recent tendency to correct for intellectuals' legacy of disrespect for the popular by privileging the fan audience, it sometimes seems to me that we need to be reminded of the fact that not all listeners bought the appeal of even the most popular shows.

34 Marchand, *Advertising the American Dream,* 353, 357.

35 I say "seems" since Benjamin is careful to state that the changes in epic forms of which he speaks are very slow and gradual; yet one cannot miss the sense of irretrievable loss in his opening claim that "the art of storytelling is coming to an end." The essay does emphasize historical disjunction and change (*Illuminations,* 88, 83). For a discussion of the "ethnographic paradigm" that juxtaposes the folk and the industrial, or *Gemeinschaft* (community) versus *Gesellschaft* (society), see Chapter 6.

36 Lawrence W. Levine, "The Folklore of Industrial Society: Popular Culture and Its Audiences," *American Historical Review* 97 (December 1992): 1372–73, 1376, 1378–80.

37 For a similar argument, see Robin D. G. Kelley's astute response to Levine's article, "Notes on Deconstructing 'The Folk,' " *American Historical Review* 97 (December 1992): 1404.

38 Benjamin, *Illuminations,* 86–87. Althusserian notions of ideology, of course, render this formulation problematic; but I venture it nevertheless, since it seems to me that Benjamin is here trying to imagine, as a kind of normative touchstone, a relation to the real that is *not* imaginary, but directly lived,

inherently meaningful. Our sense of the impossibility of such an unmediated meaning is perhaps an index of its profoundly utopian dimension.

39   T. J. Jackson Lears offers a fascinating – and I would say very Benjaminian – discussion of the uses of nostalgia in his essay "Packaging the Folk," which explores the prevalence of folksy images in the advertising of the thirties. Though he does not discuss the continuity series ads, his research raises exactly the same issues I am concerned with here:

> When the folk were invoked, the advertisers implicitly denied any rupture between tradition and modernity, trivialized the challenge of the past to the present, and ignored the destructive effects of change. Their outlook resembled the evolutionary progressiveness of Teilhard de Chardin, whose slogan they would have loved, if they had ever read it: "Nothing is ever lost to the race."
>   The denial of loss is not "nostalgia" but the erasure of its basis – and what may, indeed, be the basis of all historical memory under modern cultural conditions: the sense of the pastness of the past, the radical disjuncture between "then" and "now." (136)

The renewed experience of this disjuncture is exactly what Benjamin would have us feel. His conception of a revolutionary historiography is precisely one that seeks rupture, that aims to stop the catastrophe of history in its tracks; it is a historiography of mourning, quite opposite to Levine's optimistic historiography of continuities and of ordinary folks "making do."

40   In the rather more optimistic essay "The Work of Art in the Age of Mechanical Reproduction," the paradigmatic forms are, of course, photography and film. It is interesting, however, that in both of these major essays Benjamin seems, perhaps deliberately, to shy away from any comment on advertising: a form that for other critics (those mentioned earlier, as well as British theorists such as F. R. Leavis) has seemed to epitomize the industrial transformation of speech communities. Indeed, one of Theodor Adorno's important arguments with Benjamin concerned his failure to account for the possibility of commercial remystification: the reauraticization of the image – most notably of the movie celebrity. This is not to say that Benjamin was unaware of the importance of advertising. In *One Way Street*, for example, he contrasts the way printing seems to lie down quietly and horizontally in the book with the way it is "dragged out onto the street by advertisements" – especially by billboards, which "force the printed word entirely into the dictatorial perpendicular" (*Reflections: Essays, Aphorisms, Autobiographical Writings* [New York: Schocken, 1986], 78). Moreover, his fascination with commodities on display, with department stores, exhibitions, and so forth, in the *Arcades Project*, should be seen as an exploration of the history of advertising as an element of our everyday life and urban geography. See also Wicke, *Advertising Fictions*, 9–13, for a more detailed discussion of these matters; and on the Adorno-Benjamin debate, Susan Buck-Morss, *Origins of Negative Dialectics: Theodor W. Adorno, Walter Benjamin, and the Frankfurt Institute* (Hassocks, Sussex: Harvester Press, 1977), chap. 9.

41   Marchand, *Advertising the American Dream*, 336. This tendency to reconstruct the new, not just in the "ruins of the old" (as Jackson Lears puts it), but in its very guise, is one of the most fascinating themes of the *Arcades*

Project. Benjamin was struck by the consistency with which new technologies or new institutions (in our case these would be advertisements addressed to a vast national marketplace) assumed the *form* of whatever they replaced. To cite but the simplest of the many examples listed by Susan Buck-Morss: the first electric light bulbs were shaped like gas flames. In this tendency, Benjamin intuited what we may call the workings of the political unconscious: the wish image of society's utopian desires. The same applies to the use of the folksy in the mass-mediated culture of the American thirties. See Buck-Morss, *The Dialectics of Seeing: Walter Benjamin and the Arcades Project* (Cambridge, Mass.: MIT Press, 1989), 110-15, and Lears, "Packaging the Folk," 118, 136-37.

42   Marchand, *Advertising the American Dream,* 336.

43   Ian H. Angus, "Circumscribing Post-Modern Culture," in *Cultural Politics in Contemporary America,* ed. Ian Angus and Sut Jhally (New York: Routledge, 1989), 99.

44   Guy Debord, *Society of the Spectacle* (Detroit: Black & Red, 1983), proposition 20.

45   There is evidence that Benjamin saw the essay as his counterpart to Lukács's *Theory of the Novel*. Some years before the publication of the essay, he wrote, in a letter to Gershom Scholem, that he had conceived of "a new 'theory of the novel,' sure to gain you strong approval and a place next to Lukács." Critics have identified the piece in question as "The Storyteller." See Bernd Witte, "Benjamin and Lukács: Historical Notes on Their Relationship," *New German Critique* 5 (Spring 1975): 19.

46   Benjamin, *Reflections,* 78.

47   Georg Lukács, *Theory of the Novel: A Historico-Philosophical Essay on the Forms of Great Epic Literature,* trans. Anna Bostock (Cambridge, Mass.: MIT Press), 128.

48   Benjamin, *Illuminations,* 98-100, 88.

49   Fredric Jameson, *Marxism and Form* (Princeton, N.J.: Princeton University Press, 1971), 173.

50   John Keyes, "Nathanael West's 'New Art Form': Metamorphoses of Detective Fiction in *Miss Lonelyhearts, English Studies in Canada* 8 (March 1982): 84.

51   Jeffrey Duncan, "The Problem of Language in *Miss Lonelyhearts,*" in *Nathanael West: Modern Critical Views,* ed. Harold Bloom (New York: Chelsea House, 1986), 98-99. An essay by Martin Tropp concludes with a similarly optimistic twist. After comparing West's work to Thomas Hardy's "The Darkling Thrush," Tropp extracts this "precipitate of meaning," as André Breton might say, from the "surrounding gloom": "Nathanael West hints, at least, that there is a seemingly endless fund of belief and love in the world, which, merely by existing, helps purify the wasteland of his novels." See "Nathanael West and the Persistence of Hope," in *Nathanael West's "Miss Lonelyhearts,"* ed. Harold Bloom (New York: Chelsea House, 1987), 109.

52   Benjamin, *Illuminations,* 100.

53   Ibid., 111.

54   Jürgen Habermas, "Walter Benjamin: Consciousness Raising or Rescuing

Critique," in *On Walter Benjamin: Critical Essays and Recollections,* ed. Gary Smith (Cambridge, Mass.: MIT Press, 1988), 110.

55 Habermas's observation emerges from a discussion of Benjamin's ambivalence about aura, which I will not attempt to rehearse here. I would like, however, to try to suggest another way in which the novel, with its reliance on memory and its retrospective interpretation of the total "meaning of life," might strike Benjamin as a kind of aesthetic and political dead end – despite his great admiration for Proust and Kafka. His work on Proust, in fact, offers us two useful analytical terms: the "mémoire volontaire" and the "mémoire involontaire" (derived from Bergson but also, or so Fredric Jameson suggests, from Freud's *Beyond the Pleasure Principle*). For Freud the unconscious "memory trace," however strange and fragmentary, is privileged over the willful reconstruction of conscious memory and is far more suggestive to the analyst – far closer to the hidden "truth." Indeed, the conscious memory can be dangerous, since it tends to displace the memory trace. Similarly, for Benjamin, the story with its "short-lived reminiscences" is far more productive of a true, though fragmentary, illumination than is the "perpetuating remembrance of the novelist" (*Illuminations,* 98). And the novel, as "The Storyteller" clearly suggests, tends to displace the story; it is one of the first symptoms of the story's decline. See Jameson, *Marxism and Form,* 63–64, and Buck-Morss, *The Dialectics of Seeing: Walter Benjamin and the "Arcades Project"* (Cambridge, Mass.: MIT Press, 1989), 38–39, for further discussion.

56 Benjamin, *Illuminations,* 90.

57 Habermas, "Walter Benjamin," 117, 124.

58 Cited in Benjamin, "Surrealism: Snapshot of the Last European Intelligentsia," in *Reflections,* 178.

59 Greil Marcus, *Lipstick Traces: A Secret History of the Twentieth Century* (Cambridge, Mass.: Harvard University Press, 1989), 170.

60 Letter from West to Edmund Wilson, cited in Martin, *Nathanael West: The Art of His Life,* 334.

61 Cited in Martin, *Nathanael West: The Art of His Life,* 329.

EPILOGUE: "HAPPY ENDING"

1 *Discovery* 19 (1952): 142–53. The editorial statement of the journal reveals something about why Fearing might have chosen to publish in this venue: Aldridge and Bourjaily announced that their aim was to reach a mass audience for serious "creative writing" – the same audience, they reasoned, that had recently been reached by paperback reprints. The writing they had in mind would not be judged by any preconceived prescriptive standards or agenda that would homogenize the contents of the journal; even experimentation would be neither required nor discouraged. This venture, in other words, constituted another attempt to challenge the notion that "mass" must necessarily equal "bad," to cross that Great Divide (vii–ix).

2 Ibid., 152.

3 Ibid., 146–48.

4 Ibid., 148–52.
5 See Georg Lukács, *History and Class Consciousness* (Cambridge, Mass.: MIT Press, 1971), 100.
6 Michael Denning, "The End of Mass Culture," *International Labor and Working-Class History* 37 (Spring 1990): 11.
7 William Gibson, *Neuromancer* (New York: Ace Books, 1984), 24–25, 32.

Index

CAMBRIDGE STUDIES IN AMERICAN LITERATURE AND CULTURE

Continued from the front of the book